FIRST CANADIAN EDITION

The Essay
WORKPLACE

FIRST CANADIAN EDITION

The Essay
WORKPLACE

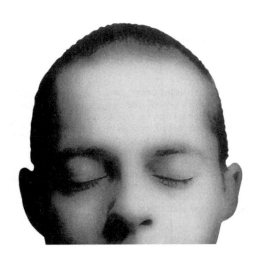

CLIFFORD WERIER   Mount Royal College, Calgary, Alberta

SANDRA SCARRY   Recently with the Office of Academic Affairs, City University of New York

JOHN SCARRY   Hostos Community College, City University of New York

THOMSON

NELSON

Australia   Canada   Mexico   Singapore   Spain   United Kingdom   United States

The Essay Workplace
First Canadian Edition
by Clifford Werier, Sandra Scarry, and John Scarry

Editorial Director and Publisher:
Evelyn Veitch

Aquisitions Editor:
Anne Williams

Marketing Manager:
Cara Yarzab

Developmental Editor:
Shefali Mehta

Production Editors:
Susan Calvert/Wendy Yano

Copy Editor:
Wayne Herrington

Production Coordinator:
Hedy Sellers

Art Director:
Angela Cluer

Cover Design:
Ken Phipps

Cover Image:
Mirek Weichsel/First Light

Compositor:
Janet Zanette

Indexer:
Edwin Durbin

Printer:
Victor Graphics

National Library of Canada Cataloguing in Publication Data

Werier, Clifford M. (Clifford Myles), 1954–
    The essay workplace

1st Canadian ed.
Includes index.
Based on: The Writer's workplace.
    Essays/Sandra Scarry,
    John Scarry
ISBN 0-7747-3763-8

1. College readers. 2. English language—Rhetoric—Problems, exercises, etc. 3. English language—Grammar—Problems, exercises, etc. 4. Report writing—Problems, exercises, etc. I. Scarry, Sandra, 1946– II. Scarry, John III. Scarry, Sandra, 1946– . Writer's workplace. IV. Title.

PE1413.W47 2002   808'.042'076
C2001-904027-X

PREFACE

Overview

The *Writer's Workplace* series of textbooks has been very popular in the United States because it offers a flexible and comprehensive approach to the teaching of basic and introductory composition. As editor of the Canadian versions of *The Writer's Workplace: Sentences to Paragraphs* and *The Writer's Workplace: Essays*, I have kept the structure of the original American texts but have added Canadian examples that make the books more attractive to both instructors and students. It was my intention to enhance the usability of the texts for a Canadian audience by choosing examples and model essays that refer directly to Canadian life and popular culture. I believe that students and instructors will enjoy both the pedagogical design of these Canadian editions and the fresh, contemporary content.

The Essay Workplace, First Canadian Edition focuses on the step-by-step development of student essays, from first draft to final copy, along with a detailed examination of grammar, sentence construction, and word choice. This book features a comprehensive examination of the traditional modes of development, plentiful exercises, and numerous opportunities for writing practice. The emphasis on exercises and practice is the greatest strength of this text—not only are the principles of good writing examined in clear language, but the teaching is linked to copious exercises that provide an effective link between theory and practice. The Answer Key to Selected Exercises at the back of the text helps students to monitor their own progress toward the mastery of each element. In addition, numerous model essays illustrate key points and provide examples of the different rhetorical modes. The readings, many by Canadian authors, provide helpful examples of how professional writers structure their ideas in full-length essays.

Organization

The Essay Workplace is divided into four parts called "Steps."

- *Step 1: Looking at the Whole* provides an overview of the entire writing process.
- *Step 2: Structuring the Essay* examines the writing process, from thesis to final draft. Separate chapters discuss the characteristics of traditional rhetorical modes and provide students with opportunities to practise and develop their own voices.
- *Step 3: Creating Effective Sentences* provides a thorough grammar review along with an examination of the relationship between correct usage and the clear expression of ideas at the sentence level.
- *Step 4: Understanding the Power of Words* discusses the implications of diction and may be especially useful for ESL students.

The Appendices contain helpful sections on documentation, irregular verbs, and parts of speech. Finally, the Readings section contains a good selection of essays that can be used as models of effective writing.

Instructors are certainly not bound by the order of these steps—they are free to choose a path that best suits their own style and syllabus. For example, some instructors may feel more comfortable integrating the grammar material in Step 3 with the examination of the essay writing processs in Step 2. No matter what the organizational choices, instructors should be delighted by the quality and number of exercises. The philosophy of this text is that students master grammatical rules and develop as writers by writing and revising, and I know of no other text that does a better job of providing thoughtful and challenging opportunities for practice.

Acknowledgments

The development and writing of *The Essay Workplace, First Canadian Edition* was a truly collaborative project that involved a number of talented writers and editors. I would like to thank Anne Williams of Nelson for initiating the project and inspiring me to get involved. I would especially like to acknowledge the contributions of Shefali Mehta, my astute editor at Nelson, who has been a delight to work with at every stage in the development of this book. I tip my hat to Lazaros and Juanita Simeon of George Brown College gifted writers who translated my unintelligible squiggles on a manuscript into the revised sentences and exercises that comprise this Canadian edition.

On a personal note, I would like to acknowledge the inspiration that I receive from my colleagues in the Department of English at Mount Royal College—a group of dedicated and innovative writing teachers. Finally, I would like to thank my family (Sabrina, Cynthia, and Alex) for putting up with the mess of papers on the dining room table and all my grumbling and complaining. I think the result will satisfy even their exacting standards.

BRIEF CONTENTS

CONTENTS

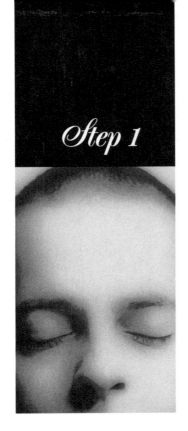

Step 1

LOOKING AT THE WHOLE

CONTENTS

The Writing Process for the Essay

Sometimes we think that people are born painters or dancers, and that their talent comes from an almost magical inspiration. It is true that a few lucky people are gifted in this way, but these people are the exceptions. Most artists, including writers, have to work long and hard to develop their skills. It might seem that an opera star like Luciano Pavarotti just opens his mouth and music pours out, but his singing is based upon years of rigorous preparation beginning with simple musical scales. When Stephen King comes out with a new novel that promises to scare us to death, the success of his story comes out of years of careful observation and writing. Like all creative individuals, these artists have learned that success is a result of hard work—daily.

Just as no two chefs or no two singers have exactly the same approach to their work, no two writers work in exactly the same way. In spite of this individuality, each writer, no matter how experienced or inexperienced, follows a remarkably similar sequence of steps to move from the blank page to the finished product.

Many students believe they can write an essay in one step—writing the essay from start to finish in one sitting. Actually, this approach often leads to a very high level of anxiety, and can even cause writer's block. These students are often the ones who complain, "I don't have anything to say."

The step-by-step approach is much more likely to ensure successful writing. It not only leads to more thoughtful and better organized work, but the writer's anxiety level is reduced. Careful preparation before writing and careful revisions afterwards lead to major improvements in what a writer can produce. You will probably be surprised as you watch your initial ideas change. Knowing there is a process that enables your ideas to take shape and blossom will help you feel more in control of your task. No longer will you feel overwhelmed by a writing assignment.

The box on page 4 lists the steps in the writing process. In the chapters that follow, you will use this basic sequence to guide you through the creation of several essays. Writing an essay is a craft like any other and can be learned through daily practice.

Whatever your level of skill right now, by the time you have practised writing several essays in the guided assignments that follow, you will be able to observe improvements in your writing.

STEPS IN THE WRITING PROCESS

1. Find a topic and controlling idea for the thesis statement.

2. Gather the information using brainstorming techniques or research.

3. Select and organize material.

4. Write the rough draft.

5. Revise the rough draft for greater clarity of ideas. (Many writers work on several drafts before a satisfactory final version is reached.)

6. Edit the revised draft for correctness. (Correct errors such as misspellings or faulty grammar.)

7. Prepare the final typed copy, print it out, and proofread.

Find the topic and controlling idea for the thesis statement

Usually when you sit down to write, you know the general topic. For a report in a history class, you may have been assigned an essay on the political parties in Canada; for a psychology take-home exam, you might have to write on the methods of coping with stress. Perhaps you are angry about a toxic waste site near your home, and you decide to write a letter to the local newspaper to convince your community to do something about the situation. Perhaps your employer has asked you to write a report to describe the ways in which productivity could be increased in your department. In all these cases, the topic is set before you and the purpose is clear. You do not have to say to yourself, "Now what in the world shall I write about?" In school, most students prefer an assigned topic or a number of topics from which to choose. Therefore, in the assignments that follow, suggestions are given to help you find a suitable topic. However, keep this fact in mind as you prepare to write any essay: You cannot hope to hold your reader if the material does not first interest you! The writer who is involved in the material puts forth more effort, and this always shows in the finished product.

Even though you may be assigned a particular topic, you will need to spend some time thinking of a possible approach that can make use of your experience or knowledge. In writing, this approach is called the ***controlling idea.*** One of our students, for example, loved to play chess. Toward the end of his final year, he described to us how he had used his interest in and knowledge of chess to help him complete several of his writing assignments. When his psychology teacher asked for a paper entitled "Stereotypes—Are They True?" he wrote about the characteristics of people who play chess. For a political science class, this same student discussed the importance of international games, including chess, of course. For a paper in his literature course, he wrote about four writers who used games in their writing. You can see from these examples how this student used his own special interests and knowledge to make his writing interesting for himself and undoubtedly interesting to the teachers who read his papers. Don't ever think that you have nothing to write about. The secret is in finding your own angle.

Once you have decided what your topic will be and what your controlling idea could be, you have what is needed to write your thesis statement. The thesis statement is a sentence that usually occurs somewhere in the first paragraph. It announces the topic and controlling idea of the essay. The thesis statement may also indicate what method of development will be used (such as explaining, comparing, defining, or persuading).

ACTIVITY 1   Composing the Thesis Statement

Below are three general topics. (1) Narrow each one down to a more specific topic, something you would be interested in writing about. (2) Give a controlling idea for the topic you select. (3) Combine the topic and controlling idea into a sentence that could become the thesis statement for an essay. An example is given.

General topic:	Pets
Narrowed topic:	Dogs
Controlling idea:	Disadvantages of owning

Thesis statement: You should be aware of the many disadvantages of owning a dog.

or (a more creative approach)

If you think you would like to own a dog, think again!

1. General Topic: Pets

   Narrowed topic: _____

   Controlling idea: _____

   Thesis statement: _____

   _____

2. General Topic: Discussion of a social problem

   Narrowed topic: _____

   Controlling idea: _____

   (Suggestion: You could discuss causes or effects.)

   Thesis statement: _____

   _____

3. General Topic: Relationships

   Narrowed topic: _____

   Controlling idea: _____

   (Suggestion: You could compare your view of the topic with your parents' or grandparents' opinion on the same topic.)

   Thesis statement: _____

   _____

Gather the information using brainstorming techniques

Once you have your topic and controlling idea in mind, a short time spent gathering ideas and details about the topic will prove helpful. If the assignment calls for your own opinions or experiences, outside research—working in the library or conducting interviews—will be unnecessary. In this case, you can begin with the technique known as *brainstorming*. Writers use brainstorming to discover what they already know and feel about a given topic.

> When you *brainstorm*, you allow your mind to roam freely around the topic, letting one idea lead to another, even if the ideas seem unrelated or irrelevant. You jot down every word and phrase that comes into your mind.

Since your brainstorming list is for your personal use, you can jot down single words, phrases, or entire sentences—whatever makes sense to you. Don't concern yourself with listing your ideas in any order. What matters is that you get all your thoughts down on paper as quickly as they come to mind. Brainstorming often stimulates your thinking, and you do not want to be sidetracked during this time. Organizing comes later.

Depending on the assignment, it can be very useful to brainstorm with another person or a group of people. With a group effort, each person's idea may bring an idea to another person's mind. In this way, you can stimulate each other's thinking and produce a wealth of material for each other's writing projects.

Finally, the details you produce during brainstorming will often get you more involved and excited about your topic. You will feel more confident as you move to the next stage of your writing.

ACTIVITY 2   Brainstorming a Topic

Choose one of the topics selected in the first activity and spend at least ten minutes jotting down every word, phrase, or thought that comes to mind as you focus on the topic. Don't judge any thought as relevant or irrelevant; just jot everything down. Let your mind follow its own path.

_____

_____

_____

_____

_____

_____

_____

_____

_____

_____

_____

_____

_____

_____

_____

_____

Select and organize material

When you brainstorm, ideas come to your mind in no particular order, and you jot them down as they come. Your next step in the writing process is to look over your list and consider ways to organize the material. At this point, try to find a logical sequence for your ideas. This need not be the final order, but this sequence will help you plan the organization of the first draft.

As you study the details on your list, do not hesitate to cross out items you know you will not use. Fill in any additional details that come to mind and continue to entertain new ideas for main points you want to make. Finally, group all the details under the three or four headings that seem to be your major points. You will want to develop each of these major points with at least one good example, a story, a description, or an explanation. Do you have the material to develop each point? If you need to, develop an outline to use for writing the draft.

ACTIVITY 3

Look at the brainstorming list in the second activity. How could you group the items on your list? Do you still want to have the same controlling idea that you selected in the first activity, or does your material seem to point you in a new direction? Group the material you wish to use into at least three different parts. (Each part would eventually become a separate paragraph in your essay.) List your three parts or main points:

1. _____

2. _____

3. _____

Write the rough draft

After you have gone through the brainstorming process, and you have organized the material into some kind of order, the time has come to write a rough draft. Some students write their drafts in the traditional way, using pen and paper. Many others, however, find it easier to compose directly on a word processor, changing or rearranging words, sentences, and even entire paragraphs as they go along.

A rough draft is just what its name implies: your first attempt to write your essay. The first attempt will undoubtedly undergo many changes before it is finished: parts may be missing, paragraphs may lack sufficient detail, or certain words may seem to be repetitious or inappropriate. Some sentences will sound awkward. They will need to be rewritten later. The experienced writer expects this. All that you should try to accomplish in the rough draft is to get down on paper as many of your initial ideas as possible. These first ideas will provide the seeds that can be developed later on.

Armed with a first draft, you will now have something with which to work. No longer is a blank paper before you; this is a great relief to most writers.

ACTIVITY 4   Developing an Idea in a Paragraph

In the third activity, you grouped your material into three parts. Refer back to your three parts and select one of those parts to develop into a paragraph. Using any material from your brainstorming list that would help to develop your point, write a paragraph (at least seven or eight sentences) to develop that idea. Keep in mind that this paragraph could become part of an essay that you will want to complete later on.

_____

_____

_____

_____

_____

_____

_____

_____

_____

_____

_____

_____

_____

_____

_____

_____

Revise the rough draft for unity and coherence

Put aside your rough draft for a day or two. Then, when you reread it, you will look at it with a fresh mind. In this important revision stage, you should be concerned with how you have organized your ideas into paragraphs and if the ideas are clear. Do not worry about grammar, spelling, and punctuation at this stage.

Ask yourself the following questions:

1. Is the essay unified? Do you stick to the topic you have announced and have you focused on the controlling idea established in the first paragraph? Go through the essay and take out irrelevant material.

2. Do you repeat yourself? Look back over your essay to determine whether or not you have said the same thing more than once. Unless you are summarizing your points at the conclusion, you should not repeat ideas. Take out any repetitious material.

3. Is the essay coherent; that is, does it make sense? Can a reader follow your logic or train of thought? You may want to give the rough draft to someone else to read at this point, to get an answer to this question. If the essay is confusing to the reader, you must decide how to fix it. Sometimes when you read your writing out loud, you will hear a sentence that seems to come suddenly out of nowhere or a paragraph that doesn't seem to follow from what came before. All that may be needed is the careful use of a transitional expression or a sentence of explanation. Reading it out loud may bring the words to mind that are needed to make one idea flow to the next.

4. Are the paragraphs roughly the same length? If you see one paragraph that has only one sentence, you know something is wrong. Each paragraph usually needs at least five sentences to develop a point. Check through your essay. Do you need to change the paragraphing? You may need to develop one point more fully, or a one-sentence "paragraph" may really belong with the paragraph that comes before or with the paragraph that follows.

5. Do you have all the types of paragraphs essential to an essay? These include the introductory paragraph with its topic sentence, at least three well-developed body paragraphs with transitional words or phrases to connect ideas, and a concluding paragraph.

6. Can you add more specific details? Most writing teachers agree that nearly every paper they read could be improved by more specific details, more descriptive verbs, and more sensory images to make the writing come alive.

7. Can you add dialogue or a quote from someone?

8. Could you make the introduction, conclusion, or title more creative?

ACTIVITY 5   Revising a Student Paragraph

The following paragraph is from the main body of a student's rough draft on the disadvantages of owning a dog. This paragraph explains what the writer thinks is the third disadvantage. At this stage in the writing process, the student must consider making revisions.

Consider how you would revise this paragraph. Without thinking about spelling, grammar, and other such corrections, concentrate on the ideas in the paragraph. Is the paragraph *unified* (all sentences help to develop a single idea)? Is the paragraph *coherent* (one idea flows into the next)? To improve the paragraph, consider adding more details, rearranging sentences, crossing out sentences that do not belong, and rewriting parts of sentences.

Another issue to consider if you think you want a dog is whether or not you are prepared for the extra expenses. Every week or so you will have to buy dog food. A family's food budget is already too high. The cost of fish, for instance, is practically out of sight. Dog food could cost you over $10.00 a week. Then there are the vitamins, medicines, or food for dogs with special diets (especially as they grow older). If the pet should become ill, you must take it to a veterinarian and now your talking big bucks. If you take any pet to an animal doctor, their professional fees are always too high. And then what about when you want to go away? You will have to pay somebody to take care of the dog. Finally, what about guilt? Most pet owners feel guilty if they don't have time every day to spend with the dog.

_____

_____

_____

_____

_____

_____

_____

_____

_____

_____

_____

_____

_____

_____

_____

_____

_____

_____

_____

_____

_____

_____

_____

_____

_____

_____

_____

Edit the second draft for correctness (look for mistakes in spelling, grammar, punctuation, and diction)

Now that you have made all the major revisions in the content of your essay, the time has come to check your paper for any mistakes in spelling, grammar, or punctuation. Most writers make mistakes as they compose. You should also expect this and be sure to leave enough time for this stage of the writing process. Use a dictionary or the spellcheck feature on the computer. Read out loud to have a clear sense of the actual sound of your writing. By doing this, you will often hear a word that has been overused, or you will think of a better word choice or a smoother way to express an idea. If you can find someone else to read your essay, that person may catch errors you may not have noticed.

Sometimes an instructor will read a rough draft and mark a number of the sentence level errors. If your instructor does this, consult the editing marks reproduced on the inside back cover of this book. These marks are the abbreviations instructors often use to correct student papers. Most important, you should concentrate on developing an awareness of your weaknesses. If you know you have a problem with spelling, plan to pay special attention to that skill area.

Many students find it helpful to keep a record of their errors. Such a record is useful because it keeps you aware of what to look for when you edit. The following is an illustration of how a student could keep a record of errors.

Sentence in student essay:

Your going to have to walk that dog in the pouring rain and more then once you'll have to leave a great party and come home to feed it.

Entries in Student Record Book:

Error	Correct to	Type of Error
1. your going	you're going . . .	confusion of *your* (a possessive pronoun) and *you're* (the contraction for *you are*)
2. more then once	more than once	confusion of *then* and *than*

While you grow as a writer, mistakes such as these will become easier to spot. You will become more analytical about your writing and thus better able to recognize your typical mistakes. Once you become aware of these errors, you will begin to avoid some of them as you write and be able to correct many others as you revise.

ACTIVITY 6   Editing a Student Paragraph

In the fifth activity, you revised a paragraph to improve the content. In the following paragraph, correct other errors such as mistakes in spelling, grammar, or punctuation.

What will you do if your pet turn out to have a terrible disposition? For example a dog may bark all night or not be good with children. In fact some dogs have been known to become very jealus of a new baby and has actually attacked infants or toddlers. If you find yourself in this situation, what will you do? Some people have gone so far as to hire special trainers or animal psycologists, these approaches do not always work. Others live for years being miserable with a dog who is never quiet housebroken. Or with a dog who may snap at it's family members and guests. The worst situation is when a pet owner decides the pet must go. This is a terribly painful and often traumatic experience for everyone in the family.

Prepare the final copy, print, and proofread it

The typing of the final version should follow the traditional rules for an acceptable submission.

CHECKLIST FOR THE FINAL COPY

Use only 8½-by-11 inch paper (never paper torn out of a spiral bound notebook).

Type on one side of the paper only.

Double space.

Leave approximately 1 inch (2.5 cm) margins on each side of the paper.

Centre the title at the top of the page. Do not put quotation marks around the title and do not underline it.

Do not hyphenate a word at the end of a line unless you are willing to consult a dictionary to check on the acceptable division of the word into syllables.

You may put your name, the date, and the title of your paper on a separate title page. Ask your instructor for specific advice on what information to include.

Indent each paragraph five spaces.

Leave two spaces after each period.

If your paper is more than one page, number the pages and paper clip the pages together so they will not get lost.

Do not forget to make a copy before you submit the paper.

Note: In most cases, teachers will not accept handwritten work. However, if you are submitting handwritten work, you must be sure to write on every other line and have good legible handwriting. Begin today to learn to type on the computer. You will be at a disadvantage if you cannot use the current technology.

Once you have typed your final version and printed it out, an important step still remains. This step can often mean the difference of an entire letter grade. You must *proofread* your paper. Even if you have used a spellcheck feature available on your word processing program, there still could be errors in your paper. The spellcheck feature only finds groupings of letters that are not words. For example, if you typed the word *van* when you meant to type *ban,* the spellcheck would not catch this error.

The secret of good proofreading is to look at each word and sentence construction by itself without thinking about the paper's contents.

> ## CHECKLIST FOR PROOFREADING
>
> Study each sentence: One way to proofread is to read backwards, starting with the last sentence and examining every sentence, one at a time. First, check that the sentence is really complete and not a fragment or a run-on. Then check the punctuation. Go on to the next sentence and do the same. In this way, you will develop a critical eye for spotting any problems with sentence level errors.
>
> Study each word: Read the paper again, this time studying each word in every sentence. Look at the letters of the words. Have you transposed any letters or have you left off an ending such as the *-ed* or the *-s?* If there are any words you are not sure how to spell, do not forget to check for the correct spelling. Is there any word you have omitted?

ACTIVITY 7   Proofread a Student Paragraph

The sentences in this activity are taken from the rough draft of a student essay. Using the guidelines for proofreading, see if you can find at least ten errors.

We are all familiar with the benefits of having a dog. Dogs offer companionchip without any complaints. You can come home everynight to a loving dog who wags his tail at the sight of you. Many expert claim that peopel who have dogs are healthier and happier than those who alone. Of course the best of all situations is if you can enjoy your dog but pass along all the work to someone else in your family. An older sister or a spouse if you are marry. Let someone else vacum the dog hair all day, take the pet out four or five times during a blizzard, go to the store in the middle of the night because you ran out of dog food, and basically stay home home all the time to be sure the dog is happy and the neighbours are happy. (Dogs have been known to drive neighbours crazy.) Can you manage this arrangement. If so by all means get a dog.

Working Together

Sometimes a writer can gather material for an essay by conducting an interview or taking a survey of a particular group of people who have something in common. For this exercise, make a survey of the students in your class to discover their attitudes and experiences with writing. Feel free to add additional questions or change the questions provided. This information could become the basis for a later essay.

Each student should answer the questionnaire below so the answers can be discussed in class and compiled to see what the range of answers are.

1. Where do you do your best writing? In the library, at home, or someplace else? What makes some places better than others?

   _____

   _____

   _____

   _____

   _____

   _____

   _____

   _____

   _____

2. Is a certain time of day better for you than other times? When do you concentrate the best?

_____

_____

3. How long can you write with concentration before you have to take a break?

_____

_____

4. What fears do you have when you write?

_____

_____

5. What do you believe is your major weakness as a writer?

_____

_____

6. Are you comfortable using a computer to compose?

_____

_____

7. In high school, how many of your classes included writing opportunities? How often did you write?

_____

_____

8. Keeping in mind that most people today use a telephone to keep in touch, how often do you find yourself writing a letter?

_____

_____

9. Which of the following best describes your feeling about writing up until this point in your school career?

_____ I enjoy writing most of the time.

_____ I occasionally like to write.

_____ I usually do not like to write.

_____ I don't have any opinion about writing at all.

How could the responses in this survey be used as the basis for an essay? What could be the purpose of such an essay?

Step 2

STRUCTURING THE ESSAY

CONTENTS

Chapter 2

Understanding Essay Form

When you studied paragraphs and their development, you realized that each paragraph you wrote had to have a topic sentence, supporting details, and an organization that was unified and coherent. Similarly, the fully developed essay must have a thesis and a unified and coherent organization with supporting details and examples. The resulting essay, however, develops a topic in greater depth than a single paragraph. Making these parts work together in a longer composition is a real challenge for every student writer.

The length of an essay is usually five or more paragraphs. This longer piece of writing can also be called a composition, a theme, or a paper. Your development of this longer piece of writing is the central work of the course you are now in, and it will be an important part of nearly every other college or university course you will take.

In this chapter, you will become familiar with what is needed for each of the three kinds of paragraphs in the essay:

- Recognizing and developing the thesis statement
- The effective introductory paragraph
- The use of transitions in the body of the essay
- The effective concluding paragraph
- Creating the title

What kinds of paragraphs are in an essay?

In addition to support paragraphs, the essay has two additional kinds of paragraphs:

1. The **introductory paragraph** is the first paragraph of the essay. Its purpose is to be so inviting that the reader will not want to stop reading. In most essays, this introduction contains a **thesis statement**.

2. **Support paragraphs** (also called **body paragraphs**) provide the evidence that shows your thesis is valid. An essay must have at least three well-developed support paragraphs. One paragraph must flow logically into the next. This is accomplished by the careful use of **transitional expressions.**

3. The **concluding paragraph** is the last paragraph of the essay. Its purpose is to give the reader a sense of coming to a satisfying conclusion. The reader should have the feeling that everything has been said that needed to be said.

Before you begin to write your own essays, study this chapter to become familiar with these special essay features:

- Thesis statement
- Introductory paragraph
- Transitional expressions
- Concluding paragraphs

What is a thesis?

> A *thesis* is a statement of the main idea of an essay.

The thesis of an essay states what you are going to explain, defend, or prove about your topic. It is usually placed at the end of the introductory paragraph.

How to recognize the thesis statement

The thesis statement is a complete sentence.

Thesis: The government should provide financial and training support for athletes who want to represent this country in Olympic events.

Do not confuse a thesis with a title. Remember that titles are usually phrases rather than complete sentences.

Title: Government support of Olympic athletes

The thesis statement presents a viewpoint about the topic that can be defended or explained in your essay. Notice that the sample thesis argues that governments should support Olympic athletes.

Thesis: The government should provide financial and training support for athletes who want to represent this country in Olympic events.

Do not confuse a thesis with a statement of fact that can be proven and is not a topic for debate. (Facts can, of course, be used to support a thesis.)

Fact: The government presently provides no direct support for athletes who want to be in the Olympics.

: PRACTICE

Read each of the following statements. If you think the statement is a thesis, write Th on the blank line. If you think the example is a title, mark T. If you think the statement is a fact, mark F.

_____   1. Jesse Owens won the 100-metre run in the 1936 Olympic Games held in Berlin.

_____   2. The procedure for getting tickets to an Olympic event

_____   3. The summer Olympics will be held in Beijing, China, in 2008.

_____   4. Several countries support their Olympic hopefuls with training, direct money allowances, and other specific forms of help.

_____   5. Citizens of this country should write to their Members of Parliament asking for more support for our Olympic athletes.

EXERCISE 1 Recognizing the Thesis Statement

Identify each of the following as a *title* (T), a *thesis* (Th), or a *fact* (F) that could be used to support a thesis.

_____   1. The United Nations' growing burden of debt

_____   2. Several celebrities, among them the singer Harry Belafonte and the actress Audrey Hepburn, have served as goodwill ambassadors for the United Nations.

_____   3. The first fifty years of the United Nations

_____   4. In 1980, the United Nations' World Health Organization announced complete victory over smallpox.

_____   5. Despite its failures in some areas, the United Nations should be supported by every nation.

_____   6. The skyrocketing number of United Nations' peacekeeping operations

_____   7. The annual United Nations' budget of nearly 5 billion dollars is excessive and must be reduced.

_____   8. The most frequently asked question of United Nations' tour guides is, "Where did Khrushchev bang his shoe?"

_____   9. One nation, Israel, was founded under United Nations' sponsorship in 1948.

_____   10. The United Nations has six official languages and 526 translators.

EXERCISE 2   Recognizing the Thesis Statement

Identify each of the following as a *title* (T), a *thesis* (Th), or a *fact* (F) that could be used to support a thesis.

_____   1. Electronic money should solve the problem of the expense of storing, moving, and protecting paper money.

_____   2. Everything from shells to cattle has been used as legal tender.

_____   3. People should welcome the coming convenience of electronic money.

_____   4. Already, Swindon, a town in England, allows 8,000 of its citizens to do all transactions using only cybermoney.

_____   5. Planning for the transformation into a cashless society

_____   6. The delicate balance of public money and individual privacy

_____   7. The millions of cheques written every year cost as much as one dollar each by the time they are processed.

_____   8. The costliness of processing cheques

_____   9. Canadians are the world's biggest users of bank cards.

_____   10. In this new cashless world, governments and banks must protect everyone against counterfeiting and other abuses likely to take place.

Writing the effective thesis statement

An effective thesis statement has the following parts:

1. **A topic that is not too broad**: Topics that are too broad usually cause trouble for the writer. Essays with broad topics end up with very general or vague ideas. Broad topics should be narrowed in scope. You can do this by *limiting the topic* (changing the term to cover a smaller part of the topic), or *qualifying the topic* (adding phrases or words to the general term).

   Broad topic: Running for office

   Limited topic: The campaign funding of political candidates in the 2000 election

   Qualified topic: Running for office in Western Canada

A topic can be narrowed in many ways. Choose what will fit into the proper essay length and what will fit your own experience and knowledge.

2. **A controlling idea that you can defend**: The controlling idea is what you want to show or prove about your topic; it is your attitude about that topic. Often the word is an adjective.

   The present campaign funding practices are *controversial*.

   Proposed reforms of campaign funding would be *beneficial* to every part of the election process.

3. **An indication of what strategy of development is to be used**: Often you can use words such as *description, steps, stages, comparison, contrast, causes, effects, reasons, advantages, disadvantages, definition, analysis, persuasion.*

Although not all writers include the strategy in the thesis statement, they must always have in mind what major strategy they plan to use to prove their thesis. Professional writers often use more than one strategy within the same essay. However, in this book, you are asked to develop your essays by using one major strategy at a time. By working in this way, you can concentrate on understanding and developing the skills needed for each specific strategy. What strategy of development does the writer plan to use in the following thesis?

In order to prevent the use of the Internet for pornographic purposes, several steps must be taken to regulate the industry.

Now look back and check the parts of this thesis statement.

General topic:	pornography
Qualified topic:	pornography on the Internet
Controlling idea:	need for regulation
Strategy of development:	steps that need to be taken to prevent improper use of the Internet

EXERCISE 1 Writing the Thesis Statement

Below are five topics. For each one, develop a thesis sentence by (1) limiting or qualifying the general topic, (2) choosing a controlling idea (what you want to explain or prove about the topic), and (3) selecting a strategy that you could use to develop that topic. An example is done for you.

General topic: Senior citizens
a. *Limit or qualify the subject:*
   Community services available to the senior citizens in my town
b. *Controlling idea:*
   To show the great variety of programs
c. *Strategy for development* (narration, process, cause and effect, definition and analysis, comparison or contrast, classification, argument):
   Classify the services into major groups

Thesis statement:
The senior citizens of Regina, Saskatchewan, are fortunate to have three major programs available that help them deal with health, housing, and leisure time.

1. Winter sports

   a. Limit or qualify the subject:

   _____

   b. Controlling idea:

   _____

c. Strategy for development (narration, process, cause and effect, definition and analysis, comparison or contrast, classification, or argument):

_____

Thesis statement:

_____

_____

2. Grocery stores

   a. Limit or qualify the subject:

   _____

   b. Controlling idea:

   _____

   c. Strategy for development (narration, process, cause and effect, definition and analysis, comparison or contrast, classification, or argument):

   _____

Thesis statement:

_____

_____

3. Public schools

   a. Limit or qualify the subject:

   _____

   b. Controlling idea:

   _____

   c. Strategy for development (narration, process, cause and effect, definition and analysis, comparison or contrast, classification, or argument):

   _____

Thesis statement:

_____

_____

4. Gambling

   a. Limit or qualify the subject:

   _____

   b. Controlling idea:

   _____

   c. Strategy for development (narration, process, cause and effect, definition and analysis, comparison or contrast, classification, or argument):

   _____

Thesis statement:

_____

_____

5. Taxes

   a. Limit or qualify the subject:

_____

   b. Controlling idea:

_____

   c. Strategy for development (narration, process, cause and effect, definition and analysis, comparison or contrast, classification, or argument):

_____

Thesis statement:

_____

_____

EXERCISE 2   Writing the Thesis Statement

Below are five topics. For each one, develop a thesis sentence by (1) limiting or qualifying the general topic, (2) choosing a controlling idea (what you want to explain or prove about the topic), and (3) selecting a strategy that you could use to develop that topic. Review the example in Exercise 1 (page 23).

1. News commentators

   a. Limit or qualify the subject:

_____

   b. Controlling idea:

_____

   c. Strategy for development (narration, process, example, cause and effect, definition and analysis, comparison or contrast, classification, or argument):

_____

Thesis statement:

_____

_____

_____

_____

2. Amusement parks

   a. Limit or qualify the subject:

_____

b. Controlling idea:

_____

c. Strategy for development (narration, process, example, cause and effect, definition and analysis, comparison or contrast, classification, or argument):

_____

Thesis statement:

_____

_____

_____

_____

3. Psychology (or another field of study)

a. Limit or qualify the subject:

_____

b. Controlling idea:

_____

c. Strategy for development (narration, process, example, cause and effect, definition and analysis, comparison or contrast, classification, or argument):

_____

Thesis statement:

_____

_____

_____

_____

4. Politicians

a. Limit or qualify the subject:

_____

b. Controlling idea:

_____

c. Strategy for development (narration, process, example, cause and effect, definition and analysis, comparison or contrast, classification, or argument):

_____

Thesis statement:

_____

_____

_____

_____

5. Part-time jobs

   a. Limit or qualify the subject:

     _____

   b. Controlling idea:

     _____

   c. Strategy for development (narration, process, example, cause and effect, definition and analysis, comparison or contrast, classification, or argument):

     _____

Thesis statement:

_____

_____

_____

_____

Ways to write an effective introductory paragraph

> An *introduction* has one main purpose: to "grab" your readers' interest so that they will keep reading.

There is no one way to write an introduction. However, since many good introductions follow the same common patterns, you will find it helpful to look at a few examples of the more typical patterns. When you are ready to create your own introductions, you can consider trying out some of these patterns.

1. *Begin with a general subject that can be narrowed down into the specific topic of your essay.* Here is an introduction to an essay about a family making cider on their farm:

> The number of children who eagerly help around a farm is rather small. Willing helpers do exist, but many more of them are five years old than fifteen. In fact, there seems to be a general law that says as long as a kid is too little to help effectively, he or she is dying to. Then, just as they reach the age when they really could drive a fence post or empty a sap bucket without spilling half of it, they lose interest. Now it's cars they want to drive, or else they want to stay in the house and listen for four straight hours to The Who. There is one exception to this rule. Almost no kid that I have ever met outgrows an interest in cidering.

> From Noel Perrin,
> "Falling for Apples"

2. *Begin with specifics (a brief anecdote, a specific example or fact) that will broaden into the more general topic of your essay.* Here is the introduction to an essay on the influenza epidemic that swept across the world in 1918:

> In the fall of 1918, an ungodly sickness coursed across the globe, killing its victims within just three to five days of infection. It would begin with sudden debilitating headaches and chills, then quickly move on to pneumonia, purpling the faces of sufferers and blackening their feet as they drowned in their own body fluids. During one month, it slew nearly 11,000 in Philadelphia; bodies lay piled three and four deep on the city morgue floor. The pandemic reached as far south as Cape Town, South Africa, and as far north as Alaska, killing 72 of the 80 residents of one Inuit village in a week. The illness even interfered with a rival killer, World War I, as it raced through army camps. This plague left a death count of between 20 and 100 million people—more than the Black Death in the 14th century. But the culprit had a name that, up until 1918, had evoked merely moderate alarm rather that widespread terror: influenza, or the common flu.

> From Gina Kolata,
> "Flu: The Story of the Great Influenza Pandemic of 1918 and the Search for the Virus That Caused It"

3. *Give a definition of the concept that will be discussed.* Here is the introduction to an essay about various ways to control obesity in our society:

> Obesity occurs when the body accumulates fat beyond the needs for its normal function. It is a common condition in Western societies. The clinical assessment and classification of obesity depends on body mass index (BMI; in kg/m²) cutoff points. Although a single cause of obesity cannot be easily identified and treated, there are various ways to help you combat it.

> From Tommy Cheung,
> "Obesity"

4. *Make a startling statement:*

> The real power of the United States is not military or economic; it is Americans' enduring belief in the importance of an informed citizenry. The degree to which this core shapes their day-to-day lives, schools and government allows Americans to think, act and interact with civic efficiency and national purpose. Thanks to an antifacts bias in our schools and an all but nonexistent national education reform movement, Canada is quickly whittling away what little civic knowledge its citizens hold in common. Like cartilage that holds us together, our common knowledge is breaking down. It may go against our instincts, but we should look to the American approach to citizenship education for clues as to how to reconstruct our body politic around a fact-based self-awareness of our own past.

> From Rudyard Griffiths,
> "From Blank to Shining Blank"

5. *Start with an idea or statement that is a widely held point of view. Then surprise the reader by stating that this idea is false or that you hold a different point of view:*

Tom Wolfe has christened today's young adults as the "me" generation, and the 1970s—obsessed with things like consciousness expansion and self-awareness—have been described as the decade of the new narcissism. The cult of "I," in fact, has taken hold with the strength and impetus of a new religion. But the joker in the pack is that it is all based on a false idea.

From Margaret Halsey,
"What's Wrong with 'Me, Me, Me'?"

6. *Start with a familiar quotation or a quotation by a famous person:*

"The very hairs of your head," says Matthew 10:30, "are all numbered." There is little reason to doubt it. Increasingly, everything tends to get numbered one way or another, everything that can be counted, measured, averaged, estimated or quantified. Intelligence is gauged by a quotient, the humidity by a ratio, pollen by its count, and the trends of birth, death, marriage and divorce by rates. In this epoch of runaway demographics, society is as often described and analyzed with statistics as with words. Politics seems more and more a game played with percentages turned up by pollsters, and economics a learned babble of ciphers and indexes that few people can translate and apparently nobody can control. Modern civilization, in sum, has begun to resemble an interminable arithmetic class in which, as Carl Sandburg put it, "numbers fly like pigeons in and out of your head."

From Frank Trippett,
"Getting Dizzy by the Numbers"

7. *Give a number of descriptive images that will lead to the thesis of your essay.* Here is the opening of an essay about the exploration of the aurora borealis:

One of the pleasures of a Canadian winter is the night. Stars spangle the heavens, and between their radiant points, the universe flows outward into endless black. We look up and feel ourselves falling into cosmic emptiness— blank space without matter or movement. But then, if luck is with us, the sky begins to ripple with soft, shimmering curtains of light that fill this seemingly empty cosmos with energy and life. Aurora borealis, or the northern lights. So faint they are seldom seen in summer, these luminous wraiths are a gift of winter's darkness.

From Candace Savage,
"Night Spirits"

8. *Ask a question that you intend to answer.* Many essays you will read in magazines and newspapers use a question in the introductory paragraph to make the reader curious about the author's viewpoint. Some writing instructors prefer that students do not use this method. Check with your instructor for his or her viewpoint. Here is an example of such an introduction:

Suppose there were no critics to tell us how to react to a picture, a play, or a new composition of music. Suppose we wandered innocent as the dawn into an art exhibition of unsigned paintings. By what standards, by what values would we decide whether they were good or bad, talented or untalented, successes or failures? How can we ever know that what we think is right?

From Marya Mannes,
"How Do You Know It's Good?"

9. *Use classification to indicate how your topic fits into the larger class to which it belongs, or how your topic can be divided into categories that you are going to discuss.* Here is how Aaron Copland began an essay on listening to music:

> We all listen to music according to our separate capacities. But, for the sake of analysis, the whole listening process may become clearer if we break it up into its component parts, so to speak. In a certain sense we all listen to music on three separate planes. For lack of a better terminology, one might name these: the sensuous plane, the expressive plane, the sheerly musical plane. The only advantage to be gained from mechanically splitting up the listening process into these hypothetical planes is the clearer view to be had of the way in which we listen.

> From Aaron Copland,
> *What to Listen For in Music*

What *not* to say in your introduction

1. *Avoid telling your reader that you are beginning your essay:*

   In this essay I will discuss . . .

   I will talk about . . .

   I am going to prove . . .

2. *Don't apologize:*

   Although I am not an expert . . .

   In my humble opinion . . .

3. *Do not refer to later parts of your essay:*

   By the end of this essay you will agree . . .

   In the next paragraph you will see . . .

4. *Don't use trite expressions.* Since they have been so overused, they will lack interest. Using such expressions shows that you have not taken the time to use your own words to express your ideas. The following are some examples of trite expressions:

   busy as a bee

   you can't tell a book by its cover

   haste makes waste

Using transitions to move the reader from one idea to the next

Successful essays help the reader understand the logic of the writer's thinking by using transitional expressions when needed. Usually this occurs when the writer is moving from one point to the next. It can also occur whenever the idea is complicated. The writer may need to summarize the points so far; the writer may need to emphasize a point already made; or the writer may want to repeat an important point. The transition may be a word, a phrase, a sentence, or even a paragraph.

- Here are some of the transitional expressions that might be used to help the reader make the right connections:

  1. To make your points stand out clearly:

the first reason	second, secondly	finally
first of all	another example	most important
in the first place	even more important	all in all
	also, next	in conclusion
	then	to summarize

  2. To show an example of what has just been said:

     for example

     for instance

  3. To show the consequence of what has just been said:

     therefore

     as a result

     then

  4. To make a contrasting point clear:

     on the other hand

     but

     contrary to current thinking

     however

  5. To admit a point:

     of course

     granted

  6. To resume your argument after admitting a point:

     nevertheless

     even though

     nonetheless

     still

  7. To call the reader's attention to your organization:

     Before attempting to answer these questions, let me . . .

     In our discussions so far, we have seen that . . .

     At this point, it is necessary to . . .

     It is beyond the scope of this paper to . . .

- A more subtle way to link one idea to another in an essay is to repeat a word or phrase from the preceding sentence. Sometimes instead of the actual word, a pronoun will take the place of the word.

  8. To repeat a word or phrase from a preceding sentence:

     I have many memories of my childhood in China. These *memories* include the aunts, uncles, grandparents, and friends I had to leave behind.

  9. To use a pronoun to refer to a word or phrase from a preceding sentence:

     Like all immigrants, my family and I have had to build a new life from almost nothing. *It* was often difficult, but I believe the struggle made us strong.

EXERCISE 1 Finding Transitional Expressions

Below are the first three paragraphs of an essay on African art. Circle all the transitional expressions including repeated words that are used to link one sentence to another or one idea to the next.

Like language and social organization, art is essential to human life. As embellishment and as creation of objects beyond the requirements of the most basic needs of living, art has accompanied man since prehistoric times. Because of its almost unfailing consistency as an element of many societies, art may be the response to some biological or psychological need. Indeed, it is one of the most constant forms of human behaviour.

However, use of the word *art* is not relevant when we describe African "art" because it is really a European term that at first grew out of Greek philosophy and was later reinforced by European culture. The use of other terms, such as *exotic art, primitive art, art sauvage,* and so on, to delineate differences is just as misleading. Most such terms are pejorative—implying that African art is on a lower cultural level. Levels of culture are irrelevant here, since African and European attitudes toward the creative act are so different. Since there is no term in our language to distinguish between the essential differences in thinking, it is best then to describe standards of African art.

African art attracts because of its powerful emotional content and its beautiful abstract form. Abstract treatment of form describes most often—with bare essentials of line, shape, texture, and pattern—intense energy and sublime spirituality. Hundreds of distinct cultures and languages and many types of people have created over one thousand different styles that defy classification. Each art and craft form has its own history and its own aesthetic content. But there are some common denominators (always with exceptions).

Ways to write an effective concluding paragraph

A concluding paragraph has one main purpose: to give the reader the sense of reaching a satisfying ending to the topic discussed. Students often feel they have nothing to say at the end. A look at how professional writers frequently end their essays can ease your anxiety about writing an effective conclusion. You have more than one possibility. Here are some of the most frequently used patterns for ending an essay:

1. *Come full circle. That is, return to the material in your introduction.* Finish what you started there. Remind your reader of the thesis. Be sure to restate the main idea using different wording. Here is the conclusion to an essay "From Blank to Shining Blank." (The introductory paragraph appears on page 28.)

   In a world of globalization and changing values, we cannot control the cultural products that wash across our borders. Nor should we burden Canadians with the task of saving the country. We can, however, decide how and what our children learn in school. National standards, modelled on the U.S. example, must be at the core of a new national strategy to promote Canadians' self-knowledge. Amnesiacs do not form meaningful relationships; nor can they build national projects.

2. *Summarize by repeating the main points.* This example is the concluding paragraph to an essay on African art. (The first three paragraphs appear on page 32.)

> In summary, African art explains the past, describes values and a way of life, helps man relate to supernatural forces, mediates his social relations, expresses emotions, and enhances man's present life as an embellishment denoting pride or status as well as providing entertainment such as with dance and music.

3. *Show the significance of your thesis by making predictions, giving a warning, giving advice, offering a solution, suggesting an alternative, or telling the results.* This example is the concluding paragraph to "Falling for Apples." (The introductory paragraph appears on page 27.)

> This pleasure goes on and on. In an average year we start making cider the second week of September, and we continue until early November. We make all we can drink ourselves, and quite a lot to give away. We have supplied whole church suppers. One year the girls sold about ten gallons to the village store, which made them some pocket money they were prouder of than any they ever earned from baby-sitting. Best of all, there are two months each year when all of us are running the farm together, just like a pioneer family.

4. *End with an anecdote that illustrates your thesis.* This example is from an essay entitled "Heritage of Storytelling" by Robert Fulford. In the essay the author suggests that storytelling is the only way that people can connect to those who lived in the distant past.

> Those who enjoy stories cherish even minor anecdotes that are charged with meaning. John Ruskin, the great art critic, went so far as to apply this criterion to buildings, which he admired for their ability to speak to him of their past—"Better the rudest work that tells a story or records a fact, than the richest without meaning," he wrote. I cherish some stories for their quirkiness, like one I encountered in *Millennium*, an 830-page account of the past 1,000 years by Felipe Fernandez-Armesto, an Oxford history professor. He tells us that in 1924, at the British Empire Exhibition at Wembley, in a suburb of London, King George V, standing in the Palace of Engineering beside a life-size statue in Canadian butter of his son, the future Edward VIII, illustrated the size of his Empire with a weirdly comical little demonstration. He sent a cabled message to himself, right around the world, and as it circled the globe it went by British wires over (except for the oceans) exclusively British territory. It arrived back at its starting point 28 seconds after he dispatched it. Why did he do it? Because it wasn't enough just to be there, and it wasn't enough just to be king. He wanted also to make a story for posterity—a story to think about, perhaps, in the next millennium.

What *not* to say in your conclusion

1. Do not introduce a new point.

2. Do not apologize.

3. Do not end up in the air, leaving the reader feeling unsatisfied. This sometimes happens if the very last sentence is not strong enough.

A note about titles

Be sure to follow the standard procedure for writing your title.

1. Capitalize all words except articles (*the, a, an*) and prepositions.

2. Do not underline the title or put quotation marks around it.

3. Try to think of a short and catchy phrase (three to six words). Often writers wait until they have written a draft before working on a title. There may be a phrase from the essay that will be perfect. If you still cannot think of a clever title after you have written a draft, choose some key words from your thesis statement.

4. Centre the title at the top of the page, and remember to leave about an inch (2.5 cm) of space between the title and the beginning of the first paragraph.

Working Together

LIFE IN FRONT OF "THE TUBE"

For years before TV took hold in Canada, families gathered in the evening to listen to their favourite radio programs, so the switch to television would seem to be a natural evolution. But "the tube" was more seductive. It made you afraid that you would miss something if you didn't pay attention. It was no longer as easy to sew, play a game, or do homework while listening; you had to be able to watch too.

Most early televisions were substantial pieces of furniture that couldn't be taken from room to room, and they were connected to a roof-top antenna cable.

So that dinner could be prepared quickly and people could eat without missing their favourite show, Swanson's introduced its line of "TV Dinners" in 1954, starting with a turkey entrée in a tray that could be taken right in front of the television set.

On September 6, 1952, the CBC opened the first Canadian TV service with a bilingual station in Montreal. Two days later, it opened an English language TV service in Toronto. For almost a decade, the government-run CBC was the sole television broadcaster in Canada. Then in 1962, the privately owned CTV began operating.

More and more companies aimed their advertisements at what would come to be called the "television generation." Ads for the latest models of television sets proliferated. Some sets, like the one mentioned in the 1949 ad shown here, could cost more than $2,000—at the time, a year's salary.

Most sets, however, were more reasonably priced, and Canadians were buying them. New developments in the technology made TV sets all the more attractive. Television sets were becoming smaller, and by 1966 the first colour TV set was introduced in Canada. Thus, in only a few years, television had become a source of information, a primary form of entertainment, a baby sitter or companion, and an important sector of the national economy.

In this chapter, you have studied the essay form. The essay above reviews the earliest years of our television era, a time when our society was still getting used to this new source of entertainment. Have a member of the class read the essay out loud, and use a period of class discussion to answer the following questions.

1. What is the purpose of the essay?

2. Look at the introductory paragraph. Which sentence has the topic and controlling idea for the essay? What word would you pick for the controlling idea? Describe how the writer has used the introductory paragraph to introduce the topic.

3. How many paragraphs form the body of the essay? How does the writer develop the ideas?

4. What does the writer do in the conclusion?

5. This article was written for an audience interested in Canadian history. How does this writer show sensitivity to this fact?

You may want to make a copy of this essay to include in your portfolio. Writing about the significance of television in Canadian life is an endlessly interesting subject and may be one you will want to write about. Many of the facts from this essay may be useful to you at that time.

THE ESSAY   *Chapter 3*

Watching a Student Essay Take Form

It's an exciting experience for most writers to see a beginning thought or inspiration evolve into a fully developed essay. In this chapter, you will follow a student writer as she works through the sequence of steps, from the initial assignment to the final proofreading of her essay.

The sequence of steps in the writing process are given here so you can review them before you study the student's development of her essay.

STEPS IN THE WRITING PROCESS

1. Find a topic and controlling idea for the thesis statement.

2. Gather the information using brainstorming techniques or research.

3. Select and organize material.

4. Write the rough draft.

5. Revise the rough draft for greater clarity of ideas. (Many writers work on several drafts before a satisfactory final version is reached.)

6. Edit the revised draft for correctness. (Correct errors such as misspellings or faulty grammar.)

7. Prepare the final typed copy, print it out, and proofread.

As you follow the student's progress through this chapter, you should maintain a critical attitude. That is, you should be prepared to analyze how well the student succeeds in producing a finished essay. Ask yourself what you might have done with the same topic. You may eventually want to write your own essay on the same topic, but with a very different controlling idea.

Choose a topic and a controlling idea for the thesis statement

The student's first task is to think over what topic would be appropriate and what approach should be taken. This leads the writer in the direction of developing a tentative thesis—the sentence that states the main idea—for the entire essay. Although not all essays come right out and state the thesis directly, the writer must always have a main idea if the writing is to be focused. A reader should never have to wonder what your main idea is.

In this case, the student has been asked to write an essay about a social issue using cause or effect as the method of development. Having this assignment from the beginning is helpful because it gives the student a good sense of direction. With the help of several members of the class, she begins by making a list of possible topics on social issues that come to mind.

The causes of children failing in school

The causes of children succeeding in school

The effects of dishonesty in business

The causes of couples choosing to have small families

The effects of growing up in a large city

The effects of consumerism on the environment

The effects on the family when both parents work

The effects of being an only child

The topic she chooses is important because her success will depend on selecting a topic that is of interest to her. Writing on a topic that you don't care about will not produce a very creative result.

The student reviews the list, talks over the ideas with others, and finds herself responding most directly to the topic of families with two wage earners. Although she doesn't work at present and her mother never worked outside the home, she intends to find a job as soon as she finishes her education. She has been thinking about the changes that going to work might mean for her family, particularly her husband. Not only is the topic of real interest to her, but she suspects most people in her class, many of whom are young mothers, will also have a strong interest in the topic.

Once a student knows the subject for the essay, there still is the question about what the point should be for this essay. Many students may find it difficult to figure this out before they actually do some brainstorming and see what material they have to develop. In this case, the instructor has already asked the students in the class to develop their essay by discussing the causes or the effects. This limits how our student can handle the material. Her main form of development will not be to tell a story about a friend who works (narration). She will not contrast a woman who works outside the home to a woman who stays at home (comparison and contrast); she will not give advice on how a woman can manage a job and a family at the same time (process). Although writing often can combine methods of development, she will focus on the *effects* on the family when both parents work.

Gathering information using brainstorming techniques

Here is what the student listed when she thought about her topic, *Working Parents:*

no time to cook
more microwavable dinners
more fast food
nobody at home for deliveries
hard to get to bank and make medical appointments
grocery shopping on weekends

moms often do most chores around the house while working full-time

moms feel too tired—no time for relaxing

dads must do more household chores and child care

moms not home for children's emergencies

moms may feel confused about roles

dads may feel resentful

some marriages could fall apart

Some writers like to cluster their ideas when they brainstorm. *Clustering* is a visual map of your ideas rather than a list. Had the student clustered her ideas, they might have looked like this:

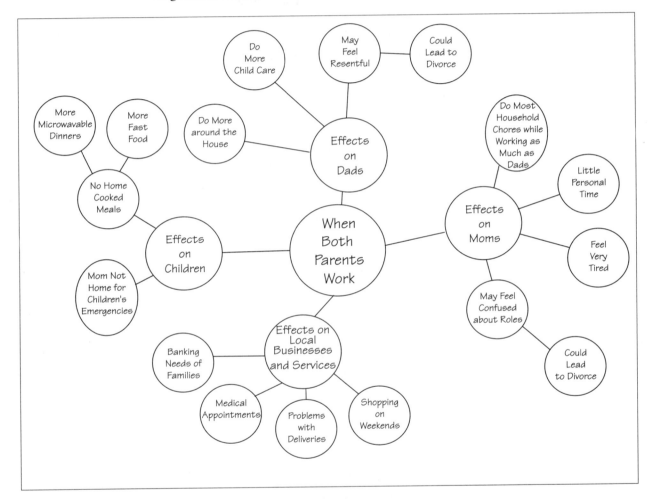

You might want to try both ways of generating ideas to see which approach works best for you.

Selecting and organizing the material

When the student has listed as many ideas as she can think of and has also asked her classmates for their ideas, she then looks over the list to see how she might group the words, phrases, or ideas into sections. Perhaps some ideas should be crossed out and not used at all. Maybe other ideas could be further developed. The student must also remember that once she starts to write, some creative flow may also direct her writing away from the exact outline she has developed by this point. That is fine. The outline is useful if it keeps the focus of the essay in mind.

Many instructors require the student to write a tentative thesis statement and an outline at this point so the instructor can verify that the student is on the right track. Here is the outline the student wrote:

Topic:	Parents who work outside the home
Method of Development:	Discuss the effects on the family
Tentative Thesis:	When economic needs force both parents to work, the effects on the family are noticeable.

I. Introductory paragraph: Economy makes it necessary for both parents to work

II. Support paragraphs: Effects on the family

    A. Effects on children
       1. No hot meals
       2. No sympathetic ear

    B. Effects on local businesses and services
       1. Medical appointments
       2. Banking and other businesses
       3. Grocery shopping

    C. Effects on dads
       1. More household chores
       2. More child care
       3. More meal preparation

    D. Effects on moms
       1. Do most household chores while working as much as dads
       2. Work never ends
       3. Little personal time
       4. Feel too tired

    E. Effects on family eating habits
       1. More convenience foods
       2. More microwavable foods

III. Concluding paragraph: Effects on marriage

    A. Dads could feel threatened

    B. Dads could feel resentful

    C. Moms could also feel resentful

    D. Moms could feel overworked

    E. Could lead to divorce

Writing the rough draft

This student went to the computer lab where she knew she could work without interruption. With her outline and brainstorming list in front of her, she wrote the first draft of her essay. At this point, she was not concerned about a polished piece of work. The writer's goal was to get all her thoughts written down as a first draft. When she finished this rough draft, she not only saved it on a diskette of her own, she also printed out her draft so she could take the hard copy (actual printed pages) with her for later review. At that time, she would be ready to consider making revisions.

Read the student's rough draft and discuss your first impressions of it with your classmates. What are the strengths and weaknesses of this draft?

When Both Parents Work

1   The economy today has made it necessary for both parents to work. Rising prices have made two-income families the norm. What has been the effect?

2   The most noticeable change for most families is that Mom is no longer home during the day. She is not there to fix hot lunches or to soothe scrape knees and bruised egos.

3   Another effect of Mom's absence from the home is that businesses are discovering she is no longer available to let meter readers in, accept furniture deliveries, take children to the doctor and dentist, or take care of banking needs. Just as many supermarkets have changed to a twenty-four-hour selling day, retail stores and service industries are beginning to realize that they must also adapt if they want to keep the working woman's business.

4   Despite the fact that she may work over eight hours a day, Mom must often come home to a dirty house and hungry family. While Dad's duties should include a share of the domestic responsibilites, rarely does he ever chip in to help around the house. He may mow the lawn and take out the garbage, but doing the laundry, taking care of the kids, and making dinner are still considered parts of Mom's household routine.

5   Sometimes mothers can leave their kids with grandparents on weekends. Grandpa and Grandma try to give Mom a break, so they take the children out for a few hours or even an entire day. This is a positive experience for the children, for they will remember these as happy hours spent with the exclusive attention of their elders.

6   What about meals? Dad may be asked to help out, but many men (and women) still feel that the kitchen is the woman's domain. The idea the women belong in the kitchen is still a popular one. Enter time-saving appliances, such as the microwave oven and convenience foods such as microwavable entrees. Mom simply doesn't have the time or the energy to prepare traditional meals. Instant meals are no longer considered a luxury and the food industry is cahsing in on the demand. Even old standby items on the grocery shelves now proclaim that they are microwavable. A fact that is not hurting sales one bit.

7   How does the family feel about Mom's new list of responsibilites? Dad may feel somewhat resentful over the fact that he may be asked to take on some of the chores around the house. Mom may feel bitter because she has to do most of household chores while working as much as Dad does. In marriages that are not solid to beging with, this mutual resentment may build up and lead to divorce.

Revising the rough draft for greater clarity of ideas

When the student has left the rough draft for a day or more and then returns to make revisions, she must consider what needs to be changed. Some of the questions that follow should help in the revision process. Go through these questions with your classmates and discuss what revisions need to be made. Remember that at this stage the writer should be concerned about the ideas and the organization of the ideas, not how a word is spelled or where a comma belongs.

1. Is the essay unified? Does the writer stick to the topic? Does any material need to be cut?

2. Does she repeat herself anywhere? If so, what needs to be cut?

3. Does the essay make sense? Can you follow her logic? If any spot is confusing, how could she make her idea clear? Sometimes the use of transitional expressions such as *another effect, the most important effect,* or *the second effect* will help show the writer is moving to the next point.

4. Are the paragraphs roughly the same length? If you see one sentence presented as a paragraph, you know something is wrong.

5. Does the essay follow essay form? Is there an introductory paragraph with the thesis statement? Are there at least three supporting paragraphs in the body of the essay? Is there a concluding paragraph?

6. Are there places where more specific details could be added to develop an idea further or to add more interest?

7. Could the introduction, conclusion, or title be more creative?

Now let's look at what the student's writing instructor suggested. Here is the rough draft again with the instructor's comments written in the margins. Notice that all corrections of punctuation, spelling, and grammar have yet to be considered. See if you agree with the instructor's comments. Think about what other comments you would have added if you had been the instructor.

When Both Parents Work

You might be able to think of a more catchy title.

Introductory paragraph needs more development. You might tell us more about the economy.

1 The economy today has made it necessary for both parents to work. Rising prices have made two-income families the norm. What has been the effect?

2 The most noticeable change for most families is that Mom is no longer home during the day. She is not there to fix hot lunches or to soothe scrape knees and bruised egos. *Is anyone available for this? More development please!*

3 Another effect of Mom's absence from the home is that businesses are discovering she is no longer available to let meter readers in, accept furniture deliveries, take children to the doctor and dentist, or take care of banking needs. Just as many supermarkets have changed to a twenty-four-hour selling day, retail stores and service industries are beginning to realize that they must also adapt if they want to keep the working woman's business. *good specific details*

4 Despite the fact that she may work over eight hours a day, Mom must often come home to a dirty house and hungry family. While Dad's duties should include a share of the domestic responsibilities, rarely does he ever chip in to help around the house. He may mow the lawn and take out the garbage, but doing the laundry, taking care of the kids, and making dinner are still considered parts of Mom's household routine. *What exactly does Dad do now? Be more specific. Give examples.*

*This ¶ is not rele-
vant to this essay,
is it? Omit it in
your next draft or
revise it.*

5 Sometimes mothers can leave their kids with grandparents on weekends. Grandpa and Grandma try to give Mom a break, so they take the children out for a few hours or even an entire day. This is a positive experience for the children, for they will remember these as happy hours spent with the exclusive attention of their elders.

6 What about meals? Dad may be asked to help out, but many men (and women) still feel that the kitchen is the woman's domain. The idea the women belong in the kitchen is still a popular one. Enter time-saving appliances, such as the microwave oven and convenience foods such as microwavable entrees. Mom simply doesn't have the time or the energy to prepare traditional meals. Instant meals are no longer considered a luxury and the food industry is cashing in on the demand. Even old standby items on the grocery shelves now proclaim that they are microwavable. A fact that is not hurting sales one bit.

*Don't these two
sentences say the
same thing?*

*In your concluding
¶, you might look
to the future for
more positive solu-
tions or summarize
all your points.*

7 How does the family feel about Mom's new list of responsibilities? Dad may feel somewhat resentful over the fact that he may be asked to take on some of the chores around the house. Mom may feel bitter because she has to do most of household chores while working as much as Dad does. In marriages that are not solid to begin with, this mutual resentment may build up and lead to divorce.

*This ¶ presents
another effect. It is
not a conclusion.*

Editing the revised draft for correctness

Until now, the student has been concerned with the content and organization of the essay. After the student is satisfied with these revisions, it is time to look at the sentences themselves for errors such as faulty grammar, misspelling, incorrect punctuation, and inappropriate diction.

Now she should take each sentence by itself, perhaps starting with the last sentence and working backwards. (This will help her focus on the correctness of the sentences and words themselves rather than on the ideas.) She should concentrate on any weaknesses that usually cause problems for her. Many of the errors we make are unconscious and therefore hard for us to spot. Some attention from another student may be helpful and may lead to finding some of her particular errors.

When you edit your draft, look for problems such as those suggested in the following list:

1. Sentence level errors: run-ons and fragments, often corrected by use of the proper punctuation.

2. Misspellings.

3. Lack of understanding about when to use the comma.

4. Possessives: *dog's* collar, but *its* collar.

5. Diction: wordiness, use of slang, informal language or abbreviated forms, wrong word.

6. Grammar errors: subject-verb agreement, parallel structure, pronoun consistency.

Here is the fourth paragraph from the student's revised draft. The student has responded to the instructor's comments and has added more specific details, along with examples. Edit the paragraph for correctness, finding at least one mistake from each of the problem areas just listed.

When Mom comes home in the evening, however, she often finds that her workday is not over. For despite the fact that she may work over eight hours a day, she must often come home to a dirty house and hungry family. Sure, Dad mows the lawn and takes out the garbage, but doing the laundry, taking are of the kids, and to make dinner are still considered parts of Moms household routine. As a result of her double responsibilities. Mom has little time for herself. She may be working as a receptionist or cashier but does not have the time to go to night school to take the courses she needs to find a more rewarding job. And though Dad may be able to relax and unwind on weekends by watching hockey or football on TV or playing golf, weekends for Mom have become a time when she catches up on her housekeeping. Most importantly, however, Mom might wish she had more time to read her favourite detective novel, she undoubtedly feels alot of remorse over the fact that she has less time to spend with her family. It is sad that the only time left for many women and their kids are the couple of ours before and after daycare.

Preparing the final copy

Read the student's final version, which she has typed, printed, and proofread. Compare it to the rough draft. Did the student make the changes suggested by the instructor? In what ways has the essay improved? What criticisms do you still have?

A Mother's Work Is Never Done

1   Inflation. Recession. No matter what you call the current state of our economy, virtually all of us have been touched by its effects. Rising prices and the shrinking dollar have made two-income families, once a rarity, now almost the norm. Besides fattening the family pocketbook (if only to buy necessities), how else has this phenomenon changed our lives?

2   The most notable change for most families is that Mom is no longer home during the day. She is not there to fix hot lunches or to soothe scraped knees and bruised egos. So who does? The answer, unfortunately, often is "No one." Countless numbers of children have become "latchkey children," left to fend for themselves after school because there aren't enough dependable, affordable baby sitters or after-school programs for them. Some children are able to handle this early independence quite well and may even become more resourceful adults because of it, but many are not. Vandalism, petty crimes, alcohol and drug abuse may all be products of this unsupervised life, problems that society must deal with eventually. Some companies (although too few) have adapted to this changing lifestyle by instituting on-site childcare facilities and/or "flextime" schedules for working mothers and fathers. Despite cutbacks in education funding, some schools continue to provide after-school activities during the school year, and summer day camps are filling the need during those months.

3   Another effect of Mom's absence from the home is that businesses are discovering that she is no longer available to let meter readers in, accept furniture deliveries, take children to the doctor and dentist, or take care of banking needs. Just as

many supermarkets have changed to a twenty-four-hour selling day, retail stores and service industries are beginning to realize that they must also adapt if they want to keep the working woman's business.

4   When Mom comes home in the evening, however, she often finds that her workday is not over. For despite the fact that she may work over eight hours a day, she must often come home to a dirty house and hungry family. Dad may mow the lawn and take out the garbage, but doing the laundry, taking care of the kids, and making dinner are still considered parts of Mom's household routine. As a result of her double responsibilities, Mom has little time for herself. She may be working as a accountant or manager but does not have the time to go to night school to take the courses she needs to advance in her career. And though Dad may be able to relax and unwind on weekends by watching hockey or football on TV or playing golf, weekends for Mom have become a time when she catches up on her house-keeping. Most importantly, however, Mom may wish she had more time to read her favourite detective novel. She undoubtedly feels a lot of remorse over the fact that she has less time to spend with her family. It is sad that the only time left for many women and their kids are the couple of hours before and after daycare.

5   The new role that Mom has taken on has also affected the family's diet. Again, Dad may be asked to help out, but many men (and women) still feel that the kitchen is the woman's domain. Enter time-saving appliances, such as the microwave oven and convenience foods such as "heat and eat" entrées. Mom simply doesn't have the time or the energy to prepare traditional meals, including pot roast and home-baked bread. Instant meals are no longer considered a luxury and the food industry is cashing in on the demand. Even old standby items on the grocery shelves are proclaiming that they are microwavable, a fact that is not hurting their sales on bit. However, even with quickie meals, Mom is just sometimes too tired to cook. At those times, fast-food restaurants enjoy the family's business. They offer no fuss, no muss, and someone to clean up after the meal. In order to preserve their share of this growing market, many grocery stores are now offering home meal replacement products. People can just stop by the local supermarket and pick up a top quality, ready-made dinner for the whole family. Maybe part of the reason for the success of take-out counters and home meal replacements is that women are beginning to realize that their time is valuable too, and if food prices are high anyway, they reason, they might as well eat out and not have to spend their few precious hours at home in the kitchen.

6   How does the family feel about Mom's new list of responsibilities? Dad may feel somewhat resentful over the fact that he may be asked to take on some of the chores around the house. Mom may feel bitter because she has to do most of the household chores while working as much as Dad does. In marriages that are not solid to begin with, this mutual resentment may build up and lead to divorce.

7   Yes, the two-income family has played havoc with our lifestyles but it hasn't been all bad. There are problems that must be solved, changes that are difficult to accept, priorities that must be rearranged. However, with increased pressure from the growing number of two-income families, these problems will be addressed. Hopefully society in general and individual families in particular will find even better ways to deal with these changes regarding how we raise our children, how we care for our homes, and how we view our marriages and ourselves.

Working Together

1. Imagine yourself in the following situation: you and your classmates are guidance counsellors in a high school. You have been asked to produce a brochure that will be entitled, "When a Young Person Quits School." This brochure is intended for students who are thinking of dropping out of school. You and the other counsellors meet to brainstorm on the topic. Divide into groups. Each group will choose a method of brainstorming: clustering, mapping, or listing. Work for 15 minutes or so, and then come together again as a class. Discuss what brainstorming method you chose and then on the board make a final grouping of the ideas for this topic.

2. In groups or as a class, construct an outline for the essay on "When a Young Person Quits School" using the information gathered in the brainstorming activity above. Organize the information into main points and supporting details under those main points.

Chapter 4

Writing an Essay Using Examples, Illustrations, or Anecdotes

Exploring the topic: Body envy

Canadians have become increasingly body-conscious. In this chapter, you will be working on an essay that emphasizes the use of *example*. As you answer the following questions, and as you read the selection in this chapter, you will be preparing to write an essay of your own, complete with examples that will illustrate and support the points you are making.

1. Based on what you have read and heard, do most people act reasonably or unreasonably when it comes to their physical appearances? Can you think of a time when you or your friends were not concerned with how you looked?

   _____

   _____

   _____

2. Based on your discussions with others, do you think that there are any risks associated with a preoccupation with one's physical appearance?

   _____

   _____

   _____

3. Some cultures have different attitudes toward how a person looks. Are there differences and similarities between these different cultural ideas of what a beautiful person looks like?

   _____

   _____

   _____

4. Have you ever looked at yourself and not been happy with a particular physical attribute? Have you considered changing that aspect of your appearance? Why or why not?

   _____

   _____

   _____

Reading a model essay to discover examples, illustrations, and anecdotes

The concern with our physical appearances has led to some startling behaviour. For example, our obsession with being thin lies at the root of a number of serious psychological disorders. Our desire to look like our favourite actors has created a booming business among plastic surgeons. In the following essay, reporter Nora Underwood details some of the effects of our obsession with physical appearance.

Body Envy
NORA UNDERWOOD

1   Dr. Stephen Mulholland is no psychic, but he can make astoundingly accurate predictions about what his clients are going to want. All he has to do is run through the movie listings and keep on top of popular television shows, and the Toronto plastic surgeon can anticipate at least some of the business that will be coming his way. Angelina Jolie is on the cover of several magazines and starring in a couple of movies? Requests for lip augmentations will soar. Jennifer Lopez displays her assets in a barely there dress at an awards ceremony and breast implants become even more of a must-have. Leonardo DiCaprio strips down in *Titanic* or *The Beach*, and requests for hair removal shoot up 20 per cent. "I have been amazed by the call of Hollywood," says Mulholland. "Younger people want to look done. They want to take on the physical attributes and characteristics of the stars of the day."

2   American writer Allen Ginsberg once said: "Whoever controls the media—the images—controls the culture." Truer words were never spoken. The media, and those they celebrate, have always influenced fashion and body shape. But what's remarkable now is how profoundly body image is affected by popular culture, and how willing—no, eager—people are to mess with Mother Nature.

3   Why the rush to retool? For one thing, baby boomers—the demographic group that can usually be counted on to rewrite the rules—are stampeding across the 50-year mark. They have long been obsessed with youth and vitality, and even before researchers mapped a rough draft of the human body's genes earlier this year, the prospects for a longer, healthier life were increasing all the time. So were the options for making changes, be they profound or merely skin-deep—from celebrity-endorsed diets and exercise crazes to fitness trainers, weight-loss or muscle-building drugs and sophisticated cosmetic surgery procedures.

4   There are best-seller lists packed with diet books (Dr. Atkins' *New Diet Revolution*, Barry Sears' *The Zone*), magazines filled with the beauty secrets of the stars ("Never eat bread!" "Do three hours of yoga every day!") and, everywhere, famous thin women and body-hair-free heavily bicepped men. "We place such a big premium on whatever the designers and image-makers have created as what's beautiful," says Mulholland. "That inspires conformity, it inspires the concept of self-worth through physical attractiveness. 'Beauty fades' just isn't true anymore."...

5   How thin is too thin? The average North American woman is five-foot-four and weighs 140 lb.; the average model, on the other hand, is five-foot-11 and weighs 117 lb. In May, the British medical establishment issued a report that blamed the media's preoccupation with the ultra-thin on the growing numbers of eating disorders among young women. "Female models are becoming thinner at a time when women are becoming heavier, and the gap between the ideal body shape and the reality is wider than ever," the British Medical Association wrote. "There is a need for more realistic body shapes to be shown on television and in fashion magazines."

At a summit in London a month later, British editors pledged to monitor images that appeared in their magazines and use "models who varied in shape and size."...

6   Others are also challenging the thin-is-in ethic. Three years ago, Allyson Mitchell and Mariko Tamaki founded Pretty, Porky and Pissed Off, a Toronto-based fat activist group. They initially handed out flyers and candy outside a fashionable clothing store that sold only small-sized items. They have since put on plays, organized regular clothing swaps with other large women and are now working on a documentary. They approach the subject of fat in a humorous way, but their message is serious. "It's important to reach out to other people because our stories are all very similar—like never having clothes that fit, crazy yo-yo diets," says Tamaki. "So we're trying to tell kids that beauty is more than fitting into a size-4 pant."...

7   Anyone who thinks men are somehow spared body-image angst hasn't looked closely at the covers of men's magazines lately, with their photo spreads and advertisements featuring brawny, chiselled studs. Not that such pressures are new—Montreal's Weider brothers began pumping up their body-building empire in the 1940s. But Dr. Harrison Pope Jr., a professor of psychiatry at Harvard Medical School and one of the authors of *The Adonis Complex*, published earlier this year, believes that men's insecurities are becoming as insidious as women's. "Men are now beginning to get a taste of the same medicine that women have had to put up with for decades," explains Pope, "namely seeing pictures of unattainably perfect bodies in the media."

8   Pope and his colleagues devised a test for college men in the United States and Europe. Each man was shown a computerized image of a male body and was asked to change it to create the look he wanted and the one he thought women would like best. On both sides of the Atlantic, the college students wanted an average of 30 lb. more muscle than they had, which they also felt would make them more attractive to women. When the researchers asked women to choose the male bodies they found attractive, they generally picked men with only slightly more muscle than average.

9   Part of what is fuelling male insecurity, says Pope, is the advent of anabolic steroids. "It's now possible to create male bodies that are more muscular and leaner than any natural male," he says. Pope also argues that many men have focused on their bodies as one of the few remaining ways to express their masculinity. "Women now can fly combat aircraft, they can go to military academies, they can be CEOs of multinational corporations," he adds, "so that men's traditional roles as soldiers and defenders and breadwinners have gradually been eroded." But no matter how much women can do, says Pope, they can't benchpress 300 lb.

10   Mark knows all about body-image pressures. He exercises like mad, is careful about what he eats and still wasn't happy with how he looked. "I wanted to look thinner and I didn't want to look quite so old," says the 45-year-old man, who does not wish to be identified. "I didn't want to look like I was 27. I wanted to look like a good 45." Mark had liposuction from his chest and abdomen, and had fat removed from under his chin and injected under his eyes to take away his tired look. Men, in fact, now comprise nine per cent of cosmetic surgeons' clients; men's liposuction procedures alone have increased 200 per cent since 1992.

11   But as John Xiros Cooper points out, obsessions with the body long predate Hollywood. "You just need one visit to the archeological museum in Athens to be impressed by how good-looking the Greeks were," laughs Cooper, an associate English professor at the University of British Columbia in Vancouver, who is interested in the cultural impact of mass media. "But the body has become a commodity and like all commodities it's in constant need of updates. Now we have the technological means of changing its shape and the genome project has opened the door to unimaginable things. So the question is, how far are we going to go?" Bodies that are more perfect? Now there's something to feel insecure about.

Analyzing the writer's strategies

1. In the first paragraph of this essay, the writer chooses a variety of examples to introduce her subject. Examine each sentence of the paragraph and underline each example. How do these different examples show the various ways that we are insecure about our bodies?

2. One of the points the writer makes throughout her essay is that our obsession with physical appearance is fuelled by the images we receive from the media— movies, TV, magazines, and advertising. How do the contents of the different paragraphs confirm the idea that the media affect our self-perceptions?

3. One method the writer uses to make her work more memorable is to be very specific when she uses examples. Choose one paragraph in the essay and judge the example in that paragraph. How has the writer made a good example even better by being specific?

4. Can you find an anecdote in this essay? (An anecdote tells a brief story in order to illustrate a point.)

Writing an essay using examples, illustrations, or anecdotes

Of the many ways writers choose to support their ideas, none is more useful or appreciated than the *example*. All of us have ideas in our minds, but these ideas will not become real for our readers until we use examples to make our concepts clear, concrete, and convincing. Writers who use good examples will be able to hold the attention of their readers.

> *Example,* one of the methods for developing a writer's ideas, provides one or more instances of the idea, either briefly or in some detail, in order to clarify, make concrete, or convince readers of the more general idea or point.

The following terms are closely related:

example:	a specific instance of something being discussed
extended example:	an example that is developed at some length, often taking up one or more complete paragraphs
illustration:	an example used to clarify or explain
anecdote:	a brief story used to illustrate a point

Find a topic and controlling idea for the thesis statement

Suggested topics for writing

Here is a list of possible topics that could lead to an essay using example as the main method of development. The section that follows this list will help you work through the various stages of the writing process.

1. Doctors I Have Encountered
2. The Quality of Medical Care

3. Crises Children Face

4. What Makes a Class Exciting

5. Features to Look for When Buying a _____

6. The World's Worst Habits

7. The Lifestyles of Students Today

8. The Increasing Problem of Homelessness

9. People I Have Admired

10. The Top Five Best Recording Artists

Using this list or ideas of your own, jot down two or three topics that appeal to you.

_____

_____

_____

From these topics, select the one you think would give you the best opportunity for writing. About which one do you feel strongest? About which one are you the most expert? Which one is most likely to interest your readers? Which one is best suited to being developed into an essay containing examples?

Selected Topic: _____

Your next step is to decide what your controlling idea should be. What is the point you want to make about the topic you have chosen? For instance, if you choose to write about "Doctors I Have Encountered," your controlling idea may be "compassionate," or it may be "egotistical."

Controlling idea: _____

Now put your topic and controlling idea together into your thesis statement.

Thesis statement: _____

_____

Gather the information (use brainstorming techniques)

Take at least fifteen minutes to jot down every example you can think of that you could use in your essay. If your topic is not of a personal nature, you might form a group to help each other think of examples, anecdotes, and illustrations. Later, you may want to refer to material from magazines or newspapers if you feel your examples need to be improved. If you do use outside sources, be sure to take notes, checking the correct spelling of names and the accuracy of dates and facts.

_____

_____

_____

_____

_____

_____

_____

_____

_____

_____

_____

_____

_____

_____

_____

Select and organize material

Review your list of examples, crossing out any ideas that are not useful. Do you have enough material to develop three body paragraphs? This might mean using three extended examples, some anecdotes, or several smaller examples that could be organized into three different groups. Decide the order in which you want to present your examples. Do you have any ideas for how you might want to write the introduction? On the lines that follow, show your plan for organizing your essay. You may want to make an outline that will show major points with supporting details under each major point.

_____

_____

_____

_____

_____

_____

_____

_____

_____

_____

_____

_____

_____

_____

_____

Write the rough draft

Now you are ready to write your rough draft. Approach the writing with the attitude that you are going to write down all your thoughts on the subject without worrying about mistakes of any kind. It is important that your mind is relaxed enough to allow your thoughts to flow freely, even if you do not follow your plan exactly. Just get your thoughts on paper. You are free to add ideas, drop others, or rearrange the order of your details at any point. Sometimes a period of freewriting leads to new ideas, ideas that could be better than the ones you had in your brainstorming session. Once a writer has something on paper, he or she usually feels a great sense of relief, even though it is obvious there are revisions ahead.

Coherence in the example essay

Keep in mind that in a paragraph with several examples, the order of these examples usually follows some logical progression. This could mean that you would start with the less serious and then move to the more serious, or you might start with the simpler one and move to the more complicated. If your examples consist of events, you might begin with examples from the more distant past and move forward to give examples from the present day. Whatever logical progression you choose, you will find it helpful to signal your examples by using some of the transitional expressions that follow.

TRANSITIONAL EXPRESSIONS IN ESSAYS USING EXAMPLES
the following illustration
to illustrate this
as an illustration
for example
for instance
specifically
an example of this is
such as
one such case
a typical case
To prove my point, listen to what happened to
Let me tell you a story.

Guidelines for revising the essay using examples

As you work on your rough draft, you may revise alone, with a group, with a peer tutor, or directly with your instructor. Here are some of the basic questions you should consider at this most important stage of your work:

1. Does the rough draft satisfy the conditions for the essay form? Is there an introductory paragraph? Are there at least three well-developed paragraphs in the body of the essay? Does each of these paragraphs have at least one example? Is there a concluding paragraph? Remember that one sentence is not usually

considered an acceptable paragraph. (Many journalistic pieces do not follow this general rule because they often have a space limitation and are not expected to develop every idea.)

2. Have you used *example* as your major method of development? Could you make your examples even better by being more specific or by looking up statistics or facts that would lend more authority to your point of view? Could you quote an expert on the subject?

3. What is the basis for the ordering of your examples? Whenever appropriate, did you use transitions to signal the beginning of an example?

4. Is any important part missing? Are there any parts that seem irrelevant or out of place?

5. Are there expressions or words that need to be better chosen? Is there any place where you have been repetitious?

6. Find at least two verbs (usually some form of the verb "to be") that could be replaced with more descriptive verbs. Add at least two adjectives that will provide better sensory images for the reader.

7. Find at least one place in the draft where you can add a sentence or two that will make an example better.

8. Can you think of a more effective way to begin or end?

9. Show your draft to two other readers and ask each one to give you at least one suggestion for improvement.

Prepare the final copy, print, and proofread it

The typing of the final version should follow the traditional rules for an acceptable submission.

CHECKLIST FOR THE FINAL COPY

Use only 8½-by-11 inch paper (never paper torn out of a spiral bound notebook).

Type on one side of the paper only.

Double space.

Leave approximately 1 inch (2.5 cm) margins on each side of the paper.

Centre the title at the top of the page. Do not put quotation marks around the title and do not underline it.

Do not hyphenate a word at the end of a line unless you are willing to consult a dictionary to check on the acceptable division of the word into syllables.

You may put your name, the date, and the title of your paper on a separate title page. Ask your instructor for specific advice on what information to include.

Indent each paragraph five spaces.

Leave two spaces after each period.

If your paper is more than one page, number the pages and paper clip the pages together so they will not get lost.

Do not forget to make a copy before you submit the paper.

Note: In most cases, teachers will not accept handwritten work. However, if you are submitting handwritten work, you must be sure to write on every other line and have good legible handwriting. Begin today to learn to type on the computer. You will be at a disadvantage if you cannot use the current technology.

Once you have typed your final version and printed it out, an important step still remains. This step can often mean the difference of an entire letter grade. You must *proofread* your paper. Even if you have used a spellcheck feature available on your word processing program, there still could be errors in your paper. The spellcheck feature only finds groupings of letters that are not words. For example, if you typed the word *van* when you meant to type *ban,* the spellcheck would not catch this error.

The secret of good proofreading is to look at each word and sentence construction by itself without thinking about the paper's contents.

CHECKLIST FOR PROOFREADING

Study each sentence: One way to proofread is to read backwards, starting with the last sentence and examining every sentence, one at a time. First, check that the sentence is really complete and not a fragment or a run-on. Then check the punctuation. Go on to the next sentence and do the same. In this way, you will develop a critical eye for spotting any problems with sentence level errors.

Study each word: Read the paper again, this time studying each word in every sentence. Look at the letters of the words. Have you transposed any letters or have you left off an ending such as the *-ed* or the *-s?* If there are any words you are not sure how to spell, do not forget to check for the correct spelling. Is there any word you have omitted?

Working Together

Brainstorming a topic as a group can create ideas and stimulate interest in the topic. A few fresh ideas will get everyone thinking and add to the list of possibilities. Students should work in groups to come up with a variety of anecdotes or illustrations that would be used in an essay on one of the following topics:

1. People who are fun to be around (or people who are annoying).

2. Courses most students like (or dislike).

3. Assignments that drive students crazy.

Twenty minutes of brainstorming may produce enough material to help everyone get started. Every person should then work on his or her own essay. Work for one hour to produce a first draft.

At the next class meeting, your instructor may want each group to discuss the drafts for possible revisions.

Chapter 5

Writing an Essay Using Narration

Exploring the topic: Confronting anxiety

At one time or another, we have all found ourselves in situations where we have been nervous or uncomfortable. Perhaps it was being overwhelmed by a large organization with its rules and regulations, or perhaps it was a new experience in an unfamiliar place. The essay you will write in this chapter will be a narrative essay, based on an experience that happened to you. As you answer the questions, and as you read the narrative selection in this chapter, you will be preparing to write your own personal experience essay.

1. From your own observation, what causes the most anxiety for a student on the first day in a new school?

   _____

   _____

   _____

2. When a person is about to go to a new school, or start a new job, or enter any other new situation, what is the best way to prepare?

   _____

   _____

   _____

3. How do you react when you are faced with an assignment such as making a report or presentation in front of a class?

   _____

   _____

   _____

4. How does it feel to be the only person in a situation where everyone else seems to know what's going on?

_____

_____

_____

Reading a model essay to discover narrative elements

First Day in Class
JAMAICA KINCAID

Jamaica Kincaid was born on the island of Antigua in the West Indies. Her work has appeared in *The Paris Review*, *Rolling Stone*, and *The New Yorker*. The following selection is taken from her 1985 novel *Annie John*, the story of a young girl's childhood and adolescence in Antigua.

1   On opening day, I walked to my new school alone. It was the first and last time that such a thing would happen. All around me were other people my age—twelve years—girls and boys, dressed in their school uniforms, marching off to school. They all seemed to know each other, and as they met they would burst into laughter, slapping each other on the shoulder and back, telling each other things that must have made for much happiness. I saw some girls wearing the same uniform as my own, and my heart just longed for them to say something to me, but the most they could do to include me was to smile and nod in my direction as they walked on arm in arm. I could hardly blame them for not paying more attention to me. Everything about me was so new: my uniform was new, my shoes were new, my hat was new, my shoulder ached from the weight of my new books in my new bag; even the road I walked on was new, and I must have put my feet down as if I weren't sure the ground was solid. At school, the yard was filled with more of these girls and their most sure-of-themselves gaits. When I looked at them, they made up a sea. They were walking in and out among the beds of flowers, all across the fields, all across the courtyard, in and out of classrooms. Except for me, no one seemed a stranger to anything or anyone. Hearing the way they greeted each other, I couldn't be sure that they hadn't all come out of the same woman's belly, and at the same time, too. Looking at them, I was suddenly glad that because I had wanted to avoid an argument with my mother I had eaten all my breakfast, for now I surely would have fainted if I had been in any more a weakened a condition.

2   I knew where my classroom was, because my mother and I had kept an appointment at the school a week before. There I met some of my teachers and was shown the ins and outs of everything. When I saw it then, it was nice and orderly and empty and smelled just scrubbed. Now it smelled of girls milling around, fresh ink in inkwells, new books, chalk and erasers. The girls in my classroom acted even more familiar with each other. I was sure I would never be able to tell them apart just from looking at them, and I was sure that I would never be able to tell them apart from the sound of their voices.

3   When the school bell rang at half past eight, we formed ourselves into the required pairs and filed into the auditorium for morning prayers and hymn-singing. Our headmistress gave us a little talk, welcoming the new students and

welcoming back the old students, saying that she hoped we had all left our bad ways behind us, that we would be good examples for each other and bring greater credit to our school than any of the other groups of girls who had been there before us. My palms were wet, and quite a few times the ground felt as if it were seesawing under my feet, but that didn't stop me from taking in a few things. For instance, the headmistress, Miss Moore. I knew right away that she had come to Antigua from England, for she looked like a prune left out of its jar a long time and she sounded as if she had borrowed her voice from an owl. The way she said, "Now, girls . . ." When she was just standing still there, listening to some of the other activities, her gray eyes going all around the room hoping to see something wrong, her throat would beat up and down as if a fish fresh out of water were caught inside. I wondered if she even smelled like a fish. Once when I didn't wash, my mother had given me a long scolding about it, and she ended by saying that it was the only thing she didn't like about English people: they didn't wash often enough, or wash properly when they finally did. My mother had said, "Have you ever noticed how they smell as if they had been bottled up in a fish?" On either side of Miss Moore stood our other teachers, women and men—mostly women. I recognized Miss George, our music teacher; Miss Nelson, our homeroom teacher; Miss Edward, our history and geography teacher; and Miss Newgate, our algebra and geometry teacher. I had met them the day my mother and I were at school. I did not know who the others were, and I did not worry about it. Since they were teachers, I was sure it wouldn't be long before, because of some misunderstanding, they would be thorns in my side.

4   We walked back to our classroom the same way we had come, quite orderly and, except for a few whispered exchanges, quite silent. But no sooner were we back in our classroom than the girls were in each other's laps, arms wrapped around necks. After peeping over my shoulder left and right, I sat down in my seat and wondered what would become of me. There were twenty of us in my class, and we were seated at desks arranged five in a row, four rows deep. I was at a desk in the third row, and this made me even more miserable. I hated to be seated so far away from the teacher, because I was sure I would miss something she said. But, even worse, if I was out of my teacher's sight all the time, how could she see my industriousness and quickness at learning things? And, besides, only dunces were seated so far to the rear, and I could not bear to be thought a dunce. I was now staring at the back of a shrubby-haired girl seated in the front row—the seat I most coveted, since it was directly in front of the teacher's desk. At that moment, the girl twisted herself around, stared at me, and said, "You are Annie John? We hear you are very bright." It was a good thing Miss Nelson walked in right then, for how would it have appeared if I had replied, "Yes, that is completely true"—the very thing that was on the tip of my tongue.

5   As soon as Miss Nelson walked in, we came to order and stood up stiffly at our desks. She said to us, "Good morning, class," half in a way that someone must have told her was the proper way to speak to us and half in a jocular way, as if we secretly amused her. We replied, "Good morning, Miss," in unison and in a respectful way, at the same time making a barely visible curtsy, also in unison. When she had seated herself at her desk, she said to us, "You may sit now," and we did. She opened the roll book, and as she called out our names each of us answered, "Present, Miss." As she called out our names, she kept her head bent over the book, but when she called out my name and I answered with the customary response she looked up and smiled at me and said, "Welcome, Annie." Everyone, of course, then turned and looked at me. I was sure it was because they could hear the loud racket my heart was making in my chest.

6   It was the first day of a new term, Miss Nelson said, so we would not be attending to any of our usual subjects; instead, we were to spend the morning in

contemplation and reflection and writing something she described as an "autobiographical essay." In the afternoon, we would read aloud to each other our autobiographical essays. (I knew quite well about "autobiography" and "essay," but reflection and contemplation! A day at school spent in such a way! Of course, in most books all the good people were always contemplating and reflecting before they did anything. Perhaps in her mind's eye she could see our futures and, against all prediction, we turned out to be good people.) On hearing this, a huge sigh went up from the girls. Half the sighs were in happiness at the thought of sitting and gazing off into clear space, the other half in unhappiness at the misdeeds that would have to go unaccomplished. I joined the happy half, because I knew it would please Miss Nelson, and, my own selfish interest aside, I liked so much the way she wore her ironed hair and her long-sleeved blouse and box-pleated skirt that I wanted to please her.

7   The morning was uneventful enough: a girl spilled ink from her inkwell all over her uniform; a girl broke her pen nib and then made a big to-do about replacing it; girls twisted and turned in their seats and pinched each other's bottoms; girls passed notes to each other. All this Miss Nelson must have seen and heard, but she didn't say anything—only kept reading her book: an elaborately illustrated edition of *The Tempest*, as later, passing by her desk, I saw. Midway in the morning, we were told to go out and stretch our legs and breathe some fresh air for a few minutes; when we returned, we were given glasses of cold lemonade and a slice of bun to refresh us.

8   As soon as the sun stood in the middle of the sky, we were sent home for lunch. The earth may have grown an inch or two larger between the time I had walked to school that morning and the time I went home to lunch, for some girls made a small space for me in their little band. But I couldn't pay much attention to them; my mind was on my new surroundings, my new teacher, what I had written in my nice new notebook with its black-all-mixed-up-with-white cover and smooth lined pages (so glad was I to get rid of my old notebooks, which had on their covers a picture of a wrinkled-up woman wearing a crown on her head and a neckful and armfuls of diamonds and pearls—their pages so coarse, as if they were made of cornmeal). I flew home. I must have eaten my food. I flew back to school. By half past one, we were sitting under a flamboyant tree in a secluded part of our schoolyard, our autobiographical essays in hand. We were about to read aloud what we had written during our morning of contemplation and reflection.

Analyzing the writer's strategies

1. Although a great deal is discussed among teachers and students on this first day of class, the selection contains only a few direct quotations. Why do you think the writer avoids the use of much dialogue in the piece? What is the effect of this on the reader?

2. Throughout the selection, the narrator shows how isolated she feels in this new situation. Starting with the first sentence of the selection, in how many places does she reveal this sense of isolation?

3. The narrator is a close observer of people and things around her. Choose five or six examples from the selection that demonstrate this ability to observe. Why do these examples strike you as outstanding?

4. In the selection, the writer's emphasis is on what happens to the young girl on the first day of school. However, we have more than one indication of her life at home. Based on details in the selection, what can you tell about the young girl's life at home and about her relationship with her mother?

Writing the essay using narration

> *Narration* is the oldest and best-known form of verbal communication. It is, quite simply, the telling of a story.

Choose a story and a point for that story

1. My worst (or best) classroom experience

2. A parent who listened (or did not listen)

3. My first _____

4. My experience with an aggressive salesperson

5. The day when nothing went right

6. A mix-up with a friend

7. Trouble at the _____

8. A day that changed my life

9. A memorable event from my childhood

10. A perfect evening

Using the list of ten topics, or using ideas of your own, jot down two or three different topics that appeal to you.

_____

_____

_____

From these two or three topics, select the one you think would give you the best opportunity for writing an interesting story. Which one do you feel strongest about? Which one is most likely to interest your readers? Which topic is most suitable for an essay?

_____

_____

_____

Selected topic: _____

Good narration should have a point. Think about your story. What is the point you could make by telling this story? In a story, a writer does not usually come right out and state the point of the story, but the reader should understand the point by the time he or she reaches the end.

Point of your story: _____

_____

_____

The introductory paragraph for a story usually sets the scene. What will be the time (time of year, time of day), place, and mood that you would like set in your introductory paragraph?

Time: _____

Place: _____

Mood: _____

Gather the information using brainstorming techniques

Take at least fifteen minutes to jot down the sequence of events for your story as you remember it. Try to remember the way things looked at the time, how people reacted (what they did, what they said), what you thought as the event was happening. If you can go to the actual spot where the event took place, you might go there and take notes of the details of the place. Later on you can sort through the material and pick out what you want to use.

_____
_____
_____
_____
_____
_____
_____
_____
_____
_____
_____
_____
_____
_____
_____

Select and organize material

Review your brainstorming list and cross out any details that are not appropriate. Prepare to build on the ideas that you like. Put these remaining ideas into an order that will serve as your temporary guide.

_____
_____
_____
_____
_____

_____

_____

_____

_____

_____

_____

_____

_____

Write the rough draft

Find a quiet place where you will not be interrupted for at least one hour. With the plan for your essay in front of you, sit down and write or type the story that is in your mind. Do not try to judge what you are putting down as right or wrong. What is important is that you let your mind relax and allow the words to flow freely. Do not worry if you find yourself not following your plan exactly. Keep in mind that you are free to add parts, drop sections of the story, or rearrange details at any point. Sometimes just allowing your thoughts to take you wherever they will lead results in new ideas. You may like these inspirations better than your original plan. Writing a rough draft is a little like setting out on an expedition; there are limitless possibilities, so it is important to be flexible.

Keep in mind that in a narrative essay, details are usually ordered according to a *time sequence.* One way to make the time sequence clear is to use transitional words that will signal a time change.

TRANSITIONAL EXPRESSIONS FOR NARRATION

A few carefully chosen transitional words will help the reader move smoothly from one part of a story to the next. Some examples are:

in December of 1980 . . .	after a little while
the following month	then
soon afterward	meanwhile
at once	next, the next day
suddenly	several weeks passed
immediately	later, later on
now, by now	at the same time
in the next month	finally

Revise the rough draft

As you work on your rough draft, you may work alone, with a group, with a peer tutor, or directly with your instructor. If you are working on a computer, making changes is so easy that you will feel encouraged to explore alternatives. Working on a computer to insert or delete material is a simple matter, unlike making changes using traditional pen and paper.

Here are some of the basic questions you should consider when the time comes to revise your narration.

1. Does the rough draft satisfy the conditions for the essay form? Is there an introductory paragraph? Are there at least three well-developed paragraphs in the body of the essay? Is there a concluding paragraph? Remember that one sentence is not a developed paragraph. One exception to this rule is when you use dialogue. When you write a story, you often include the conversation between two people. In this case, the writer makes a new paragraph each time a different person speaks. This often means that one sentence could be a separate paragraph.

2. Is your essay a narration? Does it tell the story of one particular incident that takes place in a specific time and location? Sometimes writers make the mistake of talking about incidents in a general way, and commenting on the meaning of the incidents. Be careful. This would not be considered a narration. You must be a storyteller. Where does the action take place? Can the reader see it? What time of day, week, or season is it? What is your main character in the story doing?

3. Have you put the details of the essay in a certain time order? Find the expressions you have used that show the time sequence.

4. Can you think of any part of the story that is missing and should be added? Is there any material that is irrelevant and should be omitted?

5. Are there sentences or paragraphs that seem to be repetitious?

6. Find several places where you can substitute stronger verbs or nouns. Add adjectives to give the reader better sensory images.

7. Find at least three places in your draft where you can add details. Perhaps you might add an entire paragraph that will more fully describe the person or place that is central to your story.

8. Can you think of a more effective way to begin or end?

9. Does your story have a point? If a person just told you everything he did on a certain day, that would not be a good story. A good story needs to have a point.

10. Show your rough draft to at least two other readers and ask for suggestions.

Prepare the final copy, print, and proofread it

The typing of the final version should follow the traditional rules for an acceptable submission.

CHECKLIST FOR THE FINAL COPY

Use only 8½-by-11 inch paper (never paper torn out of a spiral bound notebook).

Type on one side of the paper only.

Double space.

Leave approximately 1 inch (2.5 cm) margins on each side of the paper.

Centre the title at the top of the page. Do not put quotation marks around the title and do not underline it.

Do not hyphenate a word at the end of a line unless you are willing to consult a dictionary to check on the acceptable division of the word into syllables.

You may put your name, the date, and the title of your paper on a separate title page. Ask your instructor for specific advice on what information to include.

Indent each paragraph five spaces.

Leave two spaces after each period.

If your paper is more than one page, number the pages and paper clip the pages together so they will not get lost.

Do not forget to make a copy before you submit the paper.

Note: In most cases, teachers will not accept handwritten work. However, if you are submitting handwritten work, you must be sure to write on every other line and have good legible handwriting. Begin today to learn to type on the computer. You will be at a disadvantage if you cannot use the current technology.

Once you have typed your final version and printed it out, an important step still remains. This step can often mean the difference of an entire letter grade. You must *proofread* your paper. Even if you have used a spellcheck feature available on your word processing program, there still could be errors in your paper. The spellcheck feature only finds groupings of letters that are not words. For example, if you typed the word *van* when you meant to type *ban,* the spellcheck would not catch this error.

The secret of good proofreading is to look at each word and sentence construction by itself without thinking about the paper's contents.

CHECKLIST FOR PROOFREADING

Study each sentence: One way to proofread is to read backwards, starting with the last sentence and examining every sentence, one at a time. First, check that the sentence is really complete and not a fragment or a run-on. Then check the punctuation. Go on to the next sentence and do the same. In this way, you will develop a critical eye for spotting any problems with sentence level errors.

Study each word: Read the paper again, this time studying each word in every sentence. Look at the letters of the words. Have you transposed any letters or have you left off an ending such as the *-ed* or the *-s?* If there are any words you are not sure how to spell, do not forget to check for the correct spelling. Is there any word you have omitted?

Working Together

In this chapter, each student has written a narrative essay. This essay will be a writing project to keep in your portfolio. At some later time, you may want to return to the essay and work on it again, or use it as the basis for another piece of writing.

Divide into groups and share these narrative essays with each other. Attach a sheet of paper to each essay so that each person who reads the essay can answer the following questions:

1. In your opinion, what is one aspect of the essay that you feel is a strength?

2. In your opinion, what is one aspect of the essay that still needs improvement?

If some writers are willing to read their essays out loud to the entire class, the class would enjoy listening to a few of them, not for criticism but just for enjoyment.

Writing an Essay Using Process

Exploring the topic: Following and giving instructions

It is your sister's birthday. You have bought her a gift that tells you that "some assembly is required." You follow the instructions carefully as you try to put the item together, but something is wrong. No matter what you try, it does not work. You feel frustrated and angry and rip up the instructions in disgust.

At one time or another, all of us have found ourselves in such a situation. When we do, we understand the misery caused by poorly written instructions. Providing directions or instructions takes careful thought. These writers must be able to put themselves in the shoes of the persons following the directions. These readers may have no special background in or skill for performing the procedure. Careful writers are sensitive to those places in the directions where the readers could go wrong. Clarity and accuracy are absolutely essential.

1. Think of a time when you had to put something together, but you were not given good directions. Describe the process that was involved and what happened when you tried to accomplish it.

   _____

   _____

   _____

2. When people write instructions or give directions, what do they often leave out? Looking back on the situation you described above, why do you think you were not able to assemble the item?

   _____

   _____

   _____

3. Recall a time when you had to explain a process to someone. You might have had to show someone how to get somewhere, or you might have had to write a detailed description of how you performed a science experiment in a chemistry class. What was the process? Was it hard to explain? Why or why not?

_____

_____

_____

4. What was your worst experience in trying to follow a process? You could have been trying to work something out yourself, or you could have been trying to follow someone else's directions. How did you overcome your difficulty?

_____

_____

_____

Reading a model essay to discover steps in a process

Some of the most commonly seen examples of process writing occur in books that show readers how to complete a task. In order to be understood, a writer describing a process such as gardening must be clear, accurate, and complete. In the following selection, the expert gardener Lorraine Johnson first describes the ingredients for composting and then shows us how to "cook" compost so that what was once "garbage" turns into an essential fertilizer.

Compost Happens
LORRAINE JOHNSON

1   No matter what you do, organic materials eventually break down. Decay is inevitable. But—and it's a big but—there's a difference between controlled decomposition, as found in a healthy, working compost pile, and the smelly mess of rotting materials in a bin gone bad.

2   Anyone who has had a bad composting experience (and I confess to having had a few over the years) can tell horror stories of scary-movie magnitude, but the good news is that it's relatively straightforward to create healthy, sweet-smelling compost (often dubbed "gardener's gold" by compost enthusiasts). And the benefits are beyond doubt: compost returns nutrients and organic matter to the soil, feeds beneficial micro-organisms and earthworms, and improves the texture, oxygen-retaining capabilities and moisture-holding capacity of soil. In other words, compost helps create healthy gardens. Beyond its benefit to gardens, however, there's another compelling reason to have some form of composting system in your yard: putting garden and kitchen waste in a compost pile removes these materials (or "good garbage," as my grandmother used to say) from the waste stream. As debates about landfill sites and garbage incineration heat up across Canada, we can all do our bit to reduce the waste our households contribute by heating them up—literally—in a compost bin.

3   Composting can be seen as a kind of culinary alchemy in which a balanced recipe of ingredients is mixed in a bin or pile. As the mixture breaks down it generates heat, which accelerates the process, and it's eventually transformed into finished compost. The cooking metaphor is apt.

4   You can take the low-tech approach by simply piling garden cuttings in a corner of the yard and ignoring them for a year. But if you follow the method described on these pages, your compost should be ready to harvest in three to six months....

The Ingredients

5   Controlled and speedy decomposition is all about balance. If your compost pile is too full of "browns"—compost lingo for carbon-rich materials such as dead leaves, straw and dead plant stalks—then your pile will be slow to decompose. On the other hand, if the pile is too full of "greens"—nitrogen-rich materials such as fresh food scraps and grass clippings—it will turn slimy and smell bad. The goal is to have equal amounts, roughly by weight, of browns and greens. The ideal carbon-to-nitrogen ratio for decomposition is about 30:1. Dead leaves (browns) have a C:N ratio of approximately 40:1 to 80:1, while fresh grass clippings (greens) have a ratio of 19:1. But there's no need to obsess: your eyes, nose and common sense will tell you if you've got roughly the right balance.

6   The other ingredient you should add to the pile is soil; it supplies starter microorganisms—bacteria and other microscopic organisms that digest and excrete organic materials, breaking them down. Soil also masks the odour of food waste, which discourages pests from visiting your pile—and it's easier to keep pests out than to dislodge them once they've arrived.

7   Store-bought compost accelerators are generally nitrogen-rich to balance the bulk of compost materials—dead leaves—that are heavy on carbon. But if you're already adding a balance of green and brown materials, there's no need to include supplemental nitrogen.

Recipe Instructions

8   To achieve even greater balance and the speediest possible decomposition, layer the browns and greens, and build the pile all at once. This works well when you've got a lot of grass clippings for greens and dead leaves for browns. I always keep a big bag of dead leaves by my bin—that way, I have a ready source of browns even in spring and summer. But who wants to stockpile rotting vegetables? Add them for greens as they become available.

9   Begin with a mixture of dead plant stalks—this loose, lower layer permits air circulation at the bottom of the pile, which is important to controlled decomposition. (A densely compacted pile may start to smell bad.) Then, add a layer (approximately 15 centimetres) of greens, such as coffee grounds, vegetable peelings and grass clippings. Sprinkle a 2.5-to-five-centimetre layer of soil over the greens, and add a thick layer (approximately 30 centimetres) of dead leaves, straw or dried garden clippings. Repeat this layering process of greens, soil and browns until the bin is full.

Cooking the Pile

10   Along with the correct ratio of browns to greens, there are two other factors that contribute to speedy, effective composting: adequate moisture and oxygen flow. Again, it's a matter of balance. The materials should be as moist as a wrung-out sponge; if you've piled in dry leaves, for example, it's a good idea to run a garden hose to the top of the pile and soak it for a few minutes. Or, you can add water to each brown layer as you build the pile; chances are the green layers are already moist.

11   The best way to ensure adequate air movement is to stir the pile every week or so. You can use a commercially available compost turner, a pitchfork or a sharp stick. (I've even used an old broom handle.) While you're turning the pile, check the moisture level, and add water if necessary—think of the wrung-out sponge for guidance. Move the materials at the sides to the centre, where the temperature can reach 52°C or more, so all materials get cooked.

12   Earthworms around the base of the pile are a good sign; they help micro-organisms break down the debris.

Fresh from the Oven

13   You'll know your compost is ready when it looks and smells like soil. Dig it out; screen out any small bits of undigested materials and throw them back in. Spread compost throughout the garden: top-dress your lawn with a thin layer, dig it into new beds, or mound it around the base of established plants. You'll soon discover, as committed compost enthusiasts everywhere have, that you can never have enough.

Analyzing the writer's strategies

1. What is the writer's purpose, as she states in the second paragraph?

2. Often a process requires specialized tools. What paragraph describes the needed tools? What are these tools?

3. What are the factors that contribute to speedy, effective composting?

4. Describe the process of composting. How many steps are there in the process? Make a list of the steps and number each of them.

5. How can a gardener avoid smelly compost?

Writing the essay using process (how to . . .)

> *Process* is one method of development that shows a step-by-step progression in the accomplishment of a goal. It can be directional (explaining how to do something readers might try themselves), or it can be strictly informational (explaining how something was done or how something works, with no expectation that the readers will actually try the process).

The "how to" section of every library and bookstore is usually a busy area. People come to find books that will help them perform thousands of different tasks—from plumbing to flower arranging. If you want to learn how to cook Chinese dishes, assemble a child's bicycle, start your own business, or even remodel your bathroom, you can find a book that will tell you how to do it. Thousands of books and articles have been written that promise to help people accomplish their goals in life. What do you think are the best selling "how to" books in Canada? Perhaps you have guessed the answer: how to lose weight! In the essay that you write, be sure to choose a process with which you are already familiar.

Choose the topic and the purpose of the information for the thesis statement

1. How to get good grades
2. How to do well in a job interview
3. How to install computer software
4. How to buy a used car
5. How to burn a CD
6. How to change a tire
7. How to choose a tattoo
8. How to make sushi
9. How to find the right place to live
10. How to groom a dog

Using the above list of ten topics or using ideas of your own, jot down two or three processes with which you are familiar.

_____

_____

_____

From these two or three topics, select the one you think would give you the best opportunity for writing. Which process do you feel strongest about? Which one is most likely to interest your readers? For which topic do you have the most firsthand experience?

Selected topic: _____

Your next step is to decide your purpose in writing. Which of the two types of process writing will you be doing? Do you want to give directions on how to carry out each step in a process so that your readers can do this process themselves? For instance, would you provide directions on how to change a tire, perhaps suggesting that your readers keep these directions in the glove compartments of their cars? On the other hand, do you want to provide information as to how a certain process works because you think your readers might find the process interesting? For instance, you might explain the process involved in getting an airplane off the ground. Not many of us understand how this works, and very few of us will actually ever pilot a plane. Perhaps you know a lot about an unusual process that might amuse or entertain readers.

Directional _____ or informational _____

Now put your topic and controlling idea together into your thesis statement.

Thesis statement: _____

_____

Gather the information (use brainstorming techniques)

Take at least fifteen minutes to list as many steps or stages in the process as you can. If the process is one that others in your class or at home already know, consult with them for any additional steps that you may have overlooked. You may also need to think of the precise vocabulary words associated with the process (such as the names of tools used for building or repairing something). The more specific you can be, the more helpful and interesting the process will be for your readers. List the steps or stages in the process:

_____

_____

_____

_____

_____

_____

_____

_____

_____

_____

_____

_____

_____

_____

_____

_____

_____

Select and organize material

Review your brainstorming list and ask yourself if you now have a complete list. Have you left out any step that someone who is unfamiliar with this process might need to know? Is there some extra information you could provide along the way that would be helpful and encouraging? Do you have a special warning about something that the reader should *not* do? You might consider telling your readers exactly where in the process most people are likely to make mistakes.

Make an outline giving each stage a heading. Underneath each heading, list all of the different ideas or vocabulary words that you should keep in mind as you begin to write. In a process essay, the most essential elements for judging its success are the order, the accuracy, and the completeness of all the steps.

_____

_____

_____

_____

_____

_____

_____

_____

_____

_____

_____

Write the rough draft

Follow your outline and write your rough draft, keeping in mind that this outline is only a guide. As you write, you will find yourself re-evaluating the logic of your ideas, a perfectly natural step that may involve making some changes from your outline. You may think of some special advice that would help the reader, and if you do, feel free to add these details. Your main goal is to get the process down on paper as completely and accurately as possible.

Achieving coherence in the process essay

When you buy a product and read the instructions that go with it, the form of writing in those instructions usually consists of a list of numbered items, each telling you what to do. In an essay, you do not usually number the steps. Instead, you can signal the movement from one step to another by changing to a new paragraph and/or by using a transitional expression. As in other methods for developing ideas, *process* has its own special words and expressions that can be used to signal movement from one step to the next.

TRANSITIONAL EXPRESSIONS FOR PROCESS

the first step	while you are	the last step
in the beginning	as you are	the final step
to start with	next	finally
to begin with	then	at last
first of all	the second step	eventually
	after you have	

Revise the rough draft

A space of time is very helpful to allow you to think about your written ideas; this allows you to judge your work more objectively than you can immediately after writing. Therefore, if you can put aside your draft for a day or two before you need to revise it, your work will benefit.

When you revise, you may work alone, with a group, with a peer tutor, or directly with your instructor. Here are some of the basic questions you should consider during this most important stage of your work:

1. Does the rough draft satisfy all the conditions for the essay form? Is there an introductory paragraph? Are there at least three well-developed paragraphs in the body of the essay? Have you written a concluding paragraph? Remember that a single sentence is not a developed paragraph.

2. Does the essay describe the process, one that is either directional or informational?

3. Are the steps in the process in the correct order? In a process essay, the sequence of the steps is crucial. A step that is placed out of order could result in a disaster of major proportions.

4. Are the directions accurate and complete? Check more than once that no important piece of information has been left out. Have you considered the points where some special advice might be helpful? Are there any special tools that would be useful?

5. Is any of the material not relevant?

6. Are there sentences or words that seem to be repetitious?

7. Find several places where you can substitute more specific verbs, nouns, or adjectives. Always try to use vocabulary that is appropriate for the process being described.

8. Can you think of a more effective way to begin or end?

9. Does the essay flow logically from one idea to the next? Could you improve this flow with better use of transitional expressions?

10. Show your draft to at least two other readers and ask for suggestions.

Prepare the final copy, print it, and proofread it

The typing of the final version should follow the traditional rules for an acceptable submission.

CHECKLIST FOR THE FINAL COPY

Use only 8½-by-11 inch paper (never paper torn out of a spiral bound notebook).

Type on one side of the paper only.

Double space.

Leave approximately 1 inch (2.5 cm) margins on each side of the paper.

Centre the title at the top of the page. Do not put quotation marks around the title and do not underline it.

Do not hyphenate a word at the end of a line unless you are willing to consult a dictionary to check on the acceptable division of the word into syllables.

You may put your name, the date, and the title of your paper on a separate title page. Ask your instructor for specific advice on what information to include.

Indent each paragraph five spaces.

Leave two spaces after each period.

If your paper is more than one page, number the pages and paper clip the pages together so they will not get lost.

Do not forget to make a copy before you submit the paper.

Note: In most cases, teachers will not accept handwritten work. However, if you are submitting handwritten work, you must be sure to write on every other line and have good legible handwriting. Begin today to learn to type on the computer. You will be at a disadvantage if you cannot use the current technology.

Once you have typed your final version and printed it out, an important step still remains. This step can often mean the difference of an entire letter grade. You must *proofread* your paper. Even if you have used a spellcheck feature available on your word processing program, there still could be errors in your paper. The spellcheck feature only finds groupings of letters that are not words. For example, if you typed the word *van* when you meant to type *ban,* the spellcheck would not catch this error.

The secret of good proofreading is to look at each word and sentence construction by itself without thinking about the paper's contents.

CHECKLIST FOR PROOFREADING

Study each sentence: One way to proofread is to read backwards, starting with the last sentence and examining every sentence, one at a time. First, check that the sentence is really complete and not a fragment or a run-on. Then check the punctuation. Go on to the next sentence and do the same. In this way, you will develop a critical eye for spotting any problems with sentence level errors.

Study each word: Read the paper again, this time studying each word in every sentence. Look at the letters of the words. Have you transposed any letters or have you left off an ending such as the *-ed* or the *-s*? If there are any words you are not sure how to spell, do not forget to check for the correct spelling. Is there any word you have omitted?

Working Together

1. The students in the class should list and discuss some of the current problems on their campus today. Then the members of the class should divide into groups of three or four, each group choosing one of the problems discussed. After discussion, each group then draws up a list of steps needed to be taken in order to improve the situation.

2. Each group chooses a secretary. The group uses the list from the first activity to create sentences that will go into a letter to be sent to the appropriate college or university official, suggesting what could be done to solve the problem. The secretary will write the finished letter. Be sure there is an introductory paragraph that presents the problem and a conclusion that thanks the official for his or her attention.

Chapter 7

Writing an Essay Using Comparison or Contrast

Exploring a topic: Computers and the human brain

Computers have made it possible to explore our world and beyond. Through nano-technology, scientists are developing ways to attack diseases in the human body. As well, mobile robotics enable scientists to explore the depths of the oceans, and artificial perception enables computers to see. While many people are skeptical that any machine could ever entirely replace the human mind, many jobs are certainly changing or disappearing because of the work that computers do.

1. What are some of the jobs computers can already do better and faster than human beings can?

   _____

   _____

   _____

2. What are some of the jobs you have to do now that you would like a computer to do for you? How many of these jobs do you think a computer will take over in your lifetime?

   _____

   _____

   _____

3. Do you think a computer could ever be programmed to be as creative as the human mind? Why or why not?

   _____

   _____

   _____

4. In your opinion, what are the dangers in the sophisticated computer technology we see today?

_____

_____

_____

Reading a model essay to discover how a writer uses comparison or contrast to develop a topic

In the following selection from his book *Please Explain,* science writer Isaac Asimov compares the workings of the modern computer with the workings of the human mind.

The Computer and the Brain
ISAAC ASIMOV

1   The difference between a brain and a computer can be expressed in a single word: complexity.

2   The large mammalian brain is the most complicated thing, for its size, known to us. The human brain weighs three pounds, but in that three pounds are ten billion neurons and a hundred billion smaller cells. These many billions of cells are interconnected in a vastly complicated network that we can't begin to unravel as yet.

3   Even the most complicated computer man has yet built can't compare in intricacy with the brain. Computer switches and components number in the thousands rather than in the billions. What's more, the computer switch is just an on-off device, whereas the brain cell is itself possessed of a tremendously complex inner structure.

4   Can a computer think? That depends on what you mean by "think." If solving a mathematical problem is "thinking," then a computer can "think" and do so much faster than a man. Of course, most mathematical problems can be solved quite mechanically by repeating certain straightforward processes over and over again. Even the simple computers of today can be geared for that.

5   It is frequently said that computers solve problems only because they are "programmed" to do so. They can only do what men have them do. One must remember that human beings also can only do what they are "programmed" to do. Our genes "program" us the instant the fertilized ovum is formed, and our potentialities are limited by that "program."

6   Our "program" is so much more enormously complex, though, that we might like to define "thinking" in terms of the creativity that goes into writing a great play or composing a great symphony, in conceiving a brilliant scientific theory or a profound ethical judgment. In that sense, computers certainly can't think and neither can most humans.

7   Surely, though, if a computer can be made complex enough, it can be as creative as we. If it could be made as complex as a human brain, it could be the equivalent of a human brain and do whatever a human brain can do.

8   To suppose anything else is to suppose that there is more to the human brain than the matter that composes it. The brain is made up of cells in a certain arrangement and the cells are made up of atoms and molecules in certain arrangements. If

anything else is there, no signs of it have ever been detected. To duplicate the material complexity of the brain is therefore to duplicate everything about it.

9   But how long will it take to build a computer complex enough to duplicate the human brain? Perhaps not as long as some think. Long before we approach a computer as complex as our brain, we will perhaps build a computer that is at least complex enough to design another computer more complex than itself. This more complex computer could design one still more complex and so on and so on and so on.

10   In other words, once we pass a certain critical point, the computers take over and there is a "complexity explosion." In a very short time thereafter, computers may exist that not only duplicate the human brain—but far surpass it.

11   Then what? Well, mankind is not doing a very good job of running the earth right now. Maybe, when the time comes, we ought to step gracefully aside and hand over the job to someone who can do it better. And if we don't step aside, perhaps Supercomputer will simply move in and push us aside.

Analyzing the writer's strategies

1. An essay of comparison usually emphasizes the similarities between two subjects, while an essay of contrast emphasizes the differences. With this in mind, is the essay you have just read an essay of comparison or contrast?

2. How does this essay help to explain why a human can still beat a computer in a game of chess?

3. Does the writer provide an equal number of details that relate to both computers and the human brain or does he concentrate mostly on one part of the two-part topic? Go through the essay and underline each comparison or contrast that is made.

4. Specifically, how does the writer demonstrate the complexity of a computer and the complexity of the human brain?

5. Study the conclusion. How serious is the author's final suggestion?

Writing the essay using comparison and contrast

> *Comparison* or *Contrast,* a method for developing ideas, is the careful look at the similarities and/or differences between people, objects, or ideas, usually in order to reach some conclusion or make a judgment.

Find a topic and controlling idea for the thesis statement

1. High school classes and college or university classes

2. Studying with a friend or studying alone

3. Male and female stereotypes

4. Your best friend in childhood with your best friend now

5. Using public transportation versus using a car

6. Our current prime minister with any previous prime minister

7. Two items you have compared when shopping

8. Two apartments or houses where you have lived

9. Cooking dinner at home versus eating out

10. Watching television versus reading a book

Using the above list of ten topics or using ideas of your own, jot down a few two-part topics that appeal to you.

_____

_____

_____

From your list of two-part topics, select the one you think would give you the best opportunity for writing. Which one of these do you feel most strongly about? Which one is most likely to interest your readers? For which topic do you have the greatest firsthand experience?

Selected topic: _____

Your next step is to decide what your controlling idea should be. What is your main purpose in comparing or contrasting these two topics? Do you want to show that although people think two topics are similar, they actually differ in important ways? Do you want to show one topic is better in some ways than the other topic? Do you want to analyze how something has changed over the years (a "then-and-now" essay)?

Controlling idea: _____

At this point, combine your two-point topic and controlling idea into one thesis statement.

Thesis statement: _____

_____

Gather the information (use brainstorming techniques)

Take at least fifteen minutes to brainstorm (use listing or clustering) as many comparison or contrasting points as you can on your chosen topic. You will probably want to think of at least three or four points. Under each point, brainstorm as many details as come to mind. For instance, if you are comparing two friends and the first point covers the interests you have in common, recall as much as you can about the activities you share together. If you are brainstorming a topic that other classmates or family members might know something about, ask them to help you think of additional points to compare. If any special vocabulary comes to mind, jot that down as well. The more specific you can be, the more helpful and interesting you will make your comparison or contrast for your readers.

Points that could be compared or contrasted:

_____

_____

_____

_____

_____

_____

_____

_____

_____

_____

_____

_____

_____

Select and organize material

As a method of developing ideas, comparison or contrast involves a two-part topic. For instance, you might compare the school you attend now with a school you attended in the past. Often we need to make choices or judgments, and we can make better decisions if we can compare and/or contrast the two items in front of us. Since this is a two-part topic, there is a choice in organizing the essay:

1. **The block method:** This is when you write entirely about one item or idea, and then in a later paragraph or paragraphs you write entirely about the other topic. If you choose this method, you must be sure to bring up the same points and keep the same order as when you discussed the first topic.

2. **The point-by-point method:** This is when you discuss one point and show both topics relating to this in one paragraph. Then, in a new paragraph, you discuss the second point and relate it to both topics, and so forth.

Which method will be best for the topic you have selected: the block method or point-by-point method?

At this stage, review your brainstorming list and ask yourself if you have a list that is complete. Have you left out any point that might need to be considered? Do you have at least three points, and do you have enough material to develop both parts of the topic? You do not want the comparison or contrast to end up one-sided with all the content about only one part of the topic.

Make an outline, choosing one of the formats below, depending on whether you selected the block method or point-by-point method.

The example shown is the contrast between high school classes and college or university classes.

Outline for Block Method

I.	Topic 1	High School Classes
	A. First Point	meet 5 days a week
	B. Second Point	daily homework
	C. Third Point	no research papers
	D. Fourth Point	disciplinary problems in the class
II.	Topic 2	College or University Classes
	A. First Point	meet only 2 or 3 days a week
	B. Second Point	long term assignments
	C. Third Point	research papers required
	D. Fourth Point	no discipline problems

Outline for Point-by-Point Method

I.	First Point	How often classes meet
	A. Topic 1	high school classes
	B. Topic 2	college or university classes
II.	Second Point	Homework
	A. Topic 1	high school classes
	B. Topic 2	college or university classes
III.	Third Point	Research papers
	A. Topic 1	high school classes
	B. Topic 2	college or university classes
IV.	Fourth Point	Discipline
	A. Topic 1	high school classes
	B. Topic 2	college or university classes

_____

_____

_____

_____

_____

_____

_____

_____

_____

_____

_____

_____

_____

_____

_____

_____

_____

_____

_____

_____

_____

_____

_____

_____

_____

Write the rough draft

Follow your outline and write your rough draft. Remember the outline is a guide. Most writers find new ideas occur to them at this time, so if you have new thoughts, you should feel free to explore these ideas along the way. As you write, you will be constantly re-evaluating the logic of your ideas.

Coherence in the comparison or contrast essay

As in other methods of developing ideas, the comparison and contrast essay has its particular words and expressions that can be used to signal the movement from one point to the next.

COMMON TRANSITIONAL EXPRESSIONS		
Transitions for Comparison	**Transitions for Contrast**	
similar to	on the contrary	though
similarly	on the other hand	unlike
like	in contrast with	even though
likewise	in spite of	nevertheless
just like	despite	however
just as	instead of	but
furthermore	different from	otherwise
moreover	whereas	except for
equally	while	and yet
again	although	still
also		
too		
so		

Revise the rough draft

If you can have an interval of time between the writing of the rough draft and your work on revising it, you will be able to look at your work with a greater objectivity. Ideally, you should put aside your first draft for a day or two before you approach it again for revision.

When you revise, you may work alone, with a group, with a peer tutor, or directly with your instructor. Here are some of the basic questions you should consider during this most important stage of your work:

1. Does the rough draft satisfy the conditions for the essay form? Is there an introductory paragraph? Are there at least three well-developed paragraphs in the body of the essay? Is there a concluding paragraph? Remember that one sentence is not a developed paragraph.

2. Does the essay compare or contrast a two-part topic and come to some conclusion about the comparison or contrast?

3. Did you use either the point-by-point method or the block method to organize the essay?

4. Is any important point omitted? Is any of the material included irrelevant?

5. Are there sentences or paragraphs that are repetitious?

6. Find several places where you can substitute more specific verbs, nouns, or adjectives. Try to use the vocabulary appropriate for the topic being discussed.

7. Can you think of a more effective way to begin or end?

8. Does the essay flow logically from one idea to the next? Could you improve this flow with better use of transitional devices?

9. Show your draft to at least two other readers and ask for suggestions.

Prepare the final copy, print, and proofread it

The final version should follow the traditional rules for an acceptable submission.

CHECKLIST FOR THE FINAL COPY

Use only 8½-by-11 inch paper (never paper torn out of a spiral bound notebook).

Type on one side of the paper only.

Double space.

Leave approximately 1 inch (2.5 cm) margins on each side of the paper.

Centre the title at the top of the page. Do not put quotation marks around the title and do not underline it.

Do not hyphenate a word at the end of a line unless you are willing to consult a dictionary to check on the acceptable division of the word into syllables.

You may put your name, the date, and the title of your paper on a separate title page. Ask your instructor for specific advice on what information to include.

Indent each paragraph five spaces.

Leave two spaces after each period.

If your paper is more than one page, number the pages and paper clip the pages together so they will not get lost.

Do not forget to make a copy before you submit the paper.

Note: In most cases, teachers will not accept handwritten work. However, if you are submitting handwritten work, you must be sure to write on every other line and have good legible handwriting. Begin today to learn to type on the computer. You will be at a disadvantage if you cannot use the current technology.

Once you have typed your final version and printed it out, an important step still remains. This step can often mean the difference of an entire letter grade. You must *proofread* your paper. Even if you have used a spellcheck feature available on your word processing program, there still could be errors in your paper. The spellcheck feature only finds groupings of letters that are not words. For example, if you typed the word *van* when you meant to type *ban,* the spellcheck would not catch this error.

The secret of good proofreading is to look at each word and sentence construction by itself without thinking about the paper's contents.

CHECKLIST FOR PROOFREADING

Study each sentence: One way to proofread is to read backwards, starting with the last sentence and examining every sentence, one at a time. First, check that the sentence is really complete and not a fragment or a run-on. Then check the punctuation. Go on to the next sentence and do the same. In this way, you will develop a critical eye for spotting any problems with sentence level errors.

Study each word: Read the paper again, this time studying each word in every sentence. Look at the letters of the words. Have you transposed any letters or have you left off an ending such as the *-ed* or the *-s*? If there are any words you are not sure how to spell, do not forget to check for the correct spelling. Is there any word you have omitted?

Working Together

The selection that follows compares certain aspects of Canada to the United States. Students should read the selection out loud while others make a list of the areas being contrasted. Following the reading, put on the chalkboard the areas that have been contrasted along with specific examples. As a group, think of other areas that Canada differs from the United States. Like most writers, you will probably discover that you need to do some additional research in the library. Then work individually to write an essay of comparison or contrast. Remember, since there is an endless number of points that could be compared, limit yourself to those points that seem most significant in light of recent history.

Love It and Leave It

KEVIN NEWMAN

1   A funny thing happened on my last day at work in America. Peter Jennings, whom you know, gave me an American flag as a going-away gift in front of staff at *World News Tonight* in New York City. One Canadian giving another the Red, White and Blue of a place I had called home for seven years, and he for considerably longer. This wasn't just any flag—it had flown atop the Capitol Dome in Washington. Peter knew something in giving me that flag that I didn't until that moment: that America had found a place in my heart. I choked up. The perfect marine-folded triangle with the Stars and Stripes sat in my hands, and I felt proud.

2   Go figure. A guy who clung to his "Canadian-ness" like a shield, confident he could learn from Americans without becoming one. Someone who revelled in dis-

cussing parts of Canadian society so obviously superior to America's that friends' eyes would glaze at one more mention of Canada's gun-control laws, socialized medicine or campaign financing. Somehow, "they'd" got to me.

3   But how? By getting to know them. Canadians lament how little Americans know about Canada: the urban myth of ski racks in Toronto in July has been told many times, yet who has seen it? The truth is few Americans feel a need to know about anywhere else, including the state next to their own, so we're in good company. It's also true that we don't know as much about them as we think. Our view of America is largely the one it exports to the world through television—filled with violence, sad, attention-starved people on *Jerry Springer* and the shallow pursuits of the rich and beautiful.

4   The America I came to know had all of that, but not as much as television would have you believe. There is another, more open and generous America—different from us in often admirable ways. Consider three of them.

5   According to a 1999 Gallup poll, 56 per cent of American adults volunteer some time every year, compared with the 32 per cent of Canadians Statistics Canada found in 1997. With individuals less willing to turn to governments for social support, Americans step up to the plate more often themselves. My son, in order to graduate from Grade 8 in New Jersey, was required to perform eight hours of community service. My younger daughter helped a friend make soup and hot chocolate for the poor.

6   Another point. According to a *Maclean's* poll conducted more than a year ago, 42 per cent of Americans attend religious services weekly, while fewer than 22 per cent of Canadians do. That's a huge difference. Some might argue the strong puritan streak in American politics is one result of that (which helps explain broad support for capital punishment, the pro-life movement and the influence of the religious right). But regular religious attendance also exposes children to discussions of morality, selflessness and discipline. It may not make them behave better, but it gets them thinking.

7   Finally, there is something noble about the common thread through most of America's history. While most great nations have fought over territory, religion or money, America has fought over ideas: no taxation without representation, all men are created equal or, if you're from the South, all states are created that way, too. It's a cruel, racist and, at times, isolationist history—but also one of ideals. America's war heroes are almost always portrayed as reluctant ones, motivated more by the cause than by personal glory. America is, compared with previous empires in history, relatively benevolent. Canada exists because of it: if they wanted what we have, they could take it.

8   Those are some reasons why I find myself less likely now to engage in the age-old Canadian practice of expressing my own pride in country by dumping on theirs. I know Molson's "Joe Canada" sparked a surge of nationalist pride, but when a friend e-mailed me the ad last summer, I felt certain it was clever parody. I mean, do we really believe "the beaver is a noble creature"?

9   I have spent the past seven weeks travelling across Canada. It's a way of reconnecting, and a useful way for a journalist to measure how a place has changed. It has, in ways we should take pride in. We are bolder, more competitive and less angry than when I left in 1994. There have been explosions of creativity in the arts, high tech and print journalism. The battered Canadian dollar has meant we travelled the country more, came to know each other better, and maybe even shared more affection. If all the red Maple Leafs on Canadian heads, shirts and flagpoles are any indication, we may even have become a nation of flag-wavers. When I left, that was still considered kind of goofy.

10   It took living with Americans for my own sense of being Canadian to mature. Perspective is often enhanced with distance, but you don't have to leave to get it. Simply look around this Canada Day and judge the country for what it is. And ignore the impulse to look south for inspiration.

Writing an Essay Using Persuasion

What is persuasion?

From one point of view, all writing is persuasion since the main goal of any writer is to convince a reader to see, think, or believe in a certain way. There is, however, a more formal understanding of persuasive writing. Anyone who has ever been a member of a high school debate team knows there are techniques that the effective speaker or writer uses to present a case successfully. Learning how to recognize these techniques of persuasion and discovering how to use them in your own writing is the subject of this chapter.

> An essay of *persuasion* presents evidence intended to convince the reader that the writer's viewpoint is valid.

Guide to writing the persuasive essay

1. **State a clear thesis.** Use words such as *must, ought,* or *should.* Study the following three sample thesis statements:

   > Canada must reform its marijuana laws.
   >
   > Canada's current gun control laws ought to be changed.
   >
   > Pornography on the Internet should be banned.

2. **Give evidence or reasons for your beliefs.** Your evidence is the heart of the essay. You must show the wisdom of your logic by providing the best evidence available.

3. **Use examples.** Well-chosen examples are among the best types of evidence for an argument. People can identify with a specific example from real life in a way that is not possible with an abstract idea. Without examples, essays of persuasion would be flat, lifeless, and unconvincing.

4. **Use opinions from recognized authorities to support your points.** One of the oldest methods of supporting an argument is to use one or more

persons of authority to support your particular position. People will usually believe what well-known experts claim. However, be sure that your expert is someone who is respected in the area you are discussing. For example, if you are arguing that we must end ocean dumping, your argument will be stronger if you quote a respected scientist who can accurately predict the consequences of this approach to waste disposal. A famous movie star giving the same information might be more glamorous and get more attention, but he or she would not be as great an authority as the scientist.

5. **Answer your critics in advance.** When you point out, beforehand, what your opposition is likely to say in answer to your argument, you will be writing from a position of strength. You are letting your reader know that there is another side to the argument you are making. By pointing out this other side and then answering its objections in advance, you are strengthening your own position.

6. **Point out the results.** Here, you help your reader see what will happen if your argument is (or is not) believed or acted upon as you think it should be. You should be very specific and very rational when you point out results, making sure that you avoid exaggerations of any kind. For example, if you are arguing against the possession of guns, it would be an exaggeration to say that if we don't ban guns, "everyone will be murdered."

As in other methods of developing the essay, the essay using persuasion has its own special words that signal parts of the argument. The chart below can help you choose transitional expressions that will move you from one part of your argument to the next.

WORDS AND PHRASES THAT SIGNAL PARTS OF AN ARGUMENT

To signal the thesis of an argument

    I agree (disagree) that

    I support (do not support) the idea that

    I am in favour of (not in favour of)

    I propose

    _____ must be (must not be) changed

    _____ should be (should not be) adopted

To signal a reason

    because, just because, since, for

    in the first place

    in view of

    can be shown

    The first reason is . . .

    An additional reason is . . .

    Another reason is . . .

    The most convincing piece of evidence is . . .

To suggest another way to think about something

Most people assume that . . .

One would think that . . .

We have been told that . . .

Popular thought is that . . .

Consider the case of . . .

There is no comparison between . . .

To signal a conclusion

therefore, thus, consequently, so

as a result

We can conclude that . . .

This proves that . . .

This shows that . . .

This demonstrates that . . .

This suggests that . . .

This leads to the conclusion that . . .

It follows that . . .

Be careful not to fall into the following traps, both of which are poor ways to try to win over an opponent to your position:

1. Appeals to fear or pity:

   If we don't double the police force this year, a child in our neighbourhood might be killed.

2. Sweeping or false generalizations:

   All women belong in the kitchen.

Are We Too Connected?

ISAAC WANZAMA

Access to the Internet is easily attainable at school, the library, and even at home. In fact, a recent survey indicated that as many as 60 percent of Canadians have regular access to the Internet. In the following essay, Isaac Wanzama suggests that there should be a limit to Internet access.

As you read the essay, look for all of the elements of an effective argument. Where does the writer give his thesis statement? Where are his major examples? Does he use authorities to support his point of view? In addition, look for the paragraphs where he answers those who might not agree with him. Be sure to find the sections of the essay where he predicts the consequences of continued free Internet access. As you read the essay, try to find the weaknesses in the writer's argument.

1   The premise of the new economy is simple: enable everyone to share information with anyone anywhere at any time. It's a powerful development that has seen the emergence of e-commerce powerhouses such as Amazon, AOL and E-bay.

2   Yet sometimes sharing is not such a great thing. The state of connectivity that the world is moving towards has made the Internet a highly effective single point of attack. In a situation where 90% of the world operates on the same platform using the same software, the vulnerability cannot be overstated. Even with the amount of money corporations spend on firewalls and other similar measures, tens of thousands of viruses attack computers on a daily basis. And some, like the "Melissa" and "I Love You" viruses, hit stardom.

3   This begs the question: are we too connected? The simple answer is: any time a 15-year-old can cause billions of dollars in lost revenues from premier online businesses around the world from his mom's basement in Montreal, we are too connected.

4   The current "open" and "free" nature of the Internet will, ironically, be the ultimate downfall of the very economy that has emerged as the result of it. "Free" shouldn't mean free to handicap millions of networks around the world. We would not give a masked stranger 15 keys to the Pentagon and hope that they couldn't figure out which one to get in with.

5   A move towards regulation on the Web has caused and will continue to cause a deafening uproar from all sectors from freedom activists to politicians of all stripes. But how long can businesses, government and even personal information be at the mercy of every click-happy hacker out to prove that they're better than the last guy? Less than 50 countries have the laws, let alone the technical capabilities, in place to deal with cyber attacks.

6   It is time to understand that the Internet as it was seven years ago has changed. It is no longer a novelty application where everyone could post up their holiday pictures or little Jamie's grades on a home page and stand back saying "that's neat." The Net today represents a powerful economic engine that is becoming more and more critical to the growth strategies of companies and organizations globally. Estimates are that 5% to 10% of the world's business, representing in excess of a trillion dollars, will take place online in the next five years. This is serious stuff. Companies stand to lose more when their Web site goes down than if they have a fire in their warehouse.

7   We are in a technology age that has made millionaires overnight and given the "little guy" the opportunity to compete in the business race. But the World Wide Web has become more like the Wild Wild West, with no sheriff or even a deputy in sight.

8   There was chaos last month as IT departments tried to deal with the debilitating computer virus that originated from the Philippines. Everywhere from the Pentagon to the British House of Commons was affected. Billions of dollars were lost in productivity, files and information as people around the globe clicked on e-mails believing that they were really "loved." By the time the FBI stared to collaborate with authorities in the Philippines, the damage had already been done. More than 45 million computer users, by some estimates, had been impacted.

9   This was the second major attack in as many months. Many of these attacks have been so smoothly carried out because of how connected the planet is becoming. Consider the numbers. According to conservative estimates by the NEC Research Institute of Princeton, N.J., there are 320 million Web pages. Further, the Dublin, Ireland-based Internet consultancy Nua says that about 116 million people go online each day. And most of these people use e-mail and other electronic download methods to exchange information. Companies continue to construct intricate networks that will connect every remote corner of this planet. The medium is growing faster than any other in our history.

10   So what can be done?

11   The Internet must evolve into a tiered system with various layers with very limited access. It likely will not be the "Internet" as we know it today but rather

"pockets," or intranets, divided not by geography but by security accessibility. So it will no longer be about entering a URL to visit CNN; it will be about getting personalized security clearance to news-related sites or e-commerce sites.

12   It's time to accept that the Internet shouldn't be so "free." This may seem grim, especially because the free and open nature of the Internet is what has made it so powerful to date. But in the end, the Wild West was won by a fast-drawing sheriff and trusty deputy who drew a line in the sand to keep the bad guys out. Anyone who will intentionally release a virus or steal thousands of credit cards probably should not have been allowed into e-town in the first place.

Analyzing the writer's strategies

Many people feel that access to information should be every person's right. Isaac Wanzama's title suggests that he thinks differently, and, as readers, this immediately grabs our attention. As well, his references to recent computer viruses that were spread via the Internet give his view even more authority. In addition to relying on current events that support his point of view, Wanzama relies on facts and figures. For example, the proliferation of Web pages around the world and the rate at which computer viruses spread add credence to his argument.

The writer's position is also supported by the fact that he is very precise in his use of examples in paragraphs 6 to 9. In paragraph 11, he makes suggestions about how to curb Internet freedom. Finally, he concludes his argument in paragraph 12 by summarizing his main points and restating his thesis.

It is clear that Wanzama's argument is carefully written and complete; it has all the parts needed for a good argument. After you have studied each part of the essay, are you able to find any weaknesses in the writer's presentation?

Responding to the writer's argument

Take a position for or against one of the following topics and write an argumentative essay supporting your position. Use the "Guide to Writing the Persuasive Essay" (pp. 89–91) to help construct the essay. Be sure to include all of the important points needed for a good argument.

1. All Internet access should be free in our society.

2. Computer hackers should be given long prison sentences.

3. Corporations must ensure that their Internet security systems are impenetrable to hackers so that they can protect the safety of their customers.

4. Computer users downloading music from the Internet should have to pay copyright charges to the artists.

5. Computer knowledge is required in order to be successful in any field of study.

6. The pervasiveness of computerized technology is making people less intelligent.

7. A person who is "not connected" (does not have a computer, cell phone, pager, etc.) runs the risk of being left behind on the information highway.

8. Access to information on the World Wide Web should cost users money, which could then be used to fund other projects seeking to expand the content on the Web.

9. It is up to parents to monitor their children's use of the Internet.

10. Easy access to the Internet should be restricted in colleges and universities. Students conducting research for essays must use traditional sources of information such as libraries.

EXERCISE 1   Using Research Material to Write the Persuasive Essay

Since the advent of the Internet, the amount of information that has become readily accessible to people around the world has grown enormously. The Internet is also used as a form of communication between people. However, it has been used to harm as well as help. The following pieces of information are on the topic of controlling the uses of the Internet. You may select as many items as you want, or you may adapt the items to agree with your own way of thinking. After selecting the material you want to use, be sure to organize your points before starting the rough draft.

1. A pharmaceutical company in Toronto recently conducted a security assessment of its computer network. In the process, it discovered evidence that a hacker had broken into its databanks, gaining access to sensitive files about a new product.

2. In May 2000, a destructive computer virus called the "I Love You" bug automatically spread from computer to computer. It destroyed thousands of computers and caused an estimated $10 billion in damages around the world.

3. Onel de Guzman, the hacker who created the "I Love You" bug, believed that charging for the Internet was immoral.

4. Cultural and artistic achievements belong to the artists who made them; therefore, people should have to pay for being able to download music or movies over the Internet.

5. A Detroit man was charged by police in Windsor, Ontario, for luring a young girl to a shopping mall after he contacted her in an Internet chat room while posing as another teenage girl.

6. Some parents use software programs that attempt to restrict their children's access to inappropriate Web sites, but many computer literate children can disable this software and visit any Web site they want.

7. Whenever you fill out a personal information form on a Web site, that data is often sold to companies who use it to try to sell you a product or service later.

8. In a recent survey of college teachers in Ontario, 55 percent reported that cases of plagiarism have increased significantly over the past five years; in most of these cases, the plagiarized source was a Web site.

9. Although the purpose of e-mail is to provide a fast and inexpensive means by which people can communicate around the world, many unscrupulous individuals are sending unsolicited e-mails (or "spam") to people with get-rich-quick promises that turn out to be little more than scams.

10. On-line auctions have no way of controlling what people sell on their Web sites; people who use these sites often end up not getting what they were promised or what they paid for.

No Place Like Home

NEIL BISSOONDATH

Canada's immigration policies have often been praised because they encourage those who move here to maintain the values and customs of their homelands. Neil Bissoondath, a Canadian writer who emigrated from Trinidad, often writes about the dangers of this type of multiculturalist policy.

The following selection appeared in the journal *New Internationalist*, and in it Bissoondath suggests that immigrants are negatively ostracized because of Canada's desire to maintain a mosaic society. As Bissoondath demonstrates the detrimental effects of this policy, he is careful to maintain a steady tone, one that avoids unnecessary emotion in a debate that is already filled with strong opinions and beliefs.

1   Three or four years into the new millennium, Toronto, Canada's largest city, will mark an unusual milestone. In a city of three million, the words "minorities" and "majority" will be turned on their heads and the former will become the latter.

2   Reputed to be the most ethnically diverse city in the world, Toronto has been utterly remade by immigration, just as Canada has been remade by a quarter-century of multiculturalism.

3   It is a policy which has been quietly disastrous for the country and for immigrants themselves.

4   The stated purpose of Canada's Multiculturalism Act (1971) is to recognize "the existence of communities whose members share a common origin and their historic contribution to Canadian society." It promises to "enhance their development" and to "promote the understanding and creativity that arise from the interaction between individuals and communities of different origins." The bicultural (English and French) nature of the country is to be wilfully refashioned into a multicultural "mosaic."

5   The architects of the policy—the Government of then-Prime Minister Pierre Elliott Trudeau—were blind to the fact that their exercise in social engineering was based on two essentially false premises. First, it assumed that "culture" in the large sense could be transplanted. Second, that those who voluntarily sought a new life in a new country would wish to transport their cultures of origin.

6   But "culture" is a most complex creature; in its essence, it represents the very breath of a people. For the purposes of multiculturalism, the concept has been reduced to the simplest theatre. Canadians, neatly divided into "ethnic" and otherwise, encounter each other's mosaic tiles mainly at festivals. There's traditional music, traditional dancing, traditional food at distinctly untraditional prices, all of which is diverting as far as it goes—but such encounters remain at the level of a folkloric Disneyland.

7   We take a great deal of self-satisfaction from such festivals; they are seen as proof of our open-mindedness, of our welcoming of difference. Yet how easily we forget that none of our ethnic cultures seems to have produced poetry or literature or philosophy worthy of our consideration. How seductive it is, how reassuring, that Greeks are always Zorbas, Ukrainians always Cossacks: we come away with stereotypes reinforced.

8   Not only are differences highlighted, but individuals are defined by those differences. There are those who find pleasure in playing to the theme, those whose ethnicity ripens with the years. Yet to play the ethnic, deracinated and costumed, is to play the stereotype. It is to abdicate one's full humanity in favour of one of its exotic features. To accept the role of ethnic is also to accept a gentle marginalization. It is to accept that one will never be just a part of the landscape but always a little apart from it, not quite belonging.

9   In exoticizing and trivializing cultures, often thousands of years old, by sanctifying the mentality of the mosaic-tile, we have succeeded in creating mental ghettos for the various communities. One's sense of belonging to the larger Canadian landscape is tempered by a loyalty to a different cultural or racial heritage....

10   Often between groups one looks in vain for the quality that Canadians seem to value above all—tolerance. We pride ourselves on being a tolerant country, unlike the United States, which seems to demand of its immigrants a kind of submission to American mythology. But not only have we surrendered a great deal of ourselves in pursuit of the ideal—Christmas pageants have been replaced by "Winterfests"; the antiracist Writers Union of Canada sanctioned a 1994 conference which excluded whites—but tolerance itself may be an overrated quality, a flawed ideal.

11   The late novelist Robertson Davies pointed out that tolerance is but a weak sister to acceptance. To tolerate someone is to put up with them; it is to adopt a pose of indifference. Acceptance is far more difficult, for it implies engagement, understanding, an appreciation of the human similarities beneath the obvious differences. Tolerance then is superficial—and perhaps the highest goal one can expect of Canadian multiculturalism.

12   Another insidious effect of this approach is a kind of provisional citizenship. When 100-metre sprinter Ben Johnson won a gold medal at the Seoul Olympics, he was hailed in the media as the great Canadian star. Days later, when the medal was rescinded because of a positive drug test, Johnson became the Jamaican immigrant—Canadian when convenient, a foreigner when not. Tolerated, never truly accepted, his exoticism always part of his finery, he quickly went from being one of us to being one of them.

13   This makes for an uneasy social fabric. In replacing the old Canada, based on British and French tradition, with a mosaic (individual tiles separated by cement), we have shaken our sense of identity. In a country over 130 years old, we are still uncertain who we are.

14   A major 1993 study found that 72 per cent of the population wants, as one newspaper put it, "the mosaic to melt." Canadians were found to be "increasingly intolerant" of demands for special treatment made by ethnic groups—a Chinese group who wanted a publicly funded separate school where their children would be taught in Chinese by Chinese teachers; a Muslim group who claimed the right to opt out of the Canadian judicial system in favour of Islamic law. Canadians wanted immigrants to adopt Canada's values and way of life.

15   Many immigrants agree. They recognize that multiculturalism has not served their interests. It has exoticized, and so marginalized, them, making the realization of their dreams that much harder. The former rector of the Université du Québec à Montréal, Claude Corbo, himself the grandson of Italian immigrants, has pointed out that multiculturalism has kept many immigrants "from integrating naturally into the fabric of Canadian and Quebec society.... We tell people to preserve their original patrimony, to conserve their values, even if these values are incompatible with those of our society."

16   Which leads to the other false premise on which multiculturalism is based. It assumes that people who choose to emigrate not only can but also wish to remain what they once were.

17   The act of emigration leaves no one unscathed. From the moment you board a plane bound for a new land with a one-way ticket, a psychological metamorphosis begins—and the change occurs more quickly, more deeply and more imperceptibly than one imagines....

18   Canadian multiculturalism has emphasized difference. In so doing, it has retarded the integration of immigrants into the Canadian mainstream while dam-

aging Canada's national sense of self. Canada has an enviable record in dealing with racism—our society, while hardly perfect (we too have our racists of all colours), remains largely free of racial conflict. And yet we do ourselves a disservice in pursuing the divisive potential in multiculturalism. With an ongoing battle against separatism in Quebec, with east-west tensions, we are already a country uncomfortably riven. Our "mosaic" does not help us....

19   Canada, for the foreseeable future, will continue to be a nation open to immigrants—and one committed to combating racism, sexism and the various other forms of discrimination we share with other societies. Beyond this, because of the damage already inflicted by multiculturalism, we need to focus on programs that seek out and emphasize the experiences, values and dreams we all share as Canadians, whatever our colour, language, religion, ethnicity or historical grievance. And pursue acceptance of others—not mere tolerance of them.

20   Whatever policy follows multiculturalism it should support a new vision of Canadianness. A Canada where no one is alienated with hyphenation. A nation of cultural hybrids, where every individual is unique and every individual is a Canadian, undiluted and undivided. A nation where the following conversation, so familiar—and so enervating—to many of us will no longer take place:

21   "What nationality are you?"

22   "Canadian."

23   "No, I mean, what nationality are you really?"...

24   In the end, immigration is a personal adventure. The process of integration that follows it is a personal struggle within a social context that may make the task either more or less difficult. Multiculturalism in Canada has the latter effect but it may matter very little, because integration—the remaking of the self within a new society with one's personal heritage as invaluable texture—is finally achieved in the depths of one's soul. Many Canadians, like me, have simply ignored multiculturalism, by living our lives as fully engaged with our new society as possible, secure in the knowledge of the rich family past that has brought us here.

25   I will never forget the bright summer evening many years ago when, fresh off the plane from a trip to Europe, I stood on my apartment balcony gazing out at the Toronto skyline, at the crystal light emanating off Lake Ontario and beyond. I took a deep breath of the cooling evening air and knew, deep within my bones, that it was good to be home....

Analyzing the writer's strategies

Neil Bissoondath's essay is a provocative combination of current events and examples from history. After opening with a comment about the inadequacy of the term "minority," he states his thesis: Canada's multiculturalism policy is detrimental to Canada in general and immigrants in particular. The writer then cites the purpose of Canada's multicultural policy and accuses one of our best-known prime ministers, Pierre Trudeau, of being "blind" to its consequences. Bissoondath then suggests that our festivals, which many of his opponents feel encourage acceptance of others, actually promote the formation of stereotypes. He also states that by encouraging immigrants to be loyal to the customs of their countries of origin, people will never accept them; they will only tolerate them.

As the writer develops his argument, he goes beyond the effects of these policies on the individual and looks at the effects on Canada as a whole. According to Bissoondath, our inability to define ourselves as a nation stems from our mosaic culture.

Responding to the writer's argument

Take a position either for or against one of the following topics and write an argumentative essay supporting your position. Use the "Guide to Writing the Persuasive Essay" (pp. 89–91) to help construct the essay. Be sure to include all of the important points needed for a good argument.

1. When individuals are not encouraged to assimilate into their new culture, they do not develop allegiances to that culture.

2. Canada should adopt an immigration policy similar to that of the United States.

3. Our multiculturalism policy leads to an insidious form of racism.

4. The United States promotes assimilation for new immigrants. This policy suggests that it is possible to obliterate one's past.

5. Hyphenation of identity, as in Irish-Canadian or Italian-Canadian, only promotes different people to divide themselves along ethnic lines and ultimately leads to a form of segregation.

6. We must strive to create a society that is cohesive and enriched by cultural diversity.

7. Societies based on cultural mosaics rarely accept the various groups of which they are composed.

8. Immigrants should be forced to learn either official language.

9. Canada should decrease its level of immigration in order to assimilate more effectively those who have recently immigrated.

10. Without the diversity of Canada's immigrant population, the country would be artistically and culturally barren.

EXERCISE 1   Using Research Material to Write the Persuasive Essay

Should Canada allow more immigrants? The following pieces of information are on this controversial topic. Use this information as the basis for your own essay on immigration. You may select as many items as you want, or you may adapt the items to agree with your own way of thinking. After choosing the material you want to use, be sure to organize your major points before starting the rough draft.

1. Fifteen million immigrants have arrived in Canada over the last 150 years.

2. Without immigration, this nation would not be ranked in the top five best nations to live in by the United Nations.

3. Canada allows approximately 200,000 immigrants into the country each year, more per capita than most other nations.

4. Canada's earliest settlers were from France and Britain; now most come from Asia and Africa.

5. Many who immigrate to Canada are fleeing war and economic hardship.

6. Immigrants bring valuable knowledge and experiences to Canada.

7. Some people believe that immigrants come to Canada in order to take advantage of our generous health and welfare benefits.

8. Many important scientists, artists, and athletes have chosen Canada as their home.

9. Immigrants have often been the targets of discrimination.

10. Immigrants should be encouraged to settle in sparsely populated regions of the country.

Writing the persuasive essay: Additional topics

Choose one of the fifteen topics listed and write an essay of at least five paragraphs. Use the six points discussed on pages 89–90 and repeated below as a guide for your writing.

- Write a strong thesis statement.
- Give evidence or reasons for your beliefs.
- Provide examples for each of your reasons.
- Use at least one authority to support your thesis.
- Admit that others have a different point of view.
- Indicate the results or make predictions in the conclusion.

Essay topics   Argue for or against:

1. Legalized marijuana

2. Canada Customs' right to open mail

3. Stricter immigration laws

4. Prayer in the public schools

5. Genetically modified foods

6. Tax exemption for religious organizations

7. Tongue piercing

8. Single-parent adoption

9. Canada's role in peacekeeping

10. Homosexual marriages

11. Required courses in college or university

12. Steroid use in amateur sports

13. Expense accounts for business people

14. The use of cell phones while driving

15. Random drug testing in the workplace

EXERCISE 1 Using Research Material to Write the Persuasive Essay

The following pieces of information are on the controversial topic of ***violence in the movies and on television.*** To what extent is the violence we see in films and on television programs responsible for the degree of violence in our society? Use this information as the basis for your own essay on the topic. You may select as many of the items as you want, or you may adapt the items to agree with your way of thinking. As you study the list, decide which of your paragraphs could make use of these facts or opinions.

1. The Standing Committee on Communications and Culture concluded in 1993 that television violence is a risk factor that can lead to antisocial behaviour and aggressive tendencies.

2. In most TV series, the violence depicted shows no physical harm, no psychological harm, and no judgment about the morality of the violent act.

3. Hollywood spends over $300 million each year advertising movies that are extremely violent.

4. In a recent study, of the 188 music videos examined, 1,785 separate acts of violence were depicted, nearly one-third of them being serious in nature.

5. Television violence has increased by 65 percent since 1980.

6. Health Canada states that there is a lack of nonviolent educational and entertaining programs geared to children.

7. Horror, slasher, and violent science fiction movies have increased from 6 percent of box office receipts in 1970 to over 30 percent today.

8. In some years, more than half of the films produced by Hollywood have content that is intensely violent.

9. Over 900 research studies on violent entertainment give overwhelming evidence that violent films and other programs are having a harmful effect on people.

10. A proposal has been made that every cable TV company offering violent movie channels should also be required to offer a nonviolent channel.

EXERCISE 2 Using Research Material to Write the Persuasive Essay

To what extent can a society permit its people to read, write, and say whatever they want? The following pieces of information are on this controversial topic of ***censorship and free speech.*** Use this information as the basis for your own essay on the topic. You may select as many of the items as you want, or you may adapt the items to agree with your own way of thinking. After selecting the material to be used, be sure to organize your major points before starting the rough draft.

1. In 1949, *The Naked and the Dead,* by Norman Mailer, was banned in Canada by personal order of the Minister of National Revenue, who admitted that he had not read the entire book. The book had been a bestseller in Canada for ten months before being banned.

2. After twenty-six years on the prohibited list, James Joyce's masterpiece, *Ulysses,* was allowed into Canada in 1949—sixteen years after it was cleared of obscenity charges in the United States.

3. Such literary works as D.H. Lawrence's *Lady Chatterly's Lover,* James Joyce's *Ulysses,* and J.D. Salinger's *The Catcher in the Rye,* have been denounced as pornographic.

4. Canada's obscenity law is far-reaching. It bans the "publication, distribution or circulation [of] any obscene written matter, picture, model, phonograph record or other thing whatever."

5. In ancient Rome, the Censor was a powerful official who judged people's morals and who could even remove government officials from office.

6. *MS* magazine was banned from a number of high school libraries because it was judged to be obscene.

7. The researcher and writer Gay Talese believes that we should not allow law enforcement officials "to deny pornography to those who want it."

8. In March 1994, a group of Canadian parents attempted to have Margaret Laurence's book *The Diviners* removed from their local high school's curriculum. This classic Canadian novel has faced similar challenges since 1985.

9. Canada Customs opened domestic mail addressed to a Vancouver bookstore in search of potentially obscene material.

10. Some psychologists believe that being able to enjoy pornography helps people deal with their frustrations without having to commit criminal or antisocial acts.

Working Together

The following article by Keith Martin and Scott Sedmak appeared in the *Toronto Star*, July 6, 2001.

Fighting the Scourge of Drug Addiction

1   The illicit drug trade is destroying lives throughout our hemisphere and beyond. Collectively, we have failed miserably to come to grips with this modern day scourge. At home, we usually opt for punitive legal measures when dealing with addicts, which gives them new criminal skills, rather than enabling them to acquire the tools to live independently and drug free. Internationally, we have waged a futile military war on the ground in drug producing countries like Colombia, all to no avail. Trying to stop production without decreasing consumption has proven to be utterly useless.

2   The illicit drug trade touches millions of lives in both developed and developing countries.

3   Worldwide, more than 180 million people are addicted to heroin, cocaine, and the new so-called "designer drugs." However, the most devastating impact is felt in underdeveloped nations, which not only bear the brunt of massive drug trafficking but also of an escalating number of users.

4   In Colombia, the world's premier producer of cocaine, a guerrilla war has turned this beautiful country into a zone of destruction.

5   Guerrilla and paramilitary forces, fuelled by drug profits, kill about 80 innocent people a day, making this the bloodiest place in the Americas. Kidnapping (70 per

cent of the world's kidnappings occur in Colombia), corruption, torture and social unrest all stem from this little white powder. In shantytowns, children are prostituted to feed their parents' drug habit. Many never reach adulthood, killed in random acts of violence or by AIDS, both of which are increasing in frequency.

6   Meanwhile, in a developed country like Canada, illicit drugs have left a similar path of destruction. From the destitute people on needle row in East Vancouver, to the posh, tree-lined streets of Rosedale, addictive drugs are destroying lives and families. It is a problem shared by all of us in the Americas and, therefore, will take a combined effort to solve.

7   The first challenge for policy-makers is to implement solutions that will decrease consumption in North America. Thus, we must reevaluate our drug treatment programs. Today, far too many addicts go through a repetitive cycle of detox, treatment and release, without making real progress in kicking their habit. They remain dependent, ruled by their addictions. To address this, we need to adopt some of the newer, European treatment models that take a more holistic approach. New scientific tools, which enable us to peer into the working brain, have shown us that being in a drug environment unleashes a cascade of chemical messages that drive a person with an addiction to shoot up, snort or freebase. Thus, it is essential to remove them from their environment where drug use is often a way of life. This must also be accompanied by work and skills training so they can provide for themselves.

8   Next, we must introduce a prevention strategy that targets children. The "Just Say No" approach is not good enough. An early intervention program, like the Headstart program for children in the first 6 to 8 years of life, works well. It focuses on strengthening the parent-child bond and ensures that children live in a secure, loving, stable environment where their basic needs are met. It has proven extremely effective in dramatically reducing substance abuse later in life, decreasing youth crime by 50 per cent, keeping kids in school longer, and reducing welfare dependency. Adolescents and adults must be made aware that their consumption of heroin, cocaine and other drugs contributes to the killing and torture of innocent people half a world away.

9   Drug pushers and traffickers are a different matter. They must be met with the full force of the law. This means strengthening the power of the courts and police to prosecute the criminal organizations that thrive off this lurid business.

10   In the United States, the RICO (Racketeer Influenced Corrupt Organization) Act amendments have been used to seize the proceeds from criminal activity associated with the drug trade. The act allows for law enforcement agencies to recover the massive profits generated by these criminal organizations and use that money to fund anti-drug programs.

11   All nations in our hemisphere must adopt similar laws in order to form a united front that enables these illegally obtained profits to be used against drug traffickers. Countries in the Americas should also adopt a system of import/export permits for the chemical precursors used to manufacture illegal drugs. This will enable authorities in our hemisphere to track and halt their export to companies that are using them for illegal purposes. Collectively, if we adopt these rules it will be much more difficult for criminal organizations to engage in their nefarious activities.

12   The next challenge is what to do with subsistence farmers, who grow most of the cocoa plants used to manufacture cocaine. They will need alternative crops to grow. Thus, free trade, the elimination of barriers that are so counterproductive to developing countries, must be aggressively pursued. As United Nations Secretary-General Kofi Annan has said: "Developing countries need trade not aid." Free trade is the best thing we can do to lift the economy of the western hemisphere's developing nations.

13   In the end, the battle against the illicit drug trade requires transhemispheric co-operation. A plan must include decreasing consumption in North America through prevention programs like Headstart; treating addictions from a medical perspective rather than a punitive, judicial one; opening the hemisphere to free trade; and giving police and courts the tools to go after drug dealers and organized crime gangs.

14   We must act now to stop the scourge of drugs from taking more lives than it already has. We owe this to each other, as Canadians; we owe it to our fellow citizens of the Americas, but most of all, we owe it to our children.

1. The class should divide into groups, read the editorial together, conduct a discussion, and then individually write their answers to the following questions.

   a. What is the thesis of the editorial?

   b. What supporting evidence for the thesis is given in the editorial?

   c. Were any outside sources used to support the thesis? If so, describe the sources.

   d. Do the writers say what will or will not happen if nothing is done?

   e. Does the editorial propose a solution to the problem?

   f. Does the editorial seem reasonable to you?

   g. State why you do or do not believe this is an effective argument.

2. Write a letter to a drug user. Try to persuade this person to stop using drugs.

3. If you could gather ten drug users in a room, what do you think their arguments would be for not stopping?

4. As a class, gather material on the topic of drug use in Canada (or on another topic that interests the majority of the students). Whenever a current news story appears or an idea comes to mind, share it with the class. This material could become the research for a future essay or research paper that the class could work on together or in groups.

Writing under Pressure

Most people prefer to do their writing when they are not under the pressure of a time limit. However, many situations demand that a piece of writing be finished by a certain time. One situation is the writing of a story for a newspaper that constantly works under a very tight deadline. Another pressured situation is writing an essay exam that must be handed in by the end of a class period. This chapter will review some of the techniques for writing successful essays under pressure.

How to write well under pressure

The first rule of doing well in any test is to come to the test well rested and well prepared. Research proves that reviewing notes and reading assignments systematically throughout the semester is much more effective than cramming for a test the night before. You'll be greatly satisfied if you learn to use your time efficiently and wisely.

Coming to an exam well prepared

1. Study the textbook chapters and your notes. In your textbook, review headings and bolded words as well as information you have highlighted or underlined. Look for both chapter reviews and summaries at the ends of chapters. If you have already made an outline, study that too.

2. Avoid having to face any surprises when the exam is distributed. When the test is first announced in class, ask if it will include material from the textbook in addition to notes taken in class. Also, find out the format of the test. How many essay questions will there be, and how many points will each question be worth? How much time will you have to complete the test?

3. Form a study group if you can. One way a study group can work is the following: each person comes to the study group prepared to present at least one major question that he or she thinks the instructor will ask. Also, be prepared to give any information needed to answer that question. The other students

take notes and add whatever additional information they can. Each person in turn presents a different question along with the information needed for the answer. Members of the group can quiz each other on the information that is to be covered by the exam. For an essay exam, some material needs to be memorized. If you are unable to be part of a study group, you should still try to predict what questions will be on the exam. Prepare an outline for study and then memorize your outline.

Remember that an essay test, unlike a multiple-choice test, requires more than simply recognizing information. In an essay exam, you must be able to recall ideas and specific details and present them quickly in your own words. This ability to memorize not only concepts but also factual information is quite demanding.

Strategies for answering timed in-class essay questions

The smart test taker does not begin to answer the first question immediately. Instead, he or she takes a few moments to look over the test and form a strategy for the best way to tackle it. The following pointers will help you become "test smart."

1. When you receive the exam, *read over each essay question twice*. How many points is each question worth? The way in which you budget your time will depend heavily on the importance of each question. A well-written test should tell you how many points each question is worth. If, for example, one essay question is worth 50 points, you should spend approximately half your time planning and answering this question. However, if the test consists of ten shorter essay questions and you have a class period of 100 minutes, you should spend no more than ten minutes on each question, keeping a careful watch on your time. Tests composed of several shorter essays can be disastrous to people who do not watch their time. Students often write too much for the first four or five questions and then panic because they have very little time left to answer the final questions.

2. When you read an essay question, ask yourself *what method of development is being asked for?* We all know stories of people who failed tests because they misunderstood the question.

3. *Use key words from the test question itself* to compose your thesis statement, which in a test should be your first sentence. Don't try to be too clever on a test. State your points as directly and clearly as possible.

4. Answer the question by stating your basic point and then *using as many specific details as you have time or knowledge to give.* The more specific names, dates, and places (all spelled correctly) that you can provide will add points to your grade.

5. Since a question can have more than one part, be sure you *answer all the parts.* Check over the question to be sure your answer includes all parts.

Study the question to determine exactly what is being asked for.

Sample essay question

Define pay equity. What are some of the factors in Canadian society that have led to calls for pay equity? Be specific.

If the question given were one of ten short essay questions on a 1½ hour final examination, the following answer would probably be adequate:

*Sample essay
question
answer*

Pay equity is equal pay for work of equal or comparable value. There have been a number of factors that have led to calls for pay equity. First, more women are entering the workforce out of choice or necessity. In 1996, women accounted for about 47% of the labour force in Canada whereas twenty years before about 30% of the labour force was made up of women. Arguments for pay equity recognize the existence of the gender "wage gap." Female workers also earn, on average, 30% less in wages than male workers. A major reason for this difference in pay is due to discrimination. Male bosses and managers continue to pay their female workers less just because they are females. Another major factor is that, historically, work mostly done by women has been undervalued and underpaid in relation to work mostly done by men. Women chiefly perform the lowest paying jobs in Canada, such as baby sitters, nannies, and parents' helpers.

The first sentence provides a concise definition of the term. Notice that the second sentence uses the key words from the question to state the thesis. The answer gives not one but three examples of the factors that have contributed to arguments for pay equity. Moreover, the answer is very specific, providing key facts, dates, and statistics wherever possible. Can you spot the transitional expressions the writer uses to signal the movement from one example to the next?

Frequently used terms in essay questions

Define: A definition is the precise meaning of a word or term. When you define something in an essay you usually write an *extended definition*, in which you select an appropriate example or examples to illustrate the meaning of a term.

Comparison or Contrast: When you *compare* two people or things, you point out the similarities between them. When you *contrast* two items, you point out the differences. Sometimes you may find yourself using both comparison and contrast in an essay.

Narration: Narration is the telling of a story by the careful use of a sequence of events. The events are usually (but not always) told in chronological order.

Summary: When you write a summary, you are supplying the main ideas of a longer piece of writing.

Discussion: This is a general term that encourages you to analyze a subject at length. Inviting students to discuss some aspect of a topic is a widely used method of asking examination questions.

Classification: When you *classify* items of any kind, you place them into separate groups so that large amounts of material can be more easily understood.

Cause and Effect: When you deal with causes, you answer the question *why;* when you deal with effects you show *results* or *consequences.*

EXERCISE 1   Methods of Development

Each of the following essay questions deals with the single topic of computers. Use the above list of explanations to decide which method of development is being called for in each case. In the space provided after each question, identify the method being required.

1. Trace the development of the computer, beginning in 1937. Be sure to include all significant developments discussed in class.

   Method of development: _____

2. Choose two of the Web editing programs practised in class and discuss the similarities and differences you encountered. What in your opinion were the advantages and disadvantages of each?

   Method of development: _____

3. Explain the meaning of each of the following terms: *hard drive, RAM, network, virus,* and *software*.

   Method of development: _____

4. We have discussed many of the common business applications for the computer. Select ten applications and group them according to the functions they perform.

   Method of development: _____

5. Discuss the problems that have resulted in the typical office as a result of information technology.

   Method of development: _____

EXERCISE 2   Methods of Development/Parts of a Question

Each of the following is an example of an essay question that could be asked in different courses. In the spaces provided after each question, indicate: (a) what method of development (definition, comparison or contrast, narration, summary, or discussion) is being called for, and (b) how many parts there are to the question. This indicates how many parts there will be in your answer.

1. What does the term *sociology* mean? Include in your answer at least four different meanings the term *sociology* has had since this area of study began.

   Method of development: _____

   The different parts of the question: _____

   _____

   _____

2. Compare the reasons Canada entered the First World War with the reasons it entered the Second World War.

   Method of development: _____

   The different parts of the question: _____

   _____

   _____

3. Trace the history of our knowledge of the planet Jupiter, from the time it was first discovered until the present day. Include in your answer at least one nineteenth-century discovery and three of the most recent discoveries that have been made about Jupiter through the use of unmanned space vehicles sent near that planet.

Method of development: _____

The different parts of the question: _____

_____

_____

4. In view of the dramatic increase in cases of contagious diseases, describe the types of precautions now required for medical personnel. What changes are likely to be required in the future?

   Method of development: _____

   The different parts of the question: _____

   _____

   _____

5. Explain the three effects of high temperatures on space vehicles as they reenter the earth's atmosphere.

   Method of development: _____

   The different parts of the question: _____

   _____

   _____

6. What was the complete process of deciding whether to build a fixed link between Prince Edward Island and the mainland? Include in your answer six different steps in the process.

   Method of development: _____

   The different parts of the question: _____

   _____

   _____

7. Trace the history of the English language from its beginning to the present day. Divide the history of the language into at least three different parts, using Old English, Middle English, and Modern English as your main divisions.

   Method of development: _____

   The different parts of the question: _____

   _____

   _____

8. Discuss the events that led up to the Second World War. Be sure to include both the political and social problems of the time that directly and indirectly led to the war.

   Method of development: _____

   The different parts of the question: _____

   _____

   _____

9. Summarize the four theories that have been proposed as to why dinosaurs became extinct sixty-five million years ago.

   Method of development: _____

   The different parts of the question: _____

   _____

   _____

10. Define the term *monarchy* and discuss the relevance or irrelevance of this form of government in Canada.

    Method of development: _____

    The different parts of the question: _____

    _____

    _____

Using the thesis statement for timed in-class essay questions

One of the most effective ways to begin an essay answer is to write a thesis statement. Your thesis statement should include the important parts of the question and should also give a clear indication of the approach you intend to take in your answer. Writing your opening sentence in this way gives you a real advantage: as your professor begins to read your work, it is clear what you are going to write about and how you are going to treat your subject.

For example, suppose you were going to write an essay on the following topic:

Agree or disagree that pornography negatively portrays women and men in our society.

An effective way to write your opening sentence would be to write the following thesis sentence:

I agree that pornography negatively portrays women and men in our society.

The reader would then know that this was indeed the topic you had chosen and would also know how you intended to approach that topic.

EXERCISE 3   Writing Thesis Statements

Rewrite each of the following essay questions in thesis statement form. Read each question carefully and underline the important words or phrases in it. Then decide on the approach you would take in answering that question. An example has been done for you.

Essay question: <u>How</u> does one learn another language?

Thesis statement: The <u>process</u> of learning another language is complicated but usually follows <u>four distinct stages</u>.

1. Essay Questions: Discuss Marshall McLuhan's theories on media.

   Thesis statement: _____

   _____

2. Essay Question: What are the effects of TV violence on children?

   Thesis statement: _____

   _____

3. Essay Question: Trace the development of portrait painting from the Middle Ages to today.

   Thesis statement: _____

   _____

   _____

4. Essay Question: What are the major causes for the economic crisis facing the African nations today?

   Thesis statement: _____

   _____

5. Essay Question: What have we recently learned from ocean exploration, and what remains to be done?

   Thesis statement: _____

   _____

6. Essay Question: Is it harmful or beneficial to adopt a child from one culture and raise that child in another culture?

   Thesis statement: _____

   _____

7. Essay Question: In what ways does the new Japan differ from the old Japan?

   Thesis statement: _____

   _____

8. Essay Question: What four countries depend on tourism for the major part of their national income and why is this so?

   Thesis statement: _____

   _____

9. Essay Question: What factors should a college or university use when judging the merits of a particular student for admission?

   Thesis statement: _____

   _____

10. Essay Question: What is Alzheimer's disease, its sequence of characteristic symptoms, and the current methods of treatment?

    Thesis statement: _____

    _____

Working Together

The following passage on the consequences of the shift of human society from nomadic to agricultural is taken from *Biology*, by Helena Curtis:

> Whatever its causes, the change to agriculture had profound consequences. Populations were no longer nomadic. Thus they could store food not only in silos and granaries, but in the form of domesticated animals. In addition to food stores, other possessions could be accumulated to an extent far beyond that previously possible. Even land could be owned and accumulated and passed on by inheritance. Thus the world became divided into semipermanent groups of haves and have-nots, as it is today.
>
> Because the efforts of a few could produce enough food for everyone, the communities became diversified. People became tradesmen, artisans, bankers, scholars, poets, all the rich mixture of which a modern community is composed. And these people could live much more densely than ever before. For hunting and food-gathering economies, 2 square miles, on the average, are required to provide enough for one family to eat.
>
> One immediate and direct consequence of the agricultural revolution was an increase in populations. A striking characteristic of hunting groups is that they vigorously limit their numbers. A woman on the move cannot carry more than one infant along with her household baggage, minimal though that may be. When simple means of birth control—often just abstention—are not effective, she resorts to abortion or, more probably, infanticide. In addition, there is a high natural mortality, particularly among the very young, the very old, the ill, the disabled, and women at childbirth. As a result, populations dependent on hunting tend to remain small.

1. After you have studied the selection, construct an essay question that a professor in a biology or anthropology course could ask as part of a mid-term or final examination. At the same time, your present instructor could also make up a question based on the selection. When everyone has finished, your instructor could read his or her question first. Is it the question you had expected? How many students in the class came close to the instructor's choice of question?

2. List the questions discussed in the activity above, and use the following checklist to analyze each question.

    a. Does the question seem to be fair?
    (Some questions might be too vague or too general to be a fair test of what the student has learned.)

    b. How many parts does the question have?

    c. Does the question call for a specific method of development (for example, definition and analysis)?

    d. What are the key terms that should be used in the answer?

    e. What would be an effective opening sentence for the answer?

The Research Essay: Using Summary and Direct Quotation

Using outside sources

Most of the required writing in composition courses is done without the use of outside sources. However, during your semesters, you will be asked to produce research essays or term papers for other courses, papers that will require you to do research using *outside sources.*

> An *outside source* is any material that provides you with facts or perceptions that are not your own.

When you use outside sources, special skills are required to incorporate the ideas of others and to give credit to the original authors. In this chapter, you will study three selections, all related to the theme of valuable items people have stolen or misused. One selection describes Egypt's struggle to recover its world-famous portrait statue of the legendary Queen Nefertiti; another excerpt reports on Allied soldiers looting in war-torn Europe in 1945; a third selection gives us insight into the problem of computer hackers and vandalism. With each selection, you will have the opportunity to practise *summarizing, quoting,* and *expressing your reactions* to the ideas of others.

Before we get started, however, we need to consider a very serious problem that can occur when students use source material incorrectly. Often a student comes across material written by someone else, material that seems to be just what the student wants to say. The temptation is to copy the exact words, ideas, facts, or opinions from the other writer and present those words as if they were the student's own thoughts. This can happen when a student lacks the confidence or the experience to use material properly from other writers. The name for this dishonest practice is called *plagiarism.*

> *Plagiarism* is the use of someone else's words, ideas, facts, or opinions without proper documentation.

If an idea is not your own original thought, you must give credit to the source. Plagiarism is a very serious offence, sometimes resulting in failure in a course or, in extreme cases, expulsion from school. This does not mean you should be afraid to use the ideas of others; you may do so, but everything depends on how you present the material. As long as you cite your sources, you may summarize and quote from the work of others to produce your own essay or research paper. Please see Appendix A at the back of the text to learn how to document your sources accurately.

Direct quotations: Using quotation marks around the exact words of another writer

When you quote a source directly in your own writing, your work gains authority by using material from that published source. Occasionally you will come across phrases or sentences that are so relevant to your work and so well expressed that you will want to use those words exactly, to strengthen your own conclusions or point of view. Using quotations is one of the most effective ways to add authority to your own work. However, a few words of caution:

1. When you decide to quote, you may not add any words of your own or change any words of the original. Whatever appears within the quotation marks must be exactly the same words that appear in the original source.

2. Sometimes students use too many quotations, often because they do not feel secure enough with their own writing. Be selective in choosing your quotations. Too many quotations will ruin your report.

3. Be cautious about inserting a very long quotation into your paper. Unless every part of that quotation relates directly to what you are saying, the quotation will seem out of place.

4. In a formal paper, you will be required to provide a citation to show the source of every quotation. Every student should have the *MLA Handbook*, or a similar guide to writing a research paper, as a resource tool that is always at hand during the writing of a paper needing citations. With the use of computer technology, the task of including this information in your paper has become much easier than it used to be.

5. Some typical ways of introducing a quote are the following:

    In the words of one noted authority, . . .

    One authority has said, . . .

    As one well-known expert has observed, . . .

How to write a summary

At the heart of education is the task of extracting the main ideas from a reading selection, or taking notes of the main ideas on lectures given in class. Learning how to summarize is perhaps the most important skill needed for this kind of work. Summaries become the basis for further study and consideration, and are constantly used by writers as they research material for reports. For example, a student writing a report on a certain topic may read ten or eleven articles on that topic. Some articles, of course, will be more useful than others, but the researcher should summarize each of the articles so that when the actual writing is done, these summaries can provide information as needed.

A summary should include only main ideas. Only a few examples or supporting details from the original text will find their way into the summary because in a summary it is always necessary to reduce the amount of material. You will probably need to read and review the material more than once in order to separate the main idea statements from the details and examples. The summary will be significantly shorter than the original text, but you must be careful not to leave out any main ideas or add any of your own ideas.

Suggestions for reacting to the ideas of others

In most research essays, it is not enough to summarize the ideas others have about a topic; you will be expected to make points of your own. Since students often feel unqualified to make their own judgments, the following suggestions may be helpful when it comes to reacting to the material of others:

1. Make a suggestion of your own for further work to be done in the field.

2. Use examples from different articles to support one of your major points.

3. Make the purpose of your essay a survey of the existing information on the topic.

4. Contrast the ways different writers see the same event or subject.

5. Suggest an idea that has been overlooked, or underestimated.

6. Give your own opinion about the matter.

7. Conduct a survey of your own to determine how those around you think about some aspect of your topic.

8. Use your own experience to provide examples for added interest in the material.

Practising skills for writing research papers

ESSAY 1   The Controversy over the Statue of Nefertiti

The story of the circumstances surrounding the discovery of the famous portrait statue of Nefertiti could easily be a detective novel. In 1912, in the ancient Egyptian royal city of Amarna, German archaeologists uncovered the portrait statue of Queen Nefertiti. This beautiful image, which had not been seen for over 3,000 years, finally gave reality to the mystery that had always surrounded this legendary queen. Under the terms of the excavating agreement between Egypt and Germany, the discovery should have remained in Egypt, but the archaeologists distracted the Egyptian government by having another discovery, made at the same time, seem to be a more desirable item. This they gave to the Egyptian government. Later, after the Germans had taken the statue to Berlin, they claimed that when it had been dug up, it was in pieces and could not have been recognized for what it was.

A storm of protest broke out in Egypt, as government officials demanded the return of the statue. Newspaper stories appeared all over the world, and throughout Europe many people pressured the German government to give back the treasure. Still the Germans refused. Even when the Egyptians announced the cancellation of any further permits for German archaeological teams to dig in Egypt, the Germans would not budge. The Egyptians even offered to exchange the Nefertiti for renewed digging rights and two rare statues of ancient Egyptian kings, but this offer was also refused. Finally, all negotiations stopped, and no German archaeological team was allowed back into Egypt.

During World War II, the German authorities hid the Nefertiti, along with other works of art they did not want the approaching Allied Armies to find, in a salt mine. At the end of the war, American troops did find all of the hidden items, and when this discovery was announced, officials in Egypt once more called for the return of their national treasure. They were to be disappointed again: The Allies allowed the Germans to keep Nefertiti, and to this day she remains on display in Berlin.

Quote: What two statements would you select from the text that you feel are important enough for possible quotation in a research paper? Copy those sentences below, word for word.

1. _____

   _____

   _____

2. _____

   _____

   _____

Summarize the material: In your own words, write down the main ideas of the text. Do not forget that a summary should always be a good deal shorter than the original text.

_____

_____

_____

_____

_____

_____

_____

_____

_____

_____

_____

_____

React: What are two of your own reactions to this material, reactions that could eventually become part of your research paper?

1. _____

   _____

2. _____

   _____

Write a paragraph for your research paper: As you write, incorporate your summary, one of the quotations you copied, and a reaction of your own to the material.

_____

_____

_____

_____

_____

_____

_____

_____

_____

_____

_____

_____

_____

_____

_____

_____

_____

_____

_____

_____

_____

_____

_____

_____

_____

ESSAY 2   Looting in Wartime

from *The Spoils of World War II*
KENNETH D. ALFORD

All the occupying forces looted, and the army made it easy. Looting was done without shame or hesitation and was not regarded as stealing. Bankers, clergymen—persons who were normally honest—did not hesitate to dip into an unlimited treasure trove. There were no effective rules to control the game. The army permitted personnel to mail home captured enemy equipment provided that there was no "military need" for it. Technically, soldiers were forbidden to mail home items taken from German homes and public buildings. The ruling was admirable but rarely enforced. An occasional commanding officer attempted to apply the law, but even in respectable outfits it was possible for an enlisted man to have an officer censor his package without inspecting it, or even let it go after inspecting it. An officer's signature on a parcel was only as honest or dishonest as he was, and officers' personal baggage was not even examined.

Especially, there was the bold, unmitigated theft of motorcycles, pistols, rifles, knives, cameras, and binoculars, as these were the items most desired by the average soldier. Many of these items were expensive and beautiful, the best in the world. Once in the possession of an American, a camera, pistol, or pair of binoculars might change hands twenty times before reaching the United States. The guns included military Lugers, finely crafted civilian pistols, beautiful shotguns, and superb hunting rifles. Also into the mail pouch went priceless collections of antique ornamental swords.

Destroyed vacated towns were the most fruitful hunting grounds. The conquering American would pop through a hole in the side of a house and survey the ruins. Whatever he wanted he took. Eager hands were waiting to relieve him of his prize; if he was wounded, he was almost certain to lose the booty to ambulance drivers, medics, or hospital attendants.

Quote: What two statements would you select from the text that you feel are important enough for possible quotation in a research paper? Copy those sentences below, word for word.

1. _____

_____

_____

2. _____

_____

_____

Summarize the material: In your own words, write down the main ideas of the text. Do not forget that a summary should always be a good deal shorter than the original text.

_____

_____

_____

_____

_____

_____

_____

_____

_____

_____

_____

_____

_____

_____

React: What are two of your own reactions to this material, reactions that could eventually become part of your research paper?

1. _____

_____

2. _____

_____

Write a paragraph for your research paper: As you write, incorporate your summary, one of the quotations you copied, and a reaction of your own to the material.

_____

_____

_____

_____

_____

_____

_____

_____

_____

_____

_____

_____

_____

_____

_____

_____

_____

ESSAY 3   To Catch a Hacker

Hackers are computer-age vandals, pranksters who are driven more by their egos than a desire to damage permanently an organization's computer network. Most of the time hackers will break into an organization's network to snoop around and later brag about their adventures to other hackers. One of the most infamous hack attacks surprised the world because of the damage it caused and because of who perpetrated it—a teenaged boy from Montreal.

In February 2000, an Internet security expert in San Francisco caught wind of a self-styled hacker who was boasting on EFNet, an international chat network frequented by hackers, that he had committed a rash of recent "denial-of-service" (DoS) attacks on the Net. Using specially designed software, someone had blasted the Web sites with blocks of information, eventually shutting them down. The targeted Web sites belonged to bookseller Amazon.com, CNN.com, and auction site eBay.com, which all lost six hours of revenue to the DoS attack. The culprit was a self-styled hacker calling himself "Mafiaboy," and he began regaling others on EFNet with the tale of how he did it.

The security expert sent the transcripts of Mafiaboy's boasts to the FBI, who forwarded them to the RCMP when Mafiaboy's Canadian location was revealed. Elite computer hackers were skeptical; they had never heard of Mafiaboy, and they felt sure that the perpetrator of the world's worst DoS would have been one of their own.

But what the experts forgot is that DoS attacks are horrifyingly simple. Mafiaboy used software scripts that had been in existence for years. The software works like this: The user sends a program—something like a bug—to a local network somewhere. The bug tries to burrow in, trying thousands of passwords. Through sheer persistence, it will eventually break in at some point. It duplicates itself and sends out another bug; soon there are bugs on computers around the world, and the hacker instructs them to broadcast a barrage of data packets with false return addresses—the address of the computer the hacker really wants to attack. When those packets bounce "back" to the targeted computer, the flood of data strangles the local network. It's sort of like mailing thousands of letters with fake forwarding addresses but with the same return address. When all those letters get returned, the target's mailbox gets swamped.

On January 18, 2001, the 16-year-old Mafiaboy (whose identity is protected under the Young Offenders Act) pleaded guilty in a Montreal youth court to an array of 56 charges related to the attacks, owning up to the most expensive act of computer vandalism in history. The magnitude of his crime boggles the mind; the FBI estimates that his activities cost the U.S. economy $1.7 billion.

The Mafiaboy episode raises some serious questions about the security of the Internet. "Mafiaboy was not a good hacker, he just had a tool made by one," says Rene Hamel, an ex-Mountie turned Internet security consultant. Right now, a serious DoS attack by someone skilled and bent on specific damage—like a foreign country at war with the United States—would be unpreventable. "I keep in contact with security experts," says Hamel. "This is what keeps them awake at night."

Quote: What two statements would you select from the text that you feel are important enough for possible quotation in a research paper? Copy those sentences below, word for word.

1. _____

_____

_____

2. _____

_____

_____

Summarize the material: In your own words, write down the main ideas of the text. Do not forget that a summary should always be a good deal shorter than the original text.

_____

_____

_____

_____

_____

_____

_____

_____

_____

_____

_____

_____

_____

React: What are two of your own reactions to this material, reactions that could eventually become part of your research paper?

1. _____

_____

2. _____

_____

Write a paragraph for your research paper: As you write, incorporate your summary, one of the quotations you copied, and a reaction of your own to the material.

_____

_____

_____

_____

_____

_____

_____

_____

_____

_____

_____

_____

_____

_____

_____

_____

_____

Working Together

The following biographical information reports on the life of Nellie Cashman, an Irish-American woman who was a pioneer in many of our western mining towns in the late nineteenth and early twentieth centuries. The brief biography you are about to read covers the first thirty years of Nellie Cashman's adventurous life and takes us from her birth in 1845 in Ireland to one of her famous adventures in British Columbia in 1875.

Nellie was born in Midleton, in Ireland's County Cork, to Patrick Cashman and Frances "Fanny" Cronin in 1845. When she was about five years old, Nellie, her younger sister Fanny, and their now-widowed mother arrived in the United States, refugees from Ireland's potato famine. After 13 or 14 years in Boston, the Cashmans headed west in the late 1860s, settling in the vibrant community of San Francisco, where Irishmen were numerous and influential.

In 1872, Nellie and her elderly mother travelled to the new silver-mining district of Pioche, Nevada, opening a boarding house about ten miles from the camp. At Pioche, they found a wild environment, with thousands of boisterous miners and millmen—most of them Irish—living in a situation where filth, gun fights, and altercations between owners and employees were commonplace. The throbbing life of this mining and milling centre must have appealed to Nellie; in the coming decades, she would consistently move to similar communities.

There is no evidence that Nellie engaged in mining during her first experience at living near a mining camp. But during her two years at Pioche, she did become very involved in the affairs of the local Catholic church, participating in bazaars and other money-raising efforts.

When Nellie moved from Pioche, she left her mother with her sister Fanny in San Francisco and travelled alone to northern British Columbia. There, for a few years in the mid-1870s, she operated a boarding house in the Cassiar District, on the Stikine River, not far from modern Juneau. She also worked gold-placer ground, becoming familiar with elementary mining geology.

In the winter of 1874–75, Nellie's reputation as an "angel of mercy," for which she is best known today, was born. While on a trip to Victoria, Nellie heard that a severe winter storm had hammered her fellow miners in the Cassiar diggings and that no one could get through. She immediately purchased supplies and sleds, hired six men, sailed to Fort Wrangell, Alaska, and headed inland through heavy snows. Her success at reaching the miners with the needed medicines and food became the talk of the West, as hundreds of miners considered her their saviour.

The Victoria *Daily British Colonist* of February 5, 1875, in describing the rescue attempt, compared it to other efforts by famous prospectors and woodsmen, and declared that "Her extraordinary feat of attempting to reach the diggings in midwinter and in the face of dangers and obstacles which appalled even the stout-hearted Fannin and thrice drove him back to Wrangell for shelter is attributed by her friends to insanity." If Nellie had done nothing else for the rest of her career, that incident alone would have guaranteed her place in mining lore and tradition.

Imagine you are writing a report on pioneer women in Canadian history. This piece is one of your sources. Discuss the piece and then write a paragraph that could be a part of your final report. In the paragraph you write, summarize what you believe is significant about Nellie Cashman's life giving one quote from the piece and at the end of the paragraph providing your own commentary on her life. Begin your summary with the following words:

Another pioneer woman of the period was Nellie Cashman.

_____

_____

_____

_____

_____

_____

_____

_____

_____

_____

_____

_____

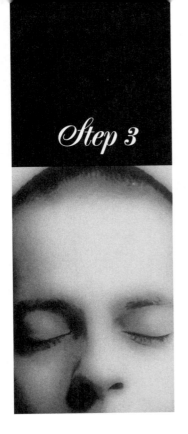

Step 3

CREATING EFFECTIVE SENTENCES

CONTENTS

THE SENTENCE

Chapter 11

Finding Subjects and Verbs in Simple Sentences

Why should we use complete sentences when we write?

We do not always speak in complete sentences. Sometimes we abbreviate a thought into a word or two, knowing that the person to whom we are talking will understand our meaning. We all do this occasionally in our conversations with friends and family.

For example, if a friend walked up to you around lunch time and said, "Lunch?" you would assume that your friend was asking to have lunch with you. While the word "lunch" is not a complete thought, the situation and the way the word was spoken allowed you to guess the probable meaning.

In writing down thoughts, however, a reader (your audience) is not likely to be totally familiar with the thoughts or the circumstances surrounding your words. The reader often cannot interpret or fill in the missing parts. Therefore, *one characteristic of good writing is that the ideas are expressed in complete sentences.*

What is a complete sentence?

> A *complete sentence* must contain a subject and a verb, as well as express a complete thought.

In this chapter, we will practise finding the subjects and the verbs in some basic sentences. These basic sentences are called *simple sentences* because they each have only one subject and verb group. (Later we will practise with compound and complex sentences in which two or more ideas are combined giving the sentence more than one subject and verb group.)

How do you find the subject of a sentence?

For most simple sentences, you can find the subject by keeping five points in mind.

1. The subject often answers the question, "Who or what is the sentence about?"

2. The subject often comes early in the sentence.

3. The subject is usually a noun or a pronoun.

4. Noun or pronoun subjects can be modified by adjectives.

5. The subject can be compound.

Understanding parts of speech: Nouns, pronouns, adjectives

> A *noun* is a word that names persons, places, or things.
> A *noun* can function as a subject, an object, or a possessive in a sentence.
>
> The *Ford* is parked outside.
> We parked the *Ford* outside.
> The *Ford's* hood is dented.

Nouns can be either *common* nouns or *proper* nouns. Most nouns in our writing are common nouns. They are not capitalized. Proper nouns name particular persons, places, or things. They are always capitalized.

NOUNS

Common	Proper
cousin	Cousin Bill
province	Alberta
car	Ford

Another way to categorize nouns is into *concrete* or *abstract* nouns. Concrete nouns are all the things we can see or touch, such as *desk, car,* or *friend.* Abstract nouns are the things we cannot see or touch, such as *justice, honesty,* or *friendship.*

NOUNS

Concrete	Abstract
store	commerce
crowd	pleasure
book	knowledge

> A *pronoun* is a word used to take the place of a noun. Just like a noun, a pronoun can be used as the subject, the object, or in some cases to show possession.
>
> *It* is parked outside.
> We parked *it* outside.
> *Its* hood is dented.

Pronouns can also be categorized or divided into groups: personal, indefinite, relative, or demonstrative.

PRONOUNS

Personal Pronouns (refer to people or things)

Personal pronouns have three forms depending on how they are used in a sentence: as a subject, an object, or a possessive.

	Subjective		*Objective*		*Possessive*	
	Singular	**Plural**	**Singular**	**Plural**	**Singular**	**Plural**
1st person	I	we	me	us	my (mine)	our (ours)
2nd person	you	you	you	you	your (yours)	your (yours)
3rd person	he	they	him	them	his (his)	their (theirs)
	she		her		her (hers)	
	it		it		its (its)	

Relative Pronouns	*Demonstrative Pronouns*	*Indefinite Pronouns*
(can introduce noun clauses and adjective clauses)	(can point out the antecedent)	(refer to non-specific persons or things)

Relative Pronouns	*Demonstrative Pronouns*	**Singular**			
who, whom, whose	this	everyone	someone	anyone	no one
which	that	everybody	somebody	anybody	nobody
that	these	everything	something	anything	nothing
what	those	each	another	either	neither
whoever					
whichever		**Singular** or **Plural** (depending on meaning)			
whatever		all	more	none	
		any	most	some	

Plural

both	few	many	several
			others

Noun or pronoun subjects can be modified by **adjectives.**

An *adjective* is a word that modifies (describes or limits) a noun or a pronoun.

   young Robert

   one boy

Adjectives usually come directly in front of the nouns they modify, but they can also appear later in the sentence and refer back to the noun.

The boy is *young*.

The subject can be *compound*.

> A *compound subject* is made up of two or more nouns or pronouns joined together by *and, or, either/or,* or *neither/nor.*
>
> *Robert* and his *dog*

The different kinds of subjects you will encounter in this chapter are illustrated in these seven sentences. Examine each of the sentences and ask yourself who or what each sentence is about. Draw a line under the word (or words) you think is the subject in each sentence. Then on the line to the right, write what kind of subject you have underlined. Be as specific as possible: *concrete noun* or *personal pronoun,* for example.

1. The young boy walked.

2. Young Robert Worthing walked. _____

3. He walked. _____

4. The road became dark. _____

5. The trees swayed. _____

6. An idea crossed his mind. _____

7. His parents and his dog would be sleeping. _____

Note: Not every noun or pronoun in a sentence is necessarily the subject for a verb. Nouns and pronouns function as subjects and as objects. In the following sentence, which noun is the subject and which noun is the object?

Helen drank the water.

For some students, the following exercises will seem easy. However, for many, analyzing the structure of a sentence is unfamiliar. As you practise, get into the habit of referring back to the definitions, charts, and examples. You can, with a little patience, develop an understanding for those words that serve as the subjects of sentences.

EXERCISE 1   Finding the Subject of a Sentence

Underline the subject in each of the following sentences. An example follows:

The Saturday <u>paper</u> had the movie listings.

1. We were a little late.

2. A long line had already formed.

3. Tickets cost six dollars.

4. The concession stand was doing a brisk business.

5. I wanted popcorn and a juice.

6. My date bought a hot dog and candy.

7. Ticket holders had already taken the best seats.

8. The movie began on time.

9. My date and I could only find front row seats.

10. The lights suddenly dimmed.

EXERCISE 2   Finding the Subject of a Sentence

Underline the subject in each of the following sentences. An example follows:

The old <u>friends</u> went shopping together.

1. Shoppers waited outside the glass doors.

2. The department store opened early.

3. The sale would last only three hours.

4. Many household items and electrical appliances were greatly reduced.

5. I needed new dinner dishes.

6. The kitchenware department was crowded.

7. I spotted my favourite dishes immediately.

8. The customers hurriedly grabbed items.

9. Salespeople worked feverishly.

10. This day would be exhausting.

How do you find the subject in sentences with prepositional phrases?

The sentences in Exercises 1 and 2 were short and basic. If we wrote only such sentences, our writing would sound choppy. Complex ideas would be difficult to express. One way to expand the simple sentence is to add prepositional phrases.

Example: The athlete was injured *on the ice.*
On is the preposition.
Ice is a noun used as the object of the preposition.
The prepositional phrase is *on the ice.*

> A *prepositional phrase* is a group of words containing a preposition and an object of the preposition with its modifiers. Prepositional phrases contain nouns or pronouns, but these nouns and pronouns are never the subject of the sentence.

In sentences with prepositional phrases, the subject may be difficult to spot. What is the subject of the following sentence?

> In the locker room, the conversation was boisterous.

In this sentence, *in the locker room* is a prepositional phrase. Since the subject can never be found within a prepositional phrase, a good idea is to cross out the prepositional phrase before you look for the subject.

> ~~In the locker room,~~ the conversation was boisterous.

Now the subject, *conversation,* is easier to identify.

> When you are looking for the subject of a sentence, do not look for it within the prepositional phrase.

You can easily recognize a prepositional phrase because it always begins with a preposition. Study the following list so that you will be able to quickly recognize all of the common prepositions.

COMMON PREPOSITIONS

about	below	in	since
above	beneath	inside	through
across	beside	into	to
after	between	like	toward
against	beyond	near	under
along	by	of	until
among	down	off	up
around	during	on	upon
at	except	outside	with
before	for	over	within
behind	from	past	without

In addition to these common prepositions, English has a number of prepositional combinations that together with other words also function as prepositions.

COMMON PREPOSITIONAL COMBINATIONS

ahead of	in addition to	in reference to
at the time of	in between	in regard to
because of	in care of	in search of
by means of	in case of	in spite of
except for	in common with	instead of
for fear of	in contrast to	on account of
for the purpose of	in the course of	similar to
for the sake of	in exchange for	

EXERCISE 1   Finding Subjects in Sentences with Prepositional Phrases

Remember that you will never find the subject of a sentence within a prepositional phrase. In each of the following sentences, cross out any prepositional phrases. Then underline the subject of each sentence. An example follows:

<del>In spite of the rainy weather</del>, <u>tourists</u> throng <del>to Vancouver</del>.

1. On Monday morning, we arrived in Vancouver.
2. Our hotel was near Stanley Park.
3. From the window, you could see Lions Gate Bridge.
4. Both of us enjoyed the view.
5. It seemed a perfect day for sightseeing.
6. On the Skytrain, we rode to the waterfront, where we could see the Expo buildings.
7. After a boat ride, the two of us ate lunch at a restaurant in Gastown.
8. By that time, the suggestion of a nap appealed to us both.
9. Toward the end of a busy day, some Vancouver boardwalks seem much too long.
10. Back in our room, two tired sightseers went to sleep.

EXERCISE 2   Finding Subjects in Sentences with Prepositional Phrases

Remember that you will never find the subject of a sentence within a prepositional phrase. In each of the following sentences, cross out any prepositional phrases. Then underline the subject of each sentence. An example follows:

<del>At some time or another</del>, <u>all</u> <del>of us</del> must go <del>without a good night's sleep</del>.

1. For those of us without a good night's sleep, herbal remedies can provide a cure to a haggard appearance.
2. Instead of preparing for the day, some of us roll over and go back to bed.
3. At the last minute in a panic, we jump out of bed and rush to our jobs.
4. A better approach for the sleep-deprived involves herbal remedies.
5. For those awful black circles under the eyes, chamomile tea bags can come to the rescue.
6. The tea bags should rest on the eyelids for at least ten minutes.
7. In addition to our physical appearance, our mental state may need some attention on these days.
8. A good wake-up call for a sleepy brain is a sniff of rosemary.
9. The ancient Greeks and Romans wore laurels of rosemary for mental alertness during exams.
10. Of course, the ideal solution is proper rest.

What are the other problems in finding subjects?

Sentences with a change in the normal subject position

Some sentences begin with words that indicate that a question is being asked. Such words as *why, where, how,* and *when* give the reader the signal that a question will follow. Such opening words are not the subjects. The subjects will be found later in the sentences. The following sentences begin with question words:

Why did Monica speak softly?

How did the fans react to the news?

Notice that in each sentence the subject is not found in the opening part of the sentence. By answering questions or changing the question into a statement, the subject is easier to spot.

Monica spoke softly because . . .

The *fans* reacted to the news by . . .

Using *there* or *here*

Such words as *there* or *here* can never be the subjects of sentences.

There have been many stories about the event.

Here is one of the stories.

Who or what is the subject of the first sentence? The answer is *stories*. What is the subject of the second sentence? Remember to cross out the prepositional phrase *of the stories*. The answer is *one*.

Commands

Sometimes a sentence contains a verb that gives an order:

Play ball.

Stay alert.

In sentences that give orders, the subject *you* is not written, but understood to be the subject. This is the only case where the subject of a sentence may be left out.

(You) play ball.

(You) stay alert.

Sentences that contain appositive phrases

> An *appositive phrase* is a group of words in a sentence that gives us extra information about a noun in the sentence. It is always separated from the rest of the sentence by commas.
>
> Monica Seles, *the tennis player*, has returned to the game.

In this sentence, the words *the tennis player* make up the appositive phrase. These words give you extra information about Ms. Seles. Notice that commas separate the appositive phrase from the rest of the sentence. If you leave out the appositive phrase when you read this sentence, the thought will still be complete.

Monica Seles has returned to the game.

Now the subject is clear: Monica Seles.

> When you are looking for the subject of a sentence, you will not find it within an appositive phrase.

EXERCISE 1   Finding Hidden Subjects

Each of the following sentences contains an example of a special problem in finding the subject of a sentence. First cross out any prepositional phrases or appositive phrases. Then underline the subject of each sentence. An example follows:

What will this new <u>job</u> be like?

1. Why was the bus on my route late?

2. There was no sign of its arrival.

3. In the middle of rush hour, the bus stop was crammed with people.

4. Luckily, I had plenty of time.

5. My job, a temporary data entry position, would last for six weeks.

6. Would I make a good impression on the manager?

7. Here is some good advice for a person with a new job.

8. Arrive on time.

9. Be ready to work.

10. In this economy, good work habits at one job may lead to another better job.

EXERCISE 2   Finding Hidden Subjects

Each of the following sentences contains an example of a special problem in finding the subject of a sentence. First cross out any prepositional phrases or appositive phrases. Then underline the subject of each sentence. An example follows:

~~In many cases~~, <u>people</u> are lactose intolerant.

1. Do you have an allergy?

2. A food intolerance, the body's inability to digest some part of a particular food, is different from an allergy.

3. Here is the best known food intolerance: milk.

4. With a food allergy, the immune system mistakes a harmless food as a dangerous invader and attacks it with irritating chemicals usually within the first 45 minutes of eating the food.

5. How can a person control an allergy or intolerance?

6. Keep a daily record of your diet for two weeks.

7. Record any adverse reactions after meals.

8. In most cases, people can pinpoint the troublesome foods.

9. There is some good news.

10. By avoidance of the offending food for a year or two, you may be able to outgrow your adverse reactions.

How do you find the verb of a sentence?

Every sentence must have a verb. Verbs can be divided into three classes.

Action: An *action verb* tells what the subject is doing.

Isaac Stern *played* a violin solo.

Linking: A *linking verb* indicates a state of being or condition.

The violinist *seemed* confident.

Helping: A *helping verb* combines with a main verb to form a verb phrase and gives the main verb a special time or meaning.

The musician *may* perform again tomorrow.

Verbs tell time. Use this fact to test for a verb. If you can put the verb into different tenses in the sentence, that word is a verb.

Present: (Today) she *performs.*

Past: (Yesterday) she *performed.*

Future: (Tomorrow) she will *perform.*

Action verbs

> *Action verbs* tell us what the subject is doing and when the subject does the action.

The student *practised* the trumpet.

What was the student doing?   practising

What is the time of the action?   past (-*ed* is the past tense ending)

ACTION VERBS

Most verbs are **action verbs.** Here are a few examples:

arrive	learn	open	watch
leave	forget	write	fly
enjoy	help	speak	catch
despise	make	teach	wait

EXERCISE 1   ## Finding Action Verbs

Each of the following sentences contains an action verb. Find the action verb by first underlining the subject of the sentence. Then circle the verb (the word that tells what the subject is doing). An example follows:

My childhood <u>friend</u> (visited) me this spring.

1. Friendship teaches patience and understanding.
2. You learn respect.
3. Friends enjoy one another's company.
4. They help each other through good and bad times.
5. Good friends watch out for one another.
6. Best friends often speak honestly to one another.
7. We forget the occasional arguments.
8. Sometimes good friends move away from each other.
9. They write and call frequently.
10. Good friends give life fuller meaning.

EXERCISE 2   ## Finding Action Verbs

Each of the following sentences contains an action verb. Find the action verb by first underlining the subject of the sentence. Then circle the verb (the word that tells what the subject is doing). An example follows:

In our house, family members(share)the housework equally.

1. Housework requires a system of organization.
2. A plan of action saves time.
3. Some people, myself included, collect all the cleaning products first.
4. Others clean in a haphazard fashion.
5. We always start with the kitchen.
6. Bathrooms and bedrooms receive our attention next.
7. The den, the most heavily used room, gets special treatment.
8. The dining and living rooms take the least amount of time.
9. Dusting, polishing, and vacuuming keep us busy every Saturday morning.
10. With help from everyone, the work goes fast.

Linking verbs

> A *linking verb* is a verb that links the subject of a sentence to one or more words that describe or identify the subject.

For example:

The social worker(is)my cousin.
She(seems)qualified.
We(feel)proud of her.

In each of these examples, the verb links the subject to a word that identifies or describes the subject. In the first example, the verb *is* links *worker* with *cousin*. The verb *seems* links the pronoun *she* with *qualified*. Finally, in the third example, the verb *feel* links the pronoun *we* with *proud*.

COMMON LINKING VERBS	
act	feel
appear	grow
be (am, is, are, was,	look
were, have been)	seem
become	taste

EXERCISE 1   Finding Linking Verbs

Each of the following sentences contains a linking verb. Find the linking verb by first underlining the subject of the sentence. Then draw an arrow to the word or words that identify or describe the subject. Finally, circle the linking verb. An example follows:

Home economics(was)a required course in my high school.

1. Sewing is a creative act.
2. It has become a less popular activity in the past decade.
3. The cost of clothing is quite expensive.
4. Homemade clothes will usually be less costly.
5. Sewing looks difficult to many people.
6. I was happy about my sewing project.
7. The finished skirt looks wonderful.
8. It felt perfectly tailored.
9. I grow more confident with each new project.
10. I feel satisfied with my sewing efforts.

EXERCISE 2 Finding Linking Verbs

Each of the following sentences contains a linking verb. Find the linking verb by first underlining the subject of the sentence. Then draw an arrow to the word or words that identify or describe the subject. Finally, circle the linking verb. An example follows:

Brain teasers(were)popular games among my friends.

1. Puzzles are tests of logic.
2. Sometimes they appear deceptively simple.
3. Most people become absorbed in a puzzle.
4. Almost everyone seems eager to find the answer.
5. Unfortunately, some people grow frustrated with the passage of time.
6. The process is fun to other people.
7. I become especially excited at the final step.
8. I feel victorious.
9. Be patient.
10. With persistence, a solution is possible.

Helping verbs (also called auxiliary verbs)

Some verbs can be used to help the main verb express a special time or meaning.

Sentence using auxiliary verb	Time expressed by auxiliary verb
He is reading.	right now
He might read.	maybe now or in the future
He should read.	ought to, now or in the future
He could have been reading.	maybe in the past

COMMON HELPING VERBS

can, could

may, might, must

shall, should

will, would

forms of the irregular verbs *be, do,* and *have.*

Remember that *be, do,* and *have* are also used as the main verbs of sentences. In such cases, *be* is a linking verb while *do* and *have* are action verbs. All the other helping verbs are usually used only as helping verbs.

Watch out for adverbs that may come in between the helping verb and the main verb.

Adverbs are words that can modify verbs, adjectives, or other adverbs.

In the following sentence, the word *often* is an adverb coming between the verb phrase *can frighten.* For a list of adverbs, see Appendix C: Parts of Speech (pp. 331–337).

A good book (can) *often* (leave) a strong impression on the reader.

EXERCISE 1   Finding Helping Verbs

Each of the following sentences contains a helping verb in addition to the main verb. In each sentence, first underline the subject. Then circle the entire verb phrase. An example follows:

<u>People</u> today (are living) longer lives and (are enjoying) those lives more fully.

1. Growing old can frighten some people.
2. Aging well will depend on your physical health and your outlook on life.
3. Adolescents do sometimes leave their teen years behind with pleasure.
4. Forty year olds will often worry about entering their fifties.
5. Attitudes about aging have changed dramatically.
6. People are taking much better care of themselves.
7. Regular exercise can insure your aging with fewer health problems.
8. You should remain physically active in later years.
9. Aging may bring unexpected pleasure to your life.
10. You might gain new insights and discover new interests.

EXERCISE 2　Finding Helping Verbs

Each of the following sentences contains a helping verb in addition to the main verb. In each sentence, first underline the subject. Then circle the entire verb phrase. An example follows:

(Did) you (wake) from your dreams refreshed?

1. Dreams should tell us something about ourselves.
2. You may dream in black and white or in colour.
3. Your dreams can seem real.
4. Did the event really happen or not?
5. Dreams can often be frightening.
6. Some people might dream of falling off a tall building.
7. The heart may race.
8. Other dreams will be delightful.
9. Have you ever had a repeating dream?
10. Do you ever try to continue your dream after waking up?
11. That, unfortunately, will rarely happen.

Parts of Speech

In this chapter you have learned how most of the words in the English language function. These categories for words are called *parts of speech*. You have learned to recognize and understand the functioning of *nouns, pronouns, adjectives, verbs, adverbs,* and *prepositions*. (In later chapters you will learn how the *conjunction* functions.) You can review your understanding of these parts of speech as you practise identifying them in the exercises provided here. You may also refer to Appendix C (at the back of the book) for a quick summary whenever you want to refresh your memory.

EXERCISE 1　Identifying Parts of Speech

In the sentences below, identify the part of speech for each underlined word. Choose from the following list.

a. noun

b. pronoun

c. adjective

d. verb

e. adverb

f. preposition

_____　　1. Chubby Checker taught the <u>world</u> how to twist.

_____　　2. Dick Clark, host of American Bandstand, <u>decided</u> he liked "The Twist" and showcased it.

_____   3. The song shot up to number one <u>on</u> the pop charts in September of 1960.

_____   4. Twisting became the biggest <u>teenage</u> fad.

_____   5. At first, <u>it</u> was considered strictly kid stuff.

_____   6. Then it became <u>respectable</u> among older groups.

_____   7. Liz Taylor and Richard Burton were seen twisting in the fashionable night spots of <u>Rome</u>.

_____   8. The dance set the pace <u>for</u> a decade.

_____   9. Soon many people were seen <u>breathlessly</u> twisting at nightclubs across North America.

_____   10. The 60s were going to be a reckless and unruly <u>time</u>.

EXERCISE 2   Identifying Parts of Speech

In the sentences below, identify the part of speech for each underlined word. Choose from the following list.

   a. noun
   b. pronoun
   c. adjective
   d. verb
   e. adverb
   f. preposition

_____   1. Japanese Canadians <u>suffered</u> enormous hardship during the Second World War.

_____   2. <u>Most</u> had lived in British Columbia for decades and were Canadian citizens.

_____   3. They were evacuated when war broke out <u>with</u> Japan in 1941.

_____   4. The <u>Canadian</u> government confiscated and sold their property.

_____   5. The <u>men</u> were separated from their families and placed in forced labour camps.

_____   6. The women and children were kept in internment camps <u>in</u> the British Columbia interior.

_____   7. These people were treated so <u>poorly</u> that citizens of wartime Japan even sent them supplemental food shipments through the Red Cross.

_____   8. The <u>majority</u> were not released until 1949, four years after Japan's surrender.

_____   9. In 1988, the Canadian government <u>formally</u> apologized to the survivors of the wartime detention.

_____   10. To many Japanese Canadians, the apology is an important <u>acknowledgment</u> of a major injustice.

Mastery and editing tests

TEST 1   ## Finding Subjects and Verbs in Simple Sentences

After reading the paragraph, use the lines that follow to write the subject and verb of each sentence.

[1]The field of red stretched out before us. [2]Red, round berries bobbed slightly in the breeze. [3]Our range of vision was filled with the sight of ripening cranberries. [4]Cranberries are symbolic of the autumn. [5]They conjure up images of cornucopias with their fruits of the harvest, or of Thanksgiving tables with their feasts of meats and pies. [6]The Cranberry, one of the native North American fruits, got its name from the earliest European settlers in the area. [7]To the Indians, cranberries were known as *sassamanash,* a source of colour for dyes, or as *pemican,* their survival cake of dried deer meat and cranberries. [8]The European settlers noticed the delicately curved pink blossoms in the spring. [9]These blossoms resemble the head and bill of the sand hill crane. [10]This explains the name *crane berry.*

	Subject	**Verb**
Sentence 1	_____	_____
Sentence 2	_____	_____
Sentence 3	_____	_____
Sentence 4	_____	_____
Sentence 5	_____	_____
Sentence 6	_____	_____
Sentence 7	_____	_____
Sentence 8	_____	_____
Sentence 9	_____	_____
Sentence 10	_____	_____

TEST 2   ## Finding Subjects and Verbs in Simple Sentences

After reading the paragraph, use the lines that follow to write the subject and verb of each sentence.

[1]On Friday the thirteenth, Jason attended his first baseball game. [2]He and his father arrived two hours early at the stadium. [3]In that way, they could watch batting practice. [4]Before the game, some of the players signed autographs. [5]With the signatures of his three favourite players, Jason accompanied his dad to their seats for the game. [6]Their seats were on field level, behind home plate. [7]During the first inning, Jason's dad bought him a hot dog, a soft drink, and a souvenir program. [8]Jason sat between his dad and a white-haired gentleman. [9]Within moments, Jason's father recognized the gentleman. [10]The man, a Hall of Fame pitcher, gladly signed his name on Jason's program.

	Subject	Verb
Sentence 1	_____	_____
Sentence 2	_____	_____
Sentence 3	_____	_____
Sentence 4	_____	_____
Sentence 5	_____	_____
Sentence 6	_____	_____
Sentence 7	_____	_____
Sentence 8	_____	_____
Sentence 9	_____	_____
Sentence 10	_____	_____

TEST 3   Finding Subjects and Verbs in Simple Sentences

After reading the paragraph, use the lines that follow to write the subject and verb of each sentence.

[1]A large number of people are afraid of flying. [2]What can those of us with a fear of flying do about our fear? [3]How can a person change irrational thought patterns? [4]Until recently, I had always preferred the train for vacations or business trips. [5]With the right therapy, most fearful fliers can be helped. [6]In the months after my participation in a seminar for people like me, I took three flights. [7]Here is the strange fact. [8]During the flights, I slept comfortably. [9]There are ways for gaining control of your symptoms. [10]Try behavioural approaches before medications like Xanex or Prozac.

	Subject	Verb
Sentence 1	_____	_____
Sentence 2	_____	_____
Sentence 3	_____	_____
Sentence 4	_____	_____
Sentence 5	_____	_____
Sentence 6	_____	_____
Sentence 7	_____	_____
Sentence 8	_____	_____
Sentence 9	_____	_____
Sentence 10	_____	_____

Making Subjects and Verbs Agree

The fact that a complete sentence must have a subject for its verb leads us to a related problem: making that subject agree with its verb.

What is subject-verb agreement?

> A verb must agree with its subject in number (singular or plural).
> When the subject is a singular noun, the verb takes an *s* in the present tense.
>
> > The athlete *rests*.
>
> When the subject is a plural noun, the verb does <u>not</u> take an *s* in the present tense.
>
> > The athletes *rest*.

Notice that when you add *s* or *es* to an ordinary noun, you form the plural of that noun. However, when you add an *s* to a verb, and you want the verb to be in the present tense, you are writing a singular verb. This causes a lot of confusion because not everyone follows this rule when speaking or writing. However, all of us must use this standard form in school and in the world of business. Mastering the material contained in this chapter is therefore of real importance to your success in college or university and beyond.

Pronouns can also present problems for subject-verb agreement

The following chart shows personal pronouns used with the verb *rest*. After you have studied the chart, what can you tell about the ending of a verb when the subject of that verb is a personal pronoun?

PERSONAL PRONOUNS

Singular	*Plural*
I rest	we rest
you rest	you rest
he, she, it rests	they rest

PRACTICE

Underline the correct verb in the following sentences.

1. The florist (arranges, arrange) the centrepiece.
2. The arrangement (includes, include) tulips and baby's breath.
3. I (likes, like) the effect of fresh flowers on a table.
4. The flowers (arrives, arrive) the day of the party.
5. The evening (promises, promise) to be a great success.

Pay special attention to the verbs *do* and *be*

Though you may have heard someone say, *it don't matter* or *we was working,* these expressions are not correct standard English usage.

THE VERB *TO DO*

	Singular	Plural	
	I do	we	
	you do	you	do
	he	they	
	she } does		
	it		

(never *he don't, she don't, it don't*)

THE VERB *TO BE*

Present Tense		Past Tense	
Singular	**Plural**	**Singular**	**Plural**
I am	we	I was	we
you are	you } are	you were	you } were
he	they	he	they
she } is		she } was	
it		it	

(never *we was, you was,* or *they was*)

PRACTICE

Underline the verb that agrees with the subject.

1. We (was, were) meeting to discuss the youth retreat.
2. The leader (was, were) concerned about the accommodations.
3. He (doesn't, don't) want boys and girls on the same floor.
4. Ann (doesn't, don't) want to chaperone unruly teenagers.
5. It (doesn't, don't) matter if some of the youth bring extra money.

EXERCISE 1 Making the Subject and Verb Agree

In the blanks next to each sentence, write the subject of the sentence and the correct form of the verb.

	Subject	Verb
1. A mystery writer (lives, live) in our town.	_____	_____
2. He (was, were) nominated for the Arthur Ellis Award for the best mystery paperback of the year.	_____	_____
3. He (doesn't, don't) live too far from me.	_____	_____
4. Sometimes we (sees, see) him out walking.	_____	_____
5. He always (wears, wear) an old wide-brimmed hat.	_____	_____
6. I (thinks, think) he enjoys his work.	_____	_____
7. His books always (centres, centre) around a sports theme.	_____	_____
8. The latest book (is, are) about a murder at the Queen's Plate horse race.	_____	_____
9. We (doesn't, don't) know yet if he will win the award.	_____	_____
10. The mystery writers of Canada (presents, present) an award called the Arthur Ellis, named after Canada's last official hangman.	_____	_____

EXERCISE 2 Making the Subject and Verb Agree

In the blanks next to each sentence, write the subject of the sentence and the correct form of the verb.

	Subject	Verb
1. Clair (was, were) at home all summer.	_____	_____
2. She (doesn't, don't) mind being at home.	_____	_____
3. Clair's parents (doesn't, don't) have the opportunity to go on vacation very often.	_____	_____
4. Next summer, however, they (plans, plan) to drive across the country.	_____	_____
5. It (is, are) fun to anticipate the places they will visit.	_____	_____
6. Her brother (lives, live) in Halifax.	_____	_____
7. He (has, have) a little baby boy.	_____	_____
8. He (doesn't, don't) care how long they stay.	_____	_____

	Subject	Verb
9. They also (does, do) plan to drive west through Saskatchewan and Alberta	_____	_____
10. Clair (dreams, dream) about the prairies and the mountains.	_____	_____

Subject-verb agreement with hard-to-find subjects

As we learned in Chapter 11, a verb does not always immediately follow the subject. Other words or groups of words called phrases (prepositional phrases or appositive phrases, for example) can come between the subject and verb. Furthermore, subjects and verbs can be inverted as they are in questions or sentences beginning with *there* or *here*.

When looking for subject-verb agreement in sentences where the subjects are more difficult to find, keep in mind two points:

- Subjects are not found in prepositional phrases or appositive phrases.
- Subjects can be found after the verb in sentences that are questions and in sentences that begin with *there* or *here*.

EXERCISE 1   Agreement with Hidden Subjects

Circle the correct verb in each sentence.

1. Sometimes there (is, are) an amazing spectacle in some European countries.
2. (Does, Do) the thought of seeing thousands of lemmings make you queasy?
3. An abundance of these little rodents (makes, make) many people afraid.
4. In "Lemming years," most individuals in their pathway (has, have) cause for concern.
5. Here (is, are) some of the things lemmings do: eat everything in sight, move in large groups, and travel in straight lines.
6. These creatures with their strange obsession (has, have) been known to run right into a lake or river and drown.
7. An automobile, unable to put on the brakes fast enough, often (runs, run) lemmings down by the hundreds.
8. (Is, Are) there other dangers with lemmings?
9. In many cases, the presence of dead lemmings in lakes and rivers (poisons, poison) the water.
10. Lack of caution on the part of many people (leads, lead) to numerous illnesses.

EXERCISE 2   Agreement with Hidden Subjects

Circle the correct verb in each sentence.

1. Every family member (needs, need) to know about first aid.
2. In what cases (is, are) the resuscitation of a loved one required?

3. Local hospitals in your town certainly (teaches, teach) resuscitation techniques.

4. Where in our homes (does, do) we keep the well-stocked first aid kit?

5. In the kit there (is, are) bandages, gauze, and antiseptic.

6. Neighbours on our street (does, do) not seem prepared for their children's accidental injuries.

7. Children with a calm, prepared parent usually (fares, fare) much better in an emergency.

8. Readiness for first aid assistance (reduces, reduce) the risk of long-term damage and can save lives.

9. Lack of preparedness often (leads, lead) to serious consequences.

10. There (is, are) too many sad cases as a result of inaction.

Special problems with subject-verb agreement

1. **Subject-verb agreement with group nouns.** Look at the list of group nouns given in the chart. Do you think a group noun should be considered singular or plural? In English, the answer to that question depends on whether the group acts as a single unit, or if the individuals in the group are acting separately.

   • A group noun takes a singular verb if the noun acts as a unit. To test this, substitute the pronoun *it* for the noun.

   The orchestra is performing today.

   Test: *It is* performing today.

   • A group noun takes a plural verb if the members of the group act as individuals. To test this, substitute the pronoun *they* for the noun.

   The orchestra are tuning their instruments.

   Test: *They are* tuning their instruments.

COMMON GROUP NOUNS		
audience	council	jury
assembly	crowd	number
board	faculty	orchestra
class	family	panel
club	group	public
committee	herd	team

EXERCISE 1　Subject-Verb Agreement with Group Nouns

Circle the correct verb in each sentence.

1. Every season the university (wants, want) to win a special swim meet.
2. The university team (trains, train) all year for the big event.
3. A crowd (gathers, gather) near the water to see the race.
4. The public (enjoys, enjoy) watching athletes who also attend the school.
5. The number of spectators (varies, vary) every year.
6. Sometimes, the police (is, are) called if the crowd becomes too large.
7. The family of each team member (is, are) not always able to be there.
8. Occasionally a school of fish (gets, get) in the way of the swimmers.
9. A crew (stands, stand) ready with a rescue boat in case of emergencies.
10. Often the panel of judges (disagrees, disagree) about issues concerning disqualification.

EXERCISE 2　Subject-Verb Agreement with Group Nouns

Circle the correct verb in each sentence.

1. The crew of carpenters (travels, travel) throughout the province looking for special old homes in disrepair.
2. A number of houses (is, are) always under review.
3. The group (forms, form) into several different committees to consider the purchase of the houses.
4. One committee (considers, consider) the cost of restoring the house in question.
5. Another committee (determines, determine) a likely selling price for the restored home.
6. A team (arrives, arrive) to plan the restoration.
7. A crowd sometimes (gathers, gather) to disagree with the plan.
8. The historical society in the town (is, are) sometimes distrustful.
9. Sometimes a town zoning board (rules, rule) what features of a particular house must be preserved.
10. Sometimes a local club of a small town (decides, decide) to save unique and crumbling old homes in the area.

2. **Subject-verb agreement with indefinite pronouns.** Care should be taken with indefinite pronouns to learn which ones are considered singular and which are considered plural.

INDEFINITE PRONOUNS

Indefinite Pronouns Taking a Singular Verb:

everyone	someone	anyone	no one
everybody	somebody	anybody	nobody
everything	something	anything	nothing
each	another	either	neither

Nobody *is* telling the truth.

Indefinite Pronouns Taking a Plural Verb:

both	few	many	several

Both *are* telling the truth.

Indefinite Pronouns Taking a Singular or Plural Verb Depending on the Meaning in the Sentence:

any	all	more	most
none	some		

The books are gone. All of them were very popular.
The sugar is gone. All of it was spilled.

EXERCISE 1   Agreement with Indefinite Pronouns

Circle the correct verb in each sentence.

1. Everyone (wants, want) a stable job.

2. Some (trains, train) for a specific job without the guarantee of a future job.

3. One of the realizations (is, are) the change in the job market.

4. Most (acknowledges, acknowledge) the importance of flexibility and a wide range of skills.

5. Both (helps, help) to adapt to the changing market.

6. Nobody (is, are) able to exactly predict the jobs of the future.

7. All of the experts (agrees, agree) on the need for computer skills.

8. All of the training for computer skills (is, are) time well invested.

9. Anybody with an interest in technical repairs (has, have) an opportunity to find employment.

10. None of the training programs (promises, promise) you success without your individual determination.

EXERCISE 2   Agreement with Indefinite Pronouns

Circle the correct verb in each sentence.

1. Few (has, have) not heard of MuchMusic.

2. Nothing (has, have) saturated television more than the MuchMusic style of quick cuts and extravagant imagery.

3. Several of the rules for pop music (has, have) changed.

4. Each of the pop songs now (requires, require) interesting visuals as well.

5. Everybody (sees, see) the combination of music and video as unique entertainment.

6. All of the ads (is, are) geared to be hip.

7. Someone (has, have) counted the number of violent videos.

8. Another (has, have) described the presentation of women as nothing more than brainless bimbos.

9. Many (does, do) not like the social message MuchMusic gives.

10. Neither of my parents ever (watches, watch) MuchMusic.

3. Subject-verb agreement with compound subjects

- If the conjunction used to connect the compound subjects is *and*, the verb is usually plural.

    Frank and Cynthia *are* helpful neighbours.

  The exception to this is if the two subjects together are thought of as a single unit.

    Bacon and eggs *is* my favourite breakfast.

- If the conjunction used to connect the compound subjects is *or, nor, either, either/or, neither, neither/nor, not only/but also*, you need to be particularly careful. The verb is singular if both subjects are singular.

    Frank or Cynthia *is* watching the children tomorrow.

  The verb is plural if both subjects are plural.

    My neighbours or my parents *are* watching the children tomorrow.

  The verb agrees with the subject closest to the verb if one subject is singular and one subject is plural.

    My neighbours or my mother *is* watching the children tomorrow.

EXERCISE 1   Subject-Verb Agreement with Compound Subjects

Circle the correct verb in each sentence below.

1. Ham and eggs (is, are) a breakfast dish too high in cholesterol for most people to eat every day.

2. My mother and father always (sits, sit) down to a large breakfast of eggs, sausage, toast, and potatoes.

3. My husband and children often (runs, run) out of the house without so much as a glass of orange juice.

4. Half a grapefruit or a banana on cereal (makes, make) a good breakfast.

5. Whole grain breads or cooked cereal (is, are) better than white bread with jam or sugared cereals.

6. Not only the adults but also the children (needs, need) energy for the day's activities.

7. A nutritious breakfast and hot lunch (has, have) a proven effect on the ability of children to concentrate in school.

8. Today, neither the busy schedules of working parents nor their interest (encourages, encourage) the cooking of large family meals.

9. A donut, a cookie, or a danish (is, are) a terrible choice for breakfast.

10. Fruits and vegetables (does, do) keep a family healthy.

EXERCISE 2   Subject-Verb Agreement with Compound Subjects

Circle the correct verb in each sentence below.

1. Pen and paper (is, are) the traditional image of a writer's tools.

2. These days, both traditional tools and added supports (helps, help) people become published writers.

3. Workshops and an experienced teacher (has, have) become necessary for the ambitious writer.

4. Novelists and poets (seems, seem) to benefit most from small seminars.

5. Not only commercial publishers but also non-profit organizations (wants, want) the work of up-and-coming writers.

6. Neither the readers nor the publisher (desires, desire) a dull book.

7. Lack of interesting content or poor style (results, result) in disappointing sales.

8. Computer skills and familiarity with the most commonly used word processing programs (continues, continue) to be important.

9. Either an agent or an editor (is, are) always an asset.

10. Good advice and a little luck (gives, give) the promising new writer a better chance for success.

4. **Subject-verb agreement with certain nouns.** Don't assume that every noun ending in *s* is plural, or that all nouns that do not end in *s* are singular. There are some exceptions. Here are a few of the most common.

Some nouns are always singular but end in *s*.

mathematics	diabetes	United States
economics	measles	St. John's

Some nouns are always plural.

clothes	scissors	fireworks
headquarters	tweezers	pants

Some nouns have an irregular plural form that does not end in *s* or *es*.

people	feet	men	data
children	mice	women	alumni (masculine)
			alumnae (feminine)

Mastery and editing tests

TEST 1   Making the Subject and Verb Agree

In the blanks next to each sentence, write the subject of the sentence and the correct form of the verb. An example follows:

	Subject	Verb
Canadian Tire stores (is, are) located in every Canadian city.	*stores*	*are*
1. Canadian Tire (has, have) a popular customer-reward program.	_____	_____
2. Every Canadian (know, knows) about Canadian Tire money.	_____	_____
3. Customers who shop at Canadian Tire (receives, receive) coupons worth 5 percent of their purchase.	_____	_____
4. Canadian Tire (like, likes) the program.	_____	_____
5. It (compels, compel) us to spend like Santa but makes us think we're saving like Scrooge.	_____	_____
6. Some people (says, say) that Canadian Tire money has become our unofficial second currency.	_____	_____
7. A bar in Cornwall, Ontario, that accepted Canadian Tire money for beer (was, were) burned down in 1998.	_____	_____
8. Some charities even (accept, accepts) Canadian Tire money as a donation.	_____	_____
9. My parents (have, has) a small fortune in Canadian Tire money in a kitchen drawer.	_____	_____
10. My dad (plans, plan) to live off of it when he retires.	_____	_____

TEST 2

Making the Subject and Verb Agree

Complete each of the following sentences being sure that the verb in each sentence agrees with the subject of that sentence. Use verbs in the present tense.

1. The board of health _____

   _____

2. One of the issues _____

   _____

3. The reports on the blood drive _____

   _____

4. Either the reporters or the editor _____

   _____

5. Neither the teacher nor the tutors _____

   _____

6. How _____

   _____

7. During this week, there _____

   _____

8. Everyone _____

   _____

9. The judge and jury _____

   _____

10. All of the _____

    _____

TEST 3

Making the Subject and Verb Agree

Complete each of the following sentences being sure that the verb in each sentence agrees with the subject of that sentence. Use verbs in the present tense.

1. The committee of citizens _____

   _____

2. When _____

   _____

3. The significance of the findings _____

   _____

4. The park or the sidewalks _____

   _____

5. The work of a few committed persons _____

_____

6. One of the speakers _____

_____

7. In the spring, there _____

_____

8. Nobody in the class _____

_____

9. The team of volunteers _____

_____

10. Neither the residents nor the visitors _____

_____

Correcting the Fragment in Simple Sentences

Fragments in everyday conversations

The fragment is a major problem for many student writers. A thought may be clear in a writer's mind, but on paper this same idea may turn out to be incomplete because it does not include a subject, a verb, or express a complete thought. In this section, you will improve your ability to spot incomplete sentences or fragments, and you will learn how to correct them. This practice will prepare you to avoid such fragments in your own writing. Here, for example, is a typical conversation between two people. It is composed entirely of fragments, but the two people who are speaking have no trouble understanding each other.

> *Betty:*   Going to the concert?
> *Veronica:* Later.
> *Betty:*   Want to meet me?
> *Veronica:* Sure.

If we use complete sentences to rewrite this brief conversation, the result might be the following:

> *Betty:*   Are you going to the concert?
> *Veronica:* I plan to go later.
> *Betty:*   Do you want to meet me there?
> *Veronica:* Sure I do.

In the first conversation, misunderstanding is unlikely since the two speakers stand face to face, see each other's gestures, and hear the intonations of each other's voice in order to help figure out the meaning. These short phrases may be enough for communication since the speakers are using more than just words to convey their thoughts. They understand each other because each one is able to complete the thoughts that are in the other person's mind.

In writing, however, readers cannot be present at the scene to observe the situation for themselves. They cannot be expected to read the author's mind. Only the words grouped into sentences and the sentences grouped into paragraphs provide the clues to the meaning. Since writing often involves thoughts that are abstract and even complex, fragments cause great difficulty and sometimes total confusion for the reader.

EXERCISE 1   Putting a Conversation into Complete Sentences

The following conversation is one that a couple of students might have at school registration. Rewrite the conversation in complete thoughts or standard sentences. Remember the definition of a sentence.

> A *complete sentence* has a subject and a verb and expresses a complete thought.

Scott:	What a disaster.
Carol:	Same every year.
Scott:	Get all your classes?
Carol:	Hardly.
Scott:	Biology still open?
Carol:	Hope so.
Scott:	Took it last year.
Carol:	Tough course?
Scott:	Guess so. Had worse.

1. _____
2. _____
3. _____
4. _____
5. _____
6. _____
7. _____
8. _____
9. _____

Remember, when you write in complete sentences, this writing may be somewhat different from the way you would express the same idea in everyday conversation with a friend.

Although you will occasionally spot incomplete sentences in professional writing, you may be sure the writer is using these fragments intentionally. In such cases, the fragment may capture the way a person thinks or speaks, or it may create a special effect. A student developing his or her writing skills should be sure to use only standard sentence form so that thoughts will be communicated effectively. Nearly all the writing you will do in your life—letters to friends, business correspondence, papers in school, or reports in your job—will demand standard sentence form. Fragments will be looked upon as a sign of ignorance rather than creative style!

What is a fragment?

> A *fragment* is a piece of a sentence.

A fragment is not a sentence for one of the following reasons:

a. The subject is missing:

      covered the roads

b. The verb is missing:

      the bus to the school

c. Both the subject and verb are missing:

      to the school

d. The subject and verb are present, but the words do not express a complete thought:

      the bus reached

EXERCISE 2   Understanding Fragments

Each of the following groups of words is a fragment. In the blank to the right of each fragment, identify what part of the sentence is missing and needs to be added to make the fragment into a sentence.

    a. Add a subject.

    b. Add a verb.

    c. Add a subject and a verb.

    d. The subject and verb are already present, but the sentence
       needs to express a complete thought.

An example is done for you.

Fragment	**Add**
the red fox	b. verb
1. melted in the streets	_____
2. the ice on the roofs	_____
3. from the roofs to the ground	_____
4. the skiers across the fields	_____
5. crows and other birds against the sky	_____
6. built on the branches of the tallest trees	_____
7. young birds in each of the nests	_____
8. the skiers found	_____
9. goes down behind the hills	_____
10. deep into the night	_____

How do you correct a fragment?

1. **Add the missing part or parts.**

   Example: Fragment: through the park
   Add: subject and verb
   Sentence: I walked through the park.

   Note: The prepositional phrase *through the park* is a fragment because a prepositional phrase cannot function as the subject or the verb in a sentence. Furthermore, the words do not express a complete thought.

2. **Join the fragment to the sentence that precedes it or to the sentence that follows it, depending on where it belongs.**

   If a writer examines a text that includes a fragment, the writer will see that a complete thought may already exist. The writer did not immediately realize that the thought belonged to the sentence that came before or just after the fragment. Study the example below.

   Wrong: In the early morning, I walked. Through the park. The day was going to be unbearably hot.

   Correct: In the early morning, I walked through the park. The day was going to be unbearably hot.

There can be more than one reason for fragments in a writer's work. A writer may be careless for a moment, or a writer may not fully understand the necessary parts of a sentence. Also, if the writer does not have a clear idea of what he or she is trying to say, fragments and other errors are more likely to occur. Sometimes further thought or another try at expressing the same idea may produce a better result.

In the following two exercises, practise correcting both kinds of fragments.

EXERCISE 3   Making Fragments into Sentences

Change the fragments of Exercise 2 into complete sentences by adding the missing part or parts that you have already identified.

1. melted in the streets

   _____

2. the ice on the roofs

   _____

3. from the roofs to the ground

   _____

4. the skiers across the fields

   _____

5. crows and other birds against the sky

   _____

6. built on the branches of the tallest trees

   _____

7. young birds in each of the nests

   _____

8. the skiers found

   _____

9. goes down behind the hills

   _____

10. deep into the night

   _____

EXERCISE 4   Finding Fragments That Belong to Other Sentences

Each of the following passages contains a fragment or two. First, read each passage. Then locate the fragment in each passage. Circle the fragment and draw an arrow to the sentence to which it should be connected. An example follows:

The students washed the cars. They worked hard. After the carwash. They decided to have a picnic.

Passage 1   People in elevators sometimes can act strangely. And can behave rudely. Most elevator passengers stare at the light above the door. Not looking at each other. Others go directly into a corner and stay there. Some people do not wait for others to leave an elevator. They just rush out the door when the elevator stops.

Passage 2   Many of the life forms that exist in the woods are never noticed. Millions of ants, invisible to us. Live, work and fight in their underground nests. Beetles hide under nearly every rock and fallen tree. Up in the highest branches, owls and hawks of many species. Hunt for food day and night. The woods are teeming with life, even if we cannot see it.

Passage 3   Over the years, Canadian writer Margaret Atwood has won several important awards for her writing. Although she had been nominated three times for it. The Booker Prize, one of the world's most important literary awards, had eluded her. People thought she should have won the prize in 1996 for her book *Alias Grace*. She finally won the Booker Prize in 2000 for her novel *The Blind Assassin*. She was so convinced that she would not win. That she didn't even have an acceptance speech ready.

What is a phrase?

> A *phrase* is a group of words that go together but that lacks one or more of the elements necessary to be classified as a sentence.

Fragments are usually made up of phrases. These phrases are often mistaken for sentences because they are words that go together as a group. However, they do not fit the definition of a sentence. *Do not confuse a phrase with a sentence.*

How many kinds of phrases are there?

The English language has six phrases (three of which you have already studied in Chapter 11). You should learn to recognize each of these phrases. Remember that a phrase is never a sentence.

1. **Noun phrase:** a noun plus its modifiers

     small pink house

2. **Prepositional phrase:** a preposition plus its object and modifiers

     above the garage

3. **Verb phrase:** the main verb plus its helping verbs

     was dancing
     might have danced
     should have been dancing

The three remaining phrases are formed from *verbs*. However, these phrases do not function as verbs in the sentence. Study carefully how to use them.

4. **Participial phrase:**
   How is the participial phrase formed?

   a. the present form of a verb ending in -*ing* and any other words necessary to complete the phrase

       walking downtown
       appearing quite healthy

   b. the past form of a verb usually ending in -*ed* and any other words necessary to complete the phrase

       extremely depressed
       explained carefully

How does the participial phrase function? Participial phrases function as *adjectives* in a sentence. Study how the above phrases could be made into complete sentences. These phrases will function as adjectives for the noun or pronoun that follows.

Walking downtown, the child looked for amusement.
Appearing quite healthy, she returned to work.
Extremely depressed, the man looked for medical help.
Explained carefully, the directions became clear.

> Do not confuse a participle that is used as an adjective with a participle that is used as part of the main verb of a sentence. A participle requires a helping verb when it is used as the main verb of the sentence.

Participial phrase: *Walking downtown*, the child felt carefree.

Verb phrase: The child *is walking* downtown.

5. **Gerund phrase:** the present form of a verb ending in *-ing*, and any other words necessary to complete the phrase.

   The gerund phrase functions as a noun. It can be the subject or the object of the sentence.

   a. subject of the sentence:

      Walking downtown was good exercise.

   b. direct object of the sentence:

      He liked *walking downtown*.

6. **Infinitive phrase:** *to* plus the verb and any other words necessary to complete the phrase

   He decided *to walk downtown*.

   Note: The word *to* can also function as a preposition.

   I walked *to school*.

EXERCISE 1   Identifying Phrases

Identify each of the underlined phrases in the following sentences.

1. <u>Becoming a professional athlete</u> takes hard work and some luck.   _____

2. The story of Mario Lemieux is known <u>to hockey fans</u> around the world.   _____

3. Coming <u>from a modest home</u> in Montreal, Mario Lemieux dreamt of being a professional hockey player.   _____

4. <u>His tall frame and prolific scoring touch</u> with the Laval Voisons of the Quebec junior hockey league earned him the attentions of NHL scouts. _____

5. In the 1984 NHL entry draft, he <u>was selected</u> first overall by the Pittsburgh Penguins.

_____

6. He became one of the NHL's highest scoring rookies <u>of all time</u>.

_____

7. Lemieux and the Penguins won back-to-back Stanley Cups in 1991 and 1992 and looked to be <u>a championship dynasty</u>.

_____

8. In the middle of what appeared to be a record-breaking season, Lemieux <u>was diagnosed</u> with Hodgkin's disease.

_____

9. Lemieux returned to action the night of his final radiation treatment, <u>scoring a goal and an assist</u> en route to again winning the scoring title.

_____

10. After retiring briefly, he <u>hesitantly returned</u> to play hockey in 2001 and led his Penguins to the NHL's semi-finals.

_____

EXERCISE 2   Identifying Phrases

Identify each of the underlined phrases in the following sentences.

1. <u>In the morning</u>, the rain became sleet.

_____

2. Then snow began <u>to fall steadily</u>, covering the hills in a thick blanket.

_____

3. <u>Shouting and laughing together</u>, the boys and girls ran to the barn.

_____

4. <u>The first job</u> of the morning was to find the skis and other equipment.

_____

5. Meanwhile, the parents worked <u>over the stove</u> in the farmhouse kitchen.

_____

6. They were preparing <u>a good breakfast</u> for the young skiers.

_____

7. Smells <u>of bacon and pancake syrup</u> mixed in the morning air.

_____

8. The skiers <u>chatted happily</u> about their plans for the day.

_____

9. <u>Finding hats, gloves, and boots</u> was the next major task.

_____

10. Before long the children <u>were racing</u> out the door.

_____

Understanding the uses of the present participle

The present participle causes a good deal of confusion for students working with the fragment. Because the participle can be used sometimes as a verb, sometimes as an adjective, and sometimes as a noun, you will want to be aware of which of these uses you intend.

EXERCISE 1   Using the Participle in a Verb Phrase

Below are five present participles. Use each of them as part of a verb phrase in a sentence. An example has been done for you.

> **Present participle:** jumping
>
> **Verb phrase:**   was jumping
>
> **Sentence:**   The boy <u>was jumping</u> on the sofa.

1. singing   _____
2. buying   _____
3. climbing   _____
4. forgetting   _____
5. fixing   _____

EXERCISE 2   Using the Participle Phrase as an Adjective

Each of the underlined words below is a present participle. Use the word along with the phrase provided to compose sentences in which the phrase functions as an adjective. An example has been done for you.

> **Present participle:**   jumping
>
> **Participial phrase:**   jumping on the sofa
>
> **Participial phrase used as an adjective phrase in the sentence:**   <u>Jumping on the sofa</u>, the boy laughed with glee.

1. <u>Singing</u> in the shower

   _____

   _____

2. <u>Buying</u> the tickets

   _____

   _____

3. <u>Climbing</u> the steps

   _____

   _____

4. <u>Forgetting</u> the address

_____

_____

5. <u>Fixing</u> the window

_____

_____

EXERCISE 3   Using the Participle Phrase as a Noun (Gerund)

Each of the underlined words below is a present participle. Use the word along with the phrase provided as a noun phrase in a sentence. An example has been done for you.

Present participle: jumping

Participial phrase: jumping on the sofa

**Participial phrase used as a
noun phrase in a sentence:**   <u>Jumping on the sofa</u> was fun.

1. <u>Singing</u> in the shower

_____

_____

2. <u>Buying</u> the tickets

_____

_____

3. <u>Climbing</u> the steps

_____

_____

4. <u>Forgetting</u> the address

_____

_____

5. <u>Fixing</u> the window

_____

_____

How do you make a complete sentence from a fragment that contains a participle?

Fragment: She <u>wishing</u> for winter to end.

1. Add a helping verb to the participle:

She <u>is wishing</u> for winter to end.

2. Change the participle to a different form of the verb:

>   She <u>wishes</u> for winter to end.

3. Use the participle as an adjective, being sure to provide a subject and verb for the sentence.

>   <u>Wishing for winter to end</u>, she read her gardening magazine.

4. Use the participle as a noun:

>   <u>Wishing for winter to end</u> is understandable.

EXERCISE 1   Correcting the Fragment That Contains a Participle

Make four complete sentences from each of the following fragments. Use the following example as your model.

Fragment: designing silver jewellery

a. He <u>is designing</u> silver jewellery.

b. He <u>designs</u> silver jewellery.

c. <u>Designing the silver jewellery</u>, he hummed and whistled all afternoon.

d. <u>Designing silver jewellery</u> is his greatest pleasure in life.

1. saving money for a computer

   a. _____

   b. _____

   c. _____

   d. _____

2. working out every morning

   a. _____

   b. _____

   c. _____

   d. _____

3. reading comic books

   a. _____

   b. _____

   c. _____

   d. _____

EXERCISE 2   Correcting the Fragment That Contains a Participle

Make four complete sentences from each of the following fragments. Use the following example as your model.

Fragment: working as a lifeguard

a. He <u>is working</u> as a lifeguard.

b. He <u>works</u> as a lifeguard.

c. <u>Working as a lifeguard,</u> he was able to save money for college.

d. <u>Working as a lifeguard</u> is an ideal summer job.

1. getting too much sun

   a. _____

   b. _____

   c. _____

   d. _____

2. working outside all day long

   a. _____

   b. _____

   c. _____

   d. _____

3. swimming every day

   a. _____

   b. _____

   c. _____

   d. _____

Now correct the fragments in the following exercises:

EXERCISE 1   Correcting Fragments

Rewrite each fragment so that it is a complete sentence.

1. the end of the day near my house

   _____

2. light fading in the sky and streetlights coming on

   _____

3. people home from work

   _____

4. children on the streets, not willing to stop their play

   _____

5. the smells of dinner coming through the open windows

   _____

6. voices floating through the evening air

   _____

7. no dogs or cats

   _____

8. empty streets and doorways

   _____

9. no voices heard in any house

   _____

10. the final silence of sleep

   _____

EXERCISE 2   Correcting Fragments

Each of the following groups of words is a phrase. First, name each phrase. Second, make each phrase into a complete sentence.

1. to create a work of art

   Name of phrase: _____

   Sentence: _____

2. to a different neighbourhood

   Name of phrase: _____

   Sentence: _____

3. working hard

   Name of phrase: _____

   Sentence: _____

4. around the city

   Name of phrase: _____

   Sentence: _____

5. making plans

   Name of phrase: _____

   Sentence: _____

6. are now making

   Name of phrase: _____

   Sentence: _____

7. to remain seated

   Name of phrase: _____

   Sentence: _____

8. at the top of the pile

   Name of phrase: _____

   Sentence: _____

9. the Renoir oil painting

   Name of phrase: _____

   Sentence: _____

10. will be visiting

    Name of phrase: _____

    Sentence: _____

Mastery and editing tests

TEST 1   Recognizing and Correcting Fragments

The following description is of a teenager on a shopping spree. The description is made up entirely of fragments. Rewrite the passage making each fragment into a complete sentence.

> Recklessly swerving down the glossy runways of the department store. Pushing aside unsuspecting shoppers. Submitting to the fury within you. A teenager on the hunt for the next new thing. Spending Ma and Pa's hard-earned cash. Exhilarating experience! New pants and running shoes. But pass on the Nike swoosh. Walkmans. Portable MP3s. Snowboards. Hockey jerseys. Admire how good you look in the full-length mirror. Too bad about the zits, though.

_____

_____

_____

_____

_____

_____

_____

_____

_____

_____

TEST 2   Recognizing and Correcting Fragments

The following paragraph contains several fragments. Read the paragraph and underline each fragment. Then rewrite the paragraph, being careful to use only complete sentences.

Mrs. Taylor, the widow with whom I lived. On the edge of the campus. She was an example of old fashioned friendliness. A motherly woman with hair done up in a bun. Her husband had been the registrar at the college. She fixed up a cozy little room for me. At the top of the stairs. In the evenings after my classes, we sat in the living room. On the two rocking chairs. Chatting about the day's events. She always fixed me a snack in the afternoon. And again before bedtime. I have a wealth of enchanting memories. The smell of her cranberry nut bread. The smell of the fragrant coffee wafting up to my room every morning. The creaking porch swing. The sweet scent of lilacs in the spring.

TEST 3   Recognizing and Correcting Fragments

The following paragraph contains several fragments. Read the paragraph and underline each fragment. Then rewrite the paragraph, being careful to use only complete sentences.

William Lyon Mackenzie King was prime minister throughout much of the first half of the twentieth century. Guided Canada through difficult times. The Depression. The Second World War. The beginning of the welfare state in Canada. Introduced old age pensions. Unemployment insurance. A gifted politician with a talent for compromise that kept the country together. During difficult times. Despite having a rather dull personality. King was also one of Canada's most intriguing leaders. Wrote diaries. Reveal he was a spiritualist. Through a medium. Consulted regularly with his dead mother. And other deceased relatives and friends. He also specially commissioned a group of Canadian soldiers during the Second World War. Collecting pieces from ancient buildings destroyed by the fighting in Europe. Returned with parts of ancient cathedrals and castles. Used to decorate the grounds of Kingsmere, King's summer home outside Ottawa.

_____

_____

_____

_____

_____

_____

_____

_____

_____

_____

_____

_____

_____

_____

_____

Chapter 14

Combining Sentences Using the Three Methods of Coordination

1st Method:	Use a comma plus a coordinating conjunction.
2nd Method:	Use a semicolon, an adverbial conjunction, and a comma.
3rd Method:	Use only a semicolon.

So far you have worked with the simple sentence. If you review some of these sentences, you will see that writing only simple sentences results in a choppy style and also makes it difficult to express more complicated ideas. You will need to understand the possible ways of combining simple sentences. In this chapter, you will practise the skill of combining sentences using *coordination.*

What is coordination?

Coordination is the combining of two simple sentences (which we will now refer to as *independent clauses*) that are related and contain ideas of equal importance. The result is a *compound sentence.*

Note: Don't be confused by the term *independent clause.* A *clause* is a group of words having a subject and a verb. An *independent clause* (IC) is a clause that could stand alone as a simple sentence. You may think of these terms in the following way:

simple sentence   =   one independent clause

compound sentence   =   two independent clauses joined by coordination

First method: Use a comma plus a coordinating conjunction

> The most common way to form a compound sentence is to combine independent clauses using a comma plus a coordinating conjunction.

IC	, *coordinating conjunction*	IC
The budget was reduced	, and	several workers were let go.

Since there are only seven common coordinating conjunctions and three pairs of coordinating conjunctions, a little time invested in memorizing the list would be time well spent. By doing this now, you will avoid confusion later on when you must use a different set of conjunctions to combine clauses.

CONNECTORS: COORDINATING CONJUNCTIONS

and	*Used in Pairs*
but	either . . . or
or, nor	neither . . . nor
for (meaning *because*)	not only . . . but also
yet	
so	

• PRACTICE

Each of the following compound sentences contains two independent clauses. Find the subject and verb in each clause and identify them by drawing a single line under the subject and a double line under the verb. Then draw a circle around the comma and coordinating conjunction that combines the two clauses. An example follows:

The actress walked to the front of the stage, and the audience became quiet.

1. The actress was nervous, for this was the night of her debut.

2. She had studied for years, and she had spent many summers on the road.

3. Now she had to win over her audience, or the critics would judge her harshly.

4. The other actors could not help her, nor could her old teacher advise her now.

5. The night was a success, but now she had to prove herself in new roles.

Did you find a subject and verb for both independent clauses in each sentence?

Now that you understand the structure of a compound sentence, you need to think about the meanings of the different coordinating conjunctions and how they can be used to show the relationship between two ideas, each idea being given equal importance.

MEANINGS OF COORDINATING CONJUNCTIONS	
to add an idea:	and
to add an idea when the first clause is in the negative:	nor
to contrast two opposing ideas:	but, yet
to introduce a reason:	for
to show a choice:	or
to introduce a result:	so

EXERCISE 1 Combining Sentences Using Coordinating Conjunctions

Each of the following examples contains two simple sentences. These two sentences could be joined by a coordinating conjunction. First, decide the relationship between the two sentences. Then join the sentences by using the correct conjunction. An example follows:

Two simple sentences:

The two girls are sisters.

They share many childhood experiences.

Relationship of 2nd sentence to 1st: result
The conjunction that introduces this meaning: so
New compound sentence:

The two girls are sisters, so they share many childhood experiences.

1. Marcia is helpful to everyone.

    Her sister is cool and distant.

    _____

    _____

2. The retired couple worry.

    Their pension money may not be enough for them to live on.

    _____

    _____

3. The baby had cried all night.

    Everyone was tired the next day.

    _____

    _____

4. The recruit was eager to prove his abilities.

    He didn't volunteer to be the first one to jump.

    _____

    _____

5. Devon decided to help out in the cafeteria at lunch.

She would make some money and meet a lot of the students.

_____

_____

6. Work was going well.

Her social life was improving.

_____

_____

7. Being popular is important to many adolescents.

Wearing the right clothes becomes a priority.

_____

_____

8. The dictionary entry was helpful.

I still wasn't sure how to use the word correctly.

_____

_____

9. I couldn't take the train.

I couldn't take the bus.

_____

_____

10. The original idea was good.

Not everyone agreed.

_____

_____

EXERCISE 2 Combining Sentences Using Coordinating Conjunctions

For each example, add a second independent clause using the given coordinating conjunction. Be certain that your new sentence makes sense.

1. (and) Bowling is my favourite recreation _____

_____

2. (but) I have played at the Maple Avenue Lanes _____

_____

3. (or) Either I bowl on Friday nights _____

_____

4. (but) I would like to play in a championship tournament _____

_____

5. (and) Last Friday, we had a blizzard _____

    _____

6. (so) We could not find anyone to do the driving _____

    _____

7. (but also) Not only was the snow too deep _____

    _____

8. (nor) We didn't go bowling _____

    _____

9. (yet) I missed the night out _____

    _____

10. (so) We are hoping for good weather next week _____

    _____

EXERCISE 3 Composing Compound Sentences

Compose ten of your own compound sentences using the coordinating conjunctions indicated.

1. and _____

    _____

2. but _____

    _____

3. or _____

    _____

4. for (meaning *because*) _____

    _____

5. yet _____

    _____

6. so _____

    _____

7. nor _____

    _____

8. neither/nor _____

    _____

9. not only/but also _____

    _____

10. either/or _____

    _____

Second method: Use a semicolon, an adverbial conjunction, and a comma

> A second way to form a compound sentence is to combine independent clauses by using a semicolon, an adverbial conjunction, and a comma.

IC	*; adverbial conjunction,*	*IC*
The budget was reduced	; therefore,	several workers were let go.

Another set of conjunctions are called **adverbial conjunctions** (or conjunctive adverbs). These conjunctions have meanings similar to the common coordinating conjunctions, but they sound slightly more formal than the shorter conjunctions such as *and* or *but*. These connecting words give a compound sentence more emphasis.

CONNECTORS: FREQUENTLY USED ADVERBIAL CONJUNCTIONS

Addition (and)	**Alternative (or)**	**Result (so)**
in addition	instead	accordingly
also	otherwise	consequently
besides		hence
furthermore		therefore
likewise		thus
moreover		

Contrast (but)	**Emphasis**	**To Show Time**
however	indeed	meanwhile
nevertheless	in fact	
nonetheless		

PRACTICE

Each of the following compound sentences contains two independent clauses. Identify the subject and verb in each clause and draw a single line under the subject and a double line under the verb. Then draw a circle around the semicolon, adverbial conjunction, and comma where they connect the two clauses. An example follows:

The hallway was newly painted; likewise, the lobby looked fresh and clean.

1. Plants had been placed on tables and counters; in addition, the windows had all been washed.

2. Comfortable new furniture had been purchased; consequently, the lobby was much more inviting.

3. The tenants were pleased; indeed, everyone felt a lift in spirits.

4. We asked the security guards about the changes; however, they did not seem to have much information.

5. My mother and I had been thinking of moving; instead, we now decided to stay.

EXERCISE 1 Combining Sentences Using Adverbial Conjunctions

Each pair of sentences below could be combined into a compound sentence. Join each pair by using a semicolon, an adverbial conjunction, and a comma. Be sure the conjunction you choose makes sense in the sentence. An example follows:

Two simple sentences:	People laugh with ease. They find it hard to laugh on command.
Compound sentence:	People laugh with ease; however, they find it hard to laugh on command.

1. Most people laugh without thinking about it.

   Some scientists are studying laughter very seriously.

   _____

   _____

2. Research has tried to observe what makes people laugh.

   It has almost become a separate branch of science.

   _____

   _____

3. We do laugh at clever jokes.

   Most of what we laugh at is simply part of everyday social conversation.

   _____

   _____

4. Laughter is one way of communicating with others.

   It is one way for us to express the state of our mood.

   _____

   _____

5. Only rare individuals can laugh on command.

   They usually have some acting experience.

   _____

   _____

6. Social scientists are looking at laughter in other cultures.

   Language experts are trying to establish common patterns for people's laughter.

   _____

   _____

7. Laughter tends to be catching.

   A child's giggle is likely to make other children laugh too.

   _____

   _____

8. Many people laugh at very ordinary things.

   A great many people often laugh at their own statements.

   _____

   _____

9. Laughter works as a mood regulator for groups of people.

   Individuals also laugh by themselves.

   _____

   _____

10. We enjoy laughing at people in positions of authority.

    Be careful not to laugh at your supervisor or manager.

    _____

    _____

EXERCISE 2   Combining Sentences Using Adverbial Conjunctions

For each example, add the suggested adverbial conjunction and another independent clause that will make sense. Remember to punctuate correctly.

1. (instead) A growing number of people do not sit down to eat the traditional three meals a day.

   _____

   _____

2. (nevertheless) Liquid meals do not appeal to most people.

   _____

   _____

3. (however) Liquid breakfasts and dinners were first developed as supplements for the elderly or the sick.

   _____

   _____

4. (in fact) Many well-known brands claim to have all the nutrients necessary for a good diet.

_____

_____

5. (consequently) Many liquid meals contain mostly water, oil, and sugar.

_____

_____

6. (therefore) Several brands of these supplements are high in fat.

_____

_____

7. (likewise) People over fifty often begin to think about supplements to keep themselves healthy.

_____

_____

8. (thus) Advertisements show professional athletes using these supplemental products.

_____

_____

9. (however) Advertisements suggest liquid supplements are better than anything else you could eat.

_____

_____

10. (furthermore) Why not eat apples or bananas?

_____

_____

Third method: Use a semicolon

> The third and less commonly used way to form a compound sentence is to combine two independent clauses by using only a semicolon.

IC	;	*IC*
The budget was reduced	;	several workers were let go.

Two independent clauses: I saw *Master Class* at the theatre last weekend. The play starred Zoe Caldwell.

Compound sentence: I saw *Master Class* at the theatre last weekend; the play starred Zoe Caldwell.

The semicolon was used in this example to show that the content of both sentences is closely related and therefore could be combined in one sentence.

When sentences are combined using a semicolon, the grammatical structure of each sentence is often similar:

> Zoe Caldwell played the part of Maria Callas; Audra McDonald played the part of a young student singer.

EXERCISE 1　Combining Sentences Using a Semicolon

For each of the independent clauses below, add your own independent clause that has a similar grammatical structure or is a closely related idea.

1. The term paper was nearly finished.

   _____

   _____

2. The topics on some television talk shows have become unacceptable.

   _____

   _____

3. The driving test was scheduled for Tuesday afternoon.

   _____

   _____

4. The milk had gone sour.

   _____

   _____

5. Her mother was encouraging.

   _____

   _____

EXERCISE 2　Combining Sentences Using a Semicolon

For each of the independent clauses below, add your own independent clause that has a similar grammatical structure or is a closely related idea.

1. The movers arrived early.

   _____

2. The beach was crowded.

   _____

   _____

3. The room suddenly fell silent.

   _____

   _____

4. The book was missing from the shelves.

    _____

    _____

5. The dancers waited backstage.

    _____

    _____

Mastery and editing tests

TEST 1   ### Combining Sentences Using Coordination

Each pair of sentences below could be combined into a compound sentence. Join each pair by using a coordinating conjunction or an adverbial conjunction that will make sense for the intended meaning of the new sentence. Be sure your punctuation is correct.

1. Everyday memory blocks are embarrassing.

    They can be easily overcome.

    _____

    _____

2. People often forget someone's name.

    People can forget their own anniversaries.

    _____

    _____

3. No one can remember everything.

    No one can rely on others to constantly remind them.

    _____

    _____

4. Boosting your memory can stop your memory lapses.

    Your life will become more problem free.

    _____

    _____

5. Visualize an item in an exaggerated form before putting it down.

    This forces your mind to pay attention to the location of the item.

    _____

    _____

6. Post a calendar with important dates.

    You can see it there every day.

    _____

    _____

7. You can blank out on a person's name.

    You can associate a name with an object (such as Michelle the sea shell).

    _____

    _____

8. Women tend to remember what they hear.

    Men are better at remembering things they see.

    _____

    _____

9. Visualize something unusual about an object such as your keys.

    This image will force your mind to remember their location.

    _____

    _____

10. Forgetting things is frustrating.

    You can improve your memory.

    _____

    _____

TEST 2   Combining Sentences Using Coordination

The following paragraph contains opportunities to combine some of the ideas using coordination. Rewrite the paragraph, creating several compound sentences. Choose conjunctions that show the correct relationship between the two clauses of these new compound sentences. Use either coordinating or adverbial conjunctions. Be sure to punctuate the newly formed compound sentences correctly.

Banff National Park was founded in 1885. It was Canada's first national park. The park is a great place to spend a vacation. It has many things to do and see. One site in the park is spectacular. It is called the Cave and Basin. It has naturally occurring, warm mineral springs inside a huge cave. The basin is emerald coloured. The park is also known for its many hot springs. The springs are heated naturally in the ground. People can take a relaxing dip in them. There is an observatory on the top of Sulphur Mountain. It was built in 1903. It was restored in 1992. In 1903, Norman Bethune Sanson became the town meteorologist. Every week, he hiked to the observatory to collect weather data. Mr. Sanson climbed to the top of Sulphur Mountain over 1,000 times in his thirty-six-year career. Today visitors can take a gondola to the top. The Banff Park Museum should also be seen. It has a rare turn-of-the-century taxidermy collection. It contains over 5,000 specimens. It thrills visitors who are curious about the animals found in the Canadian Rockies. The building itself is unique. Its architecture is distinctive. No building can match the splendour of the Banff Springs Hotel. It is built on the side of a mountain. It overlooks the town of Banff. The hotel is an imposing castle-like structure. Rumour has it that horror master Stephen King stayed in the hotel once. It gave him the inspiration for his novel *The Shining*.

_____

_____

_____

_____

_____

_____

_____

_____

_____

_____

_____

_____

_____

_____

_____

_____

_____

_____

_____

_____

_____

_____

_____

_____

TEST 3   Combining Sentences Using Coordination

The following paragraph contains opportunities to combine some of the ideas using coordination. Rewrite the paragraph, creating several compound sentences. Choose conjunctions that show the correct relationship between the two clauses of these new compound sentences. Use either coordinating or adverbial conjunctions. Be sure to punctuate the newly formed compound sentences correctly.

Patricia McDaniel is an antiques dealer. She has a very modern business. She supplies props for movies. Her name is never seen on the credits. She owns Old Storefront Antiques in Kelowna, British Columbia. She doesn't do enough business from local customers. She doesn't have many tourists coming through. This is one antique shop that depends on mail order business. Ms. McDaniel wanted to make some money on items in her shop. She could have read books and magazines about marketing. She had her own ideas. She sent out lists of her items to film companies. She would provide large numbers of old props. She would send them quickly. This made her successful. Her business became renting antique items to movie producers. These producers need props for different scenes in their films. Ms. McDaniel receives mail orders regularly from Hollywood. Her specialty is drug store items and grocery store items. Movie producers know and depend on her enormous stock and good service. She can often supply items that cannot be found anywhere else. Once she shipped out five hundred dollars worth of old Jello boxes. Once she rented out a hornet's nest.

_____

_____

_____

_____

_____

_____

_____

_____

_____

_____

_____

_____

_____

_____

_____

_____

Chapter 15

Combining Sentences Using Subordination

In Chapter 14, when you used coordination, the idea in each clause in the compound sentence carried equal weight. However, a writer often wants to combine ideas that are not equally important. This chapter will focus on *subordination*. Here you will combine clauses that are not equally important. One idea will be dependent on the other.

What is subordination?

> *Subordination* is the combining of two clauses containing ideas that are not equally important. The more important idea is called the *independent clause*, and the less important idea is called the *dependent clause*. The result is a *complex sentence*.

In coordination, you used certain connecting words called coordinating conjunctions or adverbial conjunctions to combine ideas. In subordination, you use two different sets of connecting words: subordinating conjunctions or relative pronouns.

What is the difference between an independent and dependent clause?

An independent clause stands alone as a complete thought; it could be a simple sentence.

Independent clause: She washed the car.

A dependent clause begins with a connecting word, and although the thought has a subject and a verb, it does not stand alone as a complete thought. The idea needs to be completed.

Dependent clause: When she washed the car, ...

Before you write your own complex sentences, practise the following exercises being sure you understand the difference between an independent clause and a dependent clause.

EXERCISE 1   Recognizing Dependent and Independent Clauses

In the blank to the side of each group of words, write the letters IC if the group is an independent clause (a complete thought) or DC if the group of words is a dependent clause (not a complete thought, even though it contains a subject and a verb).

_____   1.   the train was seriously delayed

_____   2.   we stood under the awning

_____   3.   since it takes two days to get there

_____   4.   I chose the wrong day to travel

_____   5.   until I sat down and talked to them

_____   6.   even though you made a reservation

_____   7.   as the telephone rang in the office

_____   8.   the beauty of the countryside will refresh you

_____   9.   whenever the track is cleared of the debris

_____   10.   while the tickets are being prepared

EXERCISE 2   Recognizing Dependent and Independent Clauses

In the blank to the side of each group of words, write the letters IC if the group is an independent clause (a complete thought) or DC if the group of words is a dependent clause (not a complete thought, even though it contains a subject and a verb).

_____   1.   after the summer months had passed

_____   2.   when the reference librarian is available

_____   3.   unless you want to read all the articles

_____   4.   unfortunately the network is down again

_____   5.   sometimes the room gets very cold

_____   6.   if Beverly returns

_____   7.   although he explained the procedure

_____   8.   in spite of the warning on the copy machine

_____   9.   everyone lost money in the machine

_____   10.   tonight the library will close early

Using Subordinating Conjunctions

Study the list of subordinating conjunctions in the chart that follows. The use of one of these connecting words signals the beginning of a dependent clause. It is a good idea to memorize them just as you did the coordinating conjunctions and adverbial conjunctions in Chapter 14. Since each group has a different principle for punctuation, you need to memorize the words in these groups.

CONNECTORS: COMMON SUBORDINATING CONJUNCTIONS		
after	if, even if	unless
although	in order that	until
as, as if	provided that	when, whenever
as long as, as though	rather than	where, wherever
because	since	whether
before	so that	while
even though	though	

The next chart contains the subordinating conjunctions grouped according to their meanings. When you use these conjunctions, you need to be absolutely sure that the connection one of these conjunctions makes between the independent and dependent clause is the meaning you intend.

FUNCTION OF SUBORDINATING CONJUNCTIONS	
To introduce a *condition*:	if, even if, as long as, provided that, unless (after a negative independent clause)
	I will go *as long as* you go with me.
	I won't go *unless* you go with me.
To introduce a *contrast*:	although, even though, though
	I will go *even though* you won't go with me.
To introduce a *cause*:	because, since
	I will go *because* the meeting is very important.
To show *time*:	after, before, when, whenever, while, until (independent clause is negative)
	I will go *whenever* you say.
	I won't go *until* you say it is time.
To show *place*:	where, wherever
	I will go *wherever* you send me.
To show *purpose*:	in order that, so that
	I will go *so that* I can hear the candidate for myself.

You have two choices of how to write a complex sentence. You can begin with the independent clause, or you can begin with the dependent clause.

First way:	**IC**	**DC**
Example:	The child cannot sleep	if the television is too loud.

Second way:	**DC**	,	**IC**
Example:	If the television is too loud	,	the child cannot sleep.

Notice that only the second version uses a comma; this is because the second version begins with the dependent clause. When a sentence begins with the independent clause, no comma is used. Your ear may help you with this punctuation. Read a sentence that begins with a dependent clause. Do you notice that there is a tendency to pause at the end of that dependent clause? This is a natural place to put a comma.

• PRACTICE

Use a subordinating conjunction to combine each of the following pairs of sentences. Remember, the independent clause will contain the more important idea in the sentence.

1. Use the subordinating conjunction *after*.

> Maria went to the party.
>
> She finished her work.

  a. Begin with the independent clause:

    _____

  b. Begin with the dependent clause:

    _____

2. Use the subordinating conjunction *when*:

> The dog scratched at the door.
>
> He wanted to go out.

  a. Begin with the independent clause:

    _____

  b. Begin with the dependent clause:

    _____

EXERCISE 1   Using Subordinating Conjunctions

Use each of the following subordinating conjunctions to compose a complex sentence. An example has been done for you.

> **Subordinating conjunction:** after
>
> **Complex sentence:**   After the storm was over, the family walked to town.

Remember that a complex sentence has one independent clause and at least one dependent clause. Every clause must have a subject and a verb. Check your sentences by underlining the subject and verb in each clause.

Can you explain why the following sentence is not a complex sentence?

> After the storm, the family walked to town.

After the storm is a prepositional phrase. *After,* in this case, is a preposition. It is not used as a subordinating conjunction to combine clauses.

1. as if

_____

_____

2. before

_____

_____

3. until

_____

_____

4. although

_____

_____

EXERCISE 2   Combining Sentences Using Subordination

Combine each pair of sentences using subordination. Look back at the list of subordinating conjunctions if you need to. An example follows:

> **Two sentences:**   Come with me to the lecture series.
> You will meet and hear Carol Shields.
>
> **Combined by subordination:** If you come with me to the lecture series, you will meet and hear Carol Shields.

1. They were sitting in class.

   News of the war was shouted from the hallways.

   _____

   _____

2. The mayor supported the city councillor.

   The people wanted the city councillor removed.

   _____

   _____

3. I will meet P.K. Page tonight.

   She is reading her poetry at the college.

   _____

   _____

4. The teacher wanted to retire.

   He had three children to put through university.

   _____

   _____

5. The teacher wanted to teach the new summer module.

   He contacted his department chairperson.

   _____

   _____

Using a relative pronoun to create a complex sentence

Often sentences can be combined with a relative pronoun.

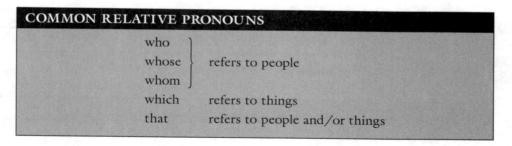

COMMON RELATIVE PRONOUNS	
who ⎤	
whose ⎬ refers to people	
whom ⎦	
which	refers to things
that	refers to people and/or things

Combining sentences with a relative pronoun

Two simple sentences: The artist paints unusually fine portraits.
The artist sits beside me in sculpture class.

These sentences could sound short and choppy. To avoid this choppiness, a writer might want to join these two related ideas with a relative pronoun.

Incorrectly combined: The artist paints unusually fine portraits who sits beside me in sculpture class.

The relative pronoun *who* and its clause *who sits beside me in sculpture class* refers to *artist*. The clause must be placed directly after the word artist.

Correctly combined: The artist *who* sits beside me in sculpture class paints unusually fine portraits.

> Remember that the relative pronoun and its clause must immediately follow the word it relates to.

Now we could join a third idea:

Third idea: She plans to exhibit her portraits in the Great Northern Arts Festival in July.

Combining sentences using two relative pronouns:

The artist *who* sits beside me in sculpture class paints unusually fine portraits, *which* she plans to exhibit in the Great Northern Arts Festival in July.

• PRACTICE 1

Combine the pairs of sentences into complex sentences by using relative pronouns. Use the relative pronoun *that*. These sentences will not require the use of commas. An example follows:

First sentence: The island is Hispaniola.

Second sentence: It lies east of Cuba.

Combined sentence: The island that lies east of Cuba is Hispaniola.

1. The island is Hispaniola.

   The island is shared by Haiti and the Dominican Republic.

   Combined: _____

   _____

2. Trade winds blow to Haiti from the northeast.

   They bring rains to the island.

   Combined: _____

   _____

3. Haiti is largely protected from storms by high mountains.

   The mountains cover two-thirds of the country.

   Combined: _____

   _____

How do you punctuate a clause with a relative pronoun?

Punctuating relative clauses can be tricky because there are two types of relative clauses:

1. Those clauses that are basic to the meaning of the sentence:

    Try to buy paper *that has been recycled.*

    The basic meaning of the sentence is not *Try to buy paper* but *Try to buy paper that has been recycled.* The relative clause is necessary to restrict the meaning. This clause is called a **restrictive clause** and does not use commas to set off the clause. *Note:* The pronoun *that* is ordinarily used in these kinds of clauses.

2. Those clauses that are not basic to the meaning of the sentence:

    The bakery's front window, *which was filled with fancy cakes,* was badly cracked.

    In this sentence, the relative clause *which was filled with fancy cakes* is not basic to the main idea. In fact, if the clause were omitted, the main idea would still be clear. This clause is called a **nonrestrictive clause**. Commas are required to indicate the information is nonessential to the main idea. *Note:* The pronoun *which* is ordinarily used in these kinds of clauses.

•PRACTICE 2

Choose whether or not to insert commas in the following sentences. Use the following examples as your models.

The student *who is standing in the doorway* is my friend.

The student can only be identified by the fact that she is the one standing in the doorway. Therefore, the relative clause *who is standing in the doorway* is essential to the meaning. No commas are necessary.

Jasmine, *who works as a DJ to earn money for college,* is my friend.

The main idea is that Jasmine is the friend. The fact that she works as a DJ is not essential to that main idea. Therefore, commas are needed to set off this nonessential information.

Insert commas as needed in each of the following sentences.

1. Canada's Walk of Fame which occupies eleven city blocks in Toronto's theatre district displays the names of world-famous Canadian artists, actors, and sports figures.

2. People who are inducted into the Walk of Fame must be born in Canada and their accomplishments must have had a national or international impact.

3. Everyone who joins the Walk of Fame has his or her name engraved on a large granite block.

4. Jacques Villeneuve who is a Formula One race car driver was the first person to be inducted into the Walk of Fame.

5. The crowds that gather during the unveiling ceremonies are often so large that busy streets must be closed to traffic.

Now you are ready to practise joining your own sentences with relative pronouns, being sure to punctuate whenever necessary. The following exercises ask you to insert a variety of relative clauses into simple sentences.

EXERCISE 1   Combining Sentences Using Relative Pronouns

Add a relative clause to each of the following ten sentences. Use each of the possibilities at least once: *who, whose, whom, which, that*. An example follows:

> **Simple sentence:**   The provincial election is one month away.
>
> **Complex sentence:**   The provincial election, which is still too close to call, is one month away.

1. The political candidates _____
   met in the television studio.

2. The leading candidate _____
   smiled and greeted the others.

3. The broadcast _____
   was to be seen throughout the country.

4. The moderator _____
   had been chosen for her fairness.

5. The studio audience _____
   filled the small space set aside for the evening.

6. Every campaign issue _____
   was permitted for discussion.

7. Each candidate _____
   shook hands with the others.

8. The debating rules _____
   were explained once again.

9. All the people in the audience _____
   gradually became quiet.

10. The debate _____
    would be helpful to voters.

EXERCISE 2   Combining Sentences Using Relative Pronouns

Add a relative clause to each of the following ten sentences. Use each of the possibilities at least once: *who, whose, whom, which, that*. Be sure to use the correct punctuation. An example follows:

> **Simple sentence:**   The trip to Quito takes ten hours.
>
> **Complex sentence:**   The trip to Quito, which is scheduled for August 16, will take ten hours.

1. The young man _____
   wanted to learn Spanish.

2. During his second year _____
   he began to plan for a semester abroad.

3. The problem _____
   was finding the right program.

4. The International Studies Department _____
   had an entire bulletin board devoted to study abroad.

5. He brought home four brochures _____

6. His Spanish teacher _____
   was very encouraging.

7. His parents _____
   were concerned about his financial arrangements as well as his health.

8. He finally selected Ecuador _____

9. In Ecuador he will live with a family _____

10. Quito _____
    has some of the most outstanding examples of eighteenth-century architecture
    in the Americas.

Mastery and editing tests

TEST 1   Combining Sentences Using Coordination and Subordination

Below is a paragraph composed of mostly simple sentences. Rewrite the paragraph combining sentences wherever you think the combining would improve the meaning or style. Don't be afraid to change the wording slightly to accommodate the changes you want to make. Combine clauses using coordination or subordination.

The fad of the 90s was in-line skating. In-line skates are a cross between ice skates and roller skates. The wheels are in a single row down the middle of the skate. They usually have only one brake. The brake is on the heel of the right foot. This skate was developed to help hockey players practise off the ice. This practice has blossomed into a multimillion dollar industry, sport, and pastime. Look around you. You can probably see in-line skaters. There are stunt teams, racing teams, and skating clubs. "Blading" is its commonly known name. It is a popular form of recreation and exercise. You should be careful when attempting in-line skating. You must wear the proper protection. Protective pads should be worn over the elbows, wrists, and knees in order to cover all joints. The head is particularly vulnerable. A helmet should be worn at all times. You can achieve speeds of 6 to 40 km per hour or more. Be prepared. You can have a lot of fun using in-line skates.

_____

_____

_____

_____

_____

_____

_____

_____

_____

_____

_____

_____

_____

_____

_____

_____

_____

_____

_____

_____

_____

_____

_____

_____

_____

TEST 2   Combining Sentences Using Coordination and Subordination

Below is a paragraph composed of mostly simple sentences. Rewrite the paragraph combining sentences wherever you think the combining would improve the meaning or style. Don't be afraid to change the wording slightly to accommodate the changes you want to make. Combine clauses using coordination or subordination.

In 1971, rich young Malcolm Bricklin decided the world needed a new kind of car. He designed a sports car that put safety first. He named it after himself. The Bricklin was a unique, futuristic vehicle. It was called a gull-wing car. Its doors opened by lifting up like the wings of a bird. The Bricklin's body was made of fibreglass. It came in only red, beige, white, orange, and yellow. There was even a song written about the Bricklin. In the 1970s, who didn't want to be seen driving in a Bricklin? The car was manufactured in Minto and Saint John, New Brunswick, from 1974 to 1975. It sold for about $9,000. The New Brunswick government decided to help out Malcolm Bricklin. Wouldn't this be a great way to expand the province's economy? The New Brunswick government came up with most of the money needed to build the cars. Critics opposed the plans from the very beginning. Should the government spend money on this project that was sure to fail? Eventually, the government cut funding to Bricklin. There were also problems getting parts to make the car. The Bricklin car company went bankrupt. There were nearly 3,000 Bricklins built. About 1,500 still exist today. It seems that neither the car nor the song were big hits in the 1970s.

_____

_____

_____

_____

_____

_____

_____

_____

_____

_____

_____

_____

_____

_____

_____

_____

_____

_____

_____

_____

_____

_____

TEST 3   Combining Sentences Using Coordination and Subordination

Below is a paragraph composed of mostly simple sentences. Rewrite the paragraph combining sentences wherever you think the combining would improve the meaning or style. Don't be afraid to change the wording slightly to accommodate the changes you want to make. Combine clauses using coordination and subordination.

The chances are that last time you saw a movie set in New York, Los Angeles, or even exotic Morocco you were probably looking at either Toronto, Montreal, or Vancouver in disguise. More and more movie producers from Hollywood have been flocking to Canada to make their films. It is cheaper to film in Canada than in the United States. The movie *Framed* starred actor Rob Lowe. Winnipeg became New York. There was a pedestrian walkway underneath the Richardson building. It was made to look like a subway platform. How did Vancouver become Vietnam? Franklin Street around the port area of the city was recently turned into Saigon circa 1975 for a TV movie. Film crews added palm trees and signs written in Vietnamese. Toronto became Morocco. Filmmakers added sand and palm trees around Sunnyside Pavilion on Lake Ontario. It looked like a Moroccan castle. Montreal's Wellington Tunnel provided a dark, urban suspense setting. It was needed for a scene in the horror thriller *The Bone Collector.* The next time you are waiting at the bus stop. A New York City bus drives up. It may not be a good idea to get on.

_____

_____

_____

_____

_____

_____

_____

_____

_____

_____

_____

_____

_____

_____

_____

_____

_____

_____

_____

_____

_____

_____

_____

_____

Correcting the Run-On

In conversation, when we tell about an event involving a series of connected actions, we may string them together as if they were part of one long thought. However, this does not mean that we should write one long sentence; that would result in run-ons. When you put your spoken narrative into written form, there are many accepted ways to separate or combine the different parts into acceptable sentences. Turning ideas into sentences calls for a careful understanding of individual clauses and how we punctuate those clauses when we combine them. This chapter is about learning how to recognize and avoid run-on sentences in your own writing.

Below is a spoken narrative that became a single run-on sentence when the writer first put it into written form. Read the paragraph. Where are the places that need punctuation or some other change?

Caitlin wanted to make a good impression on her first day of work but everything went wrong her alarm clock didn't go off and she had no time for breakfast or a shower so she hurriedly put on her work clothes and jumped into her old station wagon but the engine wouldn't start so she ran to her neighbour's house to ask for a ride but no one answered the door so Caitlin had to work on her car and the problem turned out to be a burnt fuse but luckily she had a replacement in her glove compartment but by now she only had fifteen minutes to get to work and she arrived a few minutes late and her manner was still frantic and she was preoccupied all day with the fact that she looked like she had just rolled out of bed.

What is a run-on?

Run-on sentences are independent clauses that have been combined incorrectly.

How many kinds of run-ons are there?

Run-on sentences occur when the writer is either unable to recognize where one complete idea has ended and another idea begins or is not sure of the standard ways of connecting the ideas. Certain punctuation signals where two clauses join. Other punctuation signifies the end of the thought. Three types of mistakes are commonly made:

1. *The fused run-on:* Two or more independent clauses are run together without any punctuation.

   incorrect: She woke up late she made it to work on time.

2. *The comma splice:* Two or more independent clauses are run together with only a comma.

   incorrect: She woke up late, she made it to work on time.

3. *The "and" run-on:* Two or more independent clauses are connected with a coordinating conjunction, but there is no punctuation.

   incorrect: She woke up late but she made it to work on time.

How do you make a complete sentence from a run-on?

GUIDE FOR CORRECTING RUN-ONS

1. Make two sentences with end punctuation.
   correct: She woke up late. She made it to work on time.

2. Make a compound sentence using one of the three methods of coordination.
   correct: She woke up late, but she made it to work on time.

   She woke up late; however, she made it to work on time.

   She woke up late; she made it to work on time.

3. Make a complex sentence using subordination.
   correct: Although she woke up late, she made it to work on time.

   She made it to work on time although she woke up late.

EXERCISE 1   Revising Run-Ons

Each of the following examples is a run-on. Using the Guide for Correcting Run-Ons, provide four possible ways to revise each run-on. An example is given.

Run-on:
   Lawren Harris experimented with many styles of painting it is his early landscape art that I like the most.

Two simple sentences:
   Lawren Harris experimented with many styles of painting. It is his early landscape art that I like the most.

Two kinds of compound sentences:

a. Lawren Harris experimented with many styles of painting, but it is his early landscape art that I like the most.

b. Lawren Harris experimented with many styles of painting; however, it is his early landscape art that I like the most.

Complex sentence:

Although Lawren Harris experimented with many styles of painting, it is his early landscape art that I like the most.

1. Lawren Harris, the great Canadian landscape painter, was born in Toronto in 1885 he was a member of the successful Harris farm machinery family.

   Two simple sentences:

   _____

   _____

   _____

   Two kinds of compound sentences:

   a. _____

   _____

   b. _____

   _____

   Complex sentence:

   _____

   _____

2. Harris wanted to become a better artist he went to Berlin to study art.

   Two simple sentences:

   _____

   _____

   _____

   Two kinds of compound sentences:

   a. _____

   _____

   b. _____

   _____

   Complex sentence:

   _____

   _____

3. He mostly painted landscapes he sometimes painted urban scenes to show how dreary city living could sometimes be.

   Two simple sentences:

   _____

   _____

   _____

Two kinds of compound sentences:

a. _____

_____

b. _____

_____

Complex sentence:

_____

_____

EXERCISE 2   Revising Run-Ons

Each of the following examples is a run-on. Using the guide on page 204, provide four possible ways to revise each run-on.

1. Jim wanted to travel he got a job working on a train in northern Manitoba.

   Two simple sentences:

   _____

   _____

   _____

   Two kinds of compound sentences:

   a. _____

   _____

   b. _____

   _____

   Complex sentence:

   _____

   _____

2. He worked for minimum wage he saw some great sights.

   Two simple sentences:

   _____

   _____

   _____

   Two kinds of compound sentences:

   a. _____

   _____

   b. _____

   _____

Complex sentence:

_____

_____

3. Jim fell in love with the province he might decide to stay.

Two simple sentences:

_____

_____

_____

Two kinds of compound sentences:

a. _____

_____

b. _____

_____

Complex sentence:

_____

_____

EXERCISE 1   Recognizing and Correcting Run-Ons

The following account was written as one sentence. Rewrite the account making sure to correct the run-on sentences. Put a period at the end of each complete thought. You may have to omit some of the words that loosely connect the ideas, or you may want to use coordination and subordination. Remember to make each new sentence begin with a capital letter.

> Caitlin wanted to make a good impression on her first day of work but everything went wrong her alarm clock didn't go off and she had no time for breakfast or a shower so she hurriedly put on her work clothes and jumped into her old station wagon but the engine wouldn't start so she ran to her neighbour's house to ask for a ride but no one answered the door so Caitlin had to work on her car and the problem turned out to be a burnt fuse but luckily she had a replacement in her glove compartment but by now she only had fifteen minutes to get to work and she arrived a few minutes late and her manner was still frantic and she was preoccupied all day with the fact that she looked like she had just rolled out of bed.

_____

_____

_____

_____

_____

_____

_____

_____

_____

_____

_____

_____

_____

_____

_____

_____

_____

_____

_____

_____

EXERCISE 2   Recognizing and Correcting Run-Ons

The following account was written as one sentence. Rewrite the account making sure to correct the run-on sentences. Put a period at the end of each complete thought. You may have to omit some of the words that loosely connect the ideas, or you may want to use coordination and subordination. Remember to make each new sentence begin with a capital letter.

Emily Stowe pioneered the struggle for women's equality in Canada as the first woman school principal and female physician and she organized the country's first suffrage organization and it became known as the National Council of Women and Emily Stowe was refused entry to the University of Toronto on account of her gender so she went to study medicine in New York and after she graduated from there she returned to Toronto to practise medicine and continue her studies but she faced fines, threats of imprisonment, and opposition from the Ontario College of Physicians and Surgeons so she continued her studies at the University of Toronto medical school but she endured harassment from her male professors and fellow students but she continued with her studies and she was the first woman to graduate from a medical school in Canada and she continued to practise illegally until she was finally granted a licence in 1880 and she had a daughter named Augusta Stowe-Gullen and she wanted to become a doctor but she had to endure the same hardships as her mother before her when she enrolled in medical school.

_____

_____

_____

_____

_____

_____
_____
_____
_____
_____
_____
_____
_____
_____
_____
_____
_____
_____
_____
_____
_____
_____
_____
_____

Mastery and editing tests

TEST 1   Editing for Run-Ons

The following paragraph was written as a single run-on sentence. Rewrite the paragraph making all necessary changes.

Taxi drivers are very much like football players they have that aggressive determination of the player who is going to make a first down even if it means getting his shoulders dislocated and his jaw broken so as you jump into a cab you shout your destination above the noise of the radio and the blare of beeping horns and you are off, and as the driver barrels through crowded streets you crouch in the back seat looking nervously out the window or closing your eyes tightly hoping for the best, and the driver weaves from one lane to another while cutting in front of delivery vans or buses to gain some imagined small advantage and he swerves around startled pedestrians as he turns the corners while you are thrown onto the other side of the back seat you do not have enough courage to strike up any conversation but you should busy yourself with the calculation of the steadily climbing fare, this will divert your attention to an equally sobering situation, will you have enough money to pay for the sizable tip the cab driver will expect for risking the lives of countless people in order to get you to the dentist on time?

TEST 2

Editing for Run-Ons

Edit the following paragraph, correcting all run-on sentences.

When archaeologists began to dig in Egypt in the 19th century, they were looking for royal tombs filled with gold and other treasures so many of the other items that survived the centuries were ignored by them but as the years went by and the diggers realized there were items more valuable than gold, they had new respect for even the most humble pieces from the ancient world so when workers brought up lamps and common bowls and other everyday objects, they were studied with a new respect and people could look at a dish and realize that people of another time were able to bring beauty into daily life. These pieces are like time capsules because they are able to take us back to another culture and we can examine firsthand the reality of that culture. We are also able to judge our own lives and what we produce in our own culture when we put the past next to the present but on occasion just an accident will reveal a part of the past that we never realized was there. Over a hundred years ago, a British team was digging in Egypt but there had not been much success in finding royal tombs and the only items the workers had been able to uncover were a lot of crocodile mummies left there by the ancient Egyptians so when one worker had dug up yet another crocodile mummy, he was so angry that he took a mummified crocodile and smashed it against a rock. When the mummy broke, it was seen that it had been wrapped in papyrus, the paper that was used throughout the ancient world. Scientists had never realized that many important literary works had been preserved in mummies thousands of years old and this led to a whole new area of scientific study.

TEST 3

Editing for Run-Ons

Edit the following paragraph, correcting all run-on sentences.

Most Canadians have heard of the term "brain drain," it refers to the emigration of Canada's best and brightest people to the United States. If the most talented Canadians are leaving, where will we find our future leaders, doctors, and artists? However, most Canadians don't realize that the country has really benefited from a "brain gain" and this means that the pool of talented and creative people leaving Canada has been replaced by people from abroad choosing to live and work here but the talents of Canada's recent arrivals are not always recognized or appreciated to their fullest extent. Many of the people who have immigrated to Canada were respected professionals in their own countries and they are very well educated and extremely talented so it may actually be a considerable loss to countries like Iran, Ghana, Poland, or Romania to see their best doctors, lawyers, or engineers leaving. Sadly, many of these people come to Canada and they find that their credentials are not always recognized by professional associations here and this is why we find so many doctors from Iran or engineers from Russia who are driving taxis or working as short-order cooks in Toronto, Montreal, and Vancouver.

Chapter 17

Making Sentence Parts Work Together

In Chapter 12, you focused on one major way that sentence parts must work together, namely, verbs must agree with their subjects. In this chapter, you will look at other elements in the sentence that must agree or be in balance. These include:

> Pronouns and case
>
> Pronoun-antecedent agreement
>
> Parallel structure
>
> Misplaced or dangling modifiers

With practice, you will learn to recognize these structures in your own writing.

Pronouns and case

Many personal pronouns change their form depending on how they are used in the sentence; that is, they can be used as subjects, objects, possessives, or reflexives.

> *You* gave *her your* car keys *yourself.*
>
> *She* gave *me her* car keys *herself.*

The following chart may be useful as a reference.

PRONOUNS AND CASE				
	Pronouns used as subjects	*Pronouns used as objects*	*Pronouns used as possessives*	*Pronouns used as reflexives*
Singular	I you he she it	me you him her it	my, mine you, yours his hers its	myself yourself himself herself itself
Plural	we you they	us you them	our, ours your, yours their, theirs	ourselves yourselves themselves
Singular or Plural	who	whom	whose	

- There are no such forms as *hisself* or *theirselves*.
- Do not confuse *whose* with *who's* or *its* with *it's*. (*Who's* means *who is* and *it's* means *it is*.)

In general, most of us use pronouns in the correct case without thinking. Three constructions, however, require some special attention: comparisons, compound constructions, and the use of *who/whom*.

1. Comparisons

In a comparison, choosing the correct pronoun is easier when you complete the comparison.

> His friend is a better sport than (he, him, his).

> His friend is a better sport than (he, him, his) is.

The second sentence shows that *he* is the correct form because the pronoun is used as the subject for the clause *he is*.

•PRACTICE

1. The player did not regret the loss as much as (I, me).

   Hint: Try completing the comparison:
   The player did not regret the loss as much as (I, me) did.

2. The game was more exciting for me than (she, her).

   Hint: Try completing the comparison:
   The game was more exciting for me than it was for (she, her).

EXERCISE   Choosing the Correct Pronoun in Comparisons

Circle the correct pronoun in each of the sentences.

1. Joe and Chris arrived as late as (they, them).
2. People say the Germans are unbeatable, but we ski better than (they, them).
3. Without a doubt, you are as accomplished as (he, him).
4. That topic was not as popular as (us, ours, we).
5. Jane was happier with the outcome than (I, me).
6. The "purple" group finished it faster than (we, us).
7. In the end, the judges honoured our meal over (them, they, theirs).
8. The award couldn't have meant more to (I, me) and (he, him).
9. Do those tickets belong to us, or are they (them, theirs)?
10. Maribel will stay at the hotel longer than (her, she).

2. Compound constructions

When you have a compound subject or a compound object, choosing the correct pronoun is easier if you read the sentence without one of the compound parts.

My father and (I, me) left early.

(I, me) left early.

•PRACTICE

1. The dentist and (she, her) studied the patient's chart.

Hint: Try the sentence without *dentist.*
(She, Her) studied the patient's chart.

2. They spoke to both the father and (I, me).

Hint: Try the sentence without *father.*
They spoke to (I, me).

EXERCISE ## Choosing the Correct Pronoun in Compound Constructions

Circle the correct pronoun in each of the sentences.

1. The package came addressed to Mom and (I, me).
2. It was really meant for (her, she) and Shaneil, though.
3. Among Eygir, Mohamed, and (I, me), Mohamed is the tallest.
4. Not only did he surprise us with a party, he brought Nicole and (her, she) along as well.
5. Philip and (he, him) are definitely the best chess players.
6. However, (he, him) and (I, me) always beat Igor at backgammon.
7. (Who's, Whose) shoes are these?
8. We always tell you, if you aren't home on time you must call either (I, me) or (her, she).
9. Neither (he, him) nor (I, me) felt well after eating at that new fast-food restaurant.
10. Although Dad always talks to Fran and (him, he), he asks for Fran first.

3. Who/whom constructions

Choosing between these two pronouns is confusing, partly because in daily conversation many people do not use *whom.* When in doubt, you need to consider if the pronoun is used in a subject position (who) or in an object position (whom).

Subject position:　　*Who* is the conductor of the Victoria Symphony?

Object position:　　*Whom* did the conductor select for the solo?
　　　　　　　　　　To whom did the conductor give the solo?

If there is more than one clause in the sentence, it is helpful to cross out all other clauses so you can see how *who/whom* functions in its own clause.

PRACTICE

1. He is the conductor (who, whom) I admired.

    look at:　(who, whom) I admired

2. He is the conductor (who, whom) I knew would be available.

    look at:　(who, whom) would be available

3. I am not sure (who, whom) will play the solo.

4. That is the musician (who, whom) I heard last month.

EXERCISE

Choosing the Correct Pronoun Using Who/Whom

Circle the correct pronoun in each of the sentences.

1. Do you know (who, whom) is appearing at Massey Hall tonight?
2. My favourite dancer was the one (who's, whose) solo started Act II.
3. (Whoever, Whomever) broke that plate better be prepared to pay for it.
4. I'm not sure to (who, whom) I need to speak.
5. These extra blankets will go to (whoever, whomever) needs them the most.
6. (It's, Its) difficult to choose the winner.
7. (Who's, Whose) glasses fell behind the couch?
8. I'll only consider those (who, whom) accurately completed the application.
9. (Whoever, Whomever) was the last to arrive should close the door.
10. The baby crawled toward the child (who, whom) she knew.

In order to avoid confusion, remember you can always cross out other clauses in the sentence so you can concentrate on the clause in question.

~~You must choose~~ (who, whom) ~~you believe~~ will do the best job.
~~Is that the person~~ (who, whom) ~~you think~~ you should choose?

Use the following exercises to practise all three constructions that you have now studied.

EXERCISE 1   Choosing Correct Pronoun Forms

Circle the correct pronoun in each of the sentences.

1. Do you really believe that Shirley and (he, him) were born to be together?
2. Why don't you send it to Frank and (I, me)?
3. The book is a gift to (whoever, whomever) takes the class.
4. She always gets better grades than (he, him).
5. To (who, whom) should this dish be returned?
6. I will never be as tall as (she, her).
7. Their company is working at a much higher level than (us, our, ours).
8. Extra garlic is fine for me but not (he, him).
9. Mike prefers the teacher (who's, whose) classes are limited to eight people.
10. Ann Marie is not nearly as good at math as (I, me).

EXERCISE 2   Choosing Correct Pronoun Forms

Circle the correct pronouns in the following paragraph.

Auditioning for the play can be scary, so Carol and (I, me) decided to go together. When we arrived, we weren't sure to (who, whom) we should hand our pictures. A large group of men and women had already arrived and were waiting. Our names were closer to the top of the list than (them, theirs). That meant (her, she) and (I, me) would be called sooner. Carol's number was called, and she was paired with David. He's the one (who's, whose) voice always cracks. Although a few of the others actually laughed, Carol was nicer than (they, them). Furthermore, she sang her part so beautifully that (whoever, whomever) went next would have to be especially talented to be better than (her, she). As expected, Carol got the leading role. No one was jealous. She is a better singer than (us, we).

Pronoun-antecedent agreement

When we use a pronoun in our writing, that pronoun must refer to a word used previously in the text. This word is called the ***antecedent***.

> An ***antecedent*** is a word (or words) that a pronoun replaces.
>
> The dentist's office was shabby. *It* was not a place to spend a beautiful afternoon.

In this example, the pronoun *It* replaces the word *office. Office,* in this case, is referred to as the antecedent to the pronoun *it.*

Study the following three instances where the use of pronouns can cause trouble for writers.

1. **A pronoun must agree in number (singular or plural) with any other word to which it refers.** The following sentence contains a pronoun-antecedent disagreement in number:

    Lacks agreement: *Everybody* talked about *their* first day of school.

The problem in this sentence is that *everybody* is a singular word, but *their* is a plural pronoun. You may have often heard people use the plural pronoun *their* to refer to a singular subject. In fact, the above sentence may sound correct, but it is considered a mistake in formal writing. Here are two approaches a writer might take to correct this sentence:

    Sexist: *Everybody* talked about *his* first day of school.

Although you may often encounter this approach in current writing, it is unpopular because it is widely considered a sexist construction.

    Awkward: *Everybody* talked about *his or her* first day of school.

This form is technically correct, but if it is used several times in the same paragraph it sounds awkward and repetitious.

The best solution may be to revise such a construction so that the antecedent is plural:

    All of them talked about *their* first day of school.

Another problem with pronoun-antecedent agreement in number occurs when a demonstrative pronoun (*this, that, these, those*) is used with a noun. That pronoun must agree with the noun it modifies:

    Singular: *this kind, that type*   Plural: *these kinds, those types*

    Incorrect: *Those type* of questions are difficult.

    Correct: *Those types* of questions are difficult.

                                        or

    That type of question is difficult.

• PRACTICE 1

Rewrite each of the following sentences so that the pronoun agrees with its antecedent in *number*.

1. Everyone should wear their uniforms to the picnic.

    _____

2. These kind of bathing suits will be popular this summer.

    _____

3. No one could believe what they just saw.

    _____

4. Those type of headphones can damage your hearing.

   _____

5. Each variety has their own distinguishing marks.

   _____

2. **Pronouns must also agree with their antecedents in *person*.** The following sentence contains a pronoun-antecedent disagreement in *person*.

   Incorrect: After sitting all day, *one* should do *your* basic stretching exercises.

   When you construct a piece of writing, you choose a "person" as the voice in that piece of writing. Some teachers ask students not to choose the first person *I* because they believe such writing sounds too personal. Other teachers warn students not to use *you* because it is too casual. Whatever guidelines your teacher gives you, the important point is to be consistent in person. Here are some of the possibilities for the sentence given above:

   After sitting all day, *one* should do *one's* stretching exercises.
   After sitting all day, *I* should do *my* stretching exercises.
   After sitting all day, *you* should do *your* stretching exercises.
   After sitting all day, *she* should do *her* stretching exercises.
   After sitting all day, *we* should do *our* stretching exercises.

PRACTICE 2

Correct each of the following sentences so that the pronoun agrees with its antecedent in person.

1. I love reading books because as long as you have a good book you can never be bored.

   _____

   _____

2. You may read only mysteries, but even with this limitation, one can choose from thousands.

   _____

   _____

3. When we join a book club, you may save money on the books you buy during a year.

   _____

   _____

4. One might also buy a lot of books you never read.

   _____

   _____

5. When I return an overdue book to the library, one must pay a fine of twenty cents for every day overdue.

   _____

   _____

3. The antecedent of a pronoun should not be *missing, ambiguous,* or *repetitious.*

a. **Missing antecedent:**

   They made a discovery about the human genome.

   Possible revision:

   Researchers at the University of Toronto made a discovery about the human genome.

   Explanation: In the first sentence, who is *they?* If the context has not told us that *they* refers to researchers, then the antecedent is missing. The sentence should be rewritten in order to avoid *they.*

b. **Ambiguous antecedent:**

   Dr. Stamler told his assistant that *he* needed to revise one section of the report.

   Possible revision:

   Dr. Stamler said that his assistant needed to revise one section of the report.

   Explanation: In the first version of the sentence, *he* could refer to either Dr. Stamler or the assistant. The sentence should be revised in a way that will avoid this ambiguity.

c. **Repetitious pronoun and antecedent:**

   The journal <u>Nature</u>, *it* reported that this discovery has significant implications for the treatment of blood pressure.

   Possible revision:

   The journal <u>Nature</u> reported that this discovery has significant implications for the treatment of blood pressure.

   Explanation: The subject for the verb *reported* could be the journal <u>Nature</u> or the pronoun *it,* but the subject could not be both the antecedent and the pronoun at the same time. Using both the antecedent and the pronoun results in needless repetition.

PRACTICE 3

Rewrite the following sentences so that the antecedents are not *missing, ambiguous,* or *repetitious.*

1. Mrs. Kline she asked her neighbour to listen to the local news.

   _____

2. During the rehearsal, they said we wouldn't be ready for another two weeks.

    _____

3. Mom told me to give the baby her doll.

    _____

4. I refuse to contribute because they won't tell me how the money is used.

    _____

5. The plate fell off the shelf onto the counter, and it cracked.

    _____

EXERCISE 1 Making Pronouns and Antecedents Agree

The following sentences contain errors with pronouns. Revise each sentence so that pronouns agree with their antecedents, and the antecedents are not missing, ambiguous, or repetitious.

1. No one can take out materials without their library card.

    _____

2. If you want to take the tour, one must arrive early.

    _____

3. If we want help, you have to catch the waiter's eye.

    _____

4. Those type of books scare me.

    _____

5. Those secretaries are so good, she might get a raise.

    _____

6. If you hold onto it, they won't get lost.

    _____

7. These type of socks are easily snagged.

    _____

8. If you want to lose weight, one must control the urge to eat.

    _____

9. Everyone wore their cap and gown.

    _____

10. The firefighter let the boy wear his hat.

    _____

EXERCISE 2   Making Pronouns and Antecedents Agree

The following sentences contain errors with pronouns. Revise each sentence so that pronouns agree with their antecedents, and antecedents are not missing, ambiguous, or repetitious.

1. Nobody wants his taxes increased.

    _____

2. His friend sent him his favourite leather jacket.

    _____

3. The video cassette recorder ate the cassette, so it had to be replaced.

    _____

4. In the article, they said that some cancers might be genetic.

    _____

5. If one is interested in music, you should attend as many concerts as you can.

    _____

6. Mark generally passes these kind of tests.

    _____

7. The woman she must bring her coach to the next birthing class.

    _____

8. George gave Michael a copy of his photograph.

    _____

9. They really should do more about subway graffiti.

    _____

10. Nancy told Amy that the ship she was sailing on was completely booked.

    _____

Parallel structure: Making a series of words, phrases, or clauses balanced within the sentence

Which one of the following sentences achieves a better balanced structure?

Her homework assignments include reading a chapter in psychology, writing up a lab report for biology, and an essay to compose for art history.

or

Her homework assignments include reading a chapter in psychology, writing up a lab report for biology, and composing an essay for art history.

If you selected the second sentence, you made the better choice. The second sentence uses parallel structure to balance the three phrases in the series: *reading, writing,* and *composing.* By matching each of the items in the series with the same *-ing* structure, the sentence becomes easier to understand and more pleasant to read. You can make words, phrases, and even sentences in a series parallel:

1. **Words in a series should be the same parts of speech.**

   Not parallel: The street was narrow, crowded, and the noise was terrible.
   (The series is composed of two adjectives and one clause.)

   Parallel: The street was narrow, crowded, and terribly noisy.
   (The series is composed of three adjectives: *narrow, crowded,* and *noisy.*

2. **Phrases in a series should be the same parts of speech.**

   Not parallel: The street was at the outskirts of town, along the Peace River, and it wasn't far to walk to a lovely park.
   (The series is composed of two prepositional phrases and one independent clause.)

   Parallel: The street was located at the outskirts of town, along the Peace River, and within walking distance of a lovely park.
   (The series is composed of three prepositional phrases.)

3. **Clauses in a series should be the same parts of speech.**

   Not parallel: The street was narrow, the shops were charming, and crowds in the café.
   (The series is composed of two clauses and one phrase.)

   Parallel: The street was narrow, the shops were charming, and the café was crowded.
   (The series is composed of three clauses.)

• PRACTICE

Each of the following sentences has an underlined word, phrase, or clause that is not parallel. Make the underlined section parallel.

1. The office is spacious, orderly, and <u>everything is clean</u>.

   _____

   _____

2. Her jobs include gathering the data, analyzing the data, and <u>she always prepares the annual report</u>.

   _____

   _____

3. This is the woman who designs stained glass windows, who creates beautiful glass jewellery, and <u>she is making Tiffany style shades for lamps</u>.

   _____

   _____

   _____

EXERCISE 1   Revising Sentences for Parallel Structure

Each of the following sentences needs parallel structure. Underline the word, phrase, or clause that is not parallel and revise it so that its structure will balance with the other items in the pair or series.

1. Rick prefers to make dinner than going out.

   _____

   _____

2. My singing teacher told me to practise every day, breathe deeply, and with a full interpretation.

   _____

   _____

3. Content, good grammar, and to find a signature style are all elements of writing.

   _____

   _____

4. Our apartment is sunny, newly renovated, and has lots of space.

   _____

   _____

5. The subway is crowded, smelly, and the fare is too high.

   _____

   _____

6. However, it beats the bus, taking a cab, or walking.

   _____

   _____

7. At the gym, you can take a class, use the machines, or getting a massage.

   _____

   _____

8. Before you leave, go to the bathroom, wash your hands, and turning out the lights.

   _____

   _____

9. Rachel often goes to the park rather than to stay at home.

   _____

   _____

10. A parent must be loving, patient, and provide a stable environment.

   _____

   _____

EXERCISE 2   Revising Sentences for Parallel Structure

Each of the following sentences needs parallel structure. Underline the word, phrase, or clause that is not parallel and revise it so that its structure will balance with the other items in the pair or series.

1. I want to go to the beach, cruising to the islands, and to the mountains.

   _____

   _____

2. The books must be organized by size, title, and put them in alphabetical order.

   _____

   _____

3. He painted in oils, watercolours, and sometimes using leaves and flowers on the canvases themselves for a three-dimensional effect.

   _____

   _____

4. They would rather drink to your health than to toast that angry man.

   _____

   _____

5. My ancestors came from Ireland, Switzerland, and some say there may be a bit of German.

   _____

   _____

6. Losing weight can be difficult, exhausting, and it can often be bad for your health.

   _____

   _____

7. Catherine may be the greatest actor in the group and can sing, too.

   _____

   _____

8. The garden has grubs and weeds, yet it produces the largest, firmest zucchini that taste the best.

   _____

   _____

9. You are my sister, my friend, and you inspire me.

   _____

   _____

10. Those CDs must be burned, labelled, and then putting away in the locked cabinet.

   _____

   _____

Misplaced and dangling modifiers

Notice how the meaning changes in each of the following sentences, depending on where the modifier *only* is placed:

Only Shirley talked to my sister last night.
Shirley *only* talked to my sister last night.
Shirley talked to *only* my sister last night.
Shirley talked to my *only* sister last night.
Shirley talked to my sister *only* last night.

Modifiers are words or groups of words that function as adjectives or adverbs.

Examples: my *only* sister
the nurse *who is my sister*
only last night

A modifier must be placed close to the word, phrase, or clause that it modifies in order to be understood by the reader.

Misplaced modifiers

Be especially careful in your own writing when you use the words in the following list. They are often misplaced.

MODIFIERS OFTEN MISPLACED				
almost	exactly	just	nearly	scarcely
even	hardly	merely	only	simply

A *misplaced modifier* is a modifier that has been placed in a wrong, awkward, or ambiguous position.

---

1. The modifier is in the wrong place.

   Wrong: The teacher found the missing report of the student *that needed many corrections.*

   Who or what needed correction—the student or the report?

   Revised: The teacher found the student's missing report *that needed many corrections.*

2. The modifier is positioned awkwardly, interrupting the flow of the sentence, as in the following split infinitive.

Awkward: Timothy intended *to only watch* the fight.

The infinitive *to watch* should not be split.

Revised: Timothy *only* intended *to watch* the fight.

3. The modifier is in an ambiguous position; that is, it could describe the word or words on either side of it (sometimes called a *squinting modifier*).

Squinting: The artist having painted other portraits expertly painted the portrait of the well-known leader.

Did she expertly paint other portraits or did she expertly paint the well-known leader? From the wording, the author's meaning is not clear.

Revised: Having expertly painted other portraits, the artist painted the well-known leader.

Dangling modifiers

A *dangling modifier* is a modifier without a word, phrase, or clause that the modifier can describe.

Dangling: Considering a romantic cruise, the brochure promised the couple a memorable trip.

Who is considering a romantic cruise? Is it the brochure or the couple?

Revised: Considering a romantic cruise, the couple read a brochure that promised a memorable trip.

EXERCISE 1   Revising Misplaced or Dangling Modifiers

Revise each sentence so there is no dangling modifier.

1. While writing his novel, the cat begged for food.

   _____

2. Taking a shower, the doorbell rang.

   _____

3. The baby sitter bathed the baby wearing rubber gloves.

   _____

4. Scurrying across the lawn, I noticed a group of rabbits.

   _____

5. After fetching the camera, the owl flew away.

   _____

6. At the age of five, my sister was born.

   _____

7. Bringing work home to finish the project, the teacher gave me extra credit.

   _____

8. Julian admired the ring in the case that cost $200.

   _____

9. I cleaned out the trunk wearing high heels.

   _____

10. She clutched the chair feeling dizzy.

    _____

EXERCISE 2   Revising Misplaced or Dangling Modifiers

Revise each sentence so there is no dangling modifier.

1. Walking down the street, the wind blew the umbrella inside out.

   _____

2. Kim strummed the guitar wandering through the restaurant.

   _____

3. Putting on a tuxedo, Mom said Dad looked very handsome.

   _____

4. While in the laboratory, the sign said "No Smoking."

   _____

5. The butterflies were attracted to Nancy with the blue wings.

   _____

6. Staring intently into the microscope, the microbes finally reproduced.

   _____

7. We have the room with two closets that looks out on the beach.

   _____

8. Sucking her bottle, Mother watched the baby take her first steps.

   _____

9. Hiking in the Rockies, the air was crisp and clean.

   _____

10. Lee consulted the dictionary searching for just the right word.

    _____

Mastery and editing tests

TEST 1   Making Sentence Parts Work Together

Rewrite the following paragraph, correcting any errors you find in agreement, parallel structure, and misplaced or dangling modifiers.

Every living thing has their own unique circumstances: where they live, what they do, interacting with the environment, etc. Of course, no one types of organism live alone. A certain kind of scientist study these organisms and looking specifically at their habitats. They are called ecologists, and the science of studying habitats is called ecology. The word *ecology* comes from two Greek words meaning "study of the home or surroundings." Human beings and ants frequently share environments. We are much bigger than them. Scurrying around on the ground, we frequently step on them or their homes. Likewise, building our homes on "their" ground, ants invade our kitchens as unwelcome guests. Obviously, whomever shares a habitat impacts all the other organisms in that environment. The ecologist's job is to carefully look at how all the other organisms and us interact. They attempt to ensure that none of the organisms who's habitats overlap are harming any others. Ecologists seek to learn the best way of mutual habitation.

_____

_____

_____

_____

_____

_____

_____

_____

_____

_____

_____

_____

_____

_____

_____

_____

_____

_____

_____

_____

TEST 2   Making Sentence Parts Work Together

Rewrite the following paragraph, correcting any errors you find in agreement, parallel structure, and misplaced or dangling modifiers.

When one is sick, they usually are given antibiotics. These type of drug are chemicals that are used to kill microorganisms and helping your body fight disease. Made from tiny living things called microbes, scientists choose particular antibiotics for their ability to produce certain chemicals. These chemicals actually fights disease germs in the body because antibiotic chemicals are stronger than them. These chemicals are produced in large quantities in laboratories that are made into antibiotics and sold in drugstores. Many people now have learned that it is important not to take antibiotics every time you have a cold because microorganisms are growing immune to them. When we really need them, they will be useless to us.

_____

_____

_____

_____

_____

_____

_____

_____

_____

_____

_____

_____

_____

_____

_____

_____

_____

_____

_____

_____

_____

_____

_____

_____

_____

TEST 3   Making Sentence Parts Work Together

Rewrite the following sentences, correcting any errors you find in agreement, parallel structure, and misplaced or dangling modifiers.

1. They say you can't be spoiled or pampered if you're going to live on a working farm.

    _____

    _____

2. If you want to understand what rural life is like, one should try it out for a summer.

    _____

    _____

3. I had my own idealistic views about life in the country, but these sort of views turned out to be incorrect.

    _____

    _____

4. My husband and me lived three years on a farm in Saskatchewan.

    _____

    _____

5. Our friends back in the city had much more leisure time than us.

    _____

    _____

6. We were getting up at five a.m. seven days a week, milking the cows even when we were sick, and we worked throughout the day until the sun set.

    _____

    _____

7. Putting hay into bales in 32 degree heat, the sun proved its power to us.

    _____

    _____

8. We worked among rows and rows of wheat for several hours a day to exactly find out how much our backs could stand.

    _____

    _____

9. Everyone in the city should exchange places with those whom live in the country for at least one month.

_____

_____

10. Rural people they say farm life means working from sun up to sun down, but their lives are satisfying and full.

_____

_____

Chapter 18

Practising More with Verbs

So far in this book, you have already learned a great deal about verbs. In Chapter 11, you learned how to recognize the verb in a sentence. In Chapter 12, you learned that verbs must agree with their subjects. Chapter 13 discussed how to form participles, gerunds, and infinitives from the verb. This chapter will continue your study of verbs by focusing on:

- Principal parts of irregular verbs
- How to use the present perfect and past perfect tenses
- Sequence of tenses
- How to avoid unnecessary shifts in verb tense
- The difference between active or passive voice
- The subjunctive mode
- Correct use of *should* and *would*

What are the principal parts of the irregular verbs?

The English language has more than one hundred verbs that do not form the past tense or past participle with the usual *-ed* ending. Their forms are irregular. When you listen to children aged four or five, you often hear them utter expressions such as "Yesterday I *cutted* myself." Later on, they will hear that the verb "cut" is unusual, and they will change to the irregular form, "Yesterday I *cut* myself." The best way to learn these verbs is to listen to how they sound. You will find an extensive list of these verbs in Appendix B of this book. Pronounce them out loud over and over until you have learned them. If you find that you don't know a particular verb's meaning, or you cannot pronounce a verb and its forms, ask your instructor for help. Most irregular verbs are very common words that you will be using often in your writing and speaking. You will want to know them well.

Practising 50 irregular verbs

THE THREE PRINCIPAL PARTS OF IRREGULAR VERBS		
Simple Form	*Past Form*	*Past Participle*
(also called Infinitive Form)		(used with perfect tenses after, "has," "have," or "will have" or with passive voice after the verb "to be.")
ride	rode	ridden

EIGHT VERBS THAT DO NOT CHANGE THEIR FORMS (NOTICE THEY ALL END IN -T OR -D)		
Simple Form	*Past Form*	*Past Participle*
bet	bet	bet
cost	cost	cost
cut	cut	cut
fit	fit	fit
hit	hit	hit
hurt	hurt	hurt
quit	quit	quit
spread	spread	spread

TWO VERBS THAT HAVE THE SAME SIMPLE PRESENT FORM AND THE PAST PARTICIPLE		
Simple Form	*Past Form*	*Past Participle*
come	came	come
become	became	become

PRACTICE 1

Fill in the correct form of the verb in the following sentences.

(become)　　1.　I _____ ecstatic last week to find out my sister is planning to be married in June.

(hurt)　　　2.　She had been badly _____ in a car accident two years ago.

(come)　　　3.　For more than eight months, her fiancé _____ to the hospital every day.

(cost)　　　4.　The travelling _____ the family a lot of money.

(bet)　　　　5.　In spite of their troubles, I have _____ all my friends that this marriage will last.

TWENTY VERBS THAT HAVE THE SAME PAST FORM AND PAST PARTICIPLE

Simple Form	Past Form	Past Participle
bend	bent	bent
lend	lent	lent
send	sent	sent
spend	spent	spent
creep	crept	crept
keep	kept	kept
sleep	slept	slept
sweep	swept	swept
weep	wept	wept
teach	taught	taught
catch	caught	caught
bleed	bled	bled
feed	fed	fed
lead	led	led
speed	sped	sped
bring	brought	brought
buy	bought	bought
fight	fought	fought
think	thought	thought
seek	sought	sought

PRACTICE 2

In the following paragraph, five verbs are incorrect. Underline them first, and write the correct form on the lines provided.

Last year the fish farmer carefully feeded all of the stock in his tanks. After he catched them, he had a delivery problem. The fish had to be brung to market as quickly as possible. The farmer's trucks speeded to the city. He send his eldest son with the driver.

1. _____

2. _____

3. _____

4. _____

5. _____

TWENTY VERBS THAT HAVE ALL DIFFERENT FORMS		
Simple Form	*Past Form*	*Past Participle*
blow	blew	blown
fly	flew	flown
grow	grew	grown
know	knew	known
throw	threw	thrown
begin	began	begun
drink	drank	drunk
ring	rang	rung
shrink	shrank	shrunk
sink	sank	sunk
sing	sang	sung
spring	sprang	sprung
swim	swam	swum
bite	bit	bitten (or bit)
hide	hid	hidden (or hid)
drive	drove	driven
ride	rode	ridden
stride	strode	stridden
rise	rose	risen
write	wrote	written

PRACTICE 3

Fill in the correct form of the verb in the following sentences.

(fly)   1. As children, we _____ our kites in the fields around our house beginning every April.

(throw)   2. After school in the spring we _____ ourselves completely into the neighbourhood baseball games.

(swim)   3. When summer rolled around, we _____ in the nearby creek.

(ride)   4. Sometimes we _____ our neighbour's horses.

(drink)   5. We played outside and _____ in the sun until mother called us in for dinner.

EXERCISE 1   Irregular Verbs

Supply the past form or the past participle for each verb in parentheses.

1. With an attitude of confidence, the salesperson _____ up the steps of
    (spring)
    the first office building on his new route.

2. He _____ the bell.
    (ring)

3. The job had _____ from a limited area of a few small towns to include
    (grow)
    a sizable city as well.

4. He had _____ for years, but in the city he could use public
    (drive)
    transportation.

5. He _____ all thoughts of past struggles from his mind.
    (sweep)

6. He _____ his case of samples with him on the bus.
    (bring)

7. He had _____ all of the previous evening planning his presentation.
    (spend)

8. Unfortunately he had _____ the company book, *Making a Sale,* to a
    (lend)
    new employee in the company.

9. Luckily, he had _____ all the essential information written down
    (keep)
    in his notebook.

10. He _____ happily how he finally had the chance to show what he
    (think)
    could do.

EXERCISE 2   Irregular Verbs

Rewrite the paragraph below in the past tense.

> Our city has a problem. Tax revenues keep declining. Officials spend a lot of time and effort worrying about the situation. Then it hits them. They do something very dramatic. They seek permission to open a large gambling casino complex. Other cities shrink their deficits when they open gambling casinos. The city council thinks this will sweep away all the city's financial problems. The news of the plan spreads quickly around the city. However, many people know that the gambling casino solution sends citizens a danger-ous message. These citizens fight the proposal with great conviction. The council gradually finds other solutions to the financial troubles.

_____

_____

_____

_____

_____

_____

_____

_____

_____

_____

_____

_____

Appendix B at the back of this book gives an alphabetical listing of nearly every irregular verb. Use that list to supply the correct form for each verb in the fol-lowing exercises.

EXERCISE 1   Practice with More Irregular Verbs

Supply the past form or the past participle for each verb in parentheses.

1. The storm _____ with surprising fury.
   (to strike)

2. Those who could _____ from their homes.
   (to flee)

3. Some were _____ and hid in closets or under mattresses.
   (to stick)

4. In the rush, some people _____ their pets behind.
   (to leave)

5. In many cases, people _____ the roofs of their houses.
   (to lose)

6. Luckily, most had _____ for good insurance.
   (to pay)

7. This second disaster in the same area of the country _____ the
   (to shake)

   citizens' sense of optimism about their future.

8. They _____ discouraged about starting over again.
   (to feel)

9. Those who were in construction _____ some comfort in the
   (to take)

   devastation.

10. This _____ jobs for people rebuilding and replanting.
    (to mean)

EXERCISE 2 Practice with More Irregular Verbs

Rewrite the following paragraph in the past tense.

> He swings the metal detector back and forth. Suddenly he falls to the
> ground and digs for an object in the sand. Later he tells us about all the
> objects he has found. He meets with the owner of the town's resale shop. He
> slides a few gold objects out of his pocket and holds them out to the owner
> for consideration. Eventually he sells some of these to the owner. On a chain
> around his neck, he wears two of the rings he has found. We stand watching
> the transaction and think to ourselves that all of this is quite remarkable for a
> boy who is only seven years old.

_____

_____

_____

_____

_____

_____

_____

_____

_____

_____

_____

_____

_____

_____

How many verb tenses are there in English?

Since the next sections of this chapter concern common problems with tense, a chart of the English Verb Tenses is given in case you want to refer to this list from time to time. Not all languages express time by using exactly the same verb tenses. Students for whom English is a second language know that one of their major tasks in learning English is to understand how to use each of these tenses. Along with the name of each verb tense, the chart gives a sentence using that particular tense.

ENGLISH VERB TENSES	
present	I talk
present continuous	I am talking
present perfect	I have talked
present perfect continuous	I have been talking
past	I talked
past continuous	I was talking
past perfect	I had talked
past perfect continuous	I had been talking
future	I will talk
future continuous	I will be talking
future perfect	I will have talked
future perfect continuous	I will have been talking

Note: The perfect tenses need special attention since they are generally not well understood or used consistently in the accepted way.

How do you use the present perfect and the past perfect tenses?

Forming the perfect tenses

Present perfect tense: *has* or *have* + past participle of the main verb
has studied
have studied

Past perfect tense: *had* + past participle of the main verb
had studied

What do these tenses mean?

The *present perfect tense* describes an action that started in the past and continues to the present time.

Jay *has studied* at the university for four years.

This sentence indicates that Jay began to study at the university four years ago and is still studying there now.

Examine the following time line. What does it tell you about the present perfect tense?

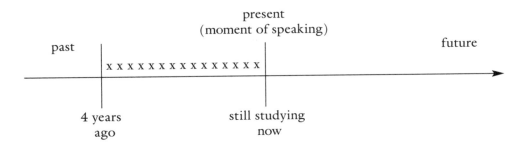

Other example sentences of the present perfect tense:

She *has lived* in this apartment since 1980.

I *have* always *walked* this way to work.

The *present perfect tense* can also describe an action that has just taken place, or an action where the exact time in the past is indefinite.

Has Jay *received* his diploma yet?

Jay *has* (just) *received* his diploma.

Have you ever *been* to the university's art gallery?

No, I *have* never *been* there.

If the time were definite, you would use the simple past:

Jay *received* his diploma last week.

Yes, I *was* there last Tuesday.

The *past perfect tense* describes an action that occurred in the past before another activity or another point of time in the past.

Jay *had studied* at the university for four years *before* he *received* his diploma.

In this sentence, there are two past actions: Jay *studied,* and Jay *received.* The action that took place first is in the past perfect (*had studied*). The action that took place later, and was also completed in the past, is in the simple past (*received*).

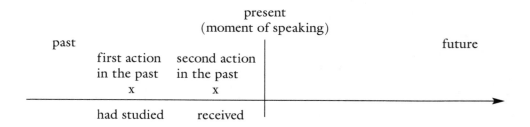

Other example sentences using the past perfect tense:

> I *had* just *finished* dinner when the phone *rang.*
>
> She *claimed* that Rafael *had discovered* a hidden bank account.
>
> He *had given* the account over to the examiner *long before* last week's meeting.

• PRACTICE

Complete each of the following sentences by filling in each blank with either the present perfect tense or past perfect tense of the verb given.

1. My brother _____ a gas-guzzling Ford Bronco.
                      (buy)

2. He _____ a Nissan Micra for seven years before buying a Bronco.
              (own)

3. _____ you ever _____ an SUV?
                                   (drive)

4. No, I _____ never even _____ in one.
                                        (be)

5. My brother's doubts about his new car _____ when he filled up
                                                (begin)
   the gas tank the first time.

What is the sequence of tenses?

The term *sequence of tenses* refers to the proper use of verb tenses in complex sentences (sentences that have an independent clause and a dependent clause).

The following guide shows the relationship between the verb in the independent clause (IC) and the verb in the dependent clause (DC).

SEQUENCE OF TENSES

Independent Clause	*Dependent Clause*	*Time of the DC in Relation to the IC*

If the tense of the independent clause is in the present (He *knows*), here are the possibilities for the dependent clause.

	that she *is* right.	same time
He knows	that she *was* right.	earlier
	that she *will be* right.	later

If the tense of the independent clause is in the past (He *knew*), here are the possibilities for the dependent clause.

	that she *was* right.	same time
He knew	that she *had been* right.	earlier
	that she *would be* right.	later

If the independent clause is in the future (He *will tell*), here are the possibilities for the dependent clause.

	if she *goes*.	same time
He will tell us	if she *has gone*.	earlier
	if she *will go*.	later

EXERCISE   Sequence of Tenses

In each of the following sentences, choose the correct verb tense for the verb in the dependent clause. Use the guide above if you need help.

1. If the artists <u>will donate</u> more of their work, the funding for the arts program _____ .
   (continue)

2. Educators <u>believe</u> that computers _____ placed in every school in the
   (to be + soon)
   country.

3. Thirty years ago, fans of the Beatles <u>did not realize</u> that one day the group _____ for a new generation of music lovers.
   (return)

4. The judge <u>did not know</u> that the witness _____ the truth at yesterday's
   (tell)
   news conference.

5. The mother <u>knew</u> from experience that her child _____ to go swim-
   (want)
   ming right after lunch.

6. The supervisor <u>realizes</u> the employee _____ his job in a few weeks.
   (lose)

7. Some federal politicians <u>want</u> divorce to be more difficult; this _____ (encourage) more couples to stay together.

8. He <u>found out</u> yesterday that the landlady _____ (raise) his rent while he was on vacation.

9. The movie director <u>thinks</u> that he _____ (make) a mistake in hiring that actress last autumn.

10. The parent <u>suspected</u> that the child _____ (take) the gum from her purse.

Avoid unnecessary shift in verb tense

Do not shift verb tenses as you write unless you intend to change the time of the action.

Shifted tense: The student *requested* (past tense) the research material again, but the librarian *informs* (present tense) him that the materials *are* (present tense) not yet available.

Revised: The student *requested* (past tense) the research material again, but the librarian *informed* (past tense) him that the materials *were* (past tense) not yet available.

Note: An exception to this occurs when the subject is a creative work such as a book, play, poem, or piece of music. In this case the present tense is always used to indicate the work is still in existence today.

The Rez Sisters remains (present tense) a frequently performed play. It <u>was</u> written by Tomson Highway.

Oedipal Dreams is (present tense) a widely read book of poetry. It <u>was</u> written by Evelyn Lau.

EXERCISE 1   Correcting Unnecessary Shift in Verb Tense

Each sentence has an unnecessary shift in verb tense. Revise each sentence so that the tense remains consistent.

1. While driving in heavy traffic, the bus driver was blinded by the sun and strikes a parked car.

   _____

   _____

2. At the start of the examination, I was nervous and unsure of myself; by the end, I am smiling and feeling pretty good.

   _____

   _____

3. The flutist performs perfectly as always and enchanted the audience.

   _____

   _____

4. After we make the change on your application, we placed a copy into your file.

   _____

   _____

5. The editorial criticized the politician, but in my opinion, it doesn't go far enough.

   _____

   _____

6. She was feeling healthy until she suddenly comes down with chicken pox.

   _____

   _____

7. The officer demanded that the recruits be up by 5 a.m. and that they will be ready to leave by 5:15.

   _____

   _____

8. He walks up to his partner and gave him the good news.

   _____

   _____

9. In the documentary, several people talk about meeting Pierre Trudeau; they recalled his charismatic personality.

   _____

   _____

10. Her research was going fine when she goes and quits the course.

    _____

    _____

EXERCISE 2   Correcting Unnecessary Shift in Verb Tense

The following paragraphs contain unnecessary shifts in verb tense. Change each incorrect verb to its proper form.

Before he died in July 2001, Mordecai Richler leaves a wealthy legacy to Canadian literature. Born in 1931, Richler was the son of a scrap-metal dealer. In many of his early novels, he writes about life on St. Urbain Street, which was the heart of the working-class Jewish community in Montreal during the 1930s and 1940s. During his career as one of Canada's most prolific writers, he goes on to win several national and international prizes for his novels and essays. He also wins Canada's Stephen Leacock Award for Humour and was appointed to the Order of Canada. Family was always very important to him. His five children probably inspire him to write the famous children's story *Jacob Two-Two Meets the Hooded Fang.*

He lives in London, England, for many years before returning to Montreal to live and work. *The Apprenticeship of Duddy Kravitz,* his most famous novel, is turned into a movie starring Richard Dreyfus. Richler is always a defender of the principles of freedom of speech and equality among people. In 1992, he angers many Quebeckers with his essay *Oh, Canada! Oh, Quebec!* In this essay, he accused many French-Canadian nationalists of being anti-Semitic. Richler goes on to write many other essays on topics as varied as his travels in Morocco to biographies of hockey and baseball players. In fact, he loves sports so much that in an acceptance speech for a literary award he jokingly acknowledges he would never win the one award that really means a lot to him: baseball's Cy Young award.

Mordecai Richler had left us a great legacy in the form of his novels and essays. His humour and sarcasm would be greatly missed by all Canadians.

_____

_____

_____

_____

_____

_____

_____

_____

_____

_____

_____

_____

_____

_____

_____

_____

_____

_____

_____

_____

_____

_____

_____

_____

What is the difference between passive and active voice?

> **PASSIVE AND ACTIVE VOICE**
>
> In the *active voice*, the subject does the acting:
>
> The board prepared the budget.
>
> **Choose the active voice generally in order to achieve direct, economical, and forceful writing. Most writing, therefore, should be in the active voice.**
>
> In the *passive voice*, the subject is acted upon:
>
> The budget was prepared by the board.
>
>   or
>
> The budget was prepared.
>
> Notice in these passive sentences, the actor is not only de-emphasized by moving out of the subject place but may be omitted entirely from the sentence.
>
> **Choose the passive voice to de-emphasize the actor or to avoid naming the actor altogether.**

Discuss the following sentences with your classmates and instructor. All three sentences state the fact of Thomas Scott's execution by Louis Riel. What makes each sentence different from the other two? By choosing a particular sentence, what would the writer be emphasizing?

1. Louis Riel, the leader of the Métis in Manitoba, tried and executed Thomas Scott in 1870.

2. Thomas Scott was tried and executed by Louis Riel in 1870.

3. Thomas Scott was tried and executed in 1870.

How do you form the passive voice?

Subject Acted Upon	+ Verb "To Be"	+ Past Participle	+ "by" Phrase (Optional)
The award	was	presented	(by the mayor)
The dress	had been	designed	(by Oscar de la Renta)
The money	is	collected	(by volunteers)

EXERCISE 1   Active and Passive Voice

Fill in the following chart by showing how the sentences in the active voice could be put into passive voice and how the sentences in the passive voice could be put into the active voice. Then discuss with your classmates and instructor the circumstances under which you would choose active or passive voice to express these ideas.

Active Voice	Passive Voice
1. The jury announced the verdict after five hours of deliberation.	1. _____ _____ _____
2. _____ _____	2. Modern pop music was created by Elvis Presley.
3. The sleet turned the old municipal building into an ice castle.	3. _____ _____ _____
4. _____ _____ _____	4. The priceless vase was smuggled by someone out of the country.
5. _____ _____ _____ _____ _____ _____	5. More attention and concern were shown by television viewers over the Stanley Cup Finals than over the provincial election in which two contentious candidates were involved.

EXERCISE 2   Active and Passive Voice

Fill in the following chart by showing how the sentences in the active voice could be put into passive voice and how the sentences in the passive voice could be put into the active voice. Then discuss with your classmates and instructor the circumstances under which you would choose active or passive voice to express these ideas.

Active Voice	Passive Voice
1. _____ _____ _____	1. The plans for peace were announced by the three world leaders.
2. _____ _____ _____	2. From the 8th to the 11th century, Spain was dominated by the Moors.

Active Voice	Passive Voice
3. The sun melted the ice, which fell in huge chunks off the bridge.	3. _____ _____ _____
4. _____ _____	4. The poem was written by Irving Layton in 1962.
5. Daniella borrowed a pickup truck to move her furniture to the new apartment.	5. _____ _____ _____

What is the subjunctive?

> The *subjunctive* is an as yet unrealized situation.

Recognize the three instances that call for the subjunctive and note the form of the verb that is used in each case.

1. Unreal conditions using *if* or *wish*, use *were:*

   If John were my brother, I would give him my advice.

   I *wish* he were my brother.

2. Clauses starting with *that* after verbs such as *ask, request, demand, suggest, order, insist,* or *command,* use the infinitive form of the verb:

   I *requested* that John bring his report.

   The family *demanded* that every document be exhibited.

3. Clauses starting with *that* after adjectives expressing urgency, as in *it is necessary, it is imperative, it is urgent, it is important,* and *it is essential,* use the infinitive form of the verb:

   It is important he be on time.

   It is imperative that he answer every question truthfully.

In each of these three instances, notice that the verb following the italicized word or phrase does not agree with its subject.

• PRACTICE

In the following sentences, circle the word or phrase that calls for using the subjunctive. Then choose the correct form of the verb. An example follows:

The college insisted that the rules be followed.

1. Mika wishes she (was, were) ready for the exam.

2. Her teacher suggested that she (waits, wait) until next semester to take it.

3. The college requires that everybody (takes, take) a writing proficiency test.

4. It is necessary she (passes, pass) this test in order to graduate in May.

5. If she (was, were) wise, she would devote herself to the preparation for this test.

Confusions with *should* and *would*

Do not use more than one modal auxiliary *(can, may, might, must, should, ought)* with the main verb.

Incorrect: Magdalene *shouldn't ought* to borrow more money.
Correct: Magdalene *shouldn't* borrow more money.

or

Magdalene *ought* not borrow more money.

Do not use *should of, would of,* or *could of* to mean *should have, would have,* or *could have.*

Incorrect: The caller *would of* told you if he had known the answer.
Correct: The caller *would have* told you if he had known the answer.

Mastery and editing tests

TEST 1   Solving Problems with Verbs

Revise each of the following sentences to avoid problems with verbs.

1. If he was my son, I would insist on a complete physical examination.

2. He has broke his arm more than once playing sports.

3. When he first begun to play hockey, his mom had worried.

4. They could of won the game if they had concentrated more.

5. The coach said that the teachers were attending the game tonight.

6. We hadn't ought to judge others.

7. The guest requested that the room is ready.

8. The blood stained the uniform. (Change to passive.)

9. I drunk the entire quart of lemonade before the game.

10. One team member weeped when they lost the championship.

TEST 2

Solving Problems with Verbs

Revise each of the following sentences to avoid problems with verbs.

1. Her family organized every detail of the wedding. (Change to passive voice.)
2. It was necessary that the mother makes the wedding gown.
3. The occasion requires that each detail is just right.
4. By the time the bride arrived, the guests are seated.
5. Most of the food was brung by the family to the reception hall.
6. If it was baked carefully, the cake would be delicious.
7. The wedding gifts were hid under a table covered with a long tablecloth.
8. She threw the bouquet to her sister.
9. Her brothers sweeped up the hall after the reception.
10. They should of taken more pictures on their honeymoon.

TEST 3

Solving Problems with Verbs

Edit the following paragraph to correct all errors with verbs. Use all that you have learned about verbs in this chapter.

I have avoided the dentist long enough. The day comes when I picked up the phone and made an appointment. The secretary should of been surprised to hear my voice, but if she was, she soon has recovered and tells me I had to wait a week for their first opening. I insisted that she gives me an appointment early in the morning. Every night after that I fall asleep and dreamed I see the dentist leaning over me and talking about "the first opening." By the time the day arrived, I feel scared. Arriving at the office, I see the white uniforms and all the gleaming equipment. My heart sinks. The receptionist smiles and takes me to one of the small rooms, but I did not feel comfortable. The large dentist's chair fills the room. As I sit there, the room becomes more and more like a cell. The venetian blinds looked like bars against the grey sky. I have sat there in solitary confinement for what seemed like years. Then the dentist came in. She is so charming that nearly all my fears have vanished.

Using Correct Capitalization and Punctuation

Ten basic rules for capitalization

Many people are often confused or careless about the use of capital letters. Sometimes writers capitalize words without thinking, or they capitalize "important" words without really understanding what makes them important enough to deserve a capital letter. The question of when to capitalize words becomes easier to answer when you study the following rules and carefully apply them to your own writing.

1. Capitalize the first word of every sentence.
2. Capitalize the names of specific things and places.

   Specific buildings:

   > The singer performed in Jack Singer Hall.
   >
   > *but*
   >
   > The singer performed in the concert hall.

   Specific streets, cities, provinces, countries:

   > He lives on Colonial Road.
   >
   > *but*
   >
   > He lives on a road near our farm.

   Specific organizations:

   > Martha donates clothes to the Red Cross.
   >
   > *but*
   >
   > Martha contributes to several charities.

   Specific institutions:

   > Ellen borrowed money from the University Credit Union.
   >
   > *but*
   >
   > Dominic went to a credit union for his car loan.

Specific bodies of water:

My cousins spend every vacation at Lake Winnipeg.

but

My cousins spend every vacation at the lake.

3. Capitalize days of the week, months of the year, and holidays. Do not capitalize the names of seasons.

The first Monday in September is Labour Day.

but

My favourite season is autumn.

4. Capitalize the names of all languages, nationalities, races, religions, deities, and sacred terms.

Veronique, who is Haitian, speaks Creole.

The Dead Sea Scrolls tell us much about ancient Judaism.

5. Capitalize the first word and every important word in a title. Do not capitalize articles, prepositions, or short connecting words in the title.

All the Anxious Girls on Earth is a novel written by Zsuzsi Gartner.

Her favourite short story is "The Lost Salt Gift of Blood."

6. Capitalize the first word of a direct quotation.

The minister said, "You are my official representative."

but

"You are," the minister said, "my official representative."

Note: *my* is not capitalized because it is not the beginning of the sentence in quotation marks.

7. Capitalize historical events, periods, and documents.

The French and Indian War

The Roaring Twenties

The Code of Hammurabi

8. Capitalize the words north, south, east, and west when they are used as places rather than as directions.

She was born in the East.

but

Their house is two kilometres east of ours.

9. Capitalize people's names.

Proper names:

   Elaine James

Professional titles when they are used with the person's proper name:

| Mayor Jean Drapeau | *but* | the mayor |
| Councillor Jane Watson | *but* | the councillor |

Term for a relative (such as mother, sister, nephew, uncle) when it is used in the place of the proper name:

   I invited Mother to attend.

   Note: terms for relatives are not capitalized if a pronoun, article, or adjective is used with the name.

   I invited my mother to attend.

10. Capitalize brand names.

| Kraft Peanut Butter | *but* | peanut butter |
| Philadelphia Cream Cheese | *but* | cream cheese |

EXERCISE 1   Capitalization

Read the paragraph and insert capitalization wherever necessary.

Although st. valentine died long before explorers to north america brought chocolate back to europe, it is easy to see the connection between chocolate and valentine's day. To begin with, the origin of our modern valentine's day as a celebration of love is in the middle ages. In england and france, it was believed that birds began to mate around february 14, a day that corresponds with st. valentine's day. This phenomenon was reported by the english poet geoffrey chaucer in his poem "parliament of fowles." Explorers brought chocolate to europe from the ancient aztecs, who considered it an aphrodisiac. They lived in what is now mexico. Back then, most chocolate was consumed in liquid form and was not sweetened with sugar. It looked and tasted nothing like our hershey's or cadbury chocolate bars. When it was first introduced to europeans, chocolate was considered a barbarous and noxious drug until the doctors in paris approved it as a beneficial potion. The europeans also heard the stories about how the aztec king montezuma drank the dark liquid chocolate all day to enhance his sex drive. Chocolate then became the perfect gift to celebrate love. But given a choice between love and chocolate, many people would rather have chocolate.

EXERCISE 2 Capitalization

Read the paragraph and insert capitalization wherever necessary.

Environmental groups have been busy putting pressure on governments to enact laws that will allow people to see a clear sky during the day. Only recently, however, have people proposed measures that will protect the night sky. After world war II, the growing population and development in the countryside meant more light everywhere. The night sky around a typical town such as penticton, british columbia, is more than ten times as bright as the natural night sky. The light over cities such as toronto and vancouver is nearly fifty times as bright as the natural light. the problem for astronomers is obvious. Astronomers at the rothney astrophysical observatory (canada's third largest observatory), located 25 kilometres from calgary, amateur astronomers, and others who dislike light pollution were thrilled to learn that the city of calgary is proposing to refit residential street lights with lower-wattage lamps so that there is no direct horizontal glare. the city has suffered very bad light pollution for many decades, making it readily visible on the "earth at night" satellite photo. Lighting bylaws have also been passed by the nearby towns of cochrane and okotoks. The desire to reduce carbon-dioxide emissions from power plants and the sharp increase in the price of electricity in alberta have caused calgary to consider using lighting more wisely.

Eight basic uses of the comma

You may feel uncertain about when to use the comma. The starting point is to concentrate on a few basic rules. These rules will cover most of your needs.

The tendency now in English is to use fewer commas than in the past. There is no one perfect complete set of rules on which everyone agrees. However, if you learn these basic eight, your common sense will help you figure out what to do in other cases. Remember that a comma usually signifies a pause in a sentence. As you read a sentence out loud, listen to where you pause within the sentence. Where you pause is often your clue that a comma is needed. Notice that in each of the examples for the following eight uses, you can pause where the comma is placed.

1. **Use a comma to separate items in a series (more than two items).**

    My friend is calm, helpful, and patient.

    She never loses her temper, never refuses to lend a hand, and never judges people harshly.

    • Some writers omit the comma before the *and* that introduces the last item.

    My friend is calm, helpful and patient.

    • When an address or date occurs in a sentence, each part is treated like an item in a series. A comma is put after each item, including the last:

    They moved to 20 King Street, Tinker's Creek, Prince Edward Island, last month.

    The twins were born October 13, 1993, in a taxicab.

- A group of adjectives may not be regarded as a series if some of the words "go together." You can test this by putting *and* between each item. If you can put *and* between two adjectives, use a comma.

  The balloon rose in the cloudless, deep blue sky.

The words *deep blue* go together. You would not say *a deep and blue sky* because *deep* is meant to qualify the colour blue. Therefore, you cannot separate the two adjectives with a comma. However, you could say *a cloudless and deep blue sky*. The lack of clouds is a separate issue from the colour of the sky. Therefore, a comma should separate *cloudless* from *deep blue*.

• PRACTICE 1

In each of the following sentences, insert commas wherever they are needed.

1. People who get enough sleep are more rested alert and focused than those who have stayed up late the night before.

2. The need for sleep varies according to age: ten to twelve hours for children nine hours for teenagers seven and a half hours for adults up to age sixty and about six and a half hours for those over sixty.

3. Our muscles relax during light sleep relax even more in deeper sleep and stop activity completely in what is called "dream sleep."

4. Have you ever seen the telltale dark blue circles under the eyes of people who regularly go without sufficient sleep?

5. Call the Genealogy and Family History Department National Library of Canada Ottawa for more information about your family's history.

2. **Use a comma along with a coordinating conjunction to combine two simple sentences (also called independent clauses) into a single compound sentence. (See Chapter 14 on coordination.)**

   The survey was brief, but the questions were carefully phrased.

   Be careful that you use the comma with the conjunction only when you are combining sentences. If you are combining only words or phrases, no comma is used:

   The survey was brief but carefully phrased.

   The weather and sports followed the news.

   She was either on the telephone or in the shower.

• PRACTICE 2

In each of the following sentences, insert commas wherever they are needed.

1. Olive oil is a very common ingredient for cooking but people do not realize the range of differences among the many kinds of olive oil.

2. You may choose an inexpensive olive oil from your supermarket or you might buy a bottle for as much as $35 at a fancy-food shop.

3. Most good olive oils are from Italy yet there are fine oils from other countries.

4. Betty Pustarfi is devoted to the virtues of olive oil and she can be found conducting free tastings of as many as twenty oils from many countries every Saturday morning.

5. At her tastings, Ms. Pustarfi provides detailed sheets to explain the properties of olive oil and the characteristics of each oil in the tasting.

3. **Use a comma to follow introductory words, expressions, phrases, or clauses.**

   A. Introductory words (such as *yes, no, oh, well*)

   Yes, I'll be there.

   B. Introductory expressions (transitions such as *as a matter of fact, finally, secondly, furthermore, consequently*)

   As a matter of fact, I plan to arrive early.

   C. Introductory phrases

Long prepositional phrase:	For the psychology of his characters, the writer draws on his own experience.
Participial phrase:	Working without an outline, she needs to make many revisions.
Infinitive phrase:	To be sure, a writer needs imagination.

   D. Introductory dependent clauses beginning with a subordinating conjunction (see Chapter 15)

   When the food arrived, we all grabbed for it.

   When the first draft is written, it is far from perfect.

PRACTICE 3

In each of the following sentences, insert commas wherever they are needed.

1. For many companies in the twenty-first century a revised dress code for employees is an idea whose time has come.

2. Taking a hint from large corporations companies of every size are relaxing the rules of dress.

3. To keep in step with the times employers want to appear flexible and up to date.

4. If an employee wants to "dress down" on a certain day the new rules allow this freedom of choice.

5. Yes the more casual atmosphere of the workplace is a welcome change for many people.

4. **Use commas surrounding a word, phrase, or clause when the word (or group of words) interrupts the main idea.**

   A. Interrupting word

       Jeff has, therefore, changed his plans.

   B. Interrupting phrase

       Jeff has, in this case, changed his plans.

       Jeff, my uncle's stepson, has changed his plans.

   C. Interrupting clause

       Jeff has, I am told, changed his plans.

       Jeff, who is my cousin, has changed his plans.

   Note: Sometimes the same word, phrase, or clause can be used in more than one way. Often this changes the rule for punctuation.

       Example: The word *therefore*

   Use commas if the word interrupts in the middle of a clause:

       Jeff has, therefore, changed his plans.

   Use a semicolon and a comma if the word connects two independent clauses:

       Jeff has won the scholarship; therefore, he has changed
       his plans.

       Example: The relative clause beginning with *who*

   Use commas if the clause interrupts and is not essential to the main idea:

       Jeff, who is my cousin, has changed his plans.

   Do not use commas if the clause is part of the identity, necessary to the main idea:

       The student who has won the scholarship is my cousin.

   The clause *who has won the scholarship* is necessary for identifying which student is the cousin.

•PRACTICE 4

In each of the following sentences, insert commas wherever they are needed.

1. Politics and public relations it must be admitted have become harder to separate.

2. Political commercials on television for example depend heavily on the use of images.

3. Ottawa, Ontario usually a political centre becomes a centre for advertising campaigns during every federal election.

4. Political debate which used to appeal to people's thinking now must use dramatic images.

5. Every voter however must make up his or her own mind how to vote.

5. Use a comma around nouns in direct address. (A noun in direct address is the name or title used in speaking to someone.)

I tell you this, Rebecca, in strictest confidence.

• PRACTICE 5

In each of the following sentences, insert commas wherever they are needed.

1. Doctor the lab results came today.

2. I hope dear that you know what you're doing.

3. Sir the taxi is waiting.

4. You don't Mother understand my point.

5. Theresa are you ready?

6. Use a comma in numbers of one thousand or larger when following the imperial system of measurement (as opposed to the metric system).

2,555

2,555,555

• PRACTICE 6

In each of the following numbers, insert commas wherever they are needed.

1. 10000000

2. 504321

3. 684977509

4. 20561

5. 9999999999

7. Use a comma to set off exact words spoken in dialogue.

"I've always depended," Blanche said, "on the kindness of strangers."

• The comma as well as the period is always placed inside the quotation marks.

•PRACTICE 7

In each of the following sentences, insert commas wherever they are necessary.

1. "Joan didn't" they explained "do an adequate job."

2. She declared "I did exactly what I was told to do."

3. "The truth of the matter is" the publisher admitted "we can't use her work."

4. "Shall the company" we ask "be forced to pay for poor quality work?"

5. The judge said "The contract must be upheld."

8. Use a comma where it is necessary to prevent a misunderstanding.

Meaning is unclear: Before slicing the cooks must wash their hands.
In this case, the reader at first thinks the cooks are being sliced up.

Meaning is clear: Before slicing, the cooks must wash their hands.

•PRACTICE 8

In each of the following sentences, insert commas wherever they are needed.

1. Striking the workers picketed the factory.

2. For Mike Mary Elizabeth Grace is his favourite poet.

3. Honking the driver alerted the biker.

4. The procedure does not hurt the child says.

5. Whatever that was was certainly strange.

EXERCISE 1   Using the Comma Correctly

Edit the following paragraph by inserting commas wherever needed.

For most people things don't get much smaller than the microscopic level but researchers at Carleton University in Ottawa Ontario are envisaging a new wave of technological devices that operate at the submicroscopic level. Nanoscience and nanotechnology refer to any activity dealing with objects measured in nanometres. Laid side by side four individual atoms of copper would measure about one nanometre. That's really really small stuff! The goal of nanoscience is in fact to create technological devices that would be able to manipulate individual atoms and create material at the molecular level. By the year 2100 people think that nanotechnology will become a normal part of life. If people wanted to build something out of steel they could release millions of nano-sized robots called nano-bots into a junkyard to scavenge iron steel and copper. They could then build the desired structure atom by atom. The medical applications which are nothing short of miraculous are even more astounding. Imagine being able to operate on a deadly form of cancer by releasing nano-devices into a patient's blood stream programming them to find the tumour and then having them destroy it one molecule at a time. There are nano-nightmares too. Imagine for a moment what might happen if someone forgets to include an off switch on these armies of nano-bots.

EXERCISE 2   Using the Comma Correctly

Edit the following paragraph by inserting commas wherever needed.

Naomi Klein is a 31-year-old writer and journalist who has made a career out of documenting criticizing and fighting against the growing intrusion of corporations in our lives. In her books and newspaper columns Klein states that huge corporations such as Nike Microsoft Coca-Cola and others with famous brands and instantly recognizable logos are trying to dominate our common culture and public spaces. They do this Klein argues by filling the world around us with their advertising messages slogans and logos. In fact it is popular today to wear the logos of companies on clothing. Logos have become fashion statements and some people will pay big bucks to wear a Nike swoosh on their hats a Puma on their shoes or a Gap logo on their T-shirts. Many of these products which sell for lots of money in Canada are made by child labourers who work for less than two dollars a day. Across Canada however more and more young people are listening carefully to Klein's words. Look for example at what happened in Toronto recently. Students protested the invasion of corporate brand names into their schools especially Pepsi Cola which has an exclusive contract to sell its products to almost 600 public schools in Toronto. In some cases the students were disciplined by the school board but many teachers have become sympathetic to the students' cause.

Three uses for the apostrophe

1. To form the possessive:

    A. Add *'s* to singular nouns:

the pen of the teacher	= the teacher*'s* pen
the strategy of the boss	= the boss*'s* strategy
the work of the week	= the week*'s* work

    Watch out that you choose the right noun to make possessive. Always ask yourself *who* or *what* possesses something. In the sentences above, the teacher possesses the pen, the boss possesses the strategy, and the week possesses the work.

    Note these unusual possessives:

    Hyphenated words: father-in-law*'s* business

    Joint possession: Ronald and Nancy*'s* children

    Individual possession: Marcia*'s* and Christopher*'s* opinions

    B. Add *'s* to irregular plural nouns that do not end in *-s*.

the games of the children	= the children*'s* games
the court for the people	= the people*'s* court

C. Add *'s* to indefinite pronouns:

anybody's guess

someone's mistake

INDEFINITE PRONOUNS

anyone	everyone	no one	someone
anybody	everybody	nobody	somebody
anything	everything	nothing	something

Possessive pronouns in English (his, hers, its, ours, yours, theirs, whose) do *not* use an apostrophe.

Whose jacket is this?

The jacket is *hers.*

The jackets are *theirs.*

D. Add an apostrophe only to regular plural nouns ending in -s.

the mothers of the babies   = the babies' mothers

the company of the brothers   = the brothers' company

- A few singular nouns ending in the *s* or *z* sound are awkward-sounding if another *s* sound is added. You may drop the final *s*. Let your ear help you make the decision.

Jesus' robe *not* Jesus's robe

Moses' law *not* Moses's law

2. To form certain plurals in order to prevent confusion, use *'s.*

A. Numbers: 100's

B. Letters: *a*'s and *b*'s

C. Years: 1800's or 1800s

D. Abbreviations: Ph.D.'s

E. Words referred to in a text: He uses too many *and's* in his writing.

- Be sure *not* to use the apostrophe to form a plural in any case other than these.

3. To show where letters have been omitted in contractions, use an apostrophe.

cannot   = can't

should not   = shouldn't

will not   = won't (the only contraction that changes its spelling)

I am   = I'm

she will   = she'll

EXERCISE 1   Using the Apostrophe

Fill in each of the blanks below, using the rules you have just studied for uses of the apostrophe.

1. the armour of the knight   the _____ armour

2. the stride of the runner   the _____ stride

3. the choir of the children   the _____ choir

4. the work of the girls   the _____ work

5. the plans of the architects   the _____ plans

6. the footprints of a bear   the _____ footprints

7. the home of John and Marlene   _____ home

8. I will not answer you.   I _____ answer you.

9. You have not told me yet.   You _____ told me yet.

10. the opinions of the mother-in-law   the _____ opinions.

EXERCISE 2   Using the Apostrophe

Rewrite each of the following sentences using an apostrophe to make a contraction or to show possession. An example follows:

The <u>title of the book</u> is *Reviving Ophelia*.

The <u>book's title is</u> *Reviving Ophelia*.

1. <u>What is happening</u> to the lives of our girls when they enter puberty?

   _____

   _____

2. <u>It does not work</u> to use the experience of any previous generation of women; girls today live in a different world.

   _____

   _____

3. <u>Reports from therapists</u> detail a tremendous increase of serious and even life-threatening problems among junior high girls.

   _____

   _____

4. The author and therapist Mary Pipher believes that <u>girls of today</u> are being poisoned by our media-saturated culture.

_____

_____

5. She claims that North America today limits <u>development of our teenagers</u>.

_____

_____

6. At puberty, girls crash into <u>the junk culture of our society</u>.

_____

_____

7. Girls know something is wrong, but they do not think of blaming it on <u>the cultural problems of society</u>; they tend to blame themselves or their own families.

_____

_____

8. <u>The lives of our adolescent girls</u> are filled with pressures to be beautiful and sophisticated; this translates into junior high girls becoming involved with chemicals and being sexual.

_____

_____

9. <u>The advice from several national leaders</u> is unmistakably clear.

_____

_____

10. <u>The environment of our culture</u> must be more nurturing and less violent and sexualized.

_____

_____

Other marks of punctuation

Four uses for quotation marks

1. For a direct quotation:

   "Certainly," he answered, "you may wait in the lobby."

   Not for an indirect quotation:

   He said that she could wait in the lobby.

2. For material copied word for word from a source:

   In *Canadian Geographic* magazine, the scientist noted, "The danger from asteroids crashing into earth is very remote."

3. For titles of shorter works such as short stories, one-act plays, poems, articles in magazines and newspapers, songs, essays, and chapters of books:

> "The Archetypes of Literature," an essay by Northrop Frye, is a Canadian masterpiece.

> "The Love of a Good Woman" is one of my favourite short stories.

4. For words used in a special way:

> "Lift" is the word used in England for an "elevator."

Underlining

> Underlining is used in handwriting or typing to indicate a title of a long work such as a book, full-length play, magazine, or newspaper. (In print, such titles are put in italics.)

In type or handwriting: Many interviews with writers appear in <u>Poets and Writers.</u>

In print: Many interviews with writers appear in *Poets and Writers*.

PRACTICE 1

In each of the following sentences, insert quotation marks or underlining wherever needed.

1. Edgar Allan Poe's The Raven was first published in the Evening Mirror in 1845.

2. In one of his plays, Shakespeare asks, What's in a name?

3. The nurse said that the patient would have to return in a week.

4. A groupie is a person who follows popular musicians from place to place.

5. Margaret Atwood's essay CanLit Crash Course appeared in the book Survival.

Three uses for the semicolon

1. To join two independent clauses whose ideas and sentence structure are related:

> He did not vote in the provincial election; he did vote in the federal election.

2. To combine two sentences using an adverbial conjunction:

> He did not vote in the provincial election; however, he did vote in the federal election.

3. To separate items in a series when the items themselves contain commas:

The mayor met with Frank Burns, Chief of Police; Shelia MacKaye, Press Officer; and James Wheatley, Crown Attorney.

If the writer had used only commas to separate items in the last example, the reader might think six people had met with the mayor.

•PRACTICE 2

In each of the following sentences, insert a semicolon or comma wherever needed.

1. Walking in the city can be stimulating relaxing in a park can be refreshing.

2. The car needs a new alternator now otherwise you could break down at any time.

3. The children spent the entire day watching *All Dogs Go to Heaven* a comedy *The Little Mermaid* an animated Disney movie and *Heidi* a classic starring Shirley Temple.

4. The town made an effort to attract tourists as a result its financial situation has improved.

5. The teacher was very patient however the paper was due last week.

Four uses for the colon

1. After a completed independent clause (often using the expressions *the following* or *as follows*) when the material that follows is a list, an illustration, or an explanation:

A. A list:

Please bring the following items: binoculars, camera, and film.

Notice colons are not used in the middle of clauses in which such expressions as *consists of, including, like,* or *such as* introduce a list.

Please bring items such as binoculars, camera, and film.

B. An explanation or illustration:

He came up the hard way: he started in the mail room.

2. For the salutation of a business letter:

To whom it may concern:

Dear Personnel Director:

3. In telling time:

The plane departs at 10:55 a.m.

4. Between the title and subtitle of a book:

Images of Canada: Canadian Banknotes

• PRACTICE 3

In each of the following sentences, insert colons as needed.

1. Three inventions have changed our lives in this century electricity, the airplane, and television.

2. The sport's fan had only one problem how to get the player's autograph.

3. She looked for a copy of *Pretty Like a White Boy Confessions of a Blue-Eyed Ojibway*.

4. She promised she would be on the 1018 from Moncton.

5. I need several items such as paper clips, tape, and a stapler.

The dash and parentheses

The comma, dash, and parentheses can all be used to show an interruption of the main idea. The particular form you choose depends on the degree of interruption.

> Use the dash for a less formal and more emphatic interruption of the main idea.

He wrote—I discovered—in code.

The prime minister spoke—and I recall this clearly—without any notes.

> Use the parentheses to insert extra information that some of your readers might want to know but that is not at all essential for the main idea. Such information is not emphasized.

Emily Carr (1871–1945) was a Canadian landscape painter and writer.

The contract clearly shows (see the last clause) that our position is valid.

• PRACTICE 4

Insert dashes or parentheses wherever needed.

1. He was or so she believed a spy from another company.

2. He will bring us at once and this is really crucial his passport and other documents of identification.

3. The study see the charts on file was completed in 1989.

4. Mary Pickford her real name was Gladys Mary Smith was a famous silent film star.

5. All public figures and I mean actors, politicians, writers, and sports figures must be sensitive to the feelings of every group of people.

EXERCISE 1   Using Other Marks of Punctuation Correctly

In each of the following sentences, insert apostrophes, quotation marks, underlining, semicolons, colons, the dash, or parentheses wherever they are needed.

1. Gordie is the essay Mordecai Richler wrote as a tribute to Gordie Howe.
2. To help your children plan their summer, you must do the following keep their interests in mind, keep an eye on their friends, and keep your budget in view.
3. Writing that letter gave him a lasting emotional satisfaction.
4. The Fall of the Roman Empire 476 A.D. was a critical point in human history.
5. She wanted to rent a car he wanted to go by train.
6. Everything she predicted came true my watch stopped, my car broke down, and it rained that night.
7. Tom Connors also known as Stompin' Tom is well known for writing songs about Canadian folklore.
8. Do you know how to say muchas gracias in any other languages?
9. Maurice Richard also known as The Rocket was one of our country's best hockey players.
10. She gave me her word I remember this clearly that she would call back today.

EXERCISE 2   Using Other Marks of Punctuation Correctly

In each of the following sentences, insert apostrophes, quotation marks, underlining, semicolons, colons, the dash, or parentheses wherever they are needed.

1. She borrowed the book entitled Understanding Media The Extensions of Man.
2. The road leading to success in business depends on two factors a lot of hard work and a little luck.
3. I cannot help you he answered but I will try to be supportive.
4. Her best jewellery the pieces she keeps in the bank came from her grandmother.
5. Mavis Gallant's Between Zero and One is a short story that has led to a lot of interpretations.
6. Movies in fact all parts of the entertainment industry depend on a system of superstars.
7. We refer to that long period after World War II as the Cold War.
8. Einsteins theory of relativity $E=mc^2$ still confuses many people.
9. The band was made up of some fine musicians including Tom Fox, guitar Betty Ahern, bass and Joyce Blake, flute.
10. The bands director called for extra rehearsals.

Mastery and editing tests

TEST 1

Editing for Correct Capitalization and Punctuation

Read the following paragraph and insert the correct marks of punctuation and capitalization wherever they are needed.

It is difficult to comprehend the meaning of terry fox's achievement. he ran a marathon every day across six provinces, for 143 consecutive days, on one leg, to raise money for cancer research. Terry's run called the marathon of hope began in st. john's newfoundland on april 12 1980. He ran across nova scotia prince edward island new brunswick and quebec. Word of his goal and accomplishment began to spread and by the time he reached ottawa huge crowds would gather to catch a glimpse of him. He stopped his run on september 1 1980 at thunder bay ontario because the cancer that had taken his right leg had recurred in his lungs. He died nine months later at the royal columbian hospital in new westminster british columbia. Annual terry fox runs have raised over $270 million since his death. today he is a canadian icon. Streets schools and parks have been named after him however his mother betty fox does not want people to think of him as a hero who did something extraordinary. She prefers people think of him as an ordinary person. She says he was ordinary and average and anybody could do as terry did.

TEST 2

Editing for Correct Capitalization and Punctuation

Read the following paragraph and insert the correct marks of punctuation and capitalization wherever they are needed.

The mother of a young student at the walker elementary school teaches an unusual subject penmanship. The son almost never uses script to write anything. He does sign a card to his mother on three occasions her birthday on valentines day and on mothers day. Like many other people this student is either printing everything letter by letter or using a computer to write. Penmanship today pretty much stops at the printing level says rose matousek of the canadian association of handwriting analysts. The post office reports that only 15 percent of all hand-written envelopes are written in script another 15 percent are hand printed. A related problem reported in macleans magazine is the legibility of what people write. Many pieces of mail end up in the dead letter office of the post office because no one is able to read the handwriting. One researcher reports that 58 percent of all information on hospital charts is also difficult or impossible to read. This is an important fact because a patient who needs seldane but who gets feldene will have a very different reaction. Dont you think handwriting is important when your life depends on it?

TEST 3   Editing for Correct Capitalization and Punctuation

Read the following paragraph and insert the correct marks of punctuation and capitalization wherever they are needed.

Perhaps the most famous comet in the world is halleys comet which visits our part of the universe very rarely. However an even more brilliant visitor to our skies is comet hale-bopp which will be remembered as one of the most spectacular comets of the twentieth century. the comet was discovered on july 23 1995 and the last time it visited the earth was in 1997. Prior to this comet hale-bopp visited the earth around 2214 b.c. and it may even have been depicted in a stone tablet dating from the old babylonian empire. In november 1997 people throughout much of canada could see the comet quite clearly with the naked eye. Some people actually had what they called viewing parties to celebrate the arrival of the comet. astronomers believe that comet hale-bopp came from the oort cloud a vast cloud of dust rock and ice that surrounds our solar system like a halo. They think that there may be over 100 billion comets in this cloud each one waiting for a pull of gravity from the sun. Unfortunately the comet will also be remembered for its association with the death of 40 members of the heaven's gate cult in southern california. These misguided souls were influenced by the rumour that a large ufo was following the comet waiting for earthlings to transport themselves up to it.

Step 3 Review: Using All You Have Learned

Revising more complicated fragments and run-ons

By now, you have learned to recognize the basic fragment or run-on error in your writing. You have worked with revising fairly uncomplicated sentences so that they are correct.

This chapter presents sentences that are more complicated. Even though a sentence may have more than one dependent clause and several phrases, you must always remember that the sentence must have an independent clause with a subject and verb. For example:

> After the investigator examined every part of the engine, which had failed during the airplane's recent Atlantic flight, he suspected that metal fatigue would be the conclusion of the government experts.

Cross out all dependent clauses and phrases. Can you find the independent clause? What is the subject? What is the verb? *He suspected* is the independent clause. All other parts of the sentence are dependent clauses that include many prepositional phrases.

The following exercises require mastery of all the skills you have learned in this unit on the sentence. See if you can now revise these more complicated sentences to rid them of fragments and run-ons.

EXERCISE 1   Correcting Fragments and Run-Ons

Read each of the following examples and mark each one as a fragment (F), a run-on (R), or a complete sentence (C). If an example is a fragment or a run-on, revise it so that it is correct. Use methods you have learned for coordination and subordination.

_____   1. As a child, Gebrselassie, the great long distance runner, shared a pair of running shoes with his older brother, Tekeye, and a younger sister, Yeshi, the family could not afford to buy each one a pair of running shoes.

_____

_____

_____

_____   2. Gebrselassie and his brothers who tended the crops with oxen and wooden plows and they walked up to four miles to haul drinking water from wells.

_____

_____

_____

_____   3. Their father wanting them to be doctors, teachers, clerks, anything but runners and discouraging the sport, believing it had no practical use.

_____

_____

_____

_____   4. When Gebrselassie was ten his mother died during childbirth so his older sister raised the children.

_____

_____

_____

_____   5. Following sports through a battery-powered transistor radio and learning of Ethiopia's Yifter winning a double victory at the 1980 Moscow Olympic Games.

_____

_____

_____

_____   6. Gebrselassie walked or ran six miles to school, and to this day, he has a slight hitch in his form that developed from carrying his books to one side.

_____

_____

_____

_____ 7. Even though Gebrselassie could afford to live in style after he became world famous, he lives in a modest house and routinely goes to bed by 9 P.M. awakening by 5:30 A.M. and goes without a personal coach or a private car because he believes that he should live as his people live.

_____

_____

_____

_____ 8. With five world records and was expected to win the gold in the 5,000 and 10,000 metres at the Atlanta Olympics.

_____

_____

_____

_____ 9. Everyone knows Ethiopia is poor but when Gebrselassie breaks a world record he hopes that people of the world see that Ethiopians do what they can with what they have.

_____

_____

_____

_____ 10. He runs with effortless grace his head is totally still some say he looks like he's out there for a fun run.

_____

_____

_____

EXERCISE 2   Correcting Fragments and Run-Ons

Read each of the following examples and mark each one as a fragment (F), a run-on (R), or a complete sentence (C). If an example is a fragment or a run-on, revise it so that it is correct. Use methods you have learned for coordination and subordination.

_____ 1. The Celtic music as we know it today with its long history.

_____

_____

_____

_____ 2. Celtic music has travelled far.

_____

_____

_____

_____   3. Such as originating in Europe, spreading to the British Isles, coming across the ocean with Scottish and Irish immigrants, and being handed down to young musicians such as Ashley MacIsaac and Natalie MacMaster.

_____

_____

_____

_____   4. Most famous of all, the island of Cape Breton in Nova Scotia was settled by Scottish immigrants who kept a very strong musical tradition.

_____

_____

_____

_____   5. Scottish musicians are now learning the old styles from their Canadian cousins.

_____

_____

_____

_____   6. Ashley MacIsaac's style of Celtic music that reflects new musical influences on old traditions, showing what the fiddle can do, he has performed in folk and rock concerts across the globe.

_____

_____

_____

_____   7. What MacIsaac is doing for the Celtic music tradition is, in essence, what rap and hip hop artists have been doing for the urban soul music of North America.

_____

_____

_____

_____   8. The music of the inner city has had a profound effect on MacIsaac, the other great musical influence is punk rock that was popular in the 1980s.

_____

_____

_____

_____   9. Brenda Stubbert is another fiddle player from Cape Breton she dances as well as plays the piano.

_____

_____

_____

_____   10. A good example of more traditional Celtic folk music.

_____

_____

_____

Mastery and editing tests

TEST 1   **Editing for Errors**

Edit the following paragraph. Hint: you will find an opportunity to correct each of the following:

Punctuation for a compound sentence using coordination

Punctuation for a complex sentence using subordination

Comma after an introductory phrase or clause

Apostrophe for possessive

Apostrophe for contraction

Punctuation for a full-length work of art

Punctuation for an appositive

Punctuation for city and province

Irregular verb form

A run-on

Using just pen and ink Canadian graphic designer Paul Arthur started a communication revolution that spread around the world. Arthur who coined the terms "signage" and "wayfinding" was a pioneer in what has become the international language of pictographs. We can find the pictographs he developed almost everywhere we look. The simple male and female figures that signify mens and womens washrooms were developed by Arthur and they were first used at Expo 67 in Montreal Quebec. The sign designating an area as non-smoking was also drew by him its a cigarette with a red slash going through it. Since these images are almost like an international language they are commonplace in airports around the world. Arthur also designed a book called Toronto No Mean City. Another of his important creations are graphic aids designed to help people find their ways around shopping malls and underground walkways. Its hard to believe how much we have come to rely on Paul Arthurs vision and creativity to communicate and to give us direction.

TEST 2   **Editing for Errors**

Edit the following paragraph. Hint: you will find an opportunity to correct each of the following:

A run-on

Incorrect use of the apostrophe

Fragment

Punctuation for a compound sentence using coordination

Punctuation for a word or phrase that interrupts

Punctuation for a complex sentence using subordination

Capitalization

Punctuation for a series

Subject-verb agreement

Need for parentheses

Many centuries ago, the Chinese pounded together a mixture of rags tree bark and old fish nets. Then they placed the mixture in a vat filled with water soon tiny fibres from the mixture were hanging suspended in the water. If a person dipped a mould into the water and lifted it out the mixture would dry and become a piece of paper. Today, paper production depends on machinery and modern technology but the basic process is the same as the one originally used by the ancient Chinese. Fine writing papers still contains a large percentage of rags although most paper made today contains a great deal of wood. The method of converting wood pulp into paper discovered only a little more than a century ago. Although the Chinese developed paper making and sold paper to merchants who travelled through China, they kept the secret of how to make paper for a long time. After a few hundred years however the Japanese learned how to produce it, and not long after that around the year 700 the Arabs learned the secret. After that, Arabs introduced paper wherever they traded, and by the year 1200 europeans were making their own paper. By the 1700s, people in Europe were consuming so much paper that they were running out of rags to use in the process. They also found a wider variety of uses for paper. They built chairs and bookcases out of paper, and in 1793 in Norway, a paper church that could hold 800 people was built. It served it's congregation for nearly 40 years.

TEST 3   Editing for Errors

Edit the following paragraph. Hint: you will find an opportunity to correct each of the following:

Inconsistency in verb tense

Capitalization

An apostrophe for possessive

Irregular verb form

Wrong pronoun form

Dangling modifier

Punctuation for compound sentence using coordination

Punctuation for a series

Subject-verb agreement

Fragment

The famous painter Paul Gauguin with an adventurous life and a troubled career. He was born in France in 1848. Three years later, the family travelled to Lima, Peru but on the way his father died. Young Paul and his mother lived for four years with relatives in the capital of Peru. After the family returns to France, Paul finished school and went to work in a business office. His marriage to a young danish woman seemed to give him a traditional lifestyle, but Gauguin now begun to turn his attention more and more to art. He bought paintings for hisself became friends with artists of the day and soon had a studio of his own in Paris. By 1883, he was so interested in art that, over his wifes objections, he quit his job and painted full time. Moving his large family from Paris to save money, his savings soon ran out. When he died several years later, Gauguin's belongings had to be sold to pay off his debts. One person paid $1.50 for the last painting he ever did. Today, any one of his hundreds of paintings are worth millions.

Step 4

UNDERSTANDING THE POWER OF WORDS

CONTENTS

Choosing Words That Work

Using words rich in meaning

Writing is a constant search to find the right word to express thoughts and feelings as accurately as possible. When a writer wants to be precise, or wants to give a flavour to a piece of writing, the possibilities are almost endless for word choice and sentence construction. The creative writer looks for words that have rich and appropriate meanings and associations.

For instance, if you were describing older people, you might choose one of these words or phrases:

retirees

pensioners

senior citizens

old fogeys

the elderly

golden agers

Some words have no associations beyond the strict dictionary meaning. These words are said to be neutral. Which word in the above list is strictly neutral, with no positive or negative emotional associations? (The answer is *the elderly*.) The person who is writing a brochure for a community centre for older people would probably choose the phrase *senior citizens* because these words respectfully identify the age of the group involved. A person who is addressing a group of people who have questions about their social security benefits might use the term *retirees*. In some cases, companies would refer to their workers who are receiving pensions as *pensioners*. A person who is trying to interest people in investing in a retirement community might use the term *golden agers* to give a glowing impression of life during retirement. Which slang phrase might an impatient person use to describe a couple of elderly people who are not up to date or aware of current thinking and events? (The answer is *old fogeys*.)

EXERCISE 1   Using Words Rich in Meaning

The following five words all have the same basic meaning: a method or program for doing something. For each word, however, an additional meaning makes the word richer and more specific. Match each word in Column A with the letter of the definition from Column B that best fits the meaning of the word.

Column A

_____ 1. blueprint

_____ 2. design

_____ 3. scheme

_____ 4. strategy

_____ 5. outline

Column B

a. a preliminary draft or plan for a piece of writing using Roman numerals and/or Arabic numerals to enumerate the points

b. a well thought out plan to achieve a goal, such as a company's plan to market a product or a team's plan to win a game

c. a plan that is usually in an artistic or graphic form

d. technical drawings rendered as white lines on a blue background often associated with architectural plans

e. a systematic plan of action, often secretive or devious

The following five words all have the basic meaning: to exchange opinions on important issues. Match each word in Column A with the letter of the definition from Column B that best fits the meaning of the word.

Column A

_____ 1. argue

_____ 2. debate

_____ 3. discuss

_____ 4. contend

_____ 5. dispute

Column B

a. to sharply oppose another person's ideas

b. to examine a subject by exchanging opinions

c. to support a position against others using facts and opinions

d. to argue formally, usually in public

e. to strive in debate or controversy

EXERCISE 2   Using Words Rich in Meaning

Listed under each word or phrase are four words that share the general meaning. Each word, however, has a more precise meaning as well. In each case, give the word's more precise definition.

to be funny

1. droll   _____

2. amusing   _____

3. comical   _____

4. hilarious   _____

to be polite

1. civil   _____

2. genteel   _____

3. mannerly   _____

4. courteous   _____

a special way of speaking

1. lingo   _____

2. gibberish   _____

3. dialect   _____

4. jargon   _____

to be frightened

1. terrorized   _____

2. startled   _____

3. alarmed   _____

4. frantic   _____

Understanding loaded words: Denotation/connotation

The careful writer must consider more than the dictionary meaning of a word. Some words have different meanings for different people.

> The *denotation* of a word is its strict dictionary meaning.
>
> The *connotation* of a word is the meaning (apart from the dictionary meaning) that a person attaches to a word because of the person's personal experience with the word.
>
> | | |
> |---|---|
> | *word:* | liberal |
> | *denotation:* | to favour nonrevolutionary progress or reform |
> | *possible connotations:* | socially active, free thinking, too generous, far left, favouring many costly government programs |

Politicians are usually experts in understanding the connotations of a word. They know, for instance, that if they want to get votes in a conservative area, they should not refer to their views as liberal. The strict dictionary meaning of *liberal* is "to favour nonrevolutionary progress or reform," certainly an idea that most people would support. However, when most people hear the words *liberal* or *conservative,* they bring to the words many political biases and experiences from their past: their parents' attitudes, the political and social history of the area in which they live, the two oldest political parties in Canada, and many other factors that may correctly or incorrectly colour their understanding of a word.

Choosing words that are not neutral but that have more exact or appropriate meanings is a powerful skill for your writing, one that will help your reader better understand the ideas you want to communicate. As your vocabulary grows, your writing will become richer and deeper. Your work will reflect your understanding of all the shades of meanings that words can have.

EXERCISE 1   Denotation/Connotation

In this exercise you have the opportunity to think of words that are richer in associations than the neutral words that are underlined in the sentences below. Write your own word choice in the space to the right of each sentence. Discuss with others in your class the associations you make with the words you have chosen.

1. Tony works on his <u>car</u> nearly every night.   _____

2. Last week he asked some <u>people he knows</u> to help.   _____

3. They <u>worked on the project</u> for three or four hours one evening.   _____

4. I could hear the <u>sounds</u> all the way down the street.   _____

5. The radio played their favourite <u>music</u>.   _____

6. After several hours, the workers went downtown to pick up some <u>refreshments</u>.   _____

7. Later, we saw their <u>vehicles</u> return.   _____

8. We thought we saw the addition of several more <u>people</u>.   _____

9. Their voices became <u>more audible</u>.   _____

10. The work had ended, and now they were having a <u>good time</u>.   _____

EXERCISE 2   Denotation/Connotation

Below are several sentences that contain words that may have positive or negative associations for the reader. Read the sentences and study the underlined words that often carry "emotional" meanings not contained in the dictionary meaning. Below each sentence, write the emotional meaning you associate with the underlined word. Discuss your answers with your classmates.

1. The young woman gazed at the photograph of her <u>father</u>.

   _____

2. He appeared to be wearing some kind of <u>uniform</u>.

   _____

3. At least two <u>airplanes</u> could be seen in the background.

   _____

4. Her mother always kept the photograph next to the <u>religious statue</u> on the nightstand.

   _____

5. The <u>ocean</u> had separated them from each other.

   _____

Wordiness: In writing, less can be more!

In *The Elements of Style,* essayist E.B. White quotes his old teacher William Strunk, Jr. who said that a sentence "should contain no unnecessary words" and a paragraph "no unnecessary sentences." Strunk's philosophy of writing included the commandment, "Omit needless words!" It was a lesson that E.B. White took to heart, with wonderful results that we see in his own writing. Often, less is more.

A summary follows of the most important ways you should cut the actual number of words in order to strengthen the power of your ideas. As you read each example of wordiness, notice how the revision has cut out unnecessary words.

Wordy Expressions	Revision

1. Avoid redundancy.

exact same	same
large jumbo size	jumbo
round in shape	round

2. Avoid wordy phrases.

due to the fact that	because
for the stated reason that	because
in this day and age	today
at this point in time	now

3. Avoid overuse of the verb *to be*.

That chair is in need of a new slipcover.	That chair needs a new slipcover.

4. Avoid repeating the same word too many times.

Dogs make great pets. Dogs provide companionship.	Dogs make great pets by providing companionship.

5. Avoid beginning a sentence with *there is* or *it is* whenever possible.

It is wonderful to travel.	Travel is wonderful.

6. Avoid flowery or pretentious language.

I am completely overwhelmed when I consider that the theatrical event that I have just witnessed will linger long in my memory.	I'll never forget this play.

7. Avoid apologetic, tentative expressions.

in my opinion

In my opinion, the grading policy for this course should be changed.	The grading policy for this course should be changed.

it seems to me

Right now, it seems to me that finding a job in my field is very difficult.	Right now, finding a job in my field is very difficult.

I will try to explain

In this paper, I will try to explain my views on censorship of the campus newspaper.	Censoring the campus newspaper is a mistake.

if I may say so

> If I may say so, the shoes you want to buy do not fit.   The shoes you want to buy do not fit.

EXERCISE 1   Revising Wordy Sentences

For each of the following sentences, underline the part that is unnecessarily wordy, and on the line below the sentence provide the revision.

1. Tuesday we will first begin the study of violence in the news media.

   _____

2. The violence in the news is making many people in the public to be very paranoid.

   _____

3. There is hardly a news program today without the graphic description of murders and other violent assaults.

   _____

4. Many children have the fear that they should not go outside their homes.

   _____

5. We are all in a need of feeling safer in our neighbourhoods.

   _____

6. As far as mothers are concerned, their children are not safe.

   _____

7. We are in the process of evaluating the quality of our lives.

   _____

8. Due to the fact of the violence, children's freedom has become limited.

   _____

9. In our opinion, it would seem to us that the need for more supervised activities for children is essential.

   _____

10. It is not good that children come home to empty apartments and houses.

    _____

EXERCISE 2   Revising Wordy Sentences

For each of the following sentences, underline the part that is unnecessarily wordy, and on the line below the sentence provide the revision.

1. In these difficult times we must make decisions based on solid information.

   _____

2. Her graduation dress is red in colour.

   _____

3. In terms of artistic expression, Mildred's playing is superb.

    _____

4. It would appear that we have a flat tire.

    _____

5. I will try to provide all the reasons for the decline of the Roman Empire.

    _____

6. There are several objections to the prime minister's plans for health care reform.

    _____

7. It thrills and excites every member of the class to talk about details of the upcoming square dance, to be followed by a full chicken dinner.

    _____

8. The war was supposed to be the last war, but many wars since then have proved this not to be true.

    _____

9. The piece of property is in the shape of a square.

    _____

10. She is desirous to be helpful.

    _____

Recognizing appropriate language for formal writing

In speaking or writing to our family and friends, an informal style is always appropriate because it is relaxed and conversational. On the other hand, writing and speaking in school or at work requires a more formal style, one that is less personal and more detached in tone. In formal writing situations, slang is not appropriate, and any use of language that is seen as sexist or disrespectful to any individual or groups of individuals is not at all acceptable.

> *Slang* is a term that refers to a special word or expression that a particular group of people use, often with the intention of keeping the meaning to themselves. A characteristic of a slang word or expression is that it is often used for a limited period of time and then is forgotten. For example:
>
> The party was *grand*. (1940s)
> The party was *awesome*. (2000s)

Slang or Informal Words	Acceptable
bucks	dollars
kids	children
cops	police
a bummer	a bad experience
off the wall	crazy
yummy	delicious

Clipped Language

doc	doctor
pro	professional
t.v.	television

Sexist Language

mailman	letter carrier
common man	average person
The teacher is an important man. He can influence the lives of many children in the community.	Teachers are important people. They can influence the lives of many children in a community.

Notice that in the last example, one way to revise sentences that contain the male references *he, him,* or *his,* is to put each singular reference into the plural. Therefore, *man* becomes *people,* and *he* becomes *they.*

EXERCISE 1   Recognizing Inappropriate Language for Formal Writing

The following sentences contain words that are informal, slang, or sexist. Circle the word in each sentence that is inappropriate for formal writing, and on the line to the right of each sentence, provide a more formal word or expression to replace the informal word.

1. The leader of that group is a screwball. _____

2. He's always wired over something. _____

3. Is it guts or just ego that makes him argue about every little thing? _____

4. Listening to him yakking even makes his followers tired sometimes. _____

5. No one can accuse him of being a slacker. _____

6. However, his opponents accuse him of being tacky. _____

7. Also, he does his own thing and never listens to anybody else. _____

8. The chairman of our committee has just published a very critical letter about his professional conduct. _____

9. Several t.v. clips have raised some questions. _____

10. His shenanigans are going to get him into trouble. _____

EXERCISE 2   Recognizing Inappropriate Language for Formal Writing

The following sentences contain words that are informal, slang, or sexist. Circle the word in each sentence that is inappropriate for formal writing, and on the line to the right of each sentence, provide a more formal word or expression to replace the informal word.

1. He's hyper tonight.   _____

2. The entire team is pumped up for the game.   _____

3. They intend to skunk the other team.   _____

4. Here come his pals Jeremy and Gia; they're an item these days.   _____

5. What's the crummy weather going to be tonight?   _____

6. The weathermen predict the continuation of this wind and rain.   _____

7. My bro' won't go with us if the weather is bad.   _____

8. He's the most up-tight person you can imagine.   _____

9. Why don't you fib and tell him the rain will stop by nine?   _____

10. He'd never be a sucker for that story.   _____

Mastery and editing tests

TEST 1   Editing for Wordiness and Inappropriate Language

The following paragraph contains examples of wordiness as well as inappropriate language (slang, clipped words, and sexist terms). Underline the problems as you come to them and then revise the paragraph. (Hint: Find and revise at least ten words or phrases.)

The discovery of insulin by Canadian doctors Frederick Banting, Charles Best, and John Macleod was one of the most revolutionary and important moments in the modern medicine of our day. In the year 1921, Frederick Banting was checking out the University of Toronto to help John Macleod and a team of other researchers find a cure for diabetes. Scientists had long thought that there was some kind of a connection between diabetes and the pancreas, an internal organ that helps in the digestive process. The team at the U of T, headed by Banting and Best, figured that the pancreas's digestive juices were destroying another important hormone. The trick, then, was to find a way to stop the pancreas from working while not impeding the production of this hormone. By August 1921, Banting and Best had made some conclusive results and discoveries. The introduction of insulin seemed literally like a miracle for mankind. One year the disease was an automatic death sentence; the next, people of all ages and backgrounds had hopes of living full and productive lives even with the disease. In 1923, Macleod and Banting were awarded the Nobel Prize in medicine. Banting became really ticked off because Charles Best's contributions were ignored. Banting accepted the prize and then shared his half with Best. There are probably about 15 million diabetics living in all corners of the globe today who would have died at an early age without insulin.

TEST 2 Editing for Wordiness and Inappropriate Language

The following paragraph contains examples of wordiness as well as inappropriate language (slang, clipped words, and sexist terms). Underline the problems as you come to them and then revise the paragraph. (Hint: Find and revise at least ten words or phrases.)

In terms of social manners, people are becoming more and more concerned. I mean like what has happened to consideration for others? Cars do not even stop for old geezers trying to cross the street, and very few people will help a gal who is trying to carry several heavy bags of groceries in the rain. There is more and more talk about this as people talk about what we can do to encourage people to be more polite. When it comes to pregnant women riding trains or buses, the situation is even more serious. All the docs say that a woman who is expecting should not be on her feet when she is all wiped out. She should be given a seat on a train or bus, especially when there are guys just sitting there, reading the paper in their snazzy business suits. One pregnant woman was really ticked off when she broke her arm in her seventh month of pregnancy. There she was, on her feet in a subway car, and not one man would get up for her.

TEST 3 Editing for Wordiness and Inappropriate Language

The following paragraph contains examples of wordiness as well as inappropriate language (slang, clipped words, and sexist terms). Underline the problems as you come to them and then revise the paragraph. (Hint: Find and revise at least ten words or phrases.)

Parents and kids often butt heads when it comes to homework, but this does not have to be the case. A number of basic points should be kept in mind when a parent helps her offspring with an assignment. First, find the right spot for the homework to be done. This usually is the kitchen table. You can even place a sign, such as "Buzz off!" in the area so that everyone in the family will respect the attempts being made by the little scholar to accomplish all the necessary tasks. Also important is the need for a regular schedule: plan a time in the p.m. when homework gets done. Also, do not do your son's homework for him; this only creates dependence and gives the teach the wrong impression. It is necessary that parents keep riding their offspring if academic things are to get done.

Paying Attention to Look-Alikes and Sound-Alikes

Many words are confusing because they either sound alike or look alike, but they are spelled differently and have different meanings. Master the words in each group before proceeding to the next group. The first column gives the word. The second column gives the definition, and the third column gives a sentence using the word correctly.

Group I: Words that sound alike

1. it's/its

it's	contraction of *it is*	*It's* raining.
its	possessive pronoun	*Its* wheel is missing.

2. they're/their/there

they're	contraction of *they are*	*They're* busy.
their	possessive pronoun	*Their* job is done.
there	at that place	The report is *there*.

3. we're/were/where

we're	contraction of *we are*	*We're* delayed.
were	past tense of *are*	We *were* delayed.
where	at or in what place	*Where* is the train?

4. who's/whose

who's	contraction of *who is*	*Who's* responsible?
whose	possessive pronoun	*Whose* job is this?

5. you're/your

you're	contraction of *you are*	*You're* the winner.
your	possessive pronoun	*Your* trophy is here.

6. aural/oral

aural	related to hearing	After the *aural* exam, he received a hearing aid.
oral	related to the mouth	Good *oral* hygiene saves your teeth.

7. buy/by

buy (verb)	to purchase	She only *buys* items on sale.
by (prep.)	near	He is waiting *by* the train.
	past	The actress walked *by* her fans.
	not later than	I will see you *by* midnight.

8. close/clothes

close	to shut	*Close* the window.
clothes	garments	His *clothes* are worn.

Note: *cloth* is a piece of fabric, not to be confused with the word *clothes*, which is always plural.

9. coarse/course

coarse (adj.)	rough	It was a *coarse* comedy.
	common or of inferior quality	The dress was made of a *coarse* fabric.
course (noun)	direction	The ship went off *course*.
	part of a meal	The main *course* was fish.
	a unit of study	She took all her required *courses*.

10. complement/compliment

complement (noun)	something that completes	The *complement* of the angle is 45 degrees.
(verb)	to complete	The hat *complements* her dress.
compliment (noun)	an expression of praise	She happily accepted the *compliment*.
(verb)	to praise	All her friends *complimented* her.

11. imminent/eminent

imminent (adj.)	impending; about to happen	The arrival of the train was *imminent*.
eminent (adj.)	distinguished; notable	The Queen of England is an *eminent* person.
		There were many *eminent* people at the Gemini Awards ceremony.

12. forward/foreword

forward	to send on to another address	She *forwarded* my mail.
	moving toward the front or the future	Please go *forward*.
	bold	He is a very *forward* child.
foreword	introduction to a book	The *foreword* was better than the book.

13. passed/past

passed (verb)	moved ahead	She *passed* every exam.
past (noun)	time before the present	He lives in the *past*.
(prep.)	beyond	She drove *past* the diner.
(adj.)	no longer current	The *past* semester was difficult.

14. plain/plane

plain (adj.)	ordinary	The children prefer *plain* vanilla ice cream.
	clear	Her *plain* dress was attractive.
(noun)	flat land without trees	The African *plains* are beautiful.
plane	an aircraft	The *plane's* arrival was delayed.
	a flat, level surface	The *plane* of the diamond gleamed.
	a carpenter's tool for levelling wood	The carpenter's *plane* broke.
	a level of development	She thinks on a different *plane*.

15. presence/presents

presence	the state of being present	Your *presence* is required.
	a person's manner	The queen's *presence* was unforgettable.
presents	gifts	They received many wedding *presents*.

16. principal/principle

principal (adj.)	most important	The *principal* singer was replaced.
	main	The *principal* task has been done.

principal (noun)	the head of a school	The *principal* announced the exam.
	a sum of money	He paid the interest but not the *principal*.
principle	a rule or standard	She would not violate her *principles*.

17. rain/reign/rein

rain	water falling to earth in drops	The *rain* turned to sleet.
reign	a period of rule for a king or queen	King Tut's *reign* was brief.
rein	a strap attached to a bridle, used to control a horse	The *rein* was useless to the jockey.

18. sight/site/cite

sight	the ability to see a view	He kept the wolf in *sight*.
site	the plot of land where something is located; the place for an event	They chose a new *site* for the gym.
cite	to quote as an authority or example	Please *cite* the correct law.

19. stationary/stationery

| stationary (adj.) | standing still | The truck was *stationary* in the mud. |
| stationery (noun) | writing paper and envelopes | The printed *stationery* was expensive. |

20. to/too/two

to (prep.)	in a direction toward	Bill came *to* the party.
too (adv.)	also	Sally came *too*.
	very	It was *too* crowded.
two	number	The *two* of them went home.

21. vain/vane/vein

vain	conceited	The film star was very vain.
	unsuccessful	They tried in *vain* to save the dog.
vane	an ornament that turns in the wind (often in the shape of a rooster, seen on tops of barns)	The weather *vane* rusted on the barn.

vein	a blood vessel	The surgeon repaired the *vein*.
	the branching framework of a leaf	We could see the *veins* on the leaf.
	an area in the earth where a mineral such as gold or silver is found	The *vein* of gold was visible in the rock.
	a passing attitude	He talked in a comic *vein*.

22. waist/waste

waist	the middle portion of a body or garment	The tailor measured his *waist*.
waste (verb)	to use carelessly	He *wasted* his money.
(noun)	discarded objects	The factory dumped its *waste* in the river.

23. weather/whether

| weather (noun) | atmospheric conditions | The *weather* was cold and rainy. |
| whether (conj.) | if it is the case that | Things happen *whether* or not you are ready. |

24. whole/hole

| whole | complete | The *whole* pie was eaten. |
| hole | an opening | Moths made a *hole* in the dress. |

25. write/right/rite

write	to form letters and words; to compose	*Write* a post card to Fred.
right	correct	Tell me the *right* approach.
	to conform to justice, law, or morality	He has a *right* to a trial.
	toward a conservative point of view	His political thinking is to the *right*.
rite	a traditional, often religious ceremony	Most societies have *rites* for newborn babies.

EXERCISE 1   Group I: Words That Sound Alike

In the following paragraph, ten words that are often confused are underlined. In the spaces provided, write C if the word is correct. If the word is incorrect, write the correct word.

In order to discover our <u>passed</u>, <u>aural</u> history is not enough; we must also recover our written heritage. Part of that heritage is the work of Boston King, an eighteenth-century African-American chronicler <u>who's</u> writings are being studied today. King was born a slave in the southern United States before the

War of Independence. Many slaves during the Revolution fled from their <u>coarse</u> masters to serve with the British, who had promised them liberty if they joined <u>they're</u> ranks. After the British were defeated, King and hundreds of other Black Loyalists, as they <u>where</u> called then, settled on land given to them by the British Crown around the towns of Shelburne and Birchtown, Nova Scotia. By 1784, the population of Birchtown had grown to 1,521 people; for a time, it was the largest settlement of free Blacks in North America. While his <u>principle</u> work was as a Methodist pastor, King had learned many skills that were in demand in Nova Scotia. He was a carpenter and shipbuilder. He also taught himself to read and <u>rite</u>, and he documented the hardship facing the Black Loyalists. When the Crown withdrew <u>it's</u> financial support for the Loyalists in Nova Scotia, King documented the famine that befell the Black Loyalists of Birchtown. Sadly, Boston King and hundreds of other Black Loyalists left Nova Scotia when they were given the opportunity to move to the West African territory of Sierra Leone. The hardships of a new life in Nova Scotia were <u>to</u> much for these poor people.

1. _____	6. _____
2. _____	7. _____
3. _____	8. _____
4. _____	9. _____
5. _____	10. _____

EXERCISE 2   Group I: Words That Sound Alike

In the following paragraph, ten words that are often confused are underlined. In the spaces provided, write C if the word is correct. If the word is incorrect, write the correct word.

Canadians have always felt the overwhelming <u>presents</u> of our large neighbour to the south, and much of our efforts have been aimed at defining our culture so as to distinguish us from Americans. That's why it came as a surprise <u>too</u> researchers that so many Canadians expect their country will become part of the United States within the next twenty years. Of those polled recently, 45 percent think <u>its</u> highly likely that <u>we're</u> going to become part of a North American union within ten years, and 47 percent believe this will be a reality within the next twenty years. While many of us feel that union with the United States is the inevitable <u>course</u> for our country, we also feel that <u>their</u> are important differences between us and Americans. When asked if Canadians and Americans were the same or different, 50 percent of Canadians said we were the same and 50 percent said we were different. Meanwhile, 71 percent of Americans think there is no difference between Canadians and Americans. At the same time, most Canadians think that our growing Americanization is not a move <u>foreword</u>. Over 80 percent of Canadians feel that we must keep our own values and <u>principals</u> and avoid becoming more American. Of course, people's attitudes and opinions are never <u>stationery</u>; they are constantly changing. Who knows <u>weather</u> or not the same poll conducted two years from now will reveal the same views?

1. _____   6. _____
2. _____   7. _____
3. _____   8. _____
4. _____   9. _____
5. _____   10. _____

Group II: Words that sound or look almost alike

1. accept/except

accept (verb)	to receive	I *accept* the invitation.
	to admit	I *accept* the blame.
	to regard as true or right	I *accept* the judge's decision.
except (prep.)	other than, but	Everyone *except* me went to the party.

2. advice/advise

advice (noun)	opinion as to what should be done about a problem	I listened to the lawyer's *advice*.
advise (verb)	to suggest; to counsel	The counsellor *advised* me to choose a different major.

3. affect/effect

affect (verb)	to influence; to change	The election *affected* the prime minister's thinking.
effect (noun)	result	The *effect* of the defeat was a change in government.
(verb)	to bring about (with a result)	The election *effected* a deep change in the country.

4. breath/breathe

breath (noun)	air that is inhaled or exhaled	He took a deep *breath*.
breathe (verb)	to inhale or exhale	*Breathe* in when the doctor tells you.

5. choose/chose

choose (present tense)	select	Please *choose* a number.
chose (past tense)	selected	Last weekend we *chose* to stay home.

6. conscience/conscious/conscientious

conscience	recognition of right and wrong	In Pinocchio, a cricket is the puppet's *conscience*.
conscious	awake; aware of one's own existence	Is the sick child *conscious*?

| conscientious | careful; thorough | The mother was very *conscientious* about the care of her children. |

7. costume/custom

| costume | a special style of dress for a particular occasion | He rented a *costume* for the play. |
| custom | a common tradition | Trick or Treating is a national *custom*. |

8. council/counsel/consul

council (noun)	a group that governs	The village *council* met last evening.
counsel (verb)	to give advice	He *counselled* troubled youth.
(noun)	advice; a lawyer	The judge appointed a *counsel*.
consul	a government official in the foreign service	The *consul* met the other diplomats.

9. desert/dessert

desert (verb)	to abandon	No soldier should *desert* an army.
(noun)	barren land	The *desert* was full of surprising plants.
dessert	last part of a meal, often sweet	The dinner ended with a fancy *dessert*.

10. diner/dinner

diner	a person eating dinner	The *diner* ate alone.
	a restaurant with a long counter and booths	I like coffee and donuts at the *diner*.
dinner	main meal of the day	*Dinner* will be served at eight.

11. emigrate/immigrate/emigrant/immigrant

emigrate	to leave a country	The family *emigrated* from Russia.
immigrate	to come into a country	A century ago, many Europeans *immigrated* to Canada.
emigrant	a person who leaves one country to settle in another	Many *emigrants* from Europe left poverty and war behind.
immigrant	a person who comes into a country to settle	Many *immigrants* to Canada have valuable skills.

12. farther/further

farther	greater distance (physically)	I cannot walk any *farther*.
further	greater distance (mentally); to help advance a person or a cause	She gave *further* evidence at the trial.

13. loose/lose

loose	not tightly fitted	Her *loose* jacket felt comfortable.
lose	unable to keep or find to fail to win	Don't *lose* the ticket. Our team cannot *lose*.

14. personal/personnel

personal	relating to an individual; private	Her *personal* life is a mystery.
personnel	people employed by an organization	The director asked all *personnel* to report Monday morning.

15. quiet/quit/quite

quiet	free from noise; calm	The *quiet* library was a retreat.
quit	to give up; to stop	She *quit* her job last week.
quite	completely	It is *quite* all right to ask for help.

16. receipt/recipe

receipt	a bill marked paid	You need a *receipt* to get a refund.
recipe	a formula to prepare a mixture, especially in cooking	The chefs exchanged *recipes* for their desserts.

17. special/especially

special (adj.)	not ordinary	He gave the dog a *special* treat.
especially (adv.)	particularly	Those cakes are *especially* delicious.

18. than/then

than	used to make a comparison	I would rather walk *than* ride.
then	at that time; in that case	I went to the bakery and *then* came home.

19. thorough/though/thought/through/threw

thorough (adj.)	finished, fully done	He made a *thorough* inspection of the house.
though (adv. conj.)	however; despite the fact	They bought the house even *though* it was old.

thought (verb)	past tense of *to think*	She *thought* about restoring the house to its original beauty.
through (prep.)	to enter one side and exit from the other side	They looked *through* dozens of decorating books.

Note: *thru* is not considered standard spelling.

threw	past tense of *to throw*	She *threw* her heart into the project.

20. use/used to

use	to bring or put into service, to make use of	I *used* the telephone a lot last year.
used to	indicates an activity that is no longer done in the present	I *used to* make too many long distance calls.
	accustomed to or familiar with	I am *used to* calling my family whenever I feel lonely.

EXERCISE 1   Group II: Words That Sound Almost Alike

In the following paragraph, ten words that are often confused are underlined. In the spaces provided, write C if the word is correct. If the word is incorrect, write the correct word.

Except for a very few people, most of us like to gossip. "Don't breath a word!" some people will say, and than they will tell you a deep secret they heard from someone else. This can be dangerous, especially if the gossip gets back to the person who has been discussed. Many friendships have been ruined because of these personnel misunderstandings, and in families, the affects of gossip can be disastrous. A farther point in all of this is the intentions that people have when they gossip. It is one thing to want to be helpful when talking about other people; it is quiet another thing to chose to gossip for its own sake. That is often a receipt for disaster.

1. _____   6. _____
2. _____   7. _____
3. _____   8. _____
4. _____   9. _____
5. _____   10. _____

EXERCISE 2   Group II: Words That Sound Almost Alike

In the following paragraph, ten words that are often confused are underlined. In the spaces provided, write C if the word is correct. If the word is incorrect, write the correct word.

Feeling disorganized is no fun. Some families sit down, have a family <u>counsel</u> and make a <u>through</u> review of everything they do in order to organize their daily lives. First, they discuss what they <u>use to</u> do, and promise each other they will mend their ways. Next, they give each other <u>advise</u> on the most important changes that should be made. If it is the <u>custom</u> in the house to hope everyone gets up on time in the morning, then an alarm clock should be purchased because a <u>lose</u> morning schedule always results in chaos. The end of the day is just as important, with <u>diner</u> being an important time for family cooperation. If everyone works in a <u>conscience</u> way to help make a good meal, there could even be time for <u>dessert</u>. One <u>effect</u> of all this will be that everyone will know what is expected every day. Routine is important if a family is to run smoothly.

1. _____   6. _____
2. _____   7. _____
3. _____   8. _____
4. _____   9. _____
5. _____   10. _____

Group III: Lie/lay; rise/raise; sit/set

These six verbs are perhaps the most troublesome verbs in the English language. First, one must learn the principal parts because they are irregular and easily confused with each other. Secondly, one set is reflexive and cannot take an object while the other set always takes a direct object.

THE PRINCIPAL PARTS OF THE REFLEXIVE VERBS LIE—RISE—SIT				
Verb Meaning	**Present**	**Present Participle**	**Past**	**Past Participle**
to recline	lie	lying	lay	has or have lain
to stand up or move upward	rise	rising	rose	has or have risen
to take a sitting position	sit	sitting	sat	has or have sat

Reflexive verbs never take an object.

I lie down.

The cat is lying on the rug.

I rise up.

The sun rose in the East.

She sits down.

The woman has sat on her hat.

Remember: When reflexive verbs are used, the subject is doing the action without any help. No other person or object is needed to accomplish the action.

THE PRINCIPAL PARTS OF THE VERBS LAY—RAISE—SET				
Verb Meaning	Present	Present Participle	Past	Past Participle
to put something	lay	laying	laid	has or have laid
to move something up	raise	raising	raised	has or have raised
to place something	set	setting	set	has or have set

These verbs always take a direct object.

I *lay the book* down.

I *raise the flag*.

I *set the table*. (Exception: The sun sets)

EXERCISE 1   Group III: Lie, Lay; Rise, Raise; Sit, Set

In the following paragraph, ten words that are often confused are underlined. In the spaces provided, write C if the word is correct. If the word is incorrect, write the correct word.

Most Canadians don't even think about what's <u>setting</u> on their dinner plates. What we eat may contain genetically modified (GM) food. Proponents of genetically modified food have tried <u>to sit</u> people's minds at ease. They assert that there is nothing to fear, that an estimated 75 percent of processed foods <u>laying</u> on the shelves of Canada's supermarkets contain genetically altered ingredients, and the use of GM foods <u>is rising</u>. They also state that farmers have modified the genes of plants and animals they <u>have raised</u> for centuries; if they hadn't, we'd probably still be eating grass instead of wheat. However, opponents of GM foods hope <u>to raise</u> awareness of the fact that it's no longer just a case of cross-breeding within different strains of the same species. Now, genes from completely different life forms are being spliced together—fish genes into tomatoes to make the latter more frost resistant. This group thinks that tampering with Mother Nature by producing GM foods <u>has risen</u> some problems that scientists might have overlooked. GM foods do not have to be labelled as such in Canada, so most of us don't know we're eating them when we <u>sit</u> down at dinner. However, this may have to change as public concern about GM foods <u>raises</u>. Recently, McCain's, one of Canada's largest producers of processed foods, announced that it would not use GM foods in any of its products. Clearly, it felt it had to respond to the public's concerns or risk losing its share of the market. In short, people have to show that tampering with their dinner is something they won't take <u>laying</u> down.

1. _____

2. _____

3. _____

4. _____

5. _____

6. _____

7. _____

8. _____

9. _____

10. _____

EXERCISE 2   Group III: Lie, Lay; Rise, Raise; Sit, Set

In the following paragraph, ten words that are often confused are underlined. In the spaces provided, write C if the word is correct. If the word is incorrect, write the correct word.

The new Boeing 777 jet is described as the plane for the 21st century. Although <u>setting</u> on the runway it may look like the 767 and the 757, only bigger, it represents a huge change in the way aircraft is built. Its reputation <u>has been rising</u> because it is the first Boeing plane to be designed entirely by a computerized system that the company calls "digital product design." Five thousand engineers <u>lay</u> down all the details about the four million parts for this airplane and entered the data into the computerized system. The computer could look at every part in three dimensions and match piece to piece before trying to put the parts together. This method <u>rose</u> the hopes of aircraft engineers everywhere. Before this, parts never matched up on the first attempt to put the parts together. Now the parts went together—snap, snap, snap! Engineers <u>raised</u> many other issues, one of them pointing out how each additional coat of paint that is applied <u>rises</u> the cost due to additional fuel needed to fly the plane. Think and test, think and test is the rule <u>laid</u> down by plane makers. Planning and construction costs have, of course, <u>raised</u> in recent years, and so the new airplane is a very expensive project. It seems impossible to <u>sit</u> a limit on the cost. However, engineers have been very excited about the construction of this aircraft. They want to see this process <u>set</u> the example for airplane construction in the next century.

1. _____	6. _____
2. _____	7. _____
3. _____	8. _____
4. _____	9. _____
5. _____	10. _____

Mastery and editing tests

TEST 1   Words Commonly Confused

In the following paragraph, ten words have been used incorrectly. Circle the words and write them correctly below the paragraph.

The Internet is becoming more popular around the world, and we Canadians are among it's leading users. A recent poll concluded that were the third-most frequent users of the Internet in the world. In fact, more Canadians then Americans use the Internet. Sixty percent of Canadians say they use the Internet, compared with 57 percent of U.S. residents. The rate of use in Canada is exceeded only in Norway, at 63 percent, and in Denmark, 62 percent. The study also shows that Canadians frequently chose the Internet to purchase goods or services but are specially concerned about giving credit card details on-line. Books are the most common purchase via the Internet, accounting for 24 percent of transactions. Next come close and computer software. Consumers have become empowered by the Internet. The Internet is also used to compliment conventional shopping methods. Even when they do not by a good or service on-line, people research on a Web sight before making a purchase at a store. No doubt, this growing trend will have a lasting affect on how we interact.

1. _____		6. _____
2. _____		7. _____
3. _____		8. _____
4. _____		9. _____
5. _____		10. _____

TEST 2   Words Commonly Confused

In the following paragraph, ten words have been used incorrectly. Circle the words and write them correctly below the paragraph.

Deadly diseases caused by exotic viruses may be coming to a town near you. These diseases are transmitted to humans through a variety of ways. For example, its thought that Lyme disease, witch is caused by a bacteria past on to humans by the blacklegged tic, migrated to parts of Canada with birds who's flight paths took them thorough infested parts of the United States. Sufferers of Lyme disease report swelling of their joints, headaches, and loosing their appetites. But migratory animals aren't quiet the only ones guilty of transporting diseases from one country to another. Humans are the principle cause of the spread of diseases. People who travel to exotic countries to experience foreign cultures and climates expose themselves to bacteria and viruses that there not used to. It is thought that a recent case of malaria, a blood disease common in the tropics and transmitted by mosquitoes, occurred when someone returned to Canada with an active case of the disease and was bit buy a mosquito, which then bit someone else. So be careful the next time you buy a plain ticket; you may find yourself being bitten by more than just the travel bug.

1. _____		6. _____
2. _____		7. _____
3. _____		8. _____
4. _____		9. _____
5. _____		10. _____

TEST 3   Words Commonly Confused

In the following paragraph, ten words have been used incorrectly. Circle the words and write them correctly below the paragraph.

During the 1600s, European explorers choose to cross the Atlantic Ocean in search of the elusive Northwest Passage that would bring them to the Orient. Hudson, an imminent sailor, was confident that he could find this shortcut to the East. In 1610, Hudson set out in search of the Northwest Passage on his ship *Discovery*. He navigated the treacherous tides and ice flows of the Arctic waters. He than entered a large body of water and assumed that it was the Pacific Ocean. Several weeks passed before Hudson and his crew realized they were well off coarse. Although they had sailed farther than any other explorers, they where not, in fact, on the Pacific. The large body of water they discovered was a bay that now bears Hudson's name: Hudson Bay. They had to spend the winter in the north, in freezing whether, without winter cloths, and short on rations. These conditions had a terrible affect on his men's morale. His crew mutinied, blaming Hudson for the failure of their mission. The deserters acted without conscious and forced Hudson and seven men, including his son, adrift in a small boat. Hudson and his men died in the wilderness; no trace has ever been found of them.

1. _____   6. _____

2. _____   7. _____

3. _____   8. _____

4. _____   9. _____

5. _____   10. _____

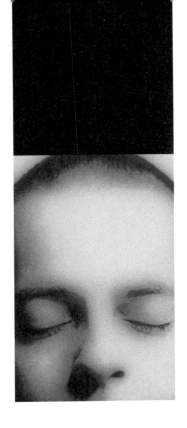

APPENDICES

CONTENTS

Handling source material

Research drafting differs from writing other essays because of outside sources. You must incorporate them smoothly into your text and document them as you draft. The bibliography can be left until last so it doesn't disrupt the flow of creation.

1. Quotations, paraphrases, and facts from other sources must flow with your paper. They are valuable only if they directly relate to *your* thesis. So you must clearly show that relationship to the reader by *smoothly introducing* all source material and by *commenting*, not just stringing quotes together like beads on a necklace. Start with simple taglines: "As one social researcher says…" or "According to the editors of *Time Magazine*…" or "After 30 years as a judge, Deborah Paine believes…." A tagline not only prepares us for a new voice but also tells us *what authority* your source has. The tagline should show us why we should trust what follows.

There are two main methods of incorporating quotations into the text. One is the smooth integration of quoted material. In this style, the quotation is simply integrated into the grammar of your sentence—it is spliced smoothly with the flow of your introductory words, as in the following example:

```
Keats describes "Negative Capability" as the experience
of living with "uncertainties, Mysteries, doubts,
without any irritable reaching after fact & reason"
(qtd. in Perkins 1209).
```

You may also introduce quotations more formally by setting them up with a tagline followed by a colon. Here is another example:

```
In a letter dated December 21-27, 1817, Keats describes
his famous theory of "Negative Capability": "I mean Neg-
ative Capability, that is when man is capable of being in
uncertainties, Mysteries, doubts, without any irritable
reaching after fact & reason" (qtd. in Perkins 1209).
```

Remember that a colon is only used after a complete sentence and gives your reader the signal that something is going to follow directly. It is almost like a pointing arrow.

If you want to omit words from the middle of your quotation, use an ellipsis, a set of spaced dots. If you are leaving out words, use three dots; if you are leaving out a complete sentence, use four dots (the last dot is the period of the sentence you've omitted from your quotation). You don't need to use an ellipsis if you are omitting something from the beginning or end of your quotation, as long as you end with a complete sentence, which is usually the case.

When choosing quotations, always keep in mind that their purpose is to provide information to support the thesis. Following is an example from the opening paragraph of a student essay. The writer begins by citing statistics about McDonald's and its labour force in order to establish a context for an argument in favour of restaurant employees having a union.

> According to <u>Report on Business Magazine</u>, "McDonald's and its franchises employ more than 65,000, largely teenage workers at 700 or so outlets across the country, and a stunning 7% of all people in Canada and the United States—1 in 15—got their first job at a McDonald's restaurant" (Kidd 48). You have seen them many times—those smiling, uniformed kids who hope you have a nice day, while they rush to and fro, madly attempting to fetch your burgers and fries before the customer standing behind you gets too grumpy. This is the story of one such employee, a 17-year-old woman from Orangeville, Ontario, and her failed attempt to organize the not-always-happy workers at McDonald's by establishing a union.

2. Condense quotations from your notes even more by paraphrasing all but the most important passages. You cover ground more quickly with paraphrases, and strings of quotes frustrate a reader, who assumes correctly that the real message is in *your* voice. If two or three writers agree on one point, quote or paraphrase the best one, and simply mention that two others agree; don't drag a reader through redundant quotes. Following is a student example of a nice paraphrase mixed with bits of quotation from a clinical description of an animal test. All of the information comes from the same page of a single source, so there's no need for more than one parenthetical citation (see below):

> The Draize Test involves testing cosmetics for eye damage that might occur to humans. Researchers smear mascara, for example, over the eyeballs of rabbits. Unlike humans, rabbits have no tear glands to wash it off. The animals are "immobilized" in a stockade device. In some cases, their eyes are held open with clips. As a result, they cannot blink to get even a moment's relief and ultimately suffer "eye ulcers, bleeding, and blindness" (O'Connor 94). And for what purpose? The tests do not even resemble how humans use the product.

Should you need a long quotation (MLA specifies more than four lines; APA specifies more than 40 words), set off the entire passage with an indentation (one inch for MLA; one-half inch for APA). No quotation marks are needed. With block-style quotations, remember to place the parenthetical reference outside the final punctuation mark, unlike the regular in-text reference, which is set within the punctuation marks of the sentence.

3. Research papers use citations in the text to document sources. Until about 15 years ago, documentation required a system of notes (either placed at the bottom of each page as footnotes or assembled on one final page as endnotes). But notes were cumbersome for both readers and writers, required Latin expressions such as "loc. cit." or "ibid.," and needlessly repeated the information contained in the bibliography. So the format has been changed, and most instructors will expect you to use one of two systems: the MLA (Modern Language Association) system for essays in the humanities, and the APA (American Psychological Association) system for essays in the social sciences and most other disciplines.

Both of these systems of documentation are based on the premise that the reader should be able to find the source of the quoted material. It's a courteous way of acknowledging that the information doesn't belong to the writer but has been borrowed from another source and incorporated into the essay. The documentation sends a signal to the reader that the information is available, should he or she wish to look it up.

Both APA and MLA are two-part systems. The first part is a reference in parentheses placed directly after a quoted, paraphrased, or summarized passage. It lists author, page number, and (in APA style) date. The second part is a list of bibliographic details in the Works Cited (MLA) or References (APA) page at the end of the document. If the reader is interested in looking up the book or article indicated by the parenthetical reference in the text, he or she can turn to the back and find all the needed information in the alphabetically arranged list.

The parenthetical references in the text show the reader which ideas or words "belong" to the writer and what has been "borrowed" to support the thesis. Documentation, then, has something to do with intellectual property—it indicates what originated with the writer and which facts or ideas have been imported to support or provide background to the argument.

MLA style of parenthetical references

The MLA system is simple. All quoted, paraphrased, or summarized material must be followed by a parenthetical citation, which usually includes the author's name and the page number (don't put a comma between them). Try to place this information as close as possible to the material it refers to, preferably at the end of a sentence:

> "The second element in the Ghost's message that squeezes
> Hamlet's life into narrowing limits is the interruption of
> the habits, such as they are, of Hamlet's life" (Frye 87).

The main idea behind this system is to try to avoid redundancy whenever possible. If Frye is your principal source and you refer to his ideas or words again soon after, your second and subsequent references only require a page number as long as it's clear you're still referring to Frye:

> The ghost speaks again to Hamlet, and it is "not a reas-
> suring recommendation" (87).

Likewise, if you mention the author's name in the introduction to the idea or quotation, there's no need to repeat it in the parenthetical citation:

> Frye goes on to suggest that "Hamlet's feelings are still fixated on his mother, and he has to keep working up his hatred of Claudius" (87-88).

If you have two books by Frye in your bibliography, then obviously a reference to Frye's name alone in parentheses will not indicate to your reader which of the two books you are referring to. In this case, you must indicate the title of the book as well (or an abbreviated version of it):

> "The second element in the Ghost's message that squeezes Hamlet's life into narrowing limits is the interruption of the habits, such as they are, of Hamlet's life" (Frye, *Shakespeare* 87).

Following are a few other examples you might run into in the course of your research. For a more exhaustive list, refer to the fifth edition of the *MLA Handbook for Writers of Research Papers*, the standard guide to MLA style published by The Modern Language Association of America.

Work by Two or More Authors

If a work is by two or three authors, give their names in the parenthetical citation: (Smith, Jones, and Brown 35–59). If a work has four or more authors, use the first author's name followed by the abbreviation "et al.": (Reed et al. 99).

Article in an Edited Collection

Your reference should indicate the name of the author of the article, not the editor of the book. If Josephine Seward has written an article in a collection edited by Stewart Snodgrass, you refer to Seward in the parenthetical reference: (Seward 87).

Work of Literature

If you are quoting from or paraphrasing a prose work (novel or short story), indicate the page number and chapter immediately after the quotation or paraphrase: (175; ch. 8). For Shakespeare and other classic verse plays and poems, omit the page number, but refer to the act, scene, and line numbers or other divisions: (*Hamlet* 1.1.22–23).

Indirect Source

If the author of the book you're using quotes from a source that you want to include in your paper, you should indicate the names of both by using the abbreviation "qtd.," which stands for "quoted": (qtd. in Cameron 450).

Multivolume Work

If you are quoting from a multivolume work, indicate which volume you are referring to by placing the volume number after the author's name, followed by a colon and the page number: (Boswell 2: 450). If you've already indicated the author's name, give only the volume and page numbers: (2: 450). If you have only one volume listed in your Works Cited, there's no need to indicate the volume number in the parenthetical citation.

Corporate Author

Use the name of the corporate author in the parenthetical citation if there's no individual author: (Government of Alberta 23). If possible, indicate the author in the introduction, rather than having a long citation in parentheses.

APA style of parenthetical references

The principle of APA style is the same as MLA: you must indicate the sources of all quoted, paraphrased, or summarized material. But the details are a little different. In APA style, the date is part of the parenthetical material because it is important in the social and natural sciences to establish quickly the currency of the information and findings. If you use the author's name to introduce the quoted material, you must place the date in parentheses immediately after the name and refer to the page number after the quotation:

```
According to Dolan (1986), "cocaine is an expensive drug
that can cost users from $500 to $5,000 per week" (p. 87).
```

The page number is not required if you are paraphrasing, but it is recommended as it allows the reader to find the reference easily.

If the author's name and year of publication don't appear in the introductory material, you must include all three elements in the parenthetical reference that follows the quotation:

```
Doctors are still not certain how cocaine works. "A
leading theory is that cocaine, like many other stimu-
lant drugs, produces an action on certain body chemicals
when it enters the bloodstream. These chemicals are
called neurotransmitters" (Dolan, 1986, p. 86).
```

Note that commas separate these elements and that page is indicated by "p." for a single page and "pp." for multiple pages.

As in the MLA system, the main idea is to avoid unnecessary repetition. For example, if you only have one book by Dolan in your References list, there's no need to include the date or author's name in subsequent references if it's clear you are still quoting Dolan—simply include the page number immediately following the quoted or paraphrased material.

If you refer to two articles by the same author and they appeared in different years, the year of publication should distinguish one from the other. If you refer to two articles written by one author in the same year, you must put them in alphabetical order on your References page with a letter beside the year (1995a). In the parenthetical references, use this designation to make it clear to your reader which one you are referring to:

```
Falk (1995a) suggests that too much television causes
the brain to turn to mush (p. 3).
```

Following are a few more examples of APA parenthetical documentation. For a more exhaustive list, refer to the fifth edition of the *Publication Manual of the American Psychological Association* (2001).

Work by Two or More Authors

If you are referring to a work by two authors, simply include their names in the introduction to the quoted or passage:

```
Arnold and Hall (1987) suggest that "there is a direct
correlation between the size of the pinkie finger and
creativity" (p. 89).
```

If you don't mention the authors' names in the text, use an ampersand (&) to link the two names in the parenthetical reference:

> Important early studies suggest that "there is a direct correlation between the size of the pinkie finger and creativity" (Arnold & Hall, 1987, p. 89).

If the work has three to five authors, refer to the last names of all the authors in the first reference, but only refer to the first author followed by "et al." in subsequent references. If you have six or more authors, use the first author and "et al." for all parenthetical citations:

> Jones, Krishna, Rosenberg, and Cooley (1990) argue that the original intention of the legislation was to provide greater access to information that had been protected by government agencies. The legislation was a good idea in theory, but the practical result is far from ideal. This discrepancy between the intent of the legislation and its implementation (Jones et al.) has not freed information, but simply created a tangled bureaucracy that gives the illusion of free access.

Note that the second parenthetical reference occurs in the middle of the sentence. In APA format, you are encouraged to place the in-text citation as close as possible to the paraphrase, even if it's in the middle of a sentence. In this case, the idea of the discrepancy between the legislation's intent and implementation comes from Jones et al., whereas the conclusion that follows belongs to the author of the paper.

Reference to Two or More Sources

If you are referring to two or more sources, alphabetize the list and separate each item with a semicolon:

> To date, research on the qualitative changes effected in writing by the word processor has been either contradictory or inconclusive (Auten, 1989; Collier, 1983; Curtis, 1988; Hawisher, 1987; Hill, Wallace, & Hass, 1991; Nydahl, 1991; Vockel & Schwartz, 1988).

Corporate Author

If there is no individual author, indicate the corporate author's name in the first reference followed by an abbreviation in brackets. For subsequent references, use the abbreviation only:

> In the report (Canadian Radio-television and Telecommunications Commission [CRTC], 1994), many of the applicants were turned down.

Bibliography

The last step in drafting a research paper is compiling a bibliography. In addition to citations in the body of your paper, you must provide complete information on book, magazine, or interview sources you used. At first glance, bibliography format may seem like a jumble, but it has an inner logic. You must give enough specific information to identify each source and allow a reader to find it.

MLA and APA formats are, as you'd expect, different in subtle ways. For one thing, bibliographies have different names. In MLA, it is called Works Cited, and in APA, the bibliography is simply called References.

Note to students: Yes, these two systems ought to be united into one simple, logical form of documentation for all areas of study so that researchers can concentrate on ideas and evidence, not on format. Check with your professors to see which system you should use for which paper.

Some publications omit identifying information. Substitute these abbreviations for missing information:

```
n.p. (no place of publication listed)
n.d. (no date given)
n.p. (no publisher given)
n. pag. (no page numbers given)
```

MLA bibliography format

The fifth edition of the *MLA Handbook for Writers of Research Papers* (1999) includes expanded sections on citing CD-ROMs and Web material. Not only is it the definitive guide to the MLA documentation style, but it also offers detailed information on the process of writing and research.

The MLA format has the following characteristics:

- The entire list is alphabetized by the authors' last names so that citations are easy to locate.
- The second and subsequent lines of each citation are indented one-half inch to keep the author's name visible.
- The entries are double spaced.
- Punctuation and the order of items in each entry are consistent.
- The list is entitled "Works Cited" and is placed on a separate page at the end of the paper.

There are three main parts to each entry: author(s), title, and publication information. Begin with the author's name: last name first, followed by the first name and initials (as you find it on the title page of the book or article) and a period. Leave two spaces and then give the title of the work. Underline it and capitalize the main words, just as you find it on the title page. Include any subtitle by separating it from the main title with a colon followed by a single space. This part also ends with a period followed by two spaces. The third part is the publication information, which includes the place of publication, followed by a colon and a space; the publisher's name, followed by a comma and a space; and the date of publication, followed by a period.

Following are sample formats for the most common sources you'll encounter.

Basic Book Format

Use the *latest* date listed on the copyright page.

Abbey, Edward. <u>The Monkey Wrench Gang</u>. New York: Avon, 1975.

Book with Two or Three Authors

Flick, Jane, and Celia Millward. <u>Handbook for Writers</u>. Toronto: Harcourt, 1993.

Book with More than Three Authors

Use "et al." after the first author's name.

Voss, Richard D., et al. <u>Mastering the Art of Documentation</u>. Toronto Scholarly, 1995.

Book with an Author and an Editor

If you refer to the primary text, the citation should begin with the author's name, followed by the editor, referred to as "ed."

Spenser, Edmund. <u>The Faerie Queene</u>. Ed. Thomas P. Roche, Jr. Markham: Penguin, 1978.

If you refer to the editor's comments, the citation should be reversed.

Roche, Jr., Thomas P., ed. <u>The Faerie Queene</u>. By Edmund Spenser. Markham: Penguin, 1978.

Corporate or Group Author

Give the full name of the group author, followed by the title.

American Psychological Association. <u>Publication Manual of the American Psychological Association</u>. 3rd ed. Washington, DC: APA, 1984.

Two or More Books by the Same Author

When listing two or more books by the same author, the second and subsequent citations should begin with three hyphens and a period, instead of with the author's name again.

Frye, Northrop. <u>Northrop Frye on Shakespeare</u>. Markham: Fitzhenry, 1986.

———. <u>Fearful Symmetry: A Study of William Blake</u>. Princeton: Princeton UP, 1974.

Book Not in First Edition

After the title, specify the edition number, because page references and wording may change from edition to edition.

        Breland, Osmond, et al. Principles of Biology. 3rd ed.
            New York: Harper, 1964.

Book in More than One Volume

Refer to the volume you use if you are citing a book in more than one volume.

        Daymond, Douglas, and Leslie Monkman. Literature in
            Canada. Vol. 2. Toronto: Gage, 1978. 2 vols.

If you use both volumes, cite the entire work.

        Daymond, Douglas, and Leslie Monkman. Literature in
            Canada. 2 vols. Toronto: Gage, 1978.

Selection from an Anthology or Edited Book

The selection is placed in quotation marks, while the book title is underlined. "Ed." refers to the editor of the collection. Page numbers must also be cited.

        Kennedy, Elizabeth. "The Marketing of Madonna." Selling
            Culture. Ed. Philippa Jones. Toronto: Oxford UP,
            1995. 145-49.

Article in an Encylopedia

Unsigned articles need no volume or page number—just the title.

        "Canada." Encyclopaedia Britannica: Micropaedia. 1993
            ed.

Signed articles require the author's name.

        Freeman, Minnie Aodia. "Inuit." The Canadian Encyclo-
            pedia. 1988 ed.

Lecture

Cite the information in the following order: speaker, title of lecture, sponsoring group, location, and date. If there is no title, label the kind of presentation: lecture, keynote address, and so on.

        Gould, Stephen Jay. "Wonderful Life." Mount Royal Col-
            lege Arts Lectures, Calgary, AB. 26 Apr. 1990.

Monthly Magazine

Cite the details in the following order: author, title of article (in quotation marks), title of magazine (underlined), date, and page numbers.

> Jervis, Nancy. "Waste Not, Want Not." <u>Natural History</u> May 1990: 70-74.

Weekly Magazine

In this case, include the precise date.

> Kael, Pauline. "The Current Cinema." <u>New Yorker</u> 29 Nov. 1982: 162-65.

Article in a Journal with Continuous Pagination

In such journals, usually published quarterly, the page numbering continues in each issue for an entire year (e.g., the page numbers in the summer issue continue where those in the spring issue left off). The volume number is followed by the date in parentheses and the page numbers.

> Collier, Richard M. "The Word Processor and Revision Strategies." <u>College Composition and Communication</u> 34 (1983): 149-55.

Article in a Journal with Separate Pagination

In this case, add a period between the volume number and the issue number.

> Bridwell-Bowles, Lillian. "Designing Research on Computer-Assisted Writing." <u>Computers and Composition</u> 7.1 (1989): 81-95.

Article in a Newspaper

If the city of publication isn't in the title, include it in brackets. The plus sign (+) indicates that the article continues on another page that isn't consecutive.

> Cernetig, Miro. "Probe Ordered into Hockey Riot." <u>Globe and Mail</u> [Toronto] 16 June 1994: A1+.

Personally Conducted Interview

Indicate what type of interview: personal or telephone.

> Raines, Tim. Personal interview. Montreal. 18 May 1990.

Pamphlet

List the author, title, publisher, and date, if available. Try to follow book format as closely as possible. If there is no author, enter the title and publishing information.

> Swinburne, Elizabeth, and Albert Roberts. <u>Gardening Tips in a Short Season</u>. Inuvik: Polar Bear Garden Supplies, 1990.

Television Program

List the program title, producer, narrator or main actors, network, station name, location, and date.

```
CBC Alberta News. Narr. Brenda Finley. Prod. Laurie
     Long. CBC. CBRT-TV, Calgary. 14 June 1995.
```

Video or Film

Be sure to include the medium after the title.

```
Antony and Cleopatra. Videocassette. Writ. William
     Shakespeare. Prod. Jonathan Miller. With Colin
     Blakely and Jane Lapotaire. BBC Enterprises, 1980.
     177 min.
```

CD-ROMs and Other Portable Databases

Most portable databases are issued on CD-ROM only, although some can be found on diskette. There is a wealth of information currently issued on CD-ROM, such as the full text of books, newspapers, periodicals, abstracts, encyclopedias, and catalogues. The entries for such databases are much like those for traditional print media, with the following special considerations:

1. You must cite the medium: CD-ROM, diskette, etc.

2. For periodically published CD-ROMs, you must cite the vendor (similar to the publisher of a book).

3. You must cite the date of electronic publication. This may be a little tricky. For example, if you are citing an article that originally appeared in print, you must cite the date it was first published as well as the date the CD-ROM database was released. Most CD-ROM databases are updated at regular intervals, and sometimes this information is only available on the title screen.

1. Periodically Published CD-ROM Database with Publication Information for a Printed Source

These CD-ROMs include material that also appears in print, either previously or simultaneously. For example, the periodical indexes and abstracts you find on computer terminals in the library are linked to a remote CD-ROM. Sometimes newspapers are made available on CD-ROM, such as the *Globe and Mail on CD-ROM* and the *New York Times Ondisc*. The bibliographic information (author, version, vendor, etc.) is usually found on the opening screen. Cite the article exactly as you would using standard MLA format, followed by the title of the database (underlined), publication medium, name of the vendor, and electronic publication date.

```
Kienetz, Alvin. "Ethnic Identity in Northern Canada."
     Journal of Ethnic Studies 14.1 (1986): 129-34. ERIC.
     CD-ROM. Knight-Ridder. Mar. 1995.
```

2. Periodically Published CD-ROM Database with No Printed Source Specified

These databases are updated regularly, but they don't refer to previously printed sources. When citing these sources, include the name of the author (if indicated), title of the material, date, title of the database, medium, vendor, and publication date.

"Aboriginal Affairs (Alberta)." 13 May 1994. <u>FundMe!</u>

   <u>Sources</u>. CD-ROM. IGW Canada. 1994.

3. Non-Periodical Publication on CD-ROM

These CD-ROMs are much like books: they are published once and may or may not be updated. They include encyclopedias, dictionaries, games, works of literature, and any number of multimedia packages. Include the following in your citation: author (if available), title of work (in quotation marks if you are citing only part of the work), title of product (underlined), edition or version, medium, city of publication, publisher, and year of publication.

<u>The Oxford English Dictionary</u>. 2nd ed. CD-ROM. Oxford:

   Oxford UP, 1992.

If citing only part of the work:

"Redundancy." <u>The Oxford English Dictionary</u>. 2nd ed. CD-

   ROM. Oxford: Oxford UP, 1992.

The Internet and the World Wide Web

Bibliographic citations for electronic sources should serve the same purpose as those for print sources. Citations for electronic texts identify their source and should provide enough information for the reader to locate them. Because electronic texts tend to be less fixed and stable than print texts, more information must be provided for them in a citation.

Although the forms of electronic sources of information vary greatly, most students prefer to conduct their research on the World Wide Web because it is easy to use and readily accessible. Citations for publications on the World Wide Web should include the author's name (if given); the title of the work (in quotation marks); the volume number, issue number, or other identifying number; the date of publication; the number range or total number of pages, paragraphs, or other sections if they are numbered; the date of retrieval; and the address (or URL).

Note: Internet addresses in Works Cited entries must be divided after a slash if they are too long to continue on a single line. Do not add a hyphen to separate the address of the entry.

The following examples of citations are consistent with the fifth edition of the *MLA Handbook for Writers of Research Papers* (1999). The same information can be found at <http://www.mla.org>.

1. An Article from an On-Line Newspaper or News Source

Derworiz, Colette. "Funding for New Schools Delayed." <u>Cal-</u>

   <u>gary Herald On-Line Edition</u> 5 Jun. 2001. 28 Jul. 2001.

   <http://www.calgaryherald.com/news/stories/010605/

   5113249.html>.

MacGuire, Katie, and Owen Wood. "TV in the Digital Age."

   <u>CBC News Online</u> Sept. 2001. 10 Sept. 2001. <http://cbc.ca/

   news/indepth/background/digitaltv/html>.

2. An Article in an On-Line Journal

```
Smith, Carol. "Safety in Public Schools." Educom Review.
     31.7 (1997). 10 October 1998. <http://educom.edu/
     web/pubs/review/reviewArticles/32945.html>.
```

3. A Professional or Personal Web Site (Authored and Anonymous)

If you know the name of the person who created the site, begin your entry with it. Otherwise, use the title of the site as it appears at the top of your browser.

```
Smith, John. Having Fun with Documentation. 17 Jan.
     2002. <http://theessayworkplace.com/MLA.html>.

Shakespeare.com home. 17 Jan. 2002. <http://www.
     shakespeare.com>.
```

4. An E-Mail Communication

It is important when you are citing from an e-mail that you include the sender's name, the subject heading of the e-mail, the recipient's name, and the date it was received.

```
Trussler, Michael. "Re: Film and Literature." E-mail to
     Derek Brown. 21 June 2001.
```

APA bibliography format

The following section reflects the format recommended in the fifth edition of the *Publication Manual of the American Psychological Association* (2001).

- APA recommends a minimum one-inch (2.5 cm) margin on all sides, as this is the default on most word processors.
- Right margins are not justified, and words are not broken at the end of a line (it's recommended that you disable the hyphenation feature of your word processor).
- As in MLA, the first line of a reference is flush-left and the second and subsequent lines are indented one-half inch.
- APA uses italics instead of underlining.
- You must indicate the volume number for magazines and newsletters as well as journals. Don't put "Vol." in front of the volume number, and be sure to include the issue number in parentheses following the volume if each issue of the publication is paginated separately.
- Electronic and on-line references must include an availability statement that generally indicates the protocol and location (see examples below).

Here is a list of general rules that distinguish APA from MLA:

1. Only initials are used for first names (middle initials are also included).

2. "Works Cited" is called "References."

3. Only the first letter of all titles of articles and books is capitalized, except proper nouns and words after colons. Capitalize all major words in the titles of journals.

4. The date appears in parentheses immediately after the author's name. The year always appears first in any date used.

5. Quotation marks are not used around the titles of articles from magazines or newspapers.

6. "p." or "pp." is used before page numbers (there are some exceptions); "p." is for a single page, "pp." for consecutive multiple pages.

Following are some sample entries done in APA format.

Basic Book Format

```
Abbey, E. (1975). The monkey wrench gang. New York:
    Avon.
```

Book with Two or Three Authors

```
Flick, J., & Millward, C. (1993). Handbook for writers.
    Toronto: Harcourt.
```

Book with More than Three Authors

List all authors in standard APA format.

```
Voss, R. D., Chow, M., Hunt, A. N., & Klaeber, L.
    (1995). Mastering the art of documentation. Toronto:
    Scholarly.
```

Book with an Author and an Editor

```
Spenser, E. (1978). The faerie queene (T. P. Roche, Jr.,
    Ed.). Markham: Penguin.
```

Corporate or Group Author

Give the full name of the group author, followed by the title. Use "author" to show that the author and publisher are the same.

```
American Psychological Association. (1994). Publication
    manual of the American psychological association
    (4th ed.). Washington, DC: Author.
```

Selection from an Anthology or Edited Book

There are no quotation marks around the title of the selection, and the word "In" tells the reader where it is found.

```
Kennedy, E. (1995). The marketing of Madonna. In P. Jones
    (Ed.), Selling culture (pp. 145-149). Toronto: Oxford.
```

Book Not in First Edition

> Wyrick, J. (1993). *Steps to writing well* (5th ed.). Fort
> Worth: Harcourt.

Book in More than One Volume

Indicate the volume(s) consulted.

> Daymond, D., & Monkman, L. (1978). *Literature in Canada*
> (Vols. 1-2). Toronto: Gage.

Article in an Encyclopedia

Remember to use "In" to introduce the title of the reference book.

> Canada. (1993). In *The new encyclopaedia Britannica* (Vol.
> 3, pp. 234-239). Chicago: Encyclopaedia Britannica.

Signed articles require the author's name.

> Freeman, M. A. (1988). Inuit. In *The Canadian*
> *encyclopedia* (Vol. 2, p. 1084). Edmonton: Hurtig.

Lecture

> Gould, S. J. (1990, April 26). *Wonderful life*. Mount
> Royal College Arts Lectures, Calgary, AB.

Monthly Magazine

Note that the titles of magazine or journal articles are not in quotation marks, while the titles of magazines are italicized. Be sure to use capitals for all periodical titles. Page references don't use the "p." or "pp." abbreviation. Include the volume number (if available).

> Cannon, M. (1995, February). No boys allowed. *Saturday*
> *Night, 110*, 18-24.

Weekly Magazine

In this case, include the precise date.

> Laver, R. (1995, January 2). Mood of a nation.
> *Maclean's, 108*, 10-12.

Article in a Journal with One Author

Note that the volume number is also italicized and that there is no abbreviation for page(s).

> Collier, R. M. (1983). The word processor and revision
> strategies. *College Composition and Communication,*
> *34*, 149-155.

Article in a Journal with Pagination by Issue

> Bridwell-Bowles, L. (1989). Designing research on com-
> puter-assisted writing. *Computers and Composition,*
> 7(1), 81–95.

Article in a Newspaper

> Cernetig, M. (1994, June 16). Probe ordered into hockey
> riot. *The Globe and Mail,* pp. A1, A4.

Personally Conducted Interview

In APA format, personal interviews are not included in your references. You must, however, give parenthetical documentation when citing an interview in your text: (personal communication, July 11, 1994).

Pamphlet

> Swinburne, E., & Roberts, A. (1990). *Gardening tips in a*
> *short season.* Inuvik: Polar Bear Garden Supplies.

Television Broadcast

Follow the standard APA format: name(s), date, title, etc.

> Long, L. (Producer), Finley, B. (Narrator). (1995, July
> 13). *The CBC Alberta news.* Calgary: CBRT-TV.

Video or Film

> Miller, J. (Producer). (1980). *Antony and Cleopatra*
> [videotape]. Toronto: BBC.

The Internet and the World Wide Web

In the fifth edition of the *Publication Manual of the American Psychological Association* (2001), the APA indicates that, at a minimum, a reference of an Internet source should include a document title, a date (either the date of publication or update or the date of retrieval), and the address (or URL). Authors' names should also be provided whenever possible. The reference should enable the reader to find the source by following the path given in the entry. The following are sample entries in a References list using the APA format:

1. An Article from an On-Line Newspaper or News Source

> Derworiz, C. (2001, June 5). Funding for new schools
> delayed. *Calgary Herald On-Line Edition.* Retrieved
> July 28, 2001, from http://www.calgaryherald.com/
> news/stories/010605/5113249.html

> MacGuire, K., & Wood, O. (2001, September). TV in the
>   digital age. *CBC News Online.* Retrieved September
>   10, 2001, from http://cbc.ca/news/indepth/
>   background/digitaltv/html

2. An Article in an On-Line Journal

> Smith, C. (1997). Safety in public schools. *Educom
>   Review.* 31(7). Retrieved October 10, 1998, from
>   http://educom.edu/web/pubs/review/reviewArticles/
>   32945.html

Note: The APA does not require e-mails to be listed in the References because they are considered personal communications.

3. A Professional or Personal Web Site (Authored and Anonymous)

Web Site with Author and Date

> Smith, J. (2001). Having fun with documentation.
>   Retrieved January 17, 2002, from
>   http://theessayworkplace.com/APA.html

Web Site with No Author and Date

> Shakespeare.com home. (n.d.) Retrieved January 17, 2002,
>   from http://www.shakespeare.com

Abstracts on CD-ROM

Most conventional databases, such as abstracts and indexes, are now available on CD-ROM. The author, date, title, and publication elements are the same as the conventional APA style. Following the title and publication information, indicate the vendor, name of database, and retrieval number. There is no period at the end of the citation.

> Kienetz, A. (1986). Ethnic identity in northern Canada
>   [CD-ROM]. *Journal of Ethnic Studies, 14*(1), 129-134.
>   Abstract from: Knight-Ridder File: ERIC Item: EJ
>   335338

Alphabetical listing of principal parts of irregular verbs

Simple Form	Past Form	Past Participle
arise	arose	arisen
bear	bore	borne
beat	beat	beat or beaten
become	became	become
begin	began	begun
bend	bent	bent
bet	bet	bet
bind	bound	bound
bite	bit	bitten, bit
bleed	bled	bled
blow	blew	blown
break	broke	broken
breed	bred	bred
bring	brought	brought
build	built	built
burst	burst	burst
buy	bought	bought
cast	cast	cast
catch	caught	caught
choose	chose	chosen
cling	clung	clung
come	came	come
cost	cost	cost
creep	crept	crept
cut	cut	cut
deal	dealt	dealt
dig	dug	dug
dive	dived, dove	dived
do	did	done
draw	drew	drawn
drink	drank	drunk
drive	drove	driven
eat	ate	eaten
fall	fell	fallen

Simple Form	Past Form	Past Participle
feed	fed	fed
feel	felt	felt
fight	fought	fought
find	found	found
fit	fit	fit
flee	fled	fled
fling	flung	flung
fly	flew	flown
forbid	forbade, forbad	forbidden
forget	forgot	forgotten
forgive	forgave	forgiven
freeze	froze	frozen
get	got	gotten
give	gave	given
go	went	gone
grind	ground	ground
grow	grew	grown
hang	hung, hanged	hung, hanged
have	had	had
hear	heard	heard
hide	hid	hidden
hit	hit	hit
hold	held	held
hurt	hurt	hurt
keep	kept	kept
kneel	knelt	knelt
know	knew	known
lay (to put)	laid	laid
lead	led	led
leave	left	left
lend	lent	lent
let	let	let
lie (to recline)	lay	lain
lose	lost	lost
make	made	made
mean	meant	meant
meet	met	met
mistake	mistook	mistaken
pay	paid	paid
prove	proved	proved, proven
put	put	put
quit	quit	quit
read	*read	*read

* Pronunciation changes in past and past participle forms.

Simple Form	Past Form	Past Participle
ride	rode	ridden
ring	rang	rung
rise	rose	risen
run	ran	run
say	said	said
see	saw	seen
seek	sought	sought
sell	sold	sold
send	sent	sent
set	set	set
sew	sewed	sewn, sewed
shake	shook	shaken
shave	shaved	shaved, shaven
shed	shed	shed
shine	shone	shone
shoot	shot	shot
show	showed	shown, showed
shrink	shrank, shrunk	shrunk, shrunken
shut	shut	shut
sing	sang	sung
sink	sank	sunk
sit	sat	sat
slay	slew	slain
sleep	slept	slept
slide	slid	slid
sling	slung	slung
slink	slunk	slunk
slit	slit	slit
sow	sowed	sown, sowed
speak	spoke	spoken
speed	sped, speeded	sped, speeded
spend	spent	spent
spin	spun	spun
spit	spat	spat
split	split	split
spread	spread	spread
spring	sprang	sprung
stand	stood	stood
steal	stole	stolen
stick	stuck	stuck
sting	stung	stung
stink	stank, stunk	stunk
stride	strode	stridden

Simple Form	Past Form	Past Participle
strike	struck	struck
string	strung	strung
swear	swore	sworn
sweep	swept	swept
swim	swam	swum
swing	swung	swung
take	took	taken
teach	taught	taught
tear	tore	torn
tell	told	told
think	thought	thought
throw	threw	thrown
wake	woke, waked	woken, waked
wear	wore	worn
weep	wept	wept
weave	wove	woven
wet	wet	wet
win	won	won
wind	wound	wound
wring	wrung	wrung
write	wrote	written

Words can be divided into categories called ***parts of speech.*** Understanding these categories will help you work with language more easily, especially when it comes to revising your own writing.

Nouns

> A ***noun*** is a word that names persons, places, or things.

Common Nouns	**Proper Nouns**
officer	Patrick Roy
station	Union Station
magazine	*Newsweek*

Nouns are said to be ***concrete*** if you can see or touch them.

> window
>
> paper
>
> river

Nouns are said to be ***abstract*** if you cannot see or touch them. These words can be concepts, ideas, or qualities.

> meditation
>
> honesty
>
> carelessness

To test for a noun, it may help to ask these questions.

- Can I make the word plural? (Most common nouns have a plural form.)
- Can I put the article *the* in front of the word?
- Is the word used as the subject or object of the sentence?

Pronouns

> A ***pronoun*** is a word used to take the place of a noun. Just like a noun, it is used as the subject or object of a sentence.

Pronouns can be divided into several classes. Here are some of them:

PRONOUNS

Note: Personal pronouns have three forms depending on how they are used in a sentence: as a subject, object, or possessive.

Personal Pronouns

	Subjective		*Objective*		*Possessive*	
	Singular	**Plural**	**Singular**	**Plural**	**Singular**	**Plural**
1st person	I	we	me	us	my (mine)	our (ours)
2nd person	you	you	you	you	your (yours)	your (yours)
3rd person	he she it	they	him her it	them	his (his) her (hers) its (its)	their (theirs)

Relative Pronouns

who, whom, whose
which
that
what
whoever, whichever

Demonstrative Pronouns

this
that
these
those

Indefinite Pronouns

Singular

everyone	someone	anyone	no one
everybody	somebody	anybody	nobody
everything	something	anything	nothing
each	another	either	neither

Singular or **Plural** (depending on meaning)

all	more	none
any	most	some

Plural

both	few	many	several
			others

Adjectives

An *adjective* is a word that modifies a noun or pronoun. Adjectives usually come before the nouns they modify, but they can also come in the predicate.

The adjective comes directly in front of the noun it modifies:

The *unusual* package was placed on my desk.

The adjective occurs in the predicate but refers back to the noun it modifies:

The package felt *cold*.

Verbs

A *verb* is a word that tells what a subject is doing as well as the time (past, present, or future) of that action.

Verbs can be divided into three classes:

1. *Action Verbs*

> *Action verbs* tell us what the subject is doing and when the subject does the action.

The action takes place in the present:

> The athlete *runs* ten kilometres every morning.

The action takes place in the past:

> The crowd *cheered* for the oldest runner.

2. *Linking Verbs*

> A *linking verb* joins the subject of a sentence to one or more words that describe or identify the subject.

The linking verb *was* identifies *He* with the noun *dancer:*

> He *was* a dancer in his twenties.

The linking verb *seemed* describes *She* as *disappointed*:

> She *seemed* disappointed with her job.

COMMON LINKING VERBS

be (am, is, are, was, were, have been)	
act	grow
appear	look
become	seem
feel	taste

3. *Helping Verbs* (also called "auxiliaries")

> A *helping verb* is any verb used before the main verb.

The helping verb could show the *tense* of the verb:

> It *will* rain tomorrow.

The helping verb could show the *passive voice:*

The new civic centre *has been* finished.

The helping verb could give a ***special meaning*** to the verb:

Nellie Furtado *may be* singing here tonight.

COMMON HELPING VERBS
can, could
may, might, must
shall, should
will, would
forms of the irregular verbs *be, have,* and *do*

Adverbs

An ***adverb*** is a word that modifies a verb, an adjective, or another adverb. It often ends in *-ly*, but a better test is to ask yourself if the word answers one of the questions *how, when,* or *where.*

The adverb could modify a ***verb***:

The student walked *happily* into the classroom.

The adverb could modify an ***adjective***:

It will be *very* cold tomorrow.

The adverb could modify another ***adverb***:

Winter has come *too* early.

Here are some adverbs to look out for:

COMMON ADVERBS	
Adverbs of Frequency	*Adverbs of Degree*
often	even
never	extremely
sometimes	just
seldom	more
always	much
ever	only
	quite
	surely
	too
	very

Prepositions

> A *preposition* is a word used to relate a noun or pronoun to some other word in the sentence. The preposition with its noun or pronoun is called a *prepositional phrase.*

The letter is *from* my father.

The envelope is addressed *to* my sister.

Read through the following list of prepositions several times so that you will be able to recognize them. Your instructor may ask you to memorize them.

COMMON PREPOSITIONS

about	below	in	since
above	beneath	inside	through
across	beside	into	to
after	between	like	toward
against	beyond	near	under
along	by	of	until
among	down	off	up
around	during	on	upon
at	except	outside	with
before	for	over	within
behind	from	past	without

Conjunctions

> A *conjunction* is a word that joins or connects other words, phrases, or clauses.

A conjunction connecting *two words:*

Sooner *or* later, you will have to pay.

A conjunction connecting *two phrases:*

The story was on the radio *and* in the newspaper.

A conjunction connecting *two clauses:*

Dinner was late *because* I had to work overtime at the office.

CONJUNCTIONS

Coordinating Conjunctions	Subordinating Conjunctions
and	after
but	although
or	as, as if, as though
nor	because
for (meaning "because")	before
yet	how
so	if, even if
	provided that
	since
	unless
	until
	when, whenever
	where, wherever
	while

Correlative Conjunctions	Adverbial Conjunctions (also known as "conjunctive adverbs")	
either . . . or	To add an idea:	furthermore
neither . . . nor		moreover
both . . . and		likewise
not only . . . but also	To contrast:	however
		nevertheless
	To show results:	consequently
		therefore
	To show an alternative:	otherwise

Interjections

> An *interjection* is a word that expresses a strong feeling and is not connected grammatically to any other part of the sentence.

Oh, I forgot my keys.

Well, that means I'll have to sit here all day.

Study the Context

Since one word can function differently or have different forms or meanings, you must often study the context in which the word is found to be sure of its part of speech.

for functioning as a preposition:

The parent makes sacrifices *for* the good of the children.

for functioning as a conjunction meaning *because:*

The parent worked two jobs, *for* her child needed a good education.

Note: Exercises with answers that may vary are not included.

Step 1   Looking at the Whole

Chapter 1   The Writing Process for the Essay

Activity 6   Editing a Student Paragraph (pages 11–12)

What would you do if your pet turned out to have a terrible disposition? For example, a dog may bark all night or not be good with children. In fact, some dogs have been known to become very jealous of a new baby and have actually attacked infants or toddlers. If you find yourself in this situation, what will you do? Some people have gone so far as to hire special trainers or animal psychologists, but these approaches do not always work. Others live for years being miserable with a dog that is never quite housebroken or with a dog who may snap at its family members and guests. The worst situation is when a pet owner decides the pet must go. This is a terribly painful and often traumatic experience for everyone in the family.

Activity 7   Proofread a Student Paragraph (page 13)

We are all familiar with the benefits of having a dog. Dogs offer companionship without any complaints. You can come home every night to a loving dog who wags his tail at the sight of you. Many experts claim that people who have dogs are healthier and happier than those who are alone. Of course, the best of all situations is if you can enjoy your dog but pass along all the work to someone else in your family, an older sister or a spouse if you are married. Let someone else vacuum the dog hair all day, take the pet out four or five times during a blizzard, go to the store in the middle of the night because you ran out of dog food, and basically stay home all the time to make sure the dog is happy and the neighbours are happy. (Dogs have been known to drive neighbours crazy.) Can you manage this arrangement? If so, by all means get a dog.

Step 2   Structuring the Essay

Chapter 2   Understanding Essay Form

Practice (page 21)
1. F
2. T
3. F
4. F
5. Th

Exercise 1   Recognizing the Thesis Statement (page 21)
1. T
2. F
3. T
4. F
5. Th
6. T
7. Th
8. F
9. F
10. F

Exercise 2   Recognizing the Thesis Statement (page 22)
1. Th
2. F
3. Th
4. F
5. T
6. T
7. F
8. T
9. F
10. Th

Chapter 9   Writing under Pressure

Exercise 1   Methods of Development (pages 107–108)
1. summary
2. comparison/contrast
3. definition
4. classification
5. discussion

Exercise 2   Methods of Development/Parts of a Question (pages 108–110)
1. definition / 4

2. comparison / 2
3. summary / 4
4. discussion / 2
5. cause-effect / 3
6. classification / 6
7. summary / classification / 3
8. discussion / 2
9. summary / 4
10. definition / discussion / 2

Step 3   Creating Effective Sentences
Chapter 11   Finding Subjects and Verbs in Simple Sentences

Practice (page 132)
1. boy: concrete noun, common noun
2. Robert Worthing: concrete noun, proper noun
3. He: personal pronoun
4. road: concrete noun, common noun
5. trees: concrete noun, common noun
6. idea: abstract noun
7. parents and dog: concrete nouns, compound subject

Note: <u>Helen</u> drank the <u>water</u>.
      S   Obj.

Exercise 1   Finding the Subject of a Sentence (pages 132–133)
1. We
2. line
3. Tickets
4. concession stand
5. I
6. date
7. Ticket holders
8. movie
9. date and I
10. lights

Exercise 2   Finding the Subject of a Sentence (page 133)
1. Shoppers
2. department store
3. sale
4. items and electrical appliances
5. I
6. department
7. I
8. customers
9. Salespeople
10. day

Exercise 1   Finding Subjects in Sentences with Prepositional Phrases (page 135)
1. ~~On Monday morning~~, <u>we</u> arrived ~~in Vancouver~~.

2. Our <u>hotel</u> was ~~near Stanley Park~~.
3. ~~From the window~~, <u>you</u> could see Lions Gate Bridge.
4. <u>Both</u> ~~of us~~ enjoyed the view.
5. <u>It</u> seemed a perfect day ~~for sightseeing~~.
6. ~~On the Skytrain~~, <u>we</u> rode ~~to the waterfront~~, where we could see the Expo buildings.
7. ~~After a boat ride~~, the <u>two</u> ~~of us~~ ate lunch ~~at a restaurant in Gastown~~.
8. ~~By that time~~, the <u>suggestion</u> ~~of a nap~~ appealed ~~to us both~~.
9. ~~Toward the end of a busy day~~, some Vancouver <u>boardwalks</u> seem much too long.
10. Back ~~in our room~~, two tired <u>sightseers</u> went to sleep.

Exercise 2   Finding Subjects in Sentences with Prepositional Phrases (page 135)
1. ~~For those of us without a good night's sleep~~, herbal <u>remedies</u> can provide a cure ~~to a haggard appearance~~.
2. ~~Instead of preparing for the day~~, <u>some</u> ~~of us~~ roll ~~over~~ and go back ~~to bed~~.
3. ~~At the last minute in a panic~~, <u>we</u> jump out ~~of bed~~ and rush ~~to our jobs~~.
4. A better <u>approach</u> ~~for the sleep deprived~~ involves herbal remedies.
5. ~~For those awful black circles under the eyes~~, chamomile tea <u>bags</u> can come ~~to the rescue~~.
6. The tea <u>bags</u> should rest ~~on the eyelids for at least ten minutes~~.
7. ~~In addition to our physical appearance~~, our mental <u>state</u> may need some attention ~~on these days~~.
8. A good wake-up <u>call</u> ~~for a sleepy brain~~ is a sniff ~~of rosemary~~.
9. The ancient <u>Greeks and Romans</u> wore laurels ~~of rosemary for mental alertness during exams~~.
10. ~~Of course~~, the ideal <u>solution</u> is proper rest.

Exercise 1   Finding Hidden Subjects (page 137)
1. Why was the <u>bus</u> ~~on my route late~~?
2. There was no <u>sign</u> ~~of its arrival~~.
3. ~~In the middle of rush hour~~, the <u>bus stop</u> was crammed ~~with people~~.
4. ~~Luckily~~, <u>I</u> had plenty ~~of time~~.
5. My <u>job</u>, ~~a temporary data entry position~~, would last ~~for six weeks~~.
6. Would <u>I</u> make a good impression ~~on the manager~~?
7. Here is some good <u>advice</u> ~~for a person with a new job~~.
8. (<u>You</u>) Arrive ~~on time~~.

9. (You) Be ready to work.
10. ~~In this economy~~, good work <u>habits</u> ~~at one job~~ may lead ~~to another better job~~.

Exercise 2 Finding Hidden Subjects (page 138)

1. Do <u>you</u> have an allergy?
2. A food <u>intolerance</u>, ~~the body's inability to digest some part of a particular food~~, is different ~~from an allergy~~.
3. Here is the best known food intolerance: <u>milk</u>.
4. ~~With a food allergy~~, the immune <u>system</u> mistakes a harmless food as a dangerous invader and attacks it ~~with irritating chemicals~~ usually ~~within the first 45 minutes of eating the food~~.
5. How can a <u>person</u> control an allergy or intolerance?
6. (You) Keep a daily record ~~of your diet for two weeks~~.
7. (You) Record any adverse reactions ~~after meals~~.
8. ~~In most cases~~, <u>people</u> can pinpoint the troublesome foods.
9. There is some good <u>news</u>.
10. ~~By avoidance of the offending food for a year or two~~, <u>you</u> may be able to outgrow your adverse reactions.

Exercise 1 Finding Action Verbs (page 139)

	Subject	Verb
1.	Friendship	teaches
2.	You	learn
3.	Friends	enjoy
4.	They	help
5.	friends	watch
6.	friends	speak
7.	We	forget
8.	friends	move
9.	They	write, call
10.	friends	give

Exercise 2 Finding Action Verbs (pages 139–140)

	Subject	Verb
1.	Housework	requires
2.	Plan	saves
3.	people	collect
4.	Others	clean
5.	We	start
6.	Bathrooms and bedrooms	receive
7.	den	gets
8.	dining and living rooms	take
9.	Dusting, polishing, and vacuuming	keep
10.	work	goes

Exercise 1 Finding Linking Verbs (pages 140–141)

1. Sewing is a creative act.
2. It (has become) a less popular activity in the past decade.
3. The cost of clothing is quite expensive.
4. Homemade clothes (will) usually be less costly.
5. Sewing (looks) difficult to many people.
6. I (was) happy about my sewing project.
7. The finished skirt (looks) wonderful.
8. It (felt) perfectly tailored.
9. I (grow) more confident with each new project.
10. I (feel) satisfied with my sewing efforts.

Exercise 2 Finding Linking Verbs (page 141)

1. Puzzles are tests of logic.
2. Sometimes they (appear) deceptively simple.
3. Most people (become) absorbed in a puzzle.
4. Almost everyone (seems) eager to find the answer.
5. Unfortunately, some people (grow) frustrated with the passage of time.
6. The process (is) fun to other people.
7. I (become) especially excited at the final step.
8. I (feel) victorious.
9. (You) (Be) patient.
10. With persistence, a solution (is) possible.

Exercise 1 Finding Helping Verbs (page 142)

	Subject	Verb
1.	Growing	can frighten
2.	Aging	will depend
3.	Adolescents	do ... leave
4.	Forty year olds	will ... worry
5.	Attitudes	have changed
6.	People	are taking

7. exercise   can ensure
8. You   should remain
9. Aging   may bring
10. You   might gain

Exercise 2   Finding Helping Verbs (page 143)

	Subject	Verb
1.	Dreams	should tell
2.	You	may dream
3.	dreams	can seem
4.	event	Did ... happen
5.	Dreams	can ... be
6.	people	might dream
7.	heart	may race
8.	dreams	will be
9.	you	Have ... had
10.	you	Do ... try
11.	That	will ... happen

Exercise 1   Identifying Parts of Speech (pages 143–144)

1. a
2. d
3. f
4. c
5. b
6. c
7. a
8. f
9. e
10. a

Exercise 2   Identifying Parts of Speech (page 144)

1. d
2. b
3. f
4. c
5. a
6. f
7. e
8. a
9. e
10. a

Mastery and editing tests

Test 1   Finding Subjects and Verbs in Simple Sentences (page 145)

	Subject	Verb
1.	field	stretched
2.	berries	bobbed
3.	range	was filled
4.	Cranberries	are
5.	They	conjure
6.	Cranberry	got
7.	cranberries	were known
8.	settlers	noticed

9. blossoms   resemble
10. This   explains

Test 2   Finding Subjects and Verbs in Simple Sentences (pages 145–146)

	Subject	Verb
1.	Jason	attended
2.	He and his father	arrived
3.	they	could watch
4.	some	signed
5.	Jason	accompanied
6.	seats	were
7.	dad	bought
8.	Jason	sat
9.	father	recognized
10.	man	signed

Test 3   Finding Subjects and Verbs in Simple Sentences (page 146)

	Subject	Verb
1.	number	are
2.	those	can do
3.	person	can change
4.	I	had preferred
5.	fliers	can be helped
6.	I	took
7.	fact	is
8.	I	slept
9.	ways	are
10.	(You)	try

Chapter 12   Making Subjects and Verbs Agree

Practice (page 148)

1. arranges
2. includes
3. like
4. arrive
5. promises

Practice (page 148)

1. were
2. was
3. doesn't
4. doesn't
5. doesn't

Exercise 1   Making the Subject and Verb Agree (page 149)

	Subject	Verb
1.	writer	lives
2.	He	was
3.	He	doesn't
4.	we	see
5.	He	wears
6.	I	think
7.	books	centre
8.	book	is

9. We   don't
10. writers   present

Exercise 2 Making the Subject and Verb Agree (pages 149–150)

	Subject	Verb
1.	Clair	was
2.	She	doesn't
3.	parents	don't
4.	they	plan
5.	It	is
6.	brother	lives
7.	He	has
8.	He	doesn't
9.	They	do
10.	Clair	dreams

Exercise 1 Agreement with Hidden Subjects (page 150)

1. is
2. Does
3. makes
4. have
5. are
6. have
7. runs
8. Are
9. poisons
10. leads

Exercise 2 Agreement with Hidden Subjects (pages 150–151)

1. needs
2. is
3. teach
4. do
5. are
6. do
7. fare
8. reduces
9. leads
10. are

Exercise 1 Subject-Verb Agreement with Group Nouns (page 152)

1. wants
2. trains
3. gathers
4. enjoys
5. varies
6. are
7. is
8. gets
9. stands
10. disagree

Exercise 2 Subject-Verb Agreement with Group Nouns (page 152)

1. travels
2. is
3. forms
4. considers
5. determines
6. arrives
7. gathers
8. is
9. rules
10. decides

Exercise 1 Agreement with Indefinite Pronouns (page 153)

1. wants
2. train
3. is
4. acknowledge
5. help
6. is
7. agree
8. is
9. has
10. promises

Exercise 2 Agreement with Indefinite Pronouns (pages 153–154)

1. have
2. has
3. have
4. requires
5. sees
6. are
7. has
8. has
9. do
10. watches

Exercise 1 Subject-Verb Agreement with Compound Subjects (pages 154–155)

1. is
2. sit
3. run
4. makes
5. is
6. need
7. have
8. encourages
9. is
10. do

Exercise 2 Subject-Verb Agreement with Compound Subjects (page 155)

1. are
2. help
3. have
4. seem

5. want
6. desires
7. results
8. continue
9. is
10. give

Mastery and editing tests

Test 1   Making the Subject and Verb Agree (page 156)

Subject	Verb
1. Canadian Tire	has
2. Canadian	knows
3. Customers	receive
4. Canadian Tire	likes
5. It	compels
6. people	say
7. bar	was
8. charities	accept
9. parents	have
10. dad	plans

Chapter 13   Correcting the Fragment in Simple Sentences

Exercise 2   Understanding Fragments (page 161)

1. a. subject
2. b. verb
3. c. subject & verb
4. b. verb
5. b. verb
6. a. subject
7. b. verb
8. d. complete thought
9. a. subject
10. c. subject & verb

Exercise 4   Finding Fragments That Belong to Other Sentences (page 163)

Passage 1   People in elevators sometimes can act strangely. (And can behave rudely.) Most elevator passengers stare at the light above the door. (Not looking at each other.) Others go directly into a corner and stay there. Some people do not wait for others to leave an elevator. They just rush out the door when the elevator stops.

Passage 2   Many of the life forms that exist in the woods are never noticed. Millions of ants, invisible to us. (Live, work and fight in their underground nests.) Beetles hide under nearly every rock and fallen tree. Up in the highest branches,

owls and hawks of many species. (Hunt for food day and night.) The woods are teeming with life, even if we cannot see it.

Passage 3   Over the years, Canadian writer Margaret Atwood has won several important awards for her writing. (Although she had been nominated three times for it.) The Booker Prize, one of the world's most important literary awards, had eluded her. People thought she should have won the prize in 1996 for her book *Alias Grace*. She finally won the Booker Prize in 2000 for her novel *The Blind Assassin*. She was so convinced that she would not win. (That she didn't even have an acceptance speech ready.)

Exercise 1   Identifying Phrases (pages 165–166)

1. gerund phrase
2. prepositional phrase
3. prepositional phrase
4. noun phrase
5. verb phrase
6. prepositional phrase
7. noun phrase
8. verb phrase
9. gerund phrase
10. verb phrase

Exercise 2   Identifying Phrase (page 166)

1. prepositional phrase
2. infinitive phrase
3. participial phrase
4. noun phrase
5. prepositional phrase
6. noun phrase
7. prepositional phrase
8. verb phrase
9. gerund phrase
10. verb phrase

Exercise 3   Using the Participle Phrase as a Noun (Gerund) (page 168)

1. Singing in the shower gave me a thrill.
2. Buying the tickets was an unforgettable experience.
3. Climbing the steps was exhausting.
4. Forgetting the address was frustrating.
5. Fixing the window required great skill.

Chapter 14 Combining Sentences Using the Three Methods of Coordination

Practice (page 176)

1. The <u>actress</u> <u>was</u> nervous⟨ for⟩ <u>this</u> <u>was</u> the night of her debut.
2. <u>She</u> <u>had studied</u> for years⟨ and⟩ <u>she</u> <u>had spent</u> many summers on the road.
3. Now <u>she</u> <u>had</u> to win over her audience⟨ or⟩ the <u>critics</u> <u>would judge</u> her harshly.
4. The other <u>actors</u> <u>could</u> not <u>help</u> her⟨ nor⟩ <u>could</u> her old <u>teacher</u> <u>advise</u> her now.
5. The <u>night</u> <u>was</u> a success⟨ but⟩ now <u>she</u> <u>had</u> to prove herself in new roles.

Exercise 1 Combining Sentences Using Coordinating Conjunctions (pages 177–178)

1. Relationship: opposite
   Marcia is helpful to everyone, but her sister is cool and distant.
2. Relationship: reason
   The retired couple worry, for their pension money may not be enough to live on.
3. Relationship: result
   The baby cried all night, so everyone was tired the next day.
4. Relationship: contrast
   The recruit was eager to prove his abilities, but he didn't volunteer to be the first one to jump.
5. Relationship: result
   Devon decided to help out in the cafeteria at lunch, so she would make some money and meet a lot of the students.
6. Relationship: addition
   Work was going well, and her social life was improving.
7. Relationship: result
   Being popular is important to many adolescents, so wearing the right clothes becomes a priority.
8. Relationship: contrast
   The dictionary entry was helpful, but I still wasn't sure how to use the word correctly.
9. Relationship: addition when clauses are negative
   I couldn't take the train, nor could I take the bus.
10. Relationship: contrast
    The original idea was good, but not everyone agreed.

Practice (pages 180–181)

1. <u>Plants</u> <u>had been placed</u> on tables and counters⟨; in addition,⟩ the <u>windows</u> <u>had</u> all <u>been washed</u>.

2. Comfortable new <u>furniture</u> <u>had been purchased</u>⟨; consequently,⟩ the <u>lobby</u> <u>was</u> much more inviting.
3. The <u>tenants</u> <u>were</u> pleased⟨; indeed,⟩ <u>everyone</u> <u>felt</u> a lift in spirits.
4. <u>We</u> <u>asked</u> the security guards about the changes⟨; however,⟩ <u>they</u> <u>did</u> not <u>seem</u> to have much information.
5. My <u>mother and I</u> <u>had been thinking</u> of moving⟨; instead,⟩ <u>we</u> now <u>decided</u> to stay.

Chapter 15 Combining Sentences Using Subordination

Exercise 1 Recognizing Dependent and Independent Clauses (page 190)

1. IC
2. IC
3. DC
4. IC
5. DC
6. DC
7. DC
8. IC
9. DC
10. DC

Exercise 2 Recognizing Dependent and Independent Clauses (page 190)

1. DC
2. DC
3. DC
4. IC
5. IC
6. DC
7. DC
8. DC
9. IC
10. IC

Practice (page 192)

1. a. Maria went to the party after she finished her work.
   b. After she finished her work, Maria went to the party.
2. a. The dog scratched at the door when he wanted to go out.
   b. When he wanted to go out, the dog scratched at the door.

Practice 1 (page 195)

1. The island that is shared by Haiti and the Dominican Republic is Hispaniola.
2. Tradewinds that blow to Haiti from the northeast bring rains to the island.
3. Haiti is largely protected from storms by high mountains that cover two-thirds of the country.

Practice 2 (page 196)

1. Canada's Walk of Fame, which occupies eleven city blocks in Toronto's theatre district, displays the names of world-famous Canadian artists, actors, and sports figures.
2. People who are inducted into the Walk of Fame must be born in Canada, and their accomplishments must have had a national or international impact.
3. Everyone who joins the Walk of Fame has his or her name engraved on a large granite block.
4. Jacques Villeneuve, who is a Formula One race car driver, was the first person to be inducted into the Walk of Fame.
5. The crowds that gather during the unveiling ceremonies are often so large that busy streets must be closed to traffic.

Chapter 16 Correcting the Run-On

Exercise 1   Revising Run-Ons
(pages 204–206)

1. Two simple sentences:
   Lawren Harris, the great Canadian landscape painter, was born in Toronto in 1885. He was a member of the successful Harris farm machinery family.
   Two kinds of compound sentences:
   a. Lawren Harris, the great Canadian landscape painter, was born in Toronto in 1885, and he was a member of the successful Harris farm machinery family.
   b. Lawren Harris, the great Canadian landscape painter, was born in Toronto in 1885; he was a member of the successful Harris farm machinery family.
   Complex sentence:
   A member of the successful Harris farm machinery family, Lawren Harris, the great Canadian landscape painter, was born in Toronto in 1885.
2. Two simple sentences:
   Harris wanted to become a better artist. He went to Berlin to study art.
   Two kinds of compound sentences:
   a. Harris wanted to become a better artist, so he went to Berlin to study art.
   b. Harris wanted to become a better artist; he went to Berlin to study art.
   Complex sentence:
   Because Harris wanted to become a better artist, he went to Berlin to study art.

3. Two simple sentences:
   He mostly painted landscapes. He sometimes painted urban scenes to show how dreary city living could sometimes be.
   Two kinds of compound sentences:
   a. He mostly painted landscapes, but he sometimes painted urban scenes to show how dreary city living could sometimes be.
   b. He mostly painted landscapes; however, he sometimes painted urban scenes to show how dreary city living could be.
   Complex sentence:
   Although he mostly painted landscapes, he sometimes painted urban scenes to show how dreary city living could sometimes be.

Exercise 2   Revising Run-Ons
(pages 206–207)

1. Two simple sentences:
   Jim wanted to travel. He got a job working on a train in northern Manitoba.
   Two kinds of compound sentences:
   a. Jim wanted to travel, so he got a job working on a train in northern Manitoba.
   b. Jim wanted to travel; consequently, he got a job working on a train in northern Manitoba.
   Complex sentence:
   Since Jim wanted to travel, he got a job working on a train in northern Manitoba.
2. Two simple sentences:
   He worked for minimum wage. He saw some great sights.
   Two kinds of compound sentences:
   a. He worked for minimum wage, yet he saw some great sights.
   b. He worked for minimum wage; however, he saw some great sights.
   Complex sentence:
   Although he worked for minimum wage, he saw some great sights.
3. Two simple sentences:
   Jim fell in love with the province. He might decide to stay.
   Two kinds of compound sentences:
   a. Jim fell in love with the province, so he might decide to stay.
   b. Jim fell in love with the province; therefore, he might decide to stay.
   Complex sentence:
   Since Jim fell in love with the province, he might decide to stay.

Chapter 17 Making Sentence Parts Work Together

Practice (page 212)
1. I
2. her

Exercise Choosing the Correct Pronoun in Comparisons (page 212)
1. they
2. they
3. he
4. ours
5. I
6. we
7. theirs
8. me, him
9. theirs
10. she

Practice (page 213)
1. she
2. me

Exercise Choosing the Correct Pronoun in Compound Constructions (page 213)
1. me
2. her
3. I
4. her
5. he
6. he, I
7. Whose
8. me, her
9. he, I
10. him

Practice (page 214)
1. whom
2. whom
3. who
4. whom

Exercise Choosing the Correct Pronoun Using Who/Whom (page 214)
1. who
2. whose
3. Whoever
4. whom
5. whoever
6. It's
7. Whose
8. who
9. Whoever
10. whom

Exercise 1 Choosing Correct Pronoun Forms (page 215)
1. he
2. me
3. whoever
4. he
5. whom
6. she
7. ours
8. him
9. whose
10. I

Exercise 2 Choosing Correct Pronoun Forms (page 215)
1. I
2. whom
3. theirs
4. she
5. I
6. whose
7. they
8. whoever
9. she
10. we

Practice 1 (pages 216–217)
1. Everyone should wear his or her uniform to the picnic.
2. These kinds of bathing suits will be popular this summer.
3. No one could believe what he or she just saw.
4. Those types of headphones can damage your hearing.
5. Each variety has its own distinguishing marks.

Practice 2 (pages 217–218)
1. I love reading books because as long as I have a good book I can never be bored.
2. You may read only mysteries, but even with this limitation, you can choose from thousands.
3. When we join a book club, we may save money on the books we buy during a year.
4. One might also buy a lot of books one never reads.
5. When I return an overdue book to the library, I must pay a fine of twenty cents for every day overdue.

Practice 3 (pages 218–219)
1. Mrs. Kline asked her neighbour to listen to the local news.
2. During the rehearsal, the producers said we wouldn't be ready for another two weeks.
3. Mom told me, "Give the baby the doll!"
4. I refuse to contribute because the committee won't tell me how the money is used.
5. The plate cracked as it fell off the shelf onto the counter.

Exercise 1   Making Pronouns and Antecedents Agree (page 219)

1. No one can take out materials without his or her library card.
2. If you want to take the tour, you must arrive early.
3. If we want help, we have to catch the waiter's eye.
4. Those types of books scare me.
5. Those secretaries are so good, they might get a raise.
6. If you hold onto it, it won't get lost.
7. These types of thin socks are easily snagged.
8. If you want to lose weight, you must control the urge to eat.
9. Everyone wore his or her cap and gown.
10. The firefighter let the boy wear the firefighter's hat.

Exercise 2   Making Pronouns and Antecedents Agree (page 220)

1. Nobody wants his or her taxes increased.
2. Bob's friend sent Bob Bob's favourite leather jacket.
3. The video cassette recorder ate the cassette, so the tape had to be replaced.
4. In the article, the authors said that some cancers might be genetic.
5. If one is interested in music, one should attend as many concerts as one can.
6. Mark generally passes these kinds of tests.
7. The woman must bring her coach to the next birthing class.
8. George gave Michael a copy of George's photograph.
9. The police really should do more about subway graffiti.
10. Nancy told Amy, "The ship you are sailing on is completely booked."

Practice (page 221)

1. The office is spacious, orderly, and clean.
2. Her jobs include gathering the data, analyzing the data, and preparing the annual report.
3. This is the woman who designs stained glass windows, who creates beautiful glass jewellery, and who makes Tiffany style shades for lamps.

Exercise 1   Revising Sentences for Parallel Structure (page 222)

1. Rick prefers to make dinner than to go out.
2. My singing teacher told me to practise every day, breathe deeply, and give a full interpretation.

3. Content, good grammar, and a signature style are all elements of writing.
4. Our apartment is sunny, newly renovated, and spacious.
5. The subway is crowded, smelly, and expensive.
6. However, it beats riding the bus, taking a cab, or going on foot.
7. At the gym, you can take a class, use the machines, or get a massage.
8. Before you leave, go to the bathroom, wash your hands, and turn out the lights.
9. Rachel often goes to the park rather than stay at home.
10. A parent must be loving, patient, and willing to provide a stable environment.

Exercise 2   Revising Sentences for Parallel Structure (page 223)

1. I want to go to the beach, to the islands, and to the mountains.
2. The books must be organized by size, title, and alphabetical order.
3. He painted in oils, watercolours, and mixed media, sometimes using leaves and flowers on the canvases themselves for a three-dimensional effect.
4. They would rather drink to your health than toast that angry man.
5. My ancestors came from Ireland, Switzerland, and Germany.
6. Losing weight can be difficult, exhausting, and often bad for your health.
7. Catherine may be the greatest actor and singer in the group.
8. The garden has grubs and weeds, yet it produces the largest, firmest, and tastiest zucchini.
9. You are my sister, my friend, and my inspiration.
10. Those CDs must be burned, labelled, and then put away in the locked cabinet.

Exercise 1   Revising Misplaced or Dangling Modifiers (pages 225–226)

1. While John was writing his novel, the cat begged for food.
2. As I was taking a shower, the doorbell rang.
3. The baby sitter wore rubber gloves as she bathed the baby.
4. As I scurried across the lawn, I noticed a group of rabbits.
5. After I fetched the camera, the owl flew away.
6. My sister was born when I was five years old.

7. Because I brought work home to finish the project, the teacher gave me extra credit.

8. Julian admired the $200 ring that was in the case.

9. While I was wearing high heels, I cleaned out the trunk.

10. Feeling dizzy, she clutched the chair.

Exercise 2 Revising Misplaced or Dangling Modifiers (page 226)

1. As I was walking down the street, the wind blew the umbrella inside out.

2. Kim strummed the guitar as she wandered through the restaurant.

3. When Dad put on a tuxedo, Mom said he looked very handsome.

4. The sign in the laboratory said, "No Smoking."

5. The butterflies with the blue wings were attracted to Nancy.

6. While I was staring intently into the microscope, the microbes finally reproduced.

7. We have the room, which looks out on the beach, with two closets.

8. As the baby sucked her bottle, Mother watched the baby take her first steps.

9. As I hiked in the Rockies, the air was crisp and clean.

10. Lee consulted the dictionary as he searched for just the right word.

Mastery and editing tests

Test 3 Making Sentence Parts Work Together (pages 229–230)

1. Farmers say, "You can't be spoiled or pampered if you're going to live on a working farm."

2. If you want to understand what rural life is like, you should try it out for a summer.

3. I had my own idealistic views about life in the country, but these idealistic views turned out to be incorrect.

4. My husband and I lived on a farm in Saskatchewan for three years.

5. Our friends in the city had much more leisure time than we.

6. We were getting up at five a.m. seven days a week, milking the cows even when we were sick, and working throughout the day until the sun set.

7. As we were putting hay into bales in 32 degree heat, the sun proved its power to us.

8. We worked among rows and rows of wheat for several hours a day to find out exactly how much our backs could stand.

9. For at least one month, everyone in the city should exchange places with those who live in the country.

10. Rural people say farm life means working from sun up to sun down, but their lives are satisfying and full.

Chapter 18 Practising More with Verbs

Practice 1 (page 233)

1. became
2. hurt
3. came
4. cost
5. bet

Practice 2 (page 234)

1. feeded / fed
2. catched /caught
3. brung / brought
4. speeded / sped
5. send / sent

Practice 3 (page 235)

1. flew
2. threw
3. swam
4. rode
5. drank

Exercise 1 Irregular Verbs (page 235)

1. sprang
2. rang
3. grown
4. driven
5. swept
6. brought
7. spent
8. lent
9. kept
10. thought

Exercise 2 Irregular Verbs (page 236)

Our city had a problem. Tax revenues kept declining. Officials spent a lot of time and effort worrying about the situation. Then it hit them. They did something very dramatic. They sought permission to open a large gambling casino complex. Other cities shrank their deficits when they opened gambling casinos. The city council thought this would sweep away all the city's financial problems. The news of the plan spread quickly around the city. However, many people knew that the gambling casino solution would send citizens a dangerous message. These citizens fought the proposal with great conviction. The council gradually found other solutions to the financial troubles.

Exercise 1   Practice with More Irregular Verbs (pages 236–237)

1. struck
2. fled
3. stuck
4. left
5. lost
6. paid
7. shook
8. felt
9. took
10. meant

Exercise 2   Practice with More Irregular Verbs (page 237)

He swung the metal detector back and forth. Suddenly he fell to the ground and dug for an object in the sand. Later he told us about all the objects he had found. He met with the owner of the town's resale shop. He slid a few gold objects out of his pocket and held them out to the owner for consideration. Eventually he sold some of these to the owner. On a chain around his neck, he wore two of the rings he had found. We stood watching the transaction and thought to ourselves that all of this was quite remarkable for a boy who was only seven years old.

Practice (page 240)

1. has bought
2. had owned
3. Have, driven
4. have, been
5. had begun

Exercise   Sequence of Tenses (pages 241–242)

1. will continue
2. will soon be
3. would return
4. had told
5. would want
6. will lose
7. will encourage
8. had raised
9. made
10. had taken

Exercise 1   Correcting Unnecessary Shift in Verb Tense (pages 242–243)

1. While driving in heavy traffic, the bus driver was blinded by the sun and struck a parked car.
2. At the start of the examination, I was nervous and unsure of myself; by the end, I was smiling and feeling pretty good.
3. The flutist performed perfectly as always and enchanted the audience.
4. After we make the change on your application, we will put a copy into your file.
5. The editorial criticized the politician, but in my opinion, it didn't go far enough.
6. She was feeling healthy until she suddenly came down with chicken pox.
7. The officer demanded that the recruits be up by 5 a.m. and that they be ready to leave by 5:15.
8. He walked up to his partner and gave him the good news.
9. In the documentary, several people talked about meeting Pierre Trudeau; they recalled his charismatic personality.
10. Her research was going fine when she went and quit the course.

Exercise 2   Correcting Unnecessary Shift in Verb Tense (pages 243–244)

Before he died in July 2001, Mordecai Richler left a wealthy legacy to Canadian literature. Born in 1931, Richler was the son of a scrap-metal dealer. In many of his early novels, he wrote about life on St. Urbain Street, which was the heart of the working-class Jewish community in Montreal during the 1930s and 1940s. During his career as one of Canada's most prolific writers, he went on to win several national and international prizes for his novels and essays. He also won Canada's Stephen Leacock Award for Humour and was appointed to the Order of Canada. Family was always very important to him. His five children probably inspired him to write the famous children's story *Jacob Two-Two Meets the Hooded Fang*.

He lived in London, England, for many years before returning to Montreal to live and work. *The Apprenticeship of Duddy Kravitz*, his most famous novel, was turned into a movie starring Richard Dreyfus. Richler was always a defender of the principles of freedom of speech and equality among people. In 1992, he angered many Quebeckers with his essay *Oh, Canada! Oh, Quebec!* In this essay, he accused many French-Canadian nationalists of being anti-Semitic. Richler went on to write many other essays on topics as varied as his travels in Morocco to biographies of hockey and baseball players. In fact, he loved sports so much that in an acceptance speech for a literary award he jokingly acknowledged he would never win the one award that really meant a lot to him: baseball's Cy Young award.

Mordecai Richler left us a great legacy in the form of his novels and essays. His humour and sarcasm will be greatly missed by all Canadians.

Exercise 1 Active and Passive Voice
(page 246)

1. The verdict was announced by the jury after five hours of deliberation.
2. Elvis Presley created modern pop music.
3. The old municipal building was turned into an ice castle by the sleet.
4. Someone smuggled the priceless vase out of the country.
5. Television viewers showed more attention and concern over the Stanley Cup Finals than over the provincial election involving two contentious candidates.

Exercise 2 Active and Passive Voice
(pages 246–247)

1. The three world leaders announced plans for peace.
2. The Moors dominated Spain from the 8th to the 11th century.
3. The ice, which fell in huge chunks off the bridge, was melted by the sun.
4. Irving Layton wrote the poem in 1962.
5. A pickup truck was borrowed by Daniella to move her furniture to the new apartment.

Practice (pages 247–248)

1. were
2. wait
3. take
4. pass
5. were

Mastery and editing tests

Test 1 Solving Problems with Verbs
(page 248)

1. If he **were** my son, I would insist on a complete physical examination.
2. He has brok**en** his arm more than once playing sports.
3. When he first **began** to play hockey, his mom had worried.
4. They could **have** won the game if they had concentrated more.
5. The coach said that the teachers **would be** attending the game tonight.
6. We **shouldn't** judge others.
7. The guest requested that the room **be** ready.
8. **The uniform was stained by blood.**
9. I **drank** the entire quart of lemonade before the game.
10. One team member wept **when** they lost the championship.

Test 2 Solving Problems with Verbs
(page 249)

1. **Every detail of the wedding was organized by her family.**
2. It was necessary that the mother **make** the wedding gown.
3. The occasion requires that each detail **be** just right.
4. By the time the bride arrived, the guests **were** seated.
5. Most of the food was **brought** by the family to the reception hall.
6. If it **were** baked carefully, the cake would be delicious.
7. The wedding gifts were **hidden** under a table covered with a long tablecloth.
8. She **threw** the bouquet to her sister.
9. Her brothers **swept** up the hall after the reception.
10. They should **have** taken more pictures on their honeymoon.

Test 3 Solving Problems with Verbs
(page 249)

I **had** avoided the dentist long enough. The day **came** when I picked up the phone and made an appointment. The secretary should **have** been surprised to hear my voice, but if she **were,** she soon recovered and **told** me I had to wait a week for their first opening. I insisted that she **give** me an appointment early in the morning. Every night after that I **fell** asleep and dreamed I **saw** the dentist leaning over me and talking about "the first opening." By the time the day arrived, I **felt** scared. Arriving at the office, I **saw** the white uniforms and all the gleaming equipment. My heart **sank.** The receptionist smil**ed** and **took** me to one of the small rooms, but I did not feel comfortable. The large dentist's chair fill**ed** the room. As I **sat** there, the room **became** more and more like a cell. The venetian blinds looked like bars against the grey sky. I sat there in solitary confinement for what seemed like years. Then the dentist came in. She **was** so charming that nearly all my fears vanished.

Chapter 19 Using Correct Capitalization and Punctuation

Exercise 1 Capitalization (page 253)

Although St. Valentine died long before explorers to North America brought chocolate back to Europe, it is easy to see the connection between chocolate and Valentine's Day. To begin with, the origin of our modern Valentine's Day as a celebration of love is in the Middle Ages. In England and France, it was believed that birds began to mate around February 14, a day that corresponds with St. Valentine's Day. This phenomenon was reported by the English poet Geoffrey Chaucer in his poem "Parliament of Fowles." Explorers brought chocolate to Europe from the ancient Aztecs, who considered it an aphrodisiac. They lived in what is now Mexico. Back then, most chocolate was consumed in liquid form and was not sweetened with sugar. It looked and tasted nothing like our Hershey's or Cadbury chocolate bars. When it was first introduced to Europeans, chocolate was considered a barbarous and noxious drug until the doctors in Paris approved it as a beneficial potion. The Europeans also heard the stories about how the Aztec king Montezuma drank the dark liquid chocolate all day to enhance his sex drive. Chocolate then became the perfect gift to celebrate love. But given a choice between love and chocolate, many people would rather have chocolate.

Exercise 2   Capitalization (page 254)

Environmental groups have been busy putting pressure on governments to enact laws that will allow people to see a clear sky during the day. Only recently, however, have people proposed measures that will protect the night sky. After World War II, the growing population and development in the countryside meant more light everywhere. The night sky around a typical town such as Penticton, British Columbia, is more than ten times as bright as the natural night sky. The light over cities such as Toronto and Vancouver is nearly fifty times as bright as the natural light. The problem for astronomers is obvious. Astronomers at the Rothney Astrophysical Observatory (Canada's third largest observatory), located 25 kilometres from Calgary, amateur astronomers, and others who dislike light pollution were thrilled to learn that the city of Calgary is proposing to refit residential street lights with lower-wattage lamps so that there is no direct horizontal glare. The city has suffered very bad light pollution for many decades, making it readily visible on the "Earth at Night" satellite photo. Lighting bylaws have also been passed by the nearby towns of Cochrane and Okotoks. The desire to reduce carbon-dioxide emissions from power plants and the sharp increase in the price of electricity in Alberta have caused Calgary to consider using lighting more wisely.

Practice 1 (page 255)

1. People who get enough sleep are more rested, alert, and focused than those who have stayed up late the night before.
2. The need for sleep varies according to age: ten to twelve hours for children, nine hours for teenagers, seven and a half hours for adults up to age sixty, and about six and a half hours for those over sixty.
3. Our muscles relax during light sleep, relax even more in deeper sleep, and stop activity completely in what is called "dream sleep."
4. Have you ever seen the telltale, dark blue circles under the eyes of people who regularly go without sufficient sleep?
5. Call the Genealogy and Family History Department, National Library of Canada, Ottawa, for more information about your family's history.

Practice 2 (pages 255–256)

1. Olive oil is a very common ingredient for cooking, but people do not realize the range of differences among the many kinds of olive oil.
2. You may choose an inexpensive olive oil from your supermarket, or you might buy a bottle for as much as $35 at a fancy-food shop.
3. Most good olive oils are from Italy, yet there are fine oils from other countries.
4. Betty Pustarfi is devoted to the virtues of olive oil, and she can be found conducting free tastings of as many as twenty oils from many countries every Saturday morning.
5. At her tastings, Ms. Pustarfi provides detailed sheets to explain the properties of olive oil and the characteristics of each oil in the tasting.

Practice 3 (page 256)

1. For many companies in the twenty-first century, a revised dress code for employees is an idea whose time has come.
2. Taking a hint from large corporations, companies of every size are relaxing the rules of dress.
3. To keep in step with the times, employers want to appear flexible and up to date.
4. If an employee wants to "dress down" on a certain day, the new rules allow this freedom of choice.
5. Yes, the more casual atmosphere of the workplace is a welcome change for many people.

Practice 4 (pages 257–258)

1. Politics and public relations, it must be admitted, have become harder to separate.
2. Political commercials on television, for example, depend heavily on the use of images.
3. Ottawa, Ontario, usually a political centre, becomes a centre for advertising campaigns during every federal election.
4. Political debate, which used to appeal to people's thinking, now must use dramatic images.
5. Every voter, however, must make up his or her own mind how to vote.

Practice 5 (page 258)

1. Doctor, the lab results came today.
2. I hope, dear, that you know what you're doing.
3. Sir, the taxi is waiting.
4. You don't, Mother, understand my point.
5. Theresa, are you ready?

Practice 6 (page 258)

1. 10,000,000
2. 504,321
3. 684,977,509
4. 20,561
5. 9,999,999,999

Practice 7 (page 259)

1. "Joan didn't," they explained, "do an adequate job."
2. She declared, "I did exactly what I was told to do."
3. "The truth of the matter is," the publisher admitted, "we can't use her work."
4. "Shall the company," we ask, "be forced to pay for poor quality work?"
5. The judge said, "The contract must be upheld."

Practice 8 (page 259)

1. Striking, the workers picketed the factory.
2. For Mike, Mary Elizabeth Grace is his favourite poet.
3. Honking, the driver alerted the biker.
4. "The procedure does not hurt," the child says.
5. Whatever that was, was certainly strange.

Exercise 1   Using the Comma Correctly (pages 259–260)

For most people, things don't get much smaller than the microscopic level, but researchers at Carleton University in Ottawa, Ontario, are envisaging a new wave of technological devices that operate at the submicroscopic level. Nanoscience and nanotechnology refer to any activity dealing with objects measured in nanometres. Laid side by side, four individual atoms of copper would measure about one nanometre. That's really, really small stuff! The goal of nanoscience is, in fact, to create technological devices that would be able to manipulate individual atoms and create materials at the molecular level. By the year 2100, people think that nanotechnology will become a normal part of life. If people wanted to build something out of steel, they could release millions of nano-sized robots, called nano-bots, into a junkyard to scavenge iron, steel, and copper. They could then build the desired structure, atom by atom. The medical applications, which are nothing short of miraculous, are even more astounding. Imagine being able to operate on a deadly form of cancer by releasing nano-devices into a patient's blood stream, programming them to find the tumour and then having them destroy it, one molecule at a time. There are nano-nightmares, too. Imagine, for a moment, what might happen if someone forgets to include an off switch on these armies of nano-bots.

Exercise 2   Using the Comma Correctly (page 260)

Naomi Klein is a 31-year-old writer and journalist who has made a career out of documenting, criticizing, and fighting against the growing intrusion of corporations in our lives. In her books and newspaper columns, Klein states that huge corporations, such as Nike, Microsoft, Coca-Cola, and others with famous brands and instantly recognizable logos, are trying to dominate our common culture and public spaces. They do this, Klein argues, by filling the world around us with their advertising messages, slogans, and logos. In fact, it is popular today to wear the logos of companies on clothing. Logos have become fashion statements, and some people will pay big bucks to wear a Nike swoosh on their hats, a Puma on their shoes, or a Gap logo on their T-shirts. Many of these products, which sell for lots of money in Canada, are made by child labourers who work for less than two dollars a day. Across Canada, however, more and more young people are listening carefully to Klein's words. Look, for example, at what happened in Toronto recently. Students protested the invasion of corporate brand names into their schools, especially Pepsi-Cola, which has an exclusive contract to sell its products to almost 600 public schools in Toronto. In some cases, the students were disciplined by the school board, but many teachers have become sympathetic to the students' cause.

Exercise 1 Using the Apostrophe (page 262)

1. the **knight's** armour
2. the **runner's** stride
3. the **children's** choir
4. the **girls'** work
5. the **architects'** plans
6. the **bear's** footprints
7. **John and Marlene's** home
8. I **won't** answer you.
9. You **haven't** told me yet.
10. the **mother-in-law's** opinions.

Exercise 2 Using the Apostrophe (pages 262–263)

1. What's happening to the lives of our girls when they enter puberty?
2. It doesn't work to use the experience of any previous generation of women; girls today live in a different world.
3. Therapists' reports detail a tremendous increase of serious and even life-threatening problems among junior high girls.
4. The author and therapist Mary Pipher believes that today's girls are being poisoned by our media-saturated culture.
5. She claims that North America today limits our teenagers' development.
6. At puberty, girls crash into our society's junk culture.
7. Girls know something is wrong, but they do not think of blaming it on society's cultural problems; they tend to blame themselves or their own families.
8. Our adolescent girls' lives are filled with pressures to be beautiful and sophisticated; this translates into junior high girls becoming involved with chemicals and being sexual.
9. Several national leaders' advice is unmistakably clear.
10. Our culture's environment must be more nurturing and less violent and sexualized.

Practice 1 (page 264)

1. Edgar Allan Poe's "The Raven" was first published in the <u>Evening Mirror</u> in 1845.
2. In one of his plays, Shakespeare asks, "What's in a name?"
3. The nurse said that the patient would have to return in a week.
4. A "groupie" is a person who follows popular musicians from place to place.
5. Margaret Atwood's essay "CanLit Crash Course" appeared in the book <u>Survival</u>.

Practice 2 (page 265)

1. Walking in the city can be stimulating; relaxing in a park can be refreshing.
2. The car needs a new alternator now; otherwise, you could break down at any time.
3. The children spent the entire day watching *All Dogs Go to Heaven*, a comedy; *The Little Mermaid*, an animated Disney movie; and *Heidi*, a classic starring Shirley Temple.
4. The town made an effort to attract tourists; as a result, its financial situation has improved.
5. The teacher was very patient; however, the paper was due last week.

Practice 3 (page 266)

1. Three inventions have changed our lives in this century: electricity, the airplane, and television.
2. The sport's fan had only one problem: how to get the player's autograph.
3. She looked for a copy of *Pretty Like a White Boy: Confessions of a Blue-Eyed Ojibway*.
4. She promised she would be on the 10:18 from Moncton.
5. I need several items such as paper clips, tape, and a stapler.

Practice 4 (page 266)

1. He was—or so she believed—a spy from another company.
2. He will bring us at once—and this is really crucial—his passport and other documentation.
3. The study (see the charts on file) was completed in 1989.
4. Mary Pickford (her real name was Gladys Mary Smith) was a famous silent film star.
5. All public figures—and I mean actors, politicians, writers, and sports figures—must be sensitive to the feelings of every group of people.

Exercise 1 Using Other Marks of Punctuation Correctly (page 267)

1. "Gordie" is the essay Mordecai Richler wrote as a tribute to Gordie Howe.
2. To help your children plan their summer, you must do the following: keep their interests in mind, keep an eye on their friends, and keep your budget in view.
3. Writing that letter gave him a lasting, emotional satisfaction.
4. The fall of the Roman Empire, 476 A.D., was a critical point in human history.
5. She wanted to rent a car; he wanted to go by train.

6. Everything she predicted came true: my watch stopped, my car broke down, and it rained that night.

7. Tom Connors, also known as Stompin' Tom, is well known for writing songs about Canadian folklore.

8. Do you know how to say "muchas gracias" in any other languages?

9. Maurice Richard (also known as The Rocket) was one of our country's best hockey players.

10. She gave me her word—I remember this clearly—that she would call back today.

Exercise 2 Using Other Marks of Punctuation Correctly (page 267)

1. She borrowed the book entitled <u>Understanding Media: The Extensions of Man</u>.

2. The road leading to success in business depends on two factors: a lot of hard work and a little luck.

3. "I cannot help you," he answered, "but I will try to be supportive."

4. Her best jewellery—the pieces she keeps in the bank—came from her grandmother.

5. Mavis Gallant's "Between Zero and One" is a short story that has led to a lot of interpretations.

6. Movies, in fact all parts of the entertainment industry, depend on a system of superstars.

7. We refer to that long period after World War II as the "Cold War."

8. Einstein's theory of relativity ($E=mc^2$) still confuses many people.

9. The band was made up of some fine musicians, including Tom Fox, guitar; Betty Ahern, bass; and Joyce Blake, flute.

10. The band's director called for extra rehearsals.

Mastery and editing tests

Test 1 Editing for Correct Capitalization and Punctuation (page 268)

It is difficult to comprehend the meaning of Terry Fox's achievement. He ran a marathon every day across six provinces, for 143 consecutive days, on one leg, to raise money for cancer research. Terry's run, called "The Marathon of Hope," began in St. John's, Newfoundland, on April 12, 1980. He ran across Nova Scotia, Prince Edward Island, New Brunswick, and Quebec. Word of his goal and accomplishment began to spread, and by the time he reached Ottawa, huge crowds would gather to catch a glimpse of him. He stopped his run on September 1, 1980, at Thunder Bay, Ontario, because the cancer that had taken his right leg had recurred in his lungs. He died nine months later, at the Royal Columbian Hospital in New Westminster, British Columbia. Annual "Terry Fox Runs" have raised over $270 million since his death. Today, he is a Canadian icon. Streets, schools, and parks have been named after him; however, his mother, Betty Fox, does not want people to think of him as a hero who did something extraordinary. She prefers people think of him as an ordinary person. She says, "He was ordinary and average, and anybody could do as Terry did."

Test 2 Editing for Correct Capitalization and Punctuation (page 268)

The mother of a young student at the Walker Elementary School teaches an unusual subject: penmanship. The son almost never uses script to write anything. He does sign a card to his mother on three occasions: her birthday, on Valentine's Day, and on Mother's Day. Like many other people, this student is either printing everything letter by letter or using a computer to write. "Penmanship today pretty much stops at the printing level," says Rose Matousek of the Canadian Association of Handwriting Analysts. The post office reports that only 15 percent of all handwritten envelopes are written in script; another 15 percent are hand printed. A related problem, reported in *Maclean's* magazine, is the legibility of what people write. Many pieces of mail end up in the Dead Letter Office of the post office because no one is able to read the handwriting. One researcher reports that 58 percent of all information on hospital charts is also difficult or impossible to read. This is an important fact because a patient who needs Seldane but who gets Feldene will have a very different reaction. Don't you think handwriting is important when your life depends on it?

Test 3 Editing for Correct Capitalization and Punctuation (page 269)

Perhaps the most famous comet in the world is Halley's Comet, which visits our part of the universe very rarely. However, an even more brilliant visitor to our skies is Comet Hale-Bopp, which will be remembered as one of the most spectacular comets of the twentieth century. The comet was discovered on July 23, 1995, and the last time it visited the Earth was in 1997. Prior to this, Comet Hale-Bopp visited the Earth around 2214 B.C., and it may even have been depicted in a stone tablet dating from the old Babylonian empire. In November 1997, people throughout much of Canada could see the comet quite clearly with the naked eye. Some people had what they called "viewing parties" to celebrate the arrival of the comet. Astronomers believe that Comet Hale-Bopp came from the Oort cloud, a vast cloud of dust, rock, and ice that surrounds our solar system like a halo. They think that there may be over 100 billion comets in this cloud, each one waiting for a pull of gravity from the sun. Unfortunately, the comet will also be remembered for its association with the death of 40 members of the Heaven's Gate Cult, in Southern California. These misguided souls were influenced by the rumour that a large UFO was following the comet, waiting for Earthlings to transport themselves up to it.

Chapter 20   Step 3 Review: Using All You Have Learned

Exercise 1   Correcting Fragments and Run-Ons (pages 271–273)

1. R   As a child, Gebrselassie, the great long distance runner, shared a pair of running shoes with his older brother, Tekeye, and a younger sister, Yeshl. The family could not afford to buy each one a pair of running shoes.
2. F   Gebrselassie and his brothers tended crops with oxen and wooden plows, and they walked up to four miles to haul drinking water from wells.
3. F   Their father wanted them to be doctors, teachers, clerks, anything but runners. He discouraged the sport, believing it had no practical use.
4. R   When Gebrselassie was ten, his mother died during childbirth, so his older sister raised the children. (Punctuation missing)
5. F   Gebrselassie followed sports through a battery-powered transistor radio and learned of Ethiopia's Yifter winning a double victory at the 1980 Moscow Olympic Games.
6. C
7. R   Even though Gebrselassie could afford to live in style after he became world famous, he lives in a modest house, routinely goes to bed by 9 p.m. awakening by 5:30 a.m., and goes without a personal coach or a private car because he believes he should live as his people live. (Punctuation and parallel structure)
8. F   With five world records, he was expected to win the gold in the 5,000 and 10,000 metres at the Atlanta Olympics.
9. R   Everyone knows Ethiopia is poor, but when Gebrselassie breaks a world record he hopes that people of the world see that

Ethiopians do what they can with what they have. (Punctuation missing)
10. R   He runs with effortless grace. His head is totally still, and some say he looks like he's out there for a fun run.

Exercise 2   Correcting Fragments and Run-Ons (pages 273–275)

1. F   The Celtic music as we know it today has a long history.
2. C
3. F   It originated in Europe, spread to the British Isles, came across the ocean with Scottish and Irish immigrants, and was handed down to young musicians such as Ashley MacIsaac and Natalie MacMaster.
4. C
5. C
6. R   Ashley MacIsaac's style of Celtic music reflects new musical influences on old traditions, showing what the fiddle can do. He has performed in folk and rock concerts across the globe.
7. C
8. R   The music of the inner city has had a profound effect on MacIsaac; the other great musical influence is punk rock that was popular in the 1980s.
9. R   Brenda Stubbert is another fiddle player from Cape Breton, who dances as well as plays the piano.
10. F   Stubbert's music is a good example of more traditional Celtic folk music.

Mastery and editing tests

Test 1   Editing for Errors (page 275)

Using just pen and ink, Canadian graphic designer Paul Arthur started a communication revolution that spread around the world. Arthur, who coined the terms "signage" and "wayfinding," was a pioneer in what has become the international language of pictographs. We can find the pictographs he developed almost everywhere we look. The simple male and female figures that signify men's and women's washrooms were developed by Arthur, and they were first used at Expo 67 in Montreal, Quebec. The sign designating an area as non-smoking was also drawn by him; it's a cigarette with a red slash going through it. Since these images are almost like an international language, they are commonplace in airports around the world. Arthur also designed a book called <u>Toronto: No Mean City</u>. Another of his important creations are graphic aids designed to help people find their ways around shopping malls and underground walkways. It's hard to believe how much we have come to rely on Paul Arthur's vision and creativity to communicate and to give us direction.

Test 2 Editing for Errors (pages 275–276)

Many centuries ago, the Chinese pounded together a mixture of rags, tree bark, and old fish nets. Then they placed the mixture in a vat filled with water. Soon tiny fibres from the mixture were hanging suspended in the water. If a person dipped a mould into the water and lifted it out, the mixture would dry and become a piece of paper. Today, paper production depends on machinery and modern technology, but the basic process is the same as the one originally used by the ancient Chinese. Fine writing papers still contain a large percentage of rags, although most paper made today contains a great deal of wood. The method of converting wood pulp into paper was discovered only a little more than a century ago. Although the Chinese developed paper making and sold paper to merchants who travelled through China, they kept the secret of how to make paper for a long time. After a few hundred years, however, the Japanese learned how to produce it, and not long after that (around the year 700), the Arabs learned the secret. After that, Arabs introduced paper wherever they traded, and by the year 1200 Europeans were making their own paper. By the 1700s, people in Europe were consuming so much paper that they were running out of rags to use in the process. They also found a wider variety of uses for paper. They built chairs and bookcases out of paper, and in 1793 in Norway, a paper church that could hold 800 people was built. It served its congregation for nearly 40 years.

Test 3 Editing for Errors (pages 276–277)

The famous painter Paul Gauguin had an adventurous life and a troubled career. He was born in France in 1848. Three years later, the family travelled to Lima, Peru, but on the way his father died. Young Paul and his mother lived for four years with relatives in the capital of Peru. After the family returned to France, Paul finished school and went to work in a business office. His marriage to a young Danish woman seemed to give him a traditional lifestyle, but Gauguin now began to turn his attention more and more to art. He bought paintings for himself, became friends with artists of the day, and soon had a studio of his own in Paris. By 1883, he was so interested in art that, over his wife's objections, he quit his job and painted full time. Gauguin moved his large family from Paris to save money, but his savings soon ran out. When he died, several years later, Gauguin's belongings had to be sold to pay off his debts. One person paid $1.50 for the last painting he ever did. Today, any one of his hundreds of paintings is worth millions.

Step 4 Understanding the Power of Words

Chapter 21 Choosing Words That Work

Exercise 1 Using Words Rich in Meaning (page 282)

1. d
2. c
3. e
4. b
5. a

1. e
2. d
3. b
4. c
5. a

Exercise 2 Using Words Rich in Meaning (pages 282–283)

to be funny
1. amusingly odd
2. entertaining
3. humorous
4. uproariously funny

to be polite
1. not rude
2. refined, well-bred
3. observing social etiquette
4. gracious consideration of others

a special way of speaking
1. terms or phrases understood only within a group
2. meaningless word-like sounds
3. a regional variety of a language
4. the specialized or technical vocabulary of a particular field or discipline

to be frightened
1. terrified by intimidation
2. frightened or taken by surprise
3. alerted to danger
4. worried to a frenzy

Exercise 1 Revising Wordy Sentences (page 286)

1. Tuesday we will begin the study of violence in the news media.
2. Violence in the news is making the public very paranoid.
3. Hardly a news program today is without the graphic description of violent assaults.

4. Many children fear going outside their homes.
5. We all need to feel safer in our neighbourhoods.
6. Mothers fear their children are not safe.
7. We are evaluating the quality of our lives.
8. Violence has limited children's freedom.
9. Children need more supervised activities.
10. Children should not come home to empty apartments and houses.

Exercise 2   Recognizing Inappropriate Language for Formal Writing (pages 288–289)

1. hyper: too active
2. pumped up: excited
3. skunk: defeat totally
4. item: pair, date
5. crummy: bad
6. weathermen: weather forecasters
7. bro': close friend
8. up-tight: nervous
9. fib: lie
10. sucker: person easily deceived

Mastery and editing tests

Test 1   Editing for Wordiness and Inappropriate Language (page 289)

The discovery of insulin by Canadian doctors Frederick Banting, Charles Best, and John Macleod was one of the most revolutionary and important moments in modern medicine. In the year 1921, Frederick Banting joined the University of Toronto to help John Macleod and a team of other researchers find a cure for diabetes. Scientists had long thought that there was a connection between diabetes and the pancreas, an internal organ that helps in the digestive process. The team at the U of T, headed by Banting and Best, thought that the pancreas's digestive juices were destroying another important hormone. The goal, then, was to find a way to stop the pancreas from working while not impeding the production of this hormone. By August 1921, Banting and Best had made some conclusive discoveries. The introduction of insulin had a great impact. One year the disease was almost always fatal; the next, people with the disease had hopes of living long lives. In 1923, Macleod and Banting were awarded the Nobel Prize in medicine. Banting was angry because Charles Best's contributions were ignored, so he accepted the prize and then shared his half with Best. Today, there are probably about 15 million diabetics in the world who would have died at an early age without insulin.

Test 2   Editing for Wordiness and Inappropriate Language (page 290)

People are becoming more concerned about social manners. What has happened to consideration for others? Cars do not even stop for elderly people trying to cross the street, and very few people will help a lady who is trying to carry several heavy bags of groceries in the rain. What can we do to encourage people to be more polite? When it comes to pregnant women riding trains and buses, the situation is even more serious. Doctors say that a pregnant woman should not be on her feet when she is tired. She should be given a seat on a train or bus, especially when men are just sitting there, reading the paper in their fashionable business suits. One pregnant woman was really angry when she broke her arm in her seventh month of pregnancy. There she was, standing in a subway car, and no one would get up for her.

Test 3   Editing for Wordiness and Inappropriate Language (page 290)

Parents and children often disagree about homework, but this does not have to be the case. Several points should be kept in mind when a parent helps a child with an assignment. First, find the right spot to do the homework. This usually is the kitchen table. You can even place a sign, such as "Do not disturb," in the area so that everyone in the family will respect the attempts the child makes to complete the tasks. A regular schedule is important. Plan a time in the afternoon or evening when homework gets done. Also, never do your child's homework for him or her; this only creates dependence and gives the teacher the wrong impression. Parents must insist that all homework be completed.

Chapter 22   Paying Attention to Look-Alikes and Sound-Alikes

Exercise 1   Group I: Words That Sound Alike (pages 295–296)

1. past
2. oral
3. whose
4. C
5. their
6. were
7. principal
8. write
9. its
10. too

Exercise 2   Group I: Words That Sound Alike (pages 296–297)

1. presence
2. to
3. it's
4. C
5. C
6. there
7. forward
8. principles
9. stationary
10. whether

Exercise 1 Group II: Words That Sound Almost Alike (page 300)

1.	C	6.	effects
2.	breathe	7.	further
3.	then	8.	quite
4.	C	9.	choose
5.	personal	10.	recipe

Exercise 2 Group II: Words That Sound Almost Alike (pages 300–301)

1.	council	6.	loose
2.	thorough	7.	dinner
3.	used to	8.	conscientious
4.	advice	9.	C
5.	C	10.	C

Exercise 1 Group III: Lie, Lay; Rise, Raise; Sit, Set (page 302)

1.	sitting	6.	C
2.	to set	7.	has raised
3.	lying	8.	C
4.	C	9.	rises
5.	C	10.	lying

Exercise 2 Group III: Lie, Lay; Rise, Raise; Sit, Set (page 303)

1.	sitting	6.	raises
2.	C	7.	C
3.	laid	8.	risen
4.	raised	9.	set
5.	C	10.	C

Mastery and editing tests

Test 1 Words Commonly Confused (pages 303–304)

The Internet is becoming more popular around the world, and we Canadians are among (it's) leading users. A recent poll concluded that (were) the third-most frequent users of the Internet in the world. In fact, more Canadians (then) Americans use the Internet. Sixty percent of Canadians say they use the Internet, compared with 57 percent of U.S. residents. The rate of use in Canada is exceeded only in Norway, at 63 percent, and in Denmark, 62 percent. The study also shows that Canadians frequently (chose) the Internet to purchase goods or services but are (specially) concerned about giving credit card details on-line. Books are the most common purchase via the Internet, accounting for 24 percent of transactions. Next come (close) and computer software. Consumers have become empowered by the Internet. The Internet is also used to (compliment) conventional shopping methods. Even when they do not (by) a good or service on-line, people research on a Web (sight) before making a purchase at a store. No doubt, this growing trend will have a lasting (affect) on how we interact.

1.	its	6.	clothes
2.	we're	7.	complement
3.	than	8.	buy
4.	choose	9.	site
5.	especially	10.	effect

Test 2 Words Commonly Confused (page 304)

Deadly diseases caused by exotic viruses may be coming to a town near you. These diseases are transmitted to humans through a variety of ways. For example, (its) thought that Lyme disease, (witch) is caused by a bacteria (past) on to humans by the blacklegged tic, migrated to parts of Canada with birds (who's) flight paths took them (thorough) infested parts of the United States. Sufferers of Lyme disease report swelling of their joints, headaches, and (loosing) their appetites. But migratory animals aren't (quiet) the only ones guilty of transporting diseases from one country to another. Humans are the (principle) cause of the spread of diseases. People who travel to exotic countries to experience foreign cultures and climates expose themselves to bacteria and viruses that (there) not used to. It is thought that a recent case of malaria, a blood disease common in the tropics and transmitted by mosquitoes, occurred when someone returned to Canada with an active case of the disease and was bit by a mosquito, which then bit someone else. So be careful the next time you buy a (plain) ticket; you may find yourself being bitten by more than just the travel bug.

1.	it's	6.	losing
2.	which	7.	quite
3.	passed	8.	principal
4.	whose	9.	they're
5.	through	10.	plane

Test 3 Words Commonly Confused (pages 304–305)

During the 1600s, European explorers (choose) to cross the Atlantic Ocean in search of the elusive Northwest Passage that would bring them to the Orient. Hudson, an (imminent) sailor, was confident that he could find this shortcut to the East. In 1610, Hudson set out in search of the Northwest Passage on his ship *Discovery*. He navigated the treacherous tides and ice (flows) of the Arctic waters. He (than) entered a large body of water and assumed that it was the Pacific Ocean. Several weeks passed before Hudson and his crew realized they were well off (coarse) Although they had sailed farther than any other explorers, they (where) not, in fact, on the Pacific. The large body of water they discovered was a bay that now bears Hudson's name: Hudson Bay. They had to spend the winter in the north, in freezing (whether) without winter (cloths,) and short on rations. These conditions had a terrible (affect) on his men's morale. His crew mutinied, blaming Hudson for the failure of their mission. The deserters acted with (conscious) and forced Hudson and seven men, including his son, adrift in a small boat. Hudson and his men died in the wilderness; no trace has ever been found of them.

1. chose
2. eminent
3. floes
4. then
5. course
6. were
7. weather
8. clothes
9. effect
10. conscience

READINGS

CONTENTS

My Father, the Liberator

ALLEN ABEL

Most people know of a family member who has fought in a war. In the following autobiographical narrative written on the 50th anniversary of VE day, Allen Abel discusses the impact war has had on his family and other people he knows.

1   Fifty years ago this spring, my father liberated Europe. It didn't take him long. He went over on a troop ship in the fall of 1944—sick as a dog all the way—and in May of '45, the Nazis quit. Later that summer, he was in California, about to be reassigned to the Pacific war, but when the Japanese heard that Sgt. Ben Abel was on his way westward, they surrendered, too.

2   I don't have many of the details of how my father beat the Germans. I know that he was in a regiment, or a battalion, or suchlike, called the Timber Wolves, and that it was a "spearhead" unit sent furiously forward through France and Belgium and into the Reich itself. And I know that my father and his comrades were ordered to ride on the outside of tanks as they rumbled towards the Rhineland, but they camouflaged themselves so well by holding boughs and branches that only about half of them were picked off by snipers.

3   My father was, and is, a small target. When he and the other Timber Wolves were fighting house to house, sometimes hand to hand, and one of his friends would have his head taken off or his body shredded by enemy fire, my father would keep very low, and he believes that's why he managed to be wounded only once, by shrapnel, near his eye. It wasn't a very deep puncture, so they sent him back to the front.

4   We haven't talked about the war that much, my father and I, not nearly as much as we've talked about hockey or baseball. He's not shy about it—not as taciturn as my wife's father, who refused to talk about the war at all—but my questions are uninformed. I never was a soldier. But my father was.

5   I have a friend named David whose father was in the RAF. He flew bombing raids over Germany. But he died when David was 17, and David says: "At 17, boys aren't really into asking their dads about wars."

6   A few years after his father died, David met an uncle. The uncle told him that David's father had been permanently altered by the war. The uncle said: "Something happened to him over there. He saw something, or he did something. He was never the same after the war." But David's father is dead now, and the son cannot ask him what the "something" was.

7   David's wife's father was in the war, too. But he lost most of his hearing firing his rifle at the Japanese, and now that he's past 80 and will not wear a hearing aid, David's wife can't get the time of day out of him, let alone war stories.

8   My mother's second husband, Freddie, was in the navy, but the only thing he ever told me about his military career was that he got to box a round or two against the great Rocky Marciano in some serviceman's exhibition. Or maybe it was Rocky Graziano. Freddie died nine years ago, so I'll never know for certain.

9   It is a precious thing, to be the son of a liberator, and a painful enterprise, to poke at unspoken wounds. Take my friend Elliott. He knows that his father was highly decorated for naval service, but he doesn't know where the medals are today or how his father earned them. This eats at him.

10   Elliott says: "He was in every major battle in the Pacific. He was blown off a destroyer. The five other guys at his gunnery position were killed. He spent two days in the water before they picked him up. He's told me nothing else. Zero. Nada. It's one of the most frustrating things of my life, not knowing."

11   Lately, Elliott's father has begun to tell Elliott's daughters about the war. But he won't tell his own son.

12   My wife's father wouldn't tell anyone. Sgt. Jim Deyo left the family farm north of Kingston, Ont., to serve king and country when the war broke out, and he didn't come home for six years. My wife's mother wanted to marry him before he left for England, but he refused, because he didn't want her to be so young a widow. So she waited for him, all that time. We have a tiny black-and-white photo of Sgt. Deyo in our bedroom: six Canadian soldiers are perched on the bonnet of a big army truck, my wife's father at the rear of the pack, suntanned and squinting a smile. He's dead now. Where he drove those trucks, across what hostile lands, carrying what cargo, he never would say. Never.

13   It's not easy to conceive of my own father as a warrior, though he was one, 50 years ago this spring. He's still an active man at 83, working part-time as a cashier in a pharmacy, and pedalling his bicycle around and around his tidy Century Village in Florida. He used to go to veterans' clubs, but not any more. Yet when we were together in Boston last year for a holiday, he suddenly recollected the name of one of his pack of Timber Wolves who hailed from Massachusetts, and he found the name in the phone book and called him time and time again. There was no answer.

14   Soon, there is going to be a lot of noise about the 50th anniversary of VE-Day. I wanted my father to know that I was thinking about it, and him. I called him recently and we talked for a moment about what to me will always be Ben Abel's war.

15   "Wasn't your unit called the Timber Wolves?" I asked.

16   "That was us," he replied. "Night fighters. That was our reputation."

17   "Did you really fight at night?"

18   "Yes," my father said, very softly. "And in the daytime, too."

Questions for Critical Thinking

1. In many ways, this narrative is both funny and painful. What do you think the author is saying about the heroism of those who fought in World War II in particular and wars in general?

2. What do we know about the men Abel portrays in his narrative? What kind of men are they?

3. Take a survey of your classmates. How many of them have had family who have fought in or survived a war? What are the effects war has had on their families?

4. In this short piece, the author lists many men he knows who have fought wars. What is Abel's purpose for doing this?

Writing in Response

1. Write a story about a soldier in a war. What kinds of experiences would be important to tell?

2. Find a photograph that depicts war. Imagine the circumstances that led to the situation depicted in the photograph. Write a story based on this situation.

3. Interview someone you know who has fought in a war. After the interview, compile your notes and write a biographical sketch of this person.

4. Think of a situation that was difficult for you to overcome and write a story about how you overcame this difficulty.

5. Many people internalize traumatic experiences such as war and, like the men in Abel's story, rarely discuss them even with close family. Why do you think this is the case? Write an essay in which you discuss this phenomenon.

6. How might children encourage their parents to share past experiences with them? Write a letter to a relative wherein you ask about his or her childhood and growing up. Be sure to include your reasons and the purpose for writing the letter.

Deficits

MICHAEL IGNATIEFF

Alzheimer's disease is a devastating illness that affects many elderly people. This story, written by Canadian journalist Michael Ignatieff, recalls the effects Alzheimer's had on his family. Ignatieff uses examples to characterize this illness.

1 It begins the minute Dad leaves the house.

2 "Where is George?"

3 "He is out now, but he'll be back soon."

4 "That's wonderful," she says.

5 About three minutes later she'll look puzzled: "But George ..."

6 "He's away at work, but he'll be back later."

7 "I see."

8 "And what are you doing here? I mean it's nice, but ..."

9 "We'll do things together."

10 "I see."

11 Sometimes I try to count the number of times she asks me these questions but I lose track.

12 I remember how it began, five or six years ago. She was 66 then. She would leave a pot to boil on the stove. I would discover it and find her tearing through the house, muttering, "My glasses, my glasses, where the hell are my glasses?"

13 I took her to buy a chain so that she could wear her glasses around her neck. She hated it because her mother used to wear *her* glasses on a chain. As we drove home, she shook her fist at the windscreen.

14 "I swore I'd never wear one of these damned things."

15 I date the beginning to the purchase of the chain, to the silence that descended over her as I drove her home from the store.

16 The deficits, as the neurologists call them, are localized. She can tell you what it felt like when the Model T Ford ran over her at the school gates when she was a girl of seven. She can tell you what a good-looking man her grandfather was. She can tell you what her grandmother used to say, "A genteel sufficiency will suffice," when turning down another helping at dinner. She remembers the Canadian summer nights when her father used to wrap her in a blanket and take her out to the lake's edge to see the stars.

17 But she can't dice an onion. She can't set the table. She can't play cards. Her grandson is five, and when they play pairs with animal cards, he knows where the second penguin will be. She just turns up cards at random.

18 He hits her because she can't remember anything, because she keeps telling him not to run around quite so much.

19 Then I punish him. I tell him he has to understand.

20 He goes down on the floor, kisses her feet, and promises not to hit her again.

21   She smiles at him, as if for the first time, and says, "Oh, your kiss is so full of sugar."

22   After a week with him, she looks puzzled and says, "He's a nice little boy. Where does he sleep? I mean, who does he belong to?"

23   "He's your grandson."

24   "I see." She looks away and puts her hand to her face.

25   My brother usually stays with her when Dad is out of town. Once or twice a year, it's my turn. I put her to bed at night. I hand her the pills—small green ones that are supposed to control her moods—and she swallows them. I help her out of her bra and slip, roll down her tights, and lift the nightie over her head. I get into the bed next to hers. Before she sleeps she picks up a Len Deighton and reads a few paragraphs, always the same paragraphs, at the place where she has folded down the page. When she falls asleep, I pick the book off her chest and I pull her down in the bed so that her head isn't leaning against the wall. Otherwise she wakes up with a crick in her neck.

26   Often when I wake in the night, I see her lying next to me, staring into the dark. She stares and then she wanders. I used to try to stop her, but now I let her go. She is trying to hold on to what is left. There is a method in this. She goes to the bathroom every time she wakes, no matter if it is five times a night. Up and down the stairs silently, in her bare feet, trying not to wake me. She turns the lights on and off. Smoothes a child's sock and puts it on the bed. Sometimes she gets dressed, after a fashion, and sits on the downstairs couch in the dark, clutching her handbag.

27   When we have guests to dinner, she sits beside me at the table, holding my hand, bent forward slightly to catch everything that is said. Her face lights up when people smile, when there is laughter. She doesn't say much any more; she is worried she will forget a name and we won't be able to help her in time. She doesn't want anything to show. The guests always say how well she does. Sometimes they say, "You'd never know, really." When I put her to bed afterward I can see the effort has left her so tired she barely knows her own name.

28   She could make it easier on herself. She could give up asking questions.

29   "Where are we now, is this our house?"

30   "Yes."

31   "Where is our house?"

32   "In France."

33   I tell her: "Hold my hand, I'm here. I'm your son."

34   "I know."

35   But she keeps asking where she is. The questions are her way of trying to orient herself, of refusing and resisting the future that is being prepared for her.

36   She always loved to swim. When she dived into the water, she never made a splash. I remember her lifting herself out of the pool, as sleek as a seal in a black swimsuit, the water pearling off her back. Now she says the water is too cold and taking off her clothes too much of a bother. She paces up and down the poolside, watching her grandson swim, stroking his towel with her hand, endlessly smoothing out the wrinkles.

37   I bathe her when she wakes. Her body is white, soft, and withered. I remember how, in the changing-huts, she would bend over as she slipped out of her bathing suit. Her body was young. Now I see her skeleton through her skin. When I wash her hair, I feel her skull. I help her from the bath, dry her legs, swathe her in towels, sit her on the edge of the bath and cut her nails: they are horny and yellow. Her feet are gnarled. She has walked a long way.

38   When I was as old as my son is now I used to sit beside her at the bedroom mirror watching her apply hot depilatory wax to her legs and upper lip. She would pull her skirt up to her knees, stretch her legs out on the dresser, and sip beer from the bottle, while waiting for the wax to dry. "Have a sip," she would say. It tasted

bitter. She used to laugh at the faces I made. When the wax had set, she would begin to peel it off, and curse and wince, and let me collect the strips, with fine black hairs embedded in them. When it was over, her legs were smooth, silky to touch.

39   Now I shave her. I soap her face and legs with my shaving brush. She sits perfectly still; as my razor comes around her chin we are as close as when I was a boy.

40   She never complains. When we walk up the hill behind the house, I feel her going slower and slower, but she does not stop until I do. If you ask her whether she is sad, she shakes her head. But she did say once, "It's strange. It was supposed to be more fun than this."

41   I try to imagine what the world is like for her. Memory is what reconciles us to the future. Because she has no past, her future rushes to her, a bat's wing brushing against her face in the dark.

42   "I told you. George returns on Monday."

43   "Could you write that down?"

44   So I do. I write it down in large letters, and she folds it in her white cardigan pocket and pats it and says she feels much less worried.

45   In half an hour, she has the paper in her hand and is showing it to me.

46   "What do I do about this?"

47   "Nothing. It just tells you what is going to happen."

48   "But I didn't know anything of this."

49   "Now you do," I say and I take the paper away and tear it up.

50   It makes no sense to get angry at her, but I do.

51   She is afraid Dad will not come back. She is afraid she has been abandoned. She is afraid she will get lost and never be able to find her way home. Beneath the fears that have come with the forgetting, there lie anxieties for which she no longer has any names.

52   She paces the floor, waiting for lunch. When it is set before her, she downs it before anyone else, and then gets up to clear the plates.

53   "Why the hurry?" I ask her.

54   She is puzzled. "I don't know," she says. She is in a hurry, and she does not know why. She drinks whatever I put before her. The wine goes quickly.

55   "You'll enjoy it more if you sip it gently."

56   "What a good idea," she says and then empties the glass with a gulp.

57   I wish I knew the history of this anxiety. But I don't. All she will tell me is about being sprawled in the middle of Regent Street amid the blood and shop glass during an air raid, watching a mother shelter a child, and thinking: I am alone.

58   In the middle of all of us, she remained alone. We didn't see it. She was the youngest girl in her family, the straggler in the pack, born cross-eyed until they straightened her eyes out with an operation. Her father was a teacher and she was dyslexic, the one left behind.

59   In her wedding photo, she is wearing her white dress and holding her bouquet. They are side by side. Dad looks excited. Her eyes are wide open with alarm. Fear gleams from its hiding place. It was her secret and she kept it well hidden. When I was a child, I thought she was faultless, amusing, regal. My mother.

60   She thinks of it as a happy family, and it was. I remember them sitting on the couch together, singing along to Fats Waller records. She still remembers the crazy lyrics they used to sing:

There's no disputin'
That's Rasputin
The high-falutin loving man

I don't know how she became so dependent on him, how she lost so many of the wishes she once had for herself, and how all her wishes came to be wishes for him.

61   She is afraid of his moods, his silences, his departures, and his returns. He has become the weather of her life. But he never lets her down. He is the one who sits with her in the upstairs room, watching television, night after night, holding her hand.

62   People say: it's worse for you, she doesn't know what is happening. She used to say the same herself. Five years ago, when she began to forget little things, she knew what was in store, and she said to me once, "Don't worry. I'll make a cheerful old nut. It's you who'll have the hard time." But that is not true. She feels everything. She has had time to count up every loss. Every night, when she lies awake, she stares at desolation.

63   What is a person? That is what she makes you wonder. What kind of a person are you if you only have your habits left? She can't remember her grandson's name, but she does remember to shake out her tights at night and she never lets a dish pass her by without trying to clean it, wipe it, clear it up, or put it away. The house is littered with dishes she is putting away in every conceivable cupboard. What kind of person is this?

64   It runs in the family. Her mother had it. I remember going to see her in the house with old carpets and dark furniture on Prince Arthur Avenue. The windows were covered with the tendrils of plants growing in enormous Atlas battery jars, and the parquet floors shone with wax. She took down the giraffe, the water buffalo, and the leopard—carved in wood—that her father had brought back from Africa in the 1880s. She sat in a chair by the fire and silently watched me play with them. Then—and it seems only a week later—I came to have Sunday lunch with her and she was old and diminished and vacant, and when she looked at me she had no idea who I was.

65   I am afraid of getting it myself. I do ridiculous things: I stand on my head every morning so that the blood will irrigate my brain; I compose suicide notes, always some variant of Captain Oates's: "I may be gone for some time." I never stop thinking about what it would be like for this thing to steal over me.

66   She has taught me something. There are moments when her pacing ceases, when her hunted look is conjured away by the stillness of the dusk, when she sits in the garden, watching the sunlight stream through all the trees they planted together over 25 years in this place, and I see something pass over her face which might be serenity.

67   And then she gets up and comes toward me looking for a glass to wash, a napkin to pick up, a child's toy to rearrange.

68   I know how the story has to end. One day I return home to see her and she puts out her hand and says: "How nice to meet you." She's always charming to strangers.

69   People say I'm already beginning to say my farewells. No, she is still here. I am not ready yet. Nor is she. She paces the floor, she still searches for what has been lost and can never be found again.

70   She wakes in the night and lies in the dark by my side. Her face, in profile, against the pillow has become like her mother's, the eye sockets deep in shadow, the cheeks furrowed and drawn, the gaze ancient and disabused. Everything she once knew is still inside her, trapped in the ruined circuits—how I was when I was little, how she was when I was a baby. But it is too late to ask her now. She turns and notices I am awake too. We lie side by side. The darkness is still. I want to say her name. She turns away from me and stares into the night. Her nightie is buttoned at the neck like a little girl's.

Questions for Critical Thinking

1. What examples of the narrator's own experiences does he discuss in this piece? What does this reveal about how he coped with this illness?

2. Compare the writer's description of Alzheimer's to a clinical definition used by doctors to diagnose this disease.

3. What does the author mean when he says, "Memory is what reconciles us to the future"?

4. How does the narrator care for his mother? What does this indicate about their relationship? Provide specific examples from the text.

5. The essay ends with a series of short sentences. What is the effect that is created by this writing style? Why did the author choose to write this portion of the essay in this way?

Writing in Response

1. Write an essay about the effects that the illness of a family member or close friend has had on you. How did you care for this person? What were some of the symptoms of this illness? Provide examples of its impact on others as well as on the individual who was sick.

2. In this essay, the narrator compares his life with his mother when he was a child to his life with her when he was an adult. How has your relationship changed with your loved ones as you've matured? Write an essay in which you discuss this change. Be sure to use examples that illustrate your points.

3. At one point in the essay, Michael Ignatieff wonders, "What kind of person are you if you only have your habits left?" What habits do you have that you think are unique? Write a humorous essay that describes some of your more unique habits. Be sure to keep in mind both your audience and your purpose for writing.

There Goes the Neighborhood
JIM SHAHIN

Although all neighbourhoods may change over time, some aspects of living in a community remain the same. In the following essay, Jim Shahin's fond memories of his old neighbourhood lead him to realize that while his life has progressed far beyond the little world of his childhood, some truths about living with others in a community will always remain.

1   There is an order to my neighborhood, a rhythm to its life. It is an order and a rhythm I've come to know during the eight years I've lived in my house. But the order has been disrupted and the rhythm set off its beat. The reason is the house next door.

2   The house next door has been empty since before Thanksgiving, maybe Halloween, I don't remember exactly. I only know it's been a while and the suspense is killing me: What's happening with the house? When is somebody going to move in? Who is it going to be?

3   I keep hoping the new occupant will be a family with a kid my son's age and parents we like. But it'll probably be me of twenty years ago—some guy with a loud stereo and weird friends.

4   Please, God, not that. Please, not all-night parties with people hanging out on the front porch drinking keg beer until dawn. Please, no hard rock blasting through the walls causing visitations from the police. And please, please, please, no colored plastic owls with little light bulbs in them illuminating the backyard with its furniture of metal folding chairs and telephone-cable-spool tables.

5   As I look back on those days, I recall the mother's curse: May you have a child just like yourself. A worse fate is to have neighbors in their twenties who are just like you when you were that age.

6   A neighborhood is a delicate thing, but a resilient thing. There are deaths and births and graduations, and tuna casseroles at all of them. Neighborhoods are also indelible. You remember everything about where you grew up—the way the misty light from the street lamp shone on the snow, the person who lived next door, the smell in the bluish evening air of roasting meats at dinner time, the closest kid your age, the mounds of raked leaves piled every year at the same place by the curb. These, anyway, are among the things I remember.

7   There are nice people, like the woman who tipped me a dime every week when I went to collect for my paper route. There are mean people, like the guy across the street who would make a face, shake his fist, and keep our ball if it rolled into his yard. (We started tormenting him by smacking crab apples onto his lawn with a tennis racket.) And there are the just plain weird people, like the guy who went a little nuts one night and, when asked by his neighbor to turn off his porch light because it was shining into their side of the duplex, responded by grabbing a shotgun and marching down the middle of the street blasting it into the air and yelling admonitions, while his wife trailed behind him in her bathrobe hollering, "You tell him, hon!"

8   I remember playing handball, stickball, and football in the street. I remember the enormous sixty-foot blue spruce on the corner of our yard and climbing to the very top and swaying back and forth in the wind and being afraid. I remember beating up a kid who was a year older than me because I caught him beating up my younger brother. I remember my friends with their unlikely names, Itchy and Rusty, and going to their houses and wondering at Rusty's why my family couldn't have hoagies for dinner like this family did and at Itchy's discovering the transcendent delight of peanut butter and butter on toast.

9   I remember the blond girl about five or six years older than me, who I thought was absolutely gorgeous and who baby-sat me. I forgave her because I adored her. She was sitting on my porch baby-sitting one summer evening when suddenly I was overcome with an uncontrollable urge to kiss her. I did. Rather than make me feel like the foolish little kid that I was, she said simply, "I could use a root beer. Let's go inside." And she rose from the lawn chair, all poise and dignity, rolled up the teen magazine she had been reading, and went into the house. I stayed on the porch, frozen with mortification at what I had done. Then I ran off into the neighborhood, hoping it hadn't seen, and looking to it for comfort.

10   As a kid growing up, your neighborhood is the world and it takes a long time before you realize that the world is not your neighborhood. These days, the world of the neighborhood belongs more to Sam, my six-year-old son, than to me. The impressions he is forming of his place will stay with him forever, shaping in some important ways his sense of the world, and I often wonder what those impressions are.

11   We live in an older neighborhood of gently rolling hills, big houses, and large old pecan and live oak trees. Geographically it is small and, depending on your viewpoint, either within walking distance of restaurants, grocery stores, doctors

offices, record stores, a nightclub, a liquor store, some fast-food joints, a coffee bar, a vintage-clothes place, a comic-book shop, and assorted other retail outlets, or it is in the ever-tightening vice grip of commercial development.

12   An in-town neighborhood a few blocks from the university, its social mix is diverse. There are retirees, twentysomethings, families, professors, graduate students, state government employees, fast-food workers, rock-and-rollers, and a few people whose lives I think it's probably best I didn't know much about. It is a quiet neighborhood. Few kids live in it. And although it is close to campus, it does not attract the bare-chested, Jeep-riding, beer-swilling crowd.

13   What will Sam remember of all this? Maybe the little girl down the street with whom he sometimes plays. Probably the ice-cream parlor a few blocks away. Undoubtedly the burger joint down the hill.

14   My wife says he'll most likely recall the sound of clomping feet. Built in 1911, our house is two stories, but, like many of the houses in the neighborhood, it was carved into a triplex years ago. We live on the first floor and rent out the two units above us. The floors are hardwood throughout. Great aesthetically. Not so hot acoustically.

15   Maybe, though, it won't be the clomping that Sam remembers. Maybe it'll be the cooing of the doves that one of the tenants keeps. Or maybe it will be the neighborhood itself, its shadings and scents and sounds, or maybe the people who comprise it, such as the large elderly man across the street who, I'm told, is a professor of English at the university and who we usually see doing something industrious like chopping wood, or the guy who walks his dogs so much it seems like it's his job.

16   Or maybe his memories will be of the house next door. Lately, there has been some activity in and around the house. We've seen a beige collie in the backyard on occasion. And we've heard music coming from the house while power drills are running. But no one lives there yet.

17   I haven't seen the guy, only glimpsed his dog and heard his music. He likes his music loud. We can hear it from our porch. It's rock. Hard rock. Hard, loud, depresso, scream, rage rock. The kind of stuff I fear I would be listening to if I was in my twenties.

18   I contemplate the possibilities. Maybe he's a carpenter doing some renovation work for the people who are moving in and he likes to bring his dog to the job site. Or maybe he's the new neighbor, getting the place ready before setting up residence.

19   And I remember my mother's words. And I figure I could do worse. The neighborhood's resilient. So am I.

20   Maybe I'll take him a tuna casserole.

Questions for Critical Thinking

1. The author's title gives the reader one impression of what the essay will be about, but it is not until paragraph 5 that we learn who is being referred to in that title. Why does the writer give us the title he does, and why does he keep us waiting before he reveals his true subject?

2. What are the sources of humour in this essay? Why are we amused at so many of the writer's details?

3. How does the conclusion bring the point of the essay into focus? What is the significance of the tuna casserole at the very end? What exactly is the author's thesis?

4. In paragraphs 6 through 9, Jim Shahin describes the neighbourhood of his youth. Make a list of the kinds of memories he has. In paragraphs 10 through 18, he describes the neighbourhood he now lives in. Does he cover the same topics that he discussed about his childhood neighbourhood? What would be the list of memories you would make of your childhood neighbourhood?

5. If a new neighbour were to move in to the apartment or house next door to you tomorrow, what kind of person would you want that neighbour to be? Take a survey in your class. Is there any agreement about what the ideal neighbour should be like?

Writing in Response

1. Write an essay in which you classify the kinds of neighbours that have moved in and out of your neighbourhood.

2. Write an essay classifying the neighbourhoods you have moved in and out of during your life.

3. Describe the best or the worst neighbour you have ever encountered.

4. Define your neighbourhood for someone who has never seen it. Study Jim Shahin's descriptions to get ideas for the kinds of details you can include.

5. Argue about the benefits of living in a culturally diverse neighbourhood as opposed to living in a neighbourhood with only one ethnic group.

6. Argue about the benefits of living in a neighbourhood with all age groups as opposed to only young families or only retired couples, or all college students.

7. Define what makes a good neighbour.

Woes of a Part-Time Parent

NICK CHILES

Many North Americans have had to adapt to difficult family situations that make being a good parent an even harder task. The following observations by Nick Chiles not only show his objectivity as a reporter, but also reveal his personal dilemma as a parent who cannot be present at all the important moments in his child's life.

1   I often feel something is missing. A living, vital part of me that sprouted under my eyes for two years is now a part-time visitor in my life. For about ten hours during the week and every waking hour every other weekend, my son, Mazi, and I tinker with our developing relationship. We laugh a lot, and sometimes he cries a lot—often in a span of ten minutes. During those few hours I can feel my heart hum along at a peaceful clip, uncluttered, dancing atop a divine Sarah Vaughan contralto.

2   But then he is gone. He's off to brighten another corner of the world with his 3-year-old's unleavened energy and infectious glee. He's out of my sight, out of my realm of knowing, until the next time.

3   What I regret most about the dissolution of my marriage is the absence of a partner conversant in Mazi, fluent in Mazispeak. Sure, I can talk with his grandparents or my friends about his latest leap in reasoning or physical advance. But

their interest doesn't compare with the undying fascination of a parent. I miss having a companion with whom I can exchange reports about Mazi's day or Mazi's behavior—or misbehavior—in day care. I miss the daily conversation about his life.

4   Being a part-time parent means being cut off from a huge portion of your child's life. It means not having any idea what he does with much of his time when you're not around. His life with Mommy is now in another place. Does that also make him another child?

5   My notions of fatherhood were formed as much by television and the mass media as my life with my own dad. For me, being a father means being the stolid protector, the rock-solid shoulder to lean on when the child gives up a homer in the last inning. It means being Mr. Brady on *The Brady Bunch*. How can you be these things when half the time you aren't there? How can you avoid missing some of the important moments when your child needs you?

6   As Mazi is carried off into the night, I can't help but wonder where he's going and if he'll be okay. If he's not, am I to blame? He seems so happy to see Mommy. Have I done something wrong? My guilt is strong. It's the gnawing ache I feel when I must go days without seeing him. The second he is in my arms, the ache disappears. The second he disappears, it resumes its burdensome place.

7   I don't foresee that ache ever leaving me. I fear it only mutates to fit new circumstances. I'm beginning to learn to live with it, however, accepting it as a cloying companion, dressing it up as parental concern, paternal responsibility, love. Perhaps one day I'll come to respect the guilt, acknowledging its power to feed my fatherly instincts and impel me to make the extra effort on behalf of my son. But for the time being the guilt just throws me into a deep funk.

8   One day I spent time in the house Mazi shares with his mother, doing some repairs in preparation for its sale. As I stumbled upon his toys and the evidence of his life there, I was shocked by how strangely unfamiliar and distant it all seemed to me. He could now walk up and down the stairs with ease. Did he have free run of all four floors? There were new toys I had never seen him play with. Did he still use the combo climber? Had he become bored with the large number mats? What did he do here? I couldn't really get the answers to these questions, even if his mother provided daily dissertations. You have to be there.

9   Things probably won't get better as Mazi's world begins to widen and his outside interests broaden. Our visits will be even more infrequent when his mother relocates to a new job out of state. I still won't know what happens during much of his waking hours. Then when he goes to school and begins to immerse himself in the awesome possibilities beyond his home, I will merely join legions of parents the world over who agonize over the same basic question every day: I wonder what he's doing now?

Questions for Critical Thinking

1. Which one of the writer's sentences best states the thesis of the essay?

2. The essay reveals much about the author's involvement in his child's life. What examples does Nick Chiles give that tell us what kind of parent he is?

3. In paragraph 3, the author makes the point that the language, "Mazispeak," he speaks with his son is a special way of communicating with the child. What are some other examples of "a special language" that two people (or a group of people) use to communicate?

4. Make a list of the part-time parent's special problems, as the writer presents them. (Do not forget to add the problems mentioned in the last paragraph.) Are there any additional problems the author has not included?

5. The father in this essay regrets the limited time he has with his son. How important is the amount of time a parent spends with a child? Do you believe it is not the *quantity* of time but the *quality* of that time that matters when it comes to taking care of a child?

6. In paragraph 5, the writer tells us that his ideas of fatherhood "were formed as much by television and the mass media as my life with my own dad." To what extent have your own ideas and beliefs about being a parent been shaped by what you have seen on television or in the movies, by your own parents, and by personal influences outside your own immediate family?

Writing in Response

1. Write a story that focuses on the struggle of a person who is trying to be a good parent.

2. Write an essay of definition and analysis that presents the essential qualities of a good parent.

3. Write an essay that classifies the types of parents you have observed.

4. Write an essay in which you give advice to parents who are separated from their children. What can they do to maintain a close relationship?

5. Write an essay about the effects on a child of growing up in a single parent household.

6. Argue for or against the following statement: Children always need to grow up in a home that has two parents if these children are to feel safe and psychologically healthy.

Visiting Rites

SUSAN MUSGRAVE

Vancouver poet and author Susan Musgrave writes about her own experiences visiting her husband in prison in this poignant story. As you read this narrative, pay close attention to the details that the author chooses to reveal.

1   At first glance it looks like a fairy tale castle-hotel: parking lots shaded by endangered oaks, crewcut lawns, a stone wall running the length of the property. But when you look again you see it's a dungeon, with bars on every window and razor-wire surrounding the yard.

2   The poet Lovelace may have been right when he wrote, "stone walls do not a prison make," but razor-wire doesn't leave a doubt.

3   Visitors call it Wilkie, as if they feel some affection for the joint, or because Vancouver Island Regional Correction Centre is too much of a mouthful. Built on Wilkinson Road near Victoria after the turn of the century, it was a mental hospital before its present incarnation. Two gold-painted lions lie in repose on either side of the steps leading up to the prison doors. I hand over my driver's licence and sign in at the front desk as though committing myself, as if shock treatment might be a

relief after everything I've been through in the last two days, since my husband was arrested for bank robbery.

4   The newspapers say I am standing by my man. I'd rather be lying by him, I think, as I start to undress, taking off my wedding ring, my belt and sandals, before walking bare-soled through the metal detector. A guard inspects my Birkenstocks, making sure I haven't concealed contraband—drugs, money, books—between the straps. I ask if I am allowed Kleenex—not that I plan to weep, but my motto has always been: if you want peace, prepare for war. The guard says he will "provide me with something."

5   My visit is to take place "under glass." I enter the small Plexiglas and concrete booth, designed by someone who had the aesthetics of the sensory-deprivation chamber in mind. The walls are off-cream, the trim around the windows a tinned-lima-bean green. All else is puce.

6   It's familiar decor. Stephen and I were married in prison, in 1986, when he was serving a twenty-year sentence for bank robbery. He was paroled a few months after we took our vows, twelve years ago almost to this day. But prison is not an easy place to escape, even if they release you. STEVE LOVES SUSAN FOREVER is etched into the Plexiglas. While I wait for my Stephen with a "ph," the guard brings me a roll of toilet paper and unwinds what he thinks I'll need. The $50,000 a year it costs to keep a man behind bars must not include the price of a box of Kleenex.

7   When the door to the prisoner's booth finally opens, the man I am supposed to be standing by is not the one standing before me. The guard picks up his telephone, I pick up mine. "He's refusing the visit," he says, point-blank.

8   I knew Stephen would be going through drug withdrawal, so I'm not surprised he can't keep our date. Part of me, though, feels betrayed. When we got married we vowed to be there for one another, in sickness and in health. The one-ply toilet paper, not meant for tears, is soon the size of a spitball in my fist.

9   I'm trying to leave when I am summoned to the office of the Director of Programs. He indicates a pile of papers on his desk and asks if I'm familiar with the "ion scanner." This device has detected microscopic particles of cocaine on my letters to Stephen; my driver's licence, too, is contaminated. Given that my husband has had a $1,000-a-day drug habit for the past six months, I expect my whole life is contaminated.

10   I ask why invisible drug particles could be a problem. "We don't want inmates in contact with individuals involved in drug-seeking activities," he explains. He will suspend my visits if I ever attempt to smuggle contraband to a prisoner. How could anyone smuggle anything through Plexiglas, over a phone? I ask. "Where there's a will, there's a way," he says.

11   Next time I visit, Stephen doesn't stand me up. I try to break the ice over the heavy telephone. "At least it's not long distance," I tell him. "It's not our dime."

12   Some previous visitor has severed the wires, and they have been repaired with electrician's tape. Our voices fade in and out, accentuating the lonely long distance between us. Stephen says that just minutes before they fetched him for our visit, the wind slipped into his cell. He knew that meant I was near.

13   My hand reaches out to the glass, and I see the reflection of my hand rest itself on Stephen's hands. My reflection travels up his arm, stutters over the track-marks, and then moves sadly on. I stroke his trembling face. Where there's a will, there's a way. A way to touch, even if it's this way.

14   I don't cry until the visit is almost over, and this time I have nothing to wipe my nose on except my T-shirt sleeve.

15   They lead Stephen away though the puce-coloured doors. I wait to be released, and to book my next visit. But when I begin to spell my name for the new guard on shift, she stops me. "I know who you are," she says. "You've been an inspiration to me all my life."

16   She has taken me by surprise. I hadn't allowed myself to see past the uniform.

17   "I used to write poetry—at university," she says. "We all did. But you didn't stop like the rest of us—we had to get jobs." Her voice drops to a whisper. "I admire everything you've ever done. Except for one thing."

18   I expect her to say, "Marrying a criminal."

19   "You know those essays you used to write for the newspapers—about family life? Well, I thought they were trite." She doesn't think domesticity a subject worthy of my inspirational words. As Stephen would say, everyone's a critic.

20   Some days I feel lost. Other days life continues without Stephen, though he is here in every grain of wood, every dustball behind the wood stove, every fixed or broken thing. Words are what I know, and I have freedom in my love. All of him washes over me, like the mystery of wind.

Questions for Critical Thinking

1. Time order is the most usual way of organizing a narrative. Underline all of the transitions that indicate the passing of time, from one event to the next, that you can find in this essay.

2. What do you think Susan Musgrave's purpose was for writing this story?

3. When narrating a story, it is important to show the experience through detail. How does Musgrave show us that this experience has affected her? What do these details reveal?

4. Study the use of dialogue or the writer's reporting of what people said. Explain the importance of both of these storytelling techniques in the essay.

Writing in Response

1. In this story, Musgrave has to reconcile the life she had hoped to have with her husband against the life she now realizes that she will have. Narrate a story about yourself (or someone you know) where reality has fallen short of your dreams.

2. Write an essay about an experience that you found particularly hard to endure. Why was this experience so difficult? How did you manage to make it through?

3. Narrate a story in which you imagine your freedom being taken away. What do you think would be the most difficult aspect of this experience? What would you miss the most?

4. Freedom is a concept we place a lot of value on, but it is something we often take for granted. Narrate a story about when you felt the most free.

5. The circumstances surrounding Susan Musgrave's relationship with her husband were highly publicized by the media in 2000. Write an essay that documents the events in their relationship. Where would you go to find out how this couple met and why her husband had to go to jail?

from *The Cure for Death by Lightning*

GAIL ANDERSON-DARGATZ

We encounter process writing almost every day in the form of directions, operating instructions, or assembly instructions. However, process writing does not necessarily have to include an overly technical procedure. In fact, recipes are perhaps the best-known examples of process writing. In the following excerpt from her novel *The Cure for Death by Lightning*, Gail Anderson-Dargatz demonstrates how to cook an old family favourite.

1   Her wire basket was filled with eggs, and she put them carefully into the washbowl and scrubbed them clean with a fingernail brush, placing them one by one on the counter of the Hosier cupboard. Some cooks, to convince you of their miracle working, maintain that sponge cake is a difficult thing of chemistry, of eggs three days old and flour just so and the temperature and humidity just right, but making a sponge cake is the easiest thing in the world. A sponge cake is nothing but eggs, flour, sugar, and air; and if you're new to the sponge cake, a little baking powder too, to ease its way against gravity. The secret is eggs, lots of eggs, and eggs we had no shortage of now that summer was almost on us. My mother used an even dozen in each daffodil cake, then two cups flour, and two cups sugar. But here she did experiment; some days felt like a little more flour or sugar, some days a little less.

2   After separating the yolks and the whites into bowls, my mother added the ingredient of air, whipping the yolks until frothy, then adding half the sugar and flour and perhaps a little lemon juice or flavoring. In another bowl, she beat the egg whites until they stiffened, but not so much that the air bubbles began to break. She then added the remaining sugar and flour and a touch of real vanilla. There it was then: two frothy bowls of air and egg, one yellow and one white.

3   There are two more secrets to the sponge cake: a knowledge of folding and a clean pan. A sponge cake is nothing without a clean baking pan. A spot of grease on the pan from some other recipe, and your sponge cake will come out flat. So wash your baking pan ever so carefully, and never, ever grease it. The folding was so important that my mother spelled it out under her recipe for daffodil cake: *Take spoon under batter and gently fold over.* The spoon is important: it should be large and flat. The gentleness is important: you want to keep those bubbles of air intact. One fold is usually enough to mix the two colors. My mother poured a layer of the egg white mixture into the pan first, covering the bottom, then added spoonfuls of yellow here and there, folding them in as she went; then another layer of white, and so on. To bake she used a moderate oven. To cool the cake, she tipped it upside down over a bottle on the kitchen table, so the tube in the middle of the cake pan suspended the cake. After a couple of hours, gravity would pull the cooling cake down, so removing it from the pan would be nothing at all. My mother would then decorate the cake with an icing of butter, icing sugar, a little hot water, and vanilla, and top it with a few spicy yellow nasturtiums.

Questions for Critical Thinking

1. Most people do not grow up learning the skills that their parents or grandparents acquired as young children. How many students in your class have learned hobbies or skills from their parents or grandparents?

2. Cooking is one of the most practical skills to learn. How is this excerpt different in style from a recipe you would see in a cookbook? Make a list of these differences.

3. What do you think would happen if you tried to cook this recipe at home? Does the writer provide an effective example of process writing?

Writing in Response

1. Choose an activity that you enjoy. Write a process essay in which you not only tell the reader how to complete the activity but also provide some commentary such as background information, the reason why you like this activity, or who taught it to you. If you are brave, you may try to add humour to your writing.

2. Many schools no longer teach cooking, sewing, or industrial shop skills. Write an essay in which you argue for or against the belief that these subjects should continue to be taught in public schools.

3. Write an essay in which you classify the different kinds of hobbies that people have. What types of personalities are attracted to various hobbies? What are the qualities needed for each of them? (For instance, if the hobby is dancing, it helps to be coordinated.)

An Invisible Woman
BHARATI MUKHERJEE

We are often affected by the way in which others view and define us. In this essay, Bharati Mukherjee discusses the racism and intolerance she experienced when she lived in Canada with her husband for fifteen years. In particular, she describes the impact that racism has had on her identity and how she defines herself.

1   This story begins in Calcutta and ends in a small town in New York State called Saratoga Springs. The very long, fifteen-year middle is set in Canada. In this story, no place or person fares well, but Canada comes off poorest of all.

2   I was born in Calcutta, that most Victorian and British of post-independence Indian cities. It was not the Calcutta of documentary films—not a hell where beggars fought off dying cattle for still-warm garbage—but a gracious, green, subtropical city where Irish nuns instructed girls from better families on how to hold their heads high and how to drop their voices to a whisper and still be heard and obeyed above the screams of the city.

3   There was never a moment when we did not know that our city and our country were past their prime. We carried with us the terrible knowledge that while our lives were comfortable, they would be safer somewhere else. Ambition dictated emigration. In the 1950s everyone was waiting for the revolution. "The first thing Communists do," my best friend told me when we were fifteen, "is feel your hands. If your hands are soft, it's *kaput* for you." In our school every girl had soft hands. But when Stalin died, the nuns prayed for his soul: this was known as "fair play," an example for us pliant, colonial girls to follow.

4   In a city continually blistered with revolutionary fervour, we plodded through our productions of *The Mikado*. At least twice I was escorted by van loads of police past striking workers outside the gates of my father's factory so that I could go to school and dance a quadrille or play a walk-on part. "Our girls can take their places with the best anywhere in the world," Mother John-Baptist, the headmistress, had

promised my father on the first day of school. (And we have, all over India and the English-speaking, even German-speaking, world.) On a sticky August night in 1961, when my younger sister, who was going to Vassar College, and I, on my way to the University of Iowa, left by Air India for New York, I felt that I could.

5   Great privilege had been conferred upon me; my struggle was to work hard enough to deserve it. And I did. This bred confidence, but not conceit. I never doubted that if I wanted something—a job, a scholarship—I could get it. And I did. I had built-in advantages: primarily those of education, secondarily those of poise and grooming. I knew that if I decided to return to India after my writing degree at Iowa was finished, my father would find me a suitable husband. I would never work, never be without servants and comfort, and I could dabble in the arts until they bored me. My daughters would attend the same school as I had, my sons a similar school. It was unthinkable that they would not be class leaders, then national leaders, and that they would not perpetuate whatever values we wished to give them. Such is the glory, and the horror, of a traditional society, even at its tattered edges.

6   I had no trouble at Iowa, and though I learned less about those Vietnam and assassination years than I might have, I liked the place well enough to stay on and arrange for extensions of my scholarship. I married an American, Clark Blaise, whose parents had come from Canada and then divorced, and whose mother had returned to Winnipeg. I stayed on for a PhD, thus cutting off forever the world of passive privilege I had come from. An MA in English is considered refined, but a doctorate is far too serious a business, indicative more of brains than beauty, and likely to lead to a quarrelsome nature. We had a son, and when that son was almost two we moved to Canada. Clark had dreamed restless dreams of Canada, especially of Montreal. Still unformed at twenty-five, he felt it was the place that would let him be himself.

7   It is now the summer of 1966, and the three of us cross at Windsor in a battered VW van. Our admission goes smoothly, for I have a lecturer's position at McGill. I say "smoothly," but I realize now that there was one curious, even comic event that foreshadowed the difficulties faced by Indians in Canada. A middle-aged immigration officer, in filling out my application, asked me the year of my birth. I told him, in that private-school accent of which I was once so proud. Mishearing, he wrote down "1914" and remarked, "Ah, we're the same age." He happened to be exactly twice my age. He corrected his error without a fuss. Ten minutes inside Canada, and I was already invisible.

8   The oldest paradox of prejudice is that it renders its victims simultaneously invisible and over-exposed. I have not met an Indian in Canada who has not suffered the humiliations of being overlooked (in jobs, in queues, in deserved recognition) and from being singled out (in hotels, department stores, on the streets, and at customs). It happened to me so regularly in Canada that I now feel relief, just entering Macy's in Albany, New York, knowing that I won't be followed out by a security guard. In America, I can stay in hotels and *not* be hauled out of elevators or stopped as I enter my room. It's perhaps a small privilege in the life of a North American housewife—not to be taken automatically for a shoplifter or a whore—but it's one that my years in Canada, and especially my two years in Toronto, have made me grateful for. I know objections will be raised; I know Canadians all too well. Which of us has *not* been harassed at customs? On a summer's night, which of us *can* walk down Yonge Street without carloads of stoned youths shouting out insults? We have all stood patiently in bakery lines, had people step in front of us, we've all waved our plastic numbers and wailed, "But I was next—"

9   If we are interested in drawing minute distinctions, we can disregard or explain away nearly anything. ("Where did it happen? Oh, *Rosedale*. Well, no *wonder* ..." or, "Oh, *we* wouldn't do such a thing. He must have been French or something ...")

And I know the pious denials of hotel clerks. In a Toronto hotel I was harassed by two house detectives who demanded to see my room key before allowing me to go upstairs to join my family—harassed me in front of an elevator-load of leering, elbow-nudging women. When I complained, I extracted only a "Some of my best friends are Pakis" from the night manager, as he fervently denied that what I had just experienced was in fact a racial incident.

10   And I know the sanctimonious denials of customs officers, even as they delight in making people like me dance on the head of a bureaucratic pin. On a return from New York to Toronto, I was told, after being forced to declare a $1 valuation on a promotional leaflet handed out by a bookstore, that even a book of matches had to be declared. ("I didn't ask if you *bought* anything. Did you hear me ask about purchases? Did you? I'll ask you again in very clear English. *Are you bringing anything into the country?*")

11   Do not think that I enjoy writing this of Canada. I remain a Canadian citizen. This is the testament of a woman who came, like most immigrants, confident of her ability to do good work, in answer to a stated need. After the unsophisticated, beer-swilling rednecks of Iowa, British-commonwealth Canada, and Montreal in particular, promised a kind of haven. At the road-stops in Iowa and Illinois, when I entered in a sari, silverware would drop, conversations cease; it was not the kind of attention I craved. It was never a hostile reaction (it might have been, in the Deep South, but I avoided that region). It was innocent, dumbfounded stupefaction, and I thought I would be happy enough to leave it behind. As we drove past Toronto on the 401, we picked up the strains of sitar music on the radio; Montreal had spice shops and was soon to have Indian restaurants. It should have been a decent country, and we should have been happy in it.

12   I have been in America, this time, for only a few months, but in that time I've been attacked by a streaker on Sixth Avenue in New York; my purse has been snatched on Fifth Avenue; our car has been rammed and our insurance defrauded in Saratoga Springs; a wallet has been stolen and our children have complained of the drinking and dope-smoking even in their schoolrooms. Yes, it's America: violent, mindlessly macho, conformist, lawless. And certainly no dark-skinned person has the right to feel comfortable inside American history. Yet I do. If I am not exempt from victimization here, neither are Clark or my sons, and neither am I exempt from redress. I am less shocked, less outraged and shaken to my core, by a purse-snatching in New York City in which I lost all of my dowry gold—everything I'd been given by my mother in marriage—than I was by a simple question asked of me in the summer of 1978 by three high-school boys on the Rosedale subway station platform in Toronto. Their question was, "Why don't you go back to Africa?"

13   It hurt because of its calculation, its calm, ignorant satisfaction, its bland assumption of the right to break into my privacy. In New York, I was violated because of my suspected affluence (a Gucci purse) and my obviously foreign, heedless, non-defensiveness. Calcutta equipped me to survive theft or even assault; it did not equip me to accept proof of my unworthiness. (Friends say, "Rosedale? Well …" or, "Teenagers, well …" and I don't dispute them. But I owe it to my friends, and I have many friends in Canada, to dig deeper.)

14   Thanks to Canadian rhetoric on the highest level, I have learned several things about myself that I never suspected. The first is that I have no country of origin. In polite company, I am an "East Indian" (the opposite, presumably, of a "West Indian"). The East Indies, in my school days, were Dutch possessions, later to become Indonesia. In impolite company I'm a "Paki" (a British slur unknown in America, I'm happy to say). For an Indian of my generation, to be called a "Paki" is about as appealing as it is for an Israeli to be called a Syrian. In an official Green Paper on Immigration and Population I learn that I'm something called a "visible minority" from a "non-traditional area of immigration" who calls into question

the "absorptive capacity" of Canada. And that big question (to which my contribution is really not invited) is, "What kind of society do we really want?"

15   A spectre is haunting Canada: the perfidious "new" (meaning "dark" and thus, self-fulfillingly, "non-assimilatable") immigrant, coming to snatch up jobs, welfare cheques, subway space, cheap apartments, and blue-eyed women.

16   The Green Paper in 1975—which seemed an admirable exercise in demographic planning, an open invitation to join in a "debate"—was really a premeditated move on the part of government to throw some bones (some immigrants) to the howling wolves. The "we" of that open question was understood to mean the Anglo-Saxon or Quebec-French "founding races": it opened up the sewers of resentment that polite, British-style forbearance had kept a lid on. My kind of Canadian was assumed, once again, not to exist, not to have a legitimate opinion to offer. ("Well, you could have made an official deposition through the proper multi-cultural channel whenever hearings were held in your community ...")

17   Most Indians would date the new up-front violence, the physical assaults, the spitting, the name-calling, the bricks through the windows, the pushing and shoving on the subways—it would be, by this time, a very isolated Indian who had not experienced one or more of those reactions—from the implied consent given to racism by that infamous document. I cannot describe the agony and the betrayal one feels, hearing oneself spoken of by one's own country as being somehow exotic to its nature—a burden, a cause for serious concern. It may have been rhetorically softened, it may have been academic in tone, but in feeling it was Nuremberg, and it unleashed its own mild but continuing *Kristallnacht*. In that ill-tempered debate, the government itself appropriated the language, the reasoning, the motivation that had belonged—until then—to disreputable fringe groups. Suddenly it was all right, even patriotic, to blame these non-assimilatable Asian hordes for urban crowding, unemployment, and welfare burdens. And the uneducated, unemployed, welfare-dependent, native-born *lumpen* teenagers leaped at the bait.

18   It is not pleasant to realize your own government has betrayed you so coldly.

19   What about the "absorptive capacity" of the ambitious immigrant to take in all these new, startling descriptions of himself? It creates double-vision when self-perception is so utterly at odds with social standing. We are split from our most confident self-assumptions. We must be blind, stupid, or egomaniacal to maintain self-respect or dignity when society consistently undervalues our contribution. In Montreal, I was, simultaneously, a full professor at McGill, an author, a confident lecturer, and (I like to think) a charming and competent hostess and guest—*and* a house-bound, fearful, aggrieved, obsessive, and unforgiving queen of bitterness. Whenever I read articles about men going berserk, or women committing suicide, and read the neighbours' dazed pronouncements ("But he was so friendly, so out-going, never a problem in the world ..."), I knew I was looking into a mirror. Knowing that the culture condescended toward me, I needed ways of bolstering my self-respect—but those ways, at least to politely raised, tightly disciplined women of my age and origin, can only be achieved in society, in the recognition of our contributions.

20   And there, of course, I am up against another Canadian dilemma. I have always been struck by an oddity, call it a gap, in the cultural consciousness of the Canadian literary establishment. For fifteen years I was a professor of English and of creative writing at McGill. I published novels, stories, essays, reviews. In a land that fills it airports with itinerant poets and story-tellers, I was invited only once to give a reading by myself (after *Days and Nights in Calcutta* appeared, Clark and I, who had written it together, were frequently invited together). On that one occasion, I learned, after arriving in a mining town at three in the morning, that I'd been invited from the jacket photo and was expected to "come across." ("The others did.") No provisions had been made for my stay, except in my host's bachelor house.

("Oh, you let him meet you at the airport at three a.m.? And you went back to his house thinking there was a wife?") Friends explained to me that really, since nothing happened (except a few shoves and pushes), I shouldn't mention it again. Until now, I haven't.

21   Of course, it is possible to interpret everything in a different light. While no one likes to be pawed, isn't it nice to be acknowledged, even this way? (Don't laugh, it was suggested.) My point is simply this: an Indian slips out of invisibility in this culture at considerable peril to body and soul. I've alluded briefly (in *Days and Nights*) to the fact that I was not invited to join the Writers' Union of Canada, back at its founding, even though at that particular moment I was a Canadian and Clark was not (my Indian citizenship conferred special dispensations that his American one did not). The first explanation for the oversight was that the invitation extended to Clark was "assumed" to include me. While even a low-grade feminist might react uncomfortably to such a concoction, another, and I think truthful, explanation was offered. "We didn't know how to spell your name, and we were afraid of insulting you," a well-known writer later wrote me. She's right; I would have been insulted (just as I'm mildly insulted by Canada Council letters to "Mr. Bharati Blaise"). And then, with a tinge of self-justification, she continued: "Your book was published by an American publisher and we couldn't get hold of it, so …"

22   Well, it's an apology and an explanation and it's easy to forgive as an instance of the persistent amateurism in the Canadian soul. But if you scrutinized just a little harder and if you've dipped into the well of forgiveness far too often, you see a very different interpretation. *If you don't have a family compact name, forget about joining us.* If you don't have Canadian content, forget about publishing here. "The only Canadian thing about the novel is that it was written by a woman who now lives in Montreal," said a reviewer of my second novel, *Wife*, in *Books in Canada* (she was herself a feminist and emerging ethnicist), not even recognizing a book aimed right at her. "How can you call yourself a Canadian writer if you didn't play in snow as a child?" asked a CBC television interviewer. And more severely: "How do you justify taking grants and then not writing about Canada?"

23   The answer to all that is that I do write about Canada, perhaps not as directly as I am writing now, but that I refuse to capitulate to the rawness of Canadian literature—and, more to the point, I refuse to set my work in Canada because to do so would be to reduce its content to the very subject of this essay: politics and paranoia and bitter disappointment. The condition of the Indian in Canada is a sociological and political subject. We've not yet achieved the ease that would permit us to write of the self and of the expanding consciousness. To set my work in Canada is necessarily to adopt an urgent and strident tone; I would find irony an ill-considered option in any such situation. I advocate, instead, fighting back.

24   In case anyone finds a copy of *Wife*, it should be read in the following way: the nominal setting is Calcutta and New York City. But in the mind of the heroine, it is always Toronto.

25 Fifteen years ago, the Indian was an exotic in America, except in university towns and maybe New York City. Now I doubt if there's a town in America without its Indian family—even Saratoga Springs has Indian dentists and pediatricians. I am no longer an exotic butterfly (people used to stagger up to me, quite unconscious that there was a young woman inside the folds of brilliant cloth, just to feel the material, and then walk away). Nor am I a grubby, dishonest, smelly, ignorant, job-snatching, baby-breeding, unassimilatable malcontent. For the first time in my adult life, I am unemployed—the price I was obliged to pay for immigration to the United States. Clark this year is teaching in the local college. Our income is less than a third of what it has been, and dark times are coming. Next year, I can take the job Clark is filling now; the college has made us an interesting proposal,

though it leaves many questions unanswered. Will Clark then stay here or return? He doesn't know.

26   America trusts confrontation; its rough sense of justice derives from slugging it out. It tolerates contradictions that seem, in retrospect, monstrous. Perhaps it trusts to the constitution and the knowledge that somehow, someday, that document will resolve all difficulties. This is not the British style, not the Canadian style, in which conflict is viewed as evidence of political failure. In Canada, Parliament's sacred duty is the preservation of order; its mandate, at least in recent years, it to anticipate disorder. I can appreciate that, and if I were a white mainstream Canadian I'd probably endorse it wholeheartedly. Toronto really is a marvellous, beautiful city, as I tell all my American friends. Good God, if ever there was a city I should have been happy in, it was Toronto.

27   But when you are part of the Canadian and Toronto underbelly, invisible and nakedly obvious, you can't afford a white man's delusions. It's in Canada that a columnist can write a glib and condescending book, attack the frail, ineffective civil liberties legislation in the country, and be called a brilliant and daring intellectual. It's Canada that struggles against a constitution of its own, and its premiers who downgrade the concept of a human rights charter.

28   While preparing to write this account, I interviewed dozens of people, mostly of Indian or Pakistani origin, in many parts of Canada. I read until I grew sick—of the assaults, the recommendations, the testimonies. I attended meetings. I talked to grandparents, and I talked to high-schoolers. I walked with the police down the troubled streets of east-end Toronto; I pursued some of the more lurid stories of the past year in Toronto. I turned down collaboration on some other stories; I did not feel Canadian enough to appear on a TV programme celebrating the accomplishments of new Canadians; nor did I wish to take part in a TV show that set out to ascribe suicides among Indo-Canadian women solely to community pressures to have male children. Friends who supported this research will probably not find their observations in this piece; they will find, instead, that I turned it all inside out.

29   To a greater or lesser extent those friends and I share a common history. We came in the mid-1960s for professional reasons. We saw scope and promise, and we were slow to acknowledge the gathering clouds. Some of us have reacted positively, working with the local or provincial governments, serving as consultants, as organizers, as impresarios of understanding. Others have taken hockey sticks on vigilante patrols to protect their people. Many, including myself, have left, unable to keep our twin halves together.

Questions for Critical Thinking

1. List Bharati Mukherjee's complaints about Canada. How is it that she establishes her credibility? Be specific with your answer.

2. This essay was written over twenty years ago. Do you think Canada has changed since Mukherjee lived here? Have Canadians become more or less tolerant? Be sure to use examples to substantiate your point of view.

3. What does Mukherjee mean when she states, "The oldest paradox of prejudice is that it renders its victims simultaneously invisible and over-exposed"? Provide an example from the essay that illustrates her point.

4. How does Mukherjee define herself? Compare this with how others define her.

Writing in Response

1. Write an essay in which you discuss how a person could be raised that would encourage this person to be accepting of others. In your essay, you might want to point out situations that you believe actively discourage acceptance of others.

2. Write an essay in which you describe how you hope to raise your children so that they will be tolerant adults. What will you tell them about your own childhood that will help them to understand the need for greater tolerance? How can a parent be frank about the realities that exist in society without discouraging the child?

3. What changes do you think need to be made in Canada to ensure that it becomes a society that welcomes and celebrates newcomers? Write an essay where you argue and defend the changes that need to be made.

"I Mean, You Know, Like..."

MARGARET VISSER

Each of us has particular verbal expressions that we use when we speak. These can sometimes be characterized as slang, but in many cases they fill a particular purpose. In the following essay, Margaret Visser explores the meanings behind some of these expressions and attempts to categorize them for the audience. As you read the essay, pay close attention to some of the phrases and expressions that you use.

1   "Shut up!" is rude, even ruder than "Keep quiet!" In the polite version, *"Do you think you would mind keeping* quiet: *this is, after all, a library, and other people are trying to concentrate,"* everything in italics is extra. It is there to soften the demand, giving an impersonal reason for the request, and avoiding the brutally direct by the taking of trouble. Conventional grammar takes little account of such strategies, even though we are all masters of both making and understanding the signs that point to what is going on beneath the surface.

2   An artificially high-pitched tone universally suggests a disarming tentativeness in the speaker. Canadians are noticeably inclined to turn a statement into a question by means of a rising intonation: this expresses hope that there are no objections, and simultaneously requests a sign from the listener that the statement has been understood. Corresponding politely hesitant questions might be *"OK?" "You know?"*

3   Set phrases (*"I guess," "I suppose," "I wonder"*) commonly mitigate the force of our remarks. We condition requests, and add extra "if" clauses: *"Would you* let me have one, *if you don't mind?"* Bad news is considerately hedged: "How far is it?"— *"Well,* it's too far to walk. *I mean, you know,* it's a very long way." Criticisms and advice, too, are politely lengthened and deprecated: *"I think perhaps* you should reconsider"; *"Could you* make this version *more or less* final?" But a reproach is rendered blatant, even as it appears to be toned down, by the addition of *"With all due respect...."*

4   It sounds superior to give information bluntly: it is advisable to assume common ground by adding *"as you know,"* or, better still, *"as you and I both know."* One sounds less opinionated saying, *"I kind of think...," "I shouldn't be surprised," "it seems to me,"* or *"don't you agree?"* Canadians particularly are fond of the genteelly

archaic additions *"if you will."* A command, of course, is often sweetened, as in: *"If you will allow me,* or *If we all agree then,* I declare this meeting open."

5   You can try to take the wind of hostility out of other people's sails by admitting an imposition, or by simply acknowledging that what you are saying should not be said. Brag, for example, beginning *"If I do say so myself...."* Launch into a tirade with *"I must say,"* or *This is none of my business but...."*

6   We sound respectful of the truth while pointing out that we are being vague (thereby pre-empting criticism for our vagueness) in using words like *roughly, basically, so to speak,* and *to some extent.* The jagged edge left by our suddenly changing the subject gives rise to a wide choice of phrases including *"I might mention at this point," "While I think of it,"* and *"Now, I was wondering if...."* (*"Now"* makes a claim for relevance, even if there is none.)

7   A popular interjection has come to be the multipurpose "like." North Americans like saying "like." The word is increasingly used for "as" or "as if"; and "likely" (which as a child I was taught to use always as an adjective) is commonly adverbial, meaning "probably." *Like,* influenced by similes ("teeth *like* tombstones"), can mean "approximately" ("He got *like* sixty per cent"); but it can also underline an exciting fact ("He scored *like* five goals!"). It prepares us for something picturesque in the sentence, a metaphor perhaps ("She *like* waltzed away with the election"), a very with-it phrase ("That's *like* so not happening!"), or any unusual word or thought ("She's reading *like* Chekhov at age seven!" or "She's reading Chekhov at *like* age seven!").

8   The particle *like* emphasizes totally new information: "And there he was, *like* stuck in the ice." *Like,* as a hedge, resembles "sort of": "His car is *like* greenish grey." And because it focuses attention, underlines, and hedges, *like* is added in requests, answers, and commands sensitive to others' feelings: "Could I *like* call you tomorrow?"; "You *like* turn left at the corner." *I'm like* can even mean "I think vividly to myself": "He goes, 'Say yes!' And *I'm like,* 'Oh no.'"

9   Conversational language conveys a lot more than straightforward sense. The rules for such expressiveness inevitably operate, but they are a good deal harder to discover than to obey.

Questions for Critical Thinking

1. Make a list of all the expressions Margaret Visser defines in her essay. Also note what she says these expressions mean. For those phrases that she doesn't define, create your own definition.

2. Why don't we always say exactly what we mean? What reasons does Visser offer for this phenomenon?

3. In the course of reading this essay, did you come across any examples of expressions that you frequently use? How do you think these expressions affect the way others perceive you?

Writing in Response

1. A uniquely Canadian expression is "Eh." Research and write an essay about the origin and purpose of this expression. Why do you think Canadians use it?

2. Describe some of the expressions that you use solely with your group of friends. Do you think that people outside your group of friends would know what you're talking about?

3. Often we use more than just verbal expressions to communicate. We also communicate through body language, facial expressions, and hand gestures. Write a classification essay on nonverbal communication. For example, you may want to discuss those gestures we use to beckon someone, gestures we use to greet someone, and gestures we use to say goodbye. Think of other possible principles by which you can classify examples of nonverbal communication.

4. Do you think that some people are more prone to communicate using slang or other informal expressions than others? Write a classification essay on these different types of people and how they communicate to each other.

Neat People vs. Sloppy People
SUZANNE BRITT JORDAN

Sometimes we learn about our vices and virtues best when we are told about them in a humorous way. This is what Suzanne Britt Jordan does in the following essay, as she invites us to look for ourselves in one of two groups: those who are organized and those who can only hope to be.

1   I've finally figured out the difference between neat people and sloppy people. The distinction is, as always, moral. Neat people are lazier and meaner than sloppy people.

2   Sloppy people, you see, are not really sloppy. Their sloppiness is merely the unfortunate consequence of their extreme moral *rectitude*. Sloppy people carry in their mind's eye a heavenly vision, a precise plan, that is so stupendous, so perfect, it can't be achieved in this world or the next.

3   Sloppy people live in Never-Never Land. Someday is their *métier*. Someday they are planning to alphabetize all their books and set up home catalogues. Someday they will go through their wardrobes and mark certain items for tentative mending and certain items for passing on to relatives of similar shape and size. Someday sloppy people will make family scrapbooks into which they will put newspaper clippings, postcards, locks of hair, and the dried corsage from their senior prom. Someday they will file everything on the surface of their desks, including the cash receipts from coffee purchases at the snack shop. Someday they will sit down and read all the back issues of *The New Yorker*.

4   For all these noble reasons and more, sloppy people never get neat. They aim too high and wide. They save everything, planning someday to file, order, and straighten out the world. But while these ambitious plans take clearer and clearer shape in their heads, the books spill from the shelves onto the floor, the clothes pile up in the hamper and closet, the family mementos accumulate in every drawer, the surface of the desk is buried under mounds of paper and the unread magazines threaten to reach the ceiling.

5   Sloppy people can't bear to part with anything. They give loving attention to every detail. When sloppy people say they're going to tackle the surface of the desk, they really mean it. Not a paper will go unturned; not a rubber band will go unboxed. Four hours or two weeks into the excavation, the desk looks exactly the same, primarily because the sloppy person is meticulously creating new piles of papers with new headings and scrupulously stopping to read all the old book catalogues before he throws them away. A neat person would just bulldoze the desk.

6   Neat people are bums and clods at heart. They have cavalier attitudes toward possessions, including family heirlooms. Everything is just another dust-catcher to them. If anything collects dust, it's got to go and that's that. Neat people will toy with the idea of throwing the children out of the house just to cut down on the clutter.

7   Neat people don't care about process. They like results. What they want to do is get the whole thing over with so they can sit down and watch the rasslin' on TV. Neat people operate on two unvarying principles: Never handle any item twice, and throw everything away.

8   The only thing messy in a neat person's house is the trash can. The minute something comes to a neat person's hand, he will look at it, try to decide if it has immediate use and, finding none, throw it in the trash.

9   Neat people are especially vicious with mail. They never go through their mail unless they are standing directly over a trash can. If the trash can is beside the mailbox, even better. All ads, catalogues, pleas for charitable contributions, church bulletins and money-saving coupons go straight into the trash can without being opened. All letters from home, postcards from Europe, bills and paychecks are opened, immediately responded to, then dropped in the trash can. Neat people keep their receipts only for tax purposes. That's it. No sentimental salvaging of birthday cards or the last letter a dying relative ever wrote. Into the trash it goes.

10   Neat people place neatness above everything, even economics. They are incredibly wasteful. Neat people throw away several toys every time they walk through the den. I knew a neat person once who threw away a perfectly good dish drainer because it had mold on it. The drainer was too much trouble to wash. And neat people sell their furniture when they move. They will sell a La-Z-Boy recliner while you are reclining in it.

11   Neat people are no good to borrow from. Neat people buy everything in expensive little single portions. They get their flour and sugar in two-pound bags. They wouldn't consider clipping a coupon, saving a leftover, reusing plastic non-dairy whipped cream containers or rinsing off tin foil and draping it over the unmoldy dish drainer. You can never borrow a neat person's newspaper to see what's playing at the movies. Neat people have the paper all wadded up and in the trash by 7:05 A.M.

12   Neat people cut a clean swath through the organic as well as the inorganic world. People, animals, and things are all one to them. They are so insensitive. After they've finished with the pantry, the medicine cabinet, and the attic, they will throw out the red geranium (too many leaves), sell the dog (too many fleas), and send the children off to boarding school (too many scuffmarks on the hardwood floors).

Questions for Critical Thinking

1. When did you first become aware that this essay is written in a humorous vein?

2. What explanation does Suzanne Britt Jordan give for a sloppy person's behaviour? Do you agree with her?

3. In paragraph 3, what examples does the writer list as projects the sloppy person plans to do? Do these plans seem admirable?

4. Does the author use the block method or the point-by-point method to contrast sloppy people with neat people?

5. In paragraph 11, the author states, "Neat people are no good to borrow from." Discuss the examples the author gives to support her statement. What makes them humorous? Suzanne Britt Jordan's ability to provide details that the reader recognizes as true about himself or herself is what makes her writing so appreciated.

6. Do you know anyone who has done the things listed in the concluding paragraph? Which type of person do you think the author is?

Writing in Response

1. Write an essay that takes the opposite viewpoint of Suzanne Britt Jordan. Defend the neat person and criticize the sloppy person.

2. Describe two people you know who have very different approaches to being neat and organized. Explain what it is like to be with each of them.

3. How would you describe the household in which you grew up? In what ways were your parents very organized? In what areas were they disorganized? What are the problems of growing up in a household that is extreme one way or the other?

4. Write an essay in which you give advice to a young couple setting up a household. How would you advise them in being neat and organized?

5. Suzanne Britt Jordan claims that sloppy people cannot part with anything. Write an essay in which you analyze your own attitude about possessions. What are the things you have a hard time parting with? What things do you especially like to collect and save?

Oh, Tannenbaum: The Tale of a Tree

DAVID ADAMS RICHARDS

Although holidays are times when we practise special traditions, the nature of these traditions may change from region to region. In the following story, David Adams Richards recounts an episode from a Christmas in New Brunswick. On a literal level the story tells about how a group of young men tried to get a tree for Christmas, but on a figurative level it explores the nature of storytelling itself.

1   "Everyone seems to have their tree up now," she said to us. She was right. Still, we reassured her that it would be easy to go into the woods and get a tree. The woods in New Brunswick is never far away. And the trees are—you guessed it—in the woods.

2   Oh, there were a few "tree lots," but what were they for? I mean, these were the days (long ago) when no New Brunswicker would ever actually think of buying a tree. Buying a tree was tantamount to admitting failure as a man. That was the way it was.

3   In fact until I was in my mid-20s—being a slow learner in my formative years—I did not know anyone in New Brunswick would ever stoop so low. We had heard that once somebody sold an artificial tree to someone in the mall.

4   "I hear they sold one of those silver trees at the mall!"

5   "Made in New York!"

6   "Prob-ly!"

7   What more could be said?

8   Still, we could not put it off. So on a blustery and freezing Dec. 23, after our game of road hockey, we set out to get the tree, my brothers and I and a little neighbourhood child about six years of age I did not know. Perhaps a cousin of someone, who decided to come along just as the hockey game broke up.

9   But in those more innocent days, not knowing a child, or even who he or she belonged to, did not mean you could not drive about with them in your car all day. The last thing on anyone's mind, good men and women naively thought, was injury to a child.

10   The only problem was the sub-zero temperature and the rising wind. I sat behind the wheel of my sky-blue 1961 Chevy, with pins at the front so the hood would stay on (though it flapped continually), and away we went. At the top of the lane, I made my decision. We could have gone any place, even a few miles down river—but I thought of someplace special. I decided that we would go to the North Pole.

11   The North Pole stream is north of Newcastle. It is near where Christmas Mountain is, surrounded by little bitty mountains, like Dasher, Rudolf and Blitxen. It would be no trouble to get a tree there, I said.

12   "Isn't that a little far?" my younger brother said.

13   It was an 80- or 90-mile round trip, but worth it, if you brought a smile to the gob of a child. So off we went, the valves in the old Chevy ticking a mile a minute, and a huge plastic-carton-top cover on my gas tank.

14   The roads were ice and snow, and by the time we got to the Renous the wind had risen to gale force, and visibility was almost zero. In fact it took everything I had to keep the car on the road. The wind under the hood gave the car an element of lift, so going downhill we were airborne.

15   Our radio did not work, the thermostat was stuck and the going was getting rougher. Then the carton cap came off my gas tank, and I had to stop and search for it. Not able to find it, I stuffed a pair of white socks I had bought for my brother-in-law into the tank.

16   In retrospect, I remember that the youngster did not seem troubled by any of this. Finally I decided, halfway to Christmas Mountain, that we were in a good enough place. "This looks like a fine place for a tree to be hiding."

17   My brothers grunted agreement.

18   "This is wonderful," the little boy finally exclaimed. "I've never seen anyone get a tree before!"

19   My brothers and I looked at him. It became evident that none of us knew who he was. I studied him carefully, for some sign of recognition. He looked like a Foley, I decided. He could pass for a Foley on a bad day. But then couldn't he be a Matheson—or a Casey? Yes! Perhaps a Casey! His hands were folded on his lap, mittens pinned with big silver pins, winter coat buttoned to his chin.

20   "Where you from?" my younger brother asked.

21   He answered with grave and solemn earnestness.

22   "I'm afraid from Dublin, sir," he said.

23   "Afraid from Doob-lun?" my brother said. "Where in heck is Doob-lun?"

24   "He means Dublin," I whispered. "Ireland."

25   "Dublin!"

26   "Yes—from Doob-lun. I'm here visiting—me grandmom. I'm Owen," he said, "and I've never seen anyone get a Christmas tree."

27   "Well, you're in luck," I said. "We're all like Paul Bunyan here—you ever hear of Big Joe Mufferah?"

28   I tucked Owen's mittens over his hands, repinned them, and out we got, my brothers leading the way, plowing over the now-frozen snowbanks and into the by

now dark, frozen woods, looking for a tree. We found one, 50 yards off the road, a fir tree about six feet tall. A perfect tree, except for a slight crookedness at the base, and an overlapping bough—but these were minor flaws. And not flaws, really, for one might appreciate them as defects that heightened beauty. In fact, I could already see it sitting in our living room. I could see it trimmed, lights glowing.

29   "It will bring you great happiness and peace," the Dubliner said suddenly.

30   What a fine little boy I thought; all the way from Dublin, standing in the middle of godforsaken nowhere up to his bum in snow, and still thinking of peace. His uncle was probably a priest, a melancholy man who drank a bit. Perhaps his mother had died, or something, of—tuberculosis—and he had come here to be with his grandmother, I thought.

31   Everyone was silent, thinking about peace. Or thinking we would take the tree home and, duty done, get back to drinking eggnog and playing another game of road hockey.

32   "How are you going to cut it down?" the Dubliner asked.

33   We were silent. All of us kept staring at the tree.

34   "Don't you need an axe?" he asked.

35   So I went back to the car. I searched the back seat, the trunk, and solemnly walked into the woods again.

36   "Don't look at me," I shrugged guiltily, when I saw them looking at me. After the road hockey, we had all jumped into the car without thinking that the axe was leaning against the garage.

37   I watched my younger brother as he tried to break the tree in two with his hands. But it proved fruitless; the tree still stood.

38   "It's getting late," my younger brother said. "Mom expects to have some kind of a tree for Christmas; I think she'd be disappointed if we came back without one."

39   That was true enough.

40   "Put a ribbon on this one, to show we found it and we will come back," I said.

41   But no one wanted to drive another 40 miles just to come back to this spot. Besides, no one had a ribbon.

42   It was decided that we would take a jaunt back to town to get an axe and cut the very first tree in the very first yard we came to. We might even cut a tree in our yard.

43   "What about that pine in the back yard?" my younger brother said. "It's useless where it is—it just keeps getting in the way when I mow the lawn."

44   "It'd look far better in the living room," I agreed. "That's the place for it."

45   "But how would we keep mom from knowing—"

46   She would soon find out, if she looked out her kitchen window, that her favourite pine tree was in the living room.

47   Then we wondered if we couldn't buy one on the sly. In fact it might be considered conservation-minded if we did. There were far too many trees being cut, and that would be our out. There were some for sale at the Irving station on the Boom Road.

48   But, we asked each other, how could we keep it quiet? What a time they would have! Three grown men off to get a tree, and having to buy one.

49   It might be possible to steal one, already decorated. But we did not entertain that thought for long.

50   Owen listened to all of this with great serenity as we drove back out along the highway. Having no radio, we asked him if he knew a Christmas song. I was waiting for Jingle Bells. But Owen, mittens folded, eyes closed, broke out singing O Tannenbaum in a voice that seemed straight from the Vienna boys choir.

51   After that we were a little dumbfounded. And we remained silent until 10 miles from home, when I slammed on the brakes and yelled: "There's my plastic carton cap!!!"

52   I jumped out and ran, with the car still sliding behind me. It proved a difficult carton cap to catch. The wind had given it life, and five or six times I missed it. But finally I was able to grab it. I went back to the car, took my brother-in-law's present out of the gas tank (I would rewrap them) and placed the cap back on.

53   Turning, I saw Owen staring past me. "There's a tree over there," he said.

54   "There are many trees, son," I said. "The woods is a veritable cornucopia of trees—"

55   "However, this one just fell out of the sky," he said simply.

56   I turned and saw a pinetop blow-down rolling back and forth in the centre of the road. It had not been there 10 seconds before.

57   "It just fell from heaven and landed there—a second ago," the child said, amazed. Anyone who has ever heard an Irish child say "it just fell from heaven" will know how I felt at that moment.

58   Owen and I walked over to inspect it. It was a beautiful tree, about seven-and-a-half feet tall. It had sustained no damage; all its boughs were still fluffy and intact. In fact, it had just broken from the top of a large pine. The only thing we would have to do was to saw the butt even.

59   Delighted at our good fortune, I tied it to the trunk of the car. "Thank God for the wind," I muttered.

60   "Yes," Owen said. And off we went.

61   Now it was night. The stars came out and the wind died down. The town was lit up top to bottom, front to back, all the houses decorated, and soon ours would be too.

62   "Thank you for letting me help get the tree," Owen said. "I've never seen anyone get a tree before." Then our little Dubliner fell fast asleep. We took him home, to where he'd said his grandmother lived. My brother carried him to the door.

63   We went back home. With some sleight of hand about where we had found it, we put up the tree. My mother loved it. My father spent the night trimming it.

64   All that was long ago; both my parents now are gone. The house is no longer ours, and most of the people I grew up with I no longer know. My brothers and I get together when we can. There is still road hockey on our lane, though the city council tried to forbid it and almost started a war, and kids still gather in droves to play there near Christmas time.

65   We still speak about a child we didn't know, who came with us to find a tree the wind blew from the sky when we had no axe—of the carton cap stopping the car, so the child, himself, could light the way. And we have come to the conclusion, over many rum and beer, that at the very least he was a kind and wonderful child from Dublin, named Owen, visiting his grandmom who lived two lanes from us.

66   Unfortunately I have never seen him again, and I expect now I never will.

Questions for Critical Thinking

1. Describe the purpose and tone of this story. What do you think was the occasion for writing it?

2. Why was the group headed to Christmas Mountain? What were some of the problems they encountered during their journey? Did they reach their destination? Why or why not?

3. The writer uses dialogue in the story to develop some of his characters. What especially does the writer try to capture through the dialogue?

4. What was the identity of the little boy who decided to join the group of young men in their quest? Find passages in the story that illustrate how the others in the group felt toward him.

5. Explain the conclusion of the story. Why do you think it ends the way it does?

Writing in Response

1. Write a narrative about a humorous family story.

2. Write a narrative about a special family gathering. Describe the nature of the occasion and any other customs and traditions that took place.

3. One of the fun things about reading a story is in trying to imagine the events that take place from a different perspective. Reread the story by David Adams Richards and write a narrative from Owen's point of view. How do you think this gang of brothers from rural New Brunswick would have looked like to a six-year-old boy from Dublin?

4. The author describes a situation in which he and his brothers are contemplating a variety of ways that they can bring home a Christmas tree. In the end, they find a tree by "miracle." Describe a time when you found yourself in a difficult situation, and your attempts to remove yourself from it only made your situation more difficult.

Dirt, Germs Can Be Healthy Additives

SUZANNE MORRISON

Recent studies that have tried to determine why some people are more susceptible to diseases and allergies have arrived at some shocking conclusions. As the article by journalist Suzanne Morrison suggests, the cleanest homes may actually be better breeding grounds for allergies and asthma.

1   In our squeaky clean world, kids who live on pig farms are least likely to suffer from allergies.

2   That's no surprise to Cathy Smith and her husband, Craig, who own a pork farm in Ancaster, on the outskirts of Hamilton.

3   It's rare for any of the Smith's three children—Julia, 12; Matt, 10; and Andrea, 8—to get sick.

4   "And they don't have any allergies," Smith said. "Our kids' friends seem to get sicker than ours."

5   Scientists know what Smith is talking about.

6   They're hot on the trail of a new theory called the "hygiene hypothesis," which suggests we all need to embrace dirt a little more because the cleanest environments may be the best breeding grounds for allergies and asthma.

7   In other words, our war against germs—from detergents and chlorine to antibiotics and vaccines to antibacterial soaps—has been far too successful. What we really need early in life is to be "marinated" in all kinds of common household germs and dust to ensure we develop a healthy immune system.

8   Hamilton allergist Dr. Joseph Greenbaum said no one understands exactly why the incidence of food and other allergies is rising but the hottest idea at the moment is the hygiene hypothesis.

9   "What's important is the first few hours and months of life, not later," Greenbaum said.

10   When a woman is pregnant, neither she nor her baby is in a fighting mode immunologically, otherwise they would both die, he said.

11   Once a baby is born, its immune system must be stimulated and get ready to fight the world. Without bugs around to make that happen, a child is more likely to develop allergies.

12   That's why children who live on farms, particularly pig farms, are less likely to suffer allergies, said Greenbaum, an assistant clinical professor of medicine in McMaster University's faculty of health sciences. "As infants, their parents are dirty from working around the pig farm. They are probably crawling around on the barn floor and breathing in all these bugs and things, and getting dirty all the time. In fact, the best thing is to be born in a field and rolled into the grass.

13   "But, when you are born in a sterile operating room, they wash you. Everybody is wearing sterile gloves. They start feeding you sterilized foods. So, your body doesn't want to fight the world and it stays in this sort of allergy non-reactive mode."

14   Greenbaum said there appears to be a general rise in allergies around the world. In Canada, the incidence has gone to almost 30 per cent of the population from five to 10 per cent in the 1950s, he said.

15   The fall of the Berlin Wall in Germany strikingly illustrates what may be happening, backing up the hygiene hypothesis.

16   Before the wall came down, the incidence of allergies in East Germany was five per cent. Children were born in less-than-optimal operating rooms, ate less sterile food and lived in apartments that weren't as clean.

17   In West Germany, at the same time, the incidence of allergies was 25 per cent.

18   Genetically, people were the same on both sides of the wall.

19   The wall came down. Ten years later, the incidence of allergies was the same because both had embraced the Western ideal of cleanliness.

20   Health Canada has no reliable data on the prevalence of food allergies or how much they may be increasing.

21   True allergic reactions to foods are not common, and many are restricting their diets unnecessarily.

22   One allergist found that, out of 23 people who thought they had a food allergy, only four actually did. Some who didn't have allergies were avoiding so many foods they had become sick and malnourished.

23   A food allergy differs from food intolerance.

24   An allergy is serious and can be fatal. The throat swells. There's difficulty breathing. A person may collapse and even die. Such an allergic reaction frequently happens with peanuts but also shellfish, fish, sesame and sunflower seeds, and even kiwi, which is a fairly common food allergy in Canada.

25   In a milder way, food allergies can pop up with fresh foods like apples. People allergic to tree pollen in the spring can have their throats swell with fruits, such as apples and oranges.

26   Food intolerance is something completely different, such as lactose intolerance in people who can't digest milk properly. Others can't tolerate a vitamin called niacin, a common component of multivitamins.

27   "People eat this multivitamin," Greenbaum said. "Suddenly, they get flushed in the face, hot and sweaty. They feel—what have I just eaten—and think they're going to die. It's a benign thing—a chemical effect of niacin."

Questions for Critical Thinking

1. According to the article, what can parents do to protect their families against allergies and asthma?

2. Describe the causal relationship that some scientists think exists between exposure to common household germs and the development of a healthy immune system.

3. How does the example of the different incidences of allergies between East and West Germans support the author's thesis?

4. Why are children who live on pig farms healthier than most other children?

5. According to the author, what are some of the misconceptions about food allergies? How does a food allergy differ from a food intolerance? What examples are provided to illustrate this difference?

Writing in Response

1. Different people have different tolerances for dirt and germs. Write an essay that classifies people according to their attitudes toward cleanliness.

2. Write an essay that argues against the central thesis of the article. What kind of evidence would you use to support your perspective?

3. What are the effects of an overly clean home on young people? Use examples from your own experiences as well as ideas you have from reading this and other essays.

4. Summarize the article in one paragraph, including the thesis statement and all major supporting details.

Keep Our Doors Open
MORTON WEINFELD

Most Canadians have relations or ancestors that they know who made sacrifices to come to Canada. Thousands of immigrants still settle here each year. In the following essay, Morton Weinfeld responds to the concerns of those who do not support Canada's liberal immigration policies.

1   Alarmist critiques of Canadian immigration policy have raised the heat of the debate but shed little light.

2   First, say critics, Canada's immigration laws, regulations and the Charter of Rights and Freedoms itself do not prevent bogus refugee claimants from queue-jumping or criminals and worse from entering and remaining in Canada. Second, Canada is becoming increasingly crowded. Third, even legitimate recent immigrants are not as economically productive as those who came in the 1970s as a result of a recent tilt toward family-class migrants over independent or business-class migrants. The charge is that newer immigrants create problems of social integration and intolerance, which will hurt both Canada and the immigrants. The critics want fewer immigrants and a greater proportion of skilled or independent immigrants.

3   These criticisms are wrong, both in their specifics and in a more fundamental sense. First, there's no evidence from the 1990s of any consistent increase in the numbers or proportions or failed refugee claimants. There are clear cases, and indeed systemic patterns, of abuse, and thousands of claims are refused. But the annual numbers (and proportions) of accepted refugees, including the more "problematic" cases of those who make their claims in Canada, have varied inconsistently, around 20,000. In fact, Canada is protected from large refugee and illegal migrant streams by the United States and two large oceans.

4   Second, the family-class immigrants make serious economic contributions to Canada. Many older parents and grandparents serve as unpaid caregivers. And other family-class immigrants help out as unpaid workers in small family-run businesses. These are missed in the statistical calculations of immigrant economic contributions.

5   Both refugee and family-class immigrant cohorts include many who are well-educated. In 1997, for example, the ratio of immigrants from these two classes with a college degree or higher was similar to that among the entire Canadian population. (To be sure, higher proportions had less than nine years of schooling, reflecting the elderly proportions in the family class.) Sadly, we continue to see immigrants whose foreign academic credentials and work experience are (for many reasons) devalued in our labour market, and are thus underemployed.

6   I'd argue that the economic contribution and integration of immigrants is perhaps not optimally measured by income statistics. My father was a lawyer in Europe, but worked in Canada as a bookkeeper—poorly paid relative to his education and previous occupation. We can look at the educational attainment of Canadians between 15 and 24 from the 1996 census, for the foreign-born and for those of visible minority background (many of these are also immigrants or children of immigrants). The evidence is clear: For both groups, their educational attainment —and we are speaking mainly of Canadian schools—matches or exceeds that of non-immigrant and white Canadians.

7   This is remarkable, given that many of these youngsters had to overcome language barriers, traumas of immigration, and forms of prejudice and discrimination.

8   Moreover, evidence from Canada's leading universities (I have looked at data from McGill and the University of Toronto) and public and private research institutes and corporations indicates that foreign students who may become immigrants, as well as immigrants or children of immigrants, are playing statistically disproportionate roles as future Canadian scientists and innovators. In short, the economic returns to immigration are long term and multigenerational.

9   The fear that Canada is becoming overcrowded should be stated with caution. Suppose Canadians only lived in the bottom one-fifth of the country's land mass and lived there with the same population density as the Netherlands (which I am not recommending). The population of that one-fifth would be 740 million people. Toronto, Montreal and Vancouver currently rank 50th, 86th and 163rd among the planet's metropolitan agglomerations, smaller than many of the world's most dynamic cities.

10   There's still little evidence of a racist explosion about to go off in Canada, though both anti-immigrant conservatives and ultra-liberal anti-racists—for their own reasons—tend to harp on the dangers of intergroup tensions and inequalities. There is no equivalent here to the large, openly racist anti-immigrant movements found in Europe. Instead, I see evidence of a steady, if not always smooth, process of immigrant integration that suffers from the "all planes land safely" syndrome of being ignored by the media.

11   The specific criticisms of recent Canadian immigrants suffer from a more basic flaw. They misunderstand the role of immigration in Canadian society, past and present. They see immigration essentially as an investment option for Canada, to

be evaluated in cost-benefit terms, usually measured in the short run. But immigrants are not "them" standing in marked contrast to the Canadian-born "us."

12   About 17 per cent of the Canadian population is foreign-born, but this figure grossly understates the impact of the immigrant experience. Many Canadian-born are children of one or two foreign-born parents, and a greater number of native-born Canadians remember immigrant grandparents. Others have married immigrants or into immigrant families. My son played local hockey on a team as diverse as the United Nations.

13   The idea of Canada as a land of freedom and opportunity is tied to the historical experience of any New World society. Immigrants to those societies included many not selected for their positive economic or social characteristics. This is true of the convicts who helped settle Australia. This is true of Holocaust survivors and Jewish refugees from Arab lands who settled in Israel in the late 1940s and early 1950s.

14   And it was certainly true for the immigrants who settled in Canada from the 1880s through the 1920s. Many were of allegedly "inferior" stock: the wrong religion, the wrong nationality or race, the wrong political ideology, the wrong social class or family background. Discrimination was legal, and their cultures were openly devalued. Many fibbed on their immigration applications, claiming skills—such as tailoring—that they did not have.

15   Admitting and integrating immigrants, and their children, is what Canada does, and does relatively well. This is the way the world thinks about Canada. There are far worse things to be than a society where immigration and refugee admissions are perceived as lax. Of course, Canada might maximize the short-term economic return by seeking only immigrants who have graduate degrees in engineering or computer science, speak English or French, and have money to invest. But there are fewer such "designer immigrants" eager to move to, or stay in, Canada. And such a tilt in immigrant intake is not, and should not be, the Canadian way.

Questions for Critical Thinking

1. Explain the significance of the title of this article.

2. In the first two paragraphs the author addresses the arguments of opponents to Canada's current immigration policy. Make a list of those arguments.

3. Rewrite, using your own words, Morton Weinfeld's thesis. Does the author do what he says he'll do?

4. At which point does the conclusion of the essay start? State the author's conclusion in your own words.

5. What specific evidence does Weinfeld use to dispute the claims of his opponents?

Writing in Response

1. Anecdotal evidence is evidence that you believe is true because of your experience but which you cannot prove by any specific means. What anecdotal information do you have about people's immigrant experiences? What stories can you tell about immigrants and how they contributed to Canadian society? What stories can you tell about immigrants where they may have caused problems? You may want to work in groups to gather stories. Then pick three of these anecdotes that you would like to write about. Each story will be a separate paragraph.

2. Do you agree with Weinfeld's argument? Why or why not? Write an editorial of your own wherein you respond to this essay. Be sure to state clearly your position and use specific examples to support your points.

3. In the essay, Weinfeld suggests that throughout Canada's history immigrants have been viewed as "inferior stock." Do you agree with this statement? Why or why not? Write an essay in which you address this historical aspect of immigration to Canada.

4. In your own words, state the solutions Weinfeld offers to change our view of immigrants and their contributions to our society.

A Dead End for Humanity

WADE DAVIS

When an animal becomes extinct, many people get concerned. Few, however, consider the extinction of a language to be of great concern. In the following essay, Wade Davis suggests that the death of a language is devastating, and it has far-reaching consequences for all of humanity.

1   A hundred years from now, the 20th century will be remembered not for wars or technological innovations but as an era when people supported—or passively endorsed—the massive destruction of biological and cultural diversity. In the past 25 years alone, as many as one million species will have been driven to extinction. Yet, even as we mourn the loss of biological life, we ignore a parallel process of loss—the erosion of the ethnosphere, which might be defined as the sum of all thoughts, dreams, myths and insights brought into being by human imagination since the dawn of consciousness.

2   Of the 6,000 languages spoken today, fully half are not being taught to children. Effectively, they are already dead. By the end of the 21st century linguistic diversity may be reduced to as few as 500 languages.

3   A language, of course, is not simply vocabulary and grammar; it's a flash of the human spirit, the vehicle by which the soul of a culture comes into the material realm. Each language represents a unique intellectual and spiritual achievement. Although many of the languages at risk are those spoken by small indigenous societies, their loss would be as great as that of any other language.

4   Even the most pessimistic biologist would not claim that 50 per cent of the world's biological diversity is currently at risk. And yet this represents the most optimistic cultural scenario. When we lose a language, as MIT linguistics professor Ken Hale says, it's like dropping a bomb on the Louvre.

5   Yet, even among those sympathetic to the plight of indigenous societies, there is a mood of resignation—as if these cultures, quaint and colourful though they may be, are somehow fated to fade away, reduced to the margins of history as the modern technological world moves inexorably forward.

6   To embrace this view, however, is to ignore the central revelation of anthropology—the idea that our own society is not absolute. Rather, it is just one model of reality, the consequence of one particular set of choices that our ancestors made generations ago. Whether it is the nomadic Penan in the forests of Borneo, Vodoun acolytes in Haiti or Yak herders in Tibet, all of these people teach us that there are other ways of being and thinking and relating to the natural world.

7   I spent some time among the Penan of Borneo, one of the last nomadic peoples of Southeast Asia. For most of human history, we were all nomads, wanderers on a pristine planet. It was only 10,000 years ago, with the neolithic revolution and the rise of agriculture, that many of us succumbed to the cult of the seed. Among nomadic societies we see an image of what we once were.

8   In nomadic societies there is no incentive to accumulate possessions, because everything must be carried on your back. The wealth of a community is the strength of the relationships among its people. Sharing is an involuntary reflex; one never knows who will be the next to secure the food.

9   Different ways of life create different human beings, and there are profound lessons to be drawn from different world views. Today, in Canada, you might pass a homeless person on the street, and understand him to be the regrettable but perhaps inevitable consequences of the economic system. A Penan is raised to believe that a poor man shames us all.

10   I'm not suggesting a Rousseau view of indigenous people as noble savage conservationists; to suggest that is to deny indigenous people their legitate place in the brutal struggle for survival. Life in the malarial swamps of New Guinea leaves little room for sentiment. Nostalgia is not a trait commonly associated with the Inuit. Nomadic hunters and gatherers in the Amazon have no consciousness sense of stewardship.

11   What these cultures have, however, is a traditional relationship with the Earth, forged through time and ritual, and based not only on deep attachment to the land but on a far more subtle intuition—the idea that the land itself is breathed into being by human consciousness. Mountains, rivers and forests are not perceived as mere props on a stage on which the drama of humanity unfolds. For these societies the land is alive, a dynamic force to be embraced and transformed by the human imagination.

12   A Kwakiut boy raised to revere the salmon forests of the Pacific Northwest as the abode of Huxwhukw and the Crooked beak of Heaven, cannibal spirits living at the North of the world, will be a different person than a Canadian child taught that such forests exist to be cut. A child raised in the Andes to believe that a mountain is the realm of a protective spirit will behave differently than a youth brought up to believe that it is an inert pile of rock ready to be mined.

13   Every view of the world that fades away, every culture that disappears, diminishes the possibilities of human life. We lose not only knowledge of the natural world but also intuitions about the meaning of the cosmos. We reduce the human repertoire of adaptive responses to the common problems that confront all humanity.

14   An anthropologist from another planet visiting contemporary North America would note wonders here, but would also perhaps be puzzled to see our environmental problems, or the fact that 20 per cent of our people control 80 per cent of the wealth, more that half of our marriages end in divorce, and that more than 90 per cent of our elders don't live with relatives. As we lose other models of living, we lose a vast archive of knowledge and expertise, the memories of countless elders, healers, farmers, midwives, poets and saints.

15   How are we to value what is being lost? That we are losing the botanical knowledge of other cultures is obvious—and less than 1 per cent of the world's flora has been thoroughly studied by Western science. But how do we value less concrete contributions of other cultures? What is the worth of family bonds that mitigate poverty and insulate the individual from loneliness? Of diverse intuitions about the spirit realm? What is the economic measure of ritual practices that result in the protection of a forest?

16   Before she died, anthropologist Margaret Mead spoke of her singular concern that as we drifted toward a more homogeneous world we were laying the foundations of a bland and generic modern culture that in the end would have no rivals.

17   The entire imagination of humanity, she feared, might become imprisoned within the limits of a single intellectual and spiritual modality. Her nightmare was the possibility that we might wake up one day and not even remember what had been lost.

18   One night, on a ridge in Sarawak, I sat by a fire with Asik Nyelit, headman of the Ubong River Penan. It was dusk and the light of a partial moon filtered through the branches of the canopy. Asik looked up at the moon and casually asked me if it was true that people had journeyed there, only to return with baskets of dirt. "If true," he asked, "why did they bother to go?"

19   It was difficult to explain a $1-trillion space program to a man who kindled fire with a flint. The proper answer to Asik's query was that we did not go into space to secure new wealth but to experience a new vision of life itself.

20   The perspective of Earth we gained from space made us begin to understand the fragility of our biosphere. Now we must understand that there is an ethnosphere, and it too is fragile—and irreplaceable.

Questions for Critical Thinking

1. This essay begins with a startling statement. Write three other statements of your own that could begin this essay.

2. How does the author characterize nomadic societies? Why do you think a discussion of nomadic cultures is important in this essay?

3. According to Wade Davis, why is it essential to have a diversity of cultures and languages in the world? List at least three reasons.

4. Davis makes references to other scholars in this essay. How do these scholars add to his discussion? Be specific.

5. How does Davis define the ethnosphere?

6. What does Davis mean by the statement, "Every view of the world that fades away, every culture that disappears, diminishes the possibility of human life"?

Writing in Response

1. In your own words, summarize the main points made by this author.

2. Write an essay in which you encourage fellow students to become concerned with the state of the ethnosphere.

3. Construct an argument on a topic of your choosing. In your argument use details drawn from your personal experience to support your own position. You may wish to choose from one of the statements below.

   Canada should have only one official language.

   Each Canadian should be required to speak at least two languages fluently.

   Governments should subsidize language training for languages other than English and French.

Get Beyond Babel

KEN WIWA

In the following essay, Ken Wiwa argues that the loss of a language is not only common but inevitable as time progresses. As you are reading this essay, keep in mind Wade Davis's article "A Dead End for Humanity."

1   Earlier this week I received compelling evidence that I am doomed to extinction. According to figures released by the Worldwatch Institute, half of the world's 6,800 languages face annihilation; that's because they are spoken by fewer than 2,500 people. Here in Canada, only three of 50 aboriginal languages may survive the coming cultural Armageddon. Lurking in the reaction to this news, I suspect, is the fear that we will end up speaking English in some monocultural flatland called "Disney."

2   There is an impassioned school of thought that says that unless we take active steps to preserve our "cultural diversity"—read "languages"—the human race is in danger. When we lose a language, these doomsday prophets say, we lose its knowledge base and world-view; this, they assure us, impoverishes us all.

3   As a member of an indigenous people, and as someone actively concerned about the fate of my culture, I used to subscribe to this view. I'd soak up the arguments of philologists and writers I admired warning about the implications of losing our languages. I bought all these arguments. Then I started examining my own community's experience.

4   I am Ogoni. We number an estimated 500,000, and speak six mutually unintelligible dialects—languages, by now—on an overpopulated but fertile floodplain in southern Nigeria. The Ogoni languages and culture are threatened by Nigeria's socioeconomic realities. Our environment has been compromised by aggressive and irresponsible oil exploration. Unemployment, inadequate health care and neglect by the country's rulers has ripped out my community's heart.

5   The young, the energetic and the ambitious have no option but to leave in search of better opportunities. The community is left in the care of the old and the infirm. A whole generation of Ogoni is growing up elsewhere, speaking English, forgetting our languages, exiled from our villages and our traditions. When the elders die, they take our traditions, our folktales, our myths, our history and our cultural memories with them. As we say in Africa, "When an old man dies it is like a library has been burned down."

6   Which is why I started looking into Ogoni history, thinking about my language, trying to shoehorn our myths and folktales into a compelling story to keep them alive for another generation. But the more I study our history, especially the way our culture and our language has evolved, the more I suspect that those of us who have set out with the intention of reviving a culture by fixing it in time and space may actually be doing more harm than good.

7   Take the development of my language. According to one of our creation myths, the original Ogoni settlement was at a place called Nama. Here the first Ogoni people cleared the surrounding forest, left one tree standing and established our roots. Over time our community grew, and people migrated westward into the rain forests until there were 128 villages in Ogoni. Because these settlements were isolated, the language altered subtly. If you go to Ogoni today you can still hear the effects. In the eastern villages we speak a different dialect from the villages on the western fringes.

8   The point I am making here is that language is in constant flux. To fix it in a particular time and place is to arrest the movement and vitality that shapes a language's evolution. The more I examine the way my language has evolved, the more

I believe that the best a language can do in response is to go with the flow. As far as I know, no Ogoni language has a word for "computer," but we do say *faa-bu-yon* (car of the sky)—or airplane.

9 Unless we make a huge effort to open up the language and the culture to embrace our experience of contact with other cultures and the modern world, we will always be vulnerable. To say that is not to diminish the past or our culture, but to acknowledge a simple truth: Indigenous peoples must not turn inward and cling to nostalgia for sustenance. Though we look back, we must always go forward.

10 For me, that's the great poetic insight in Gabriel Garcia Marquez's novel, *One Hundred Years of Solitude*. The community of Macondo begins amid vibrant energy, but ossifies into a parochialism trapped in a cycle of self-repeating prophecies that refuse to embrace or even acknowledge the passage of time. When Marquez delivers his verdict on Macondo (races condemned to 100 years of solitude do not get a second chance), it seems to me to be a warning to all the language curators and conservationists working to preserve our cultures in some cultural museum.

11 It is a warning that the guardians of the French language, the Academie Française, might heed. Once French was the international language of the world; thanks to the Academie's fastidious custody, it is becoming inflexible. English, on the other hand, has rarely been as neurotic about its purity. Most English words are borrowed from other languages; little Anglo-Saxon survives. Only an incurable romantic would attempt to revive Old English for general use. No, English has evolved, absorbed and adapted. Open to foreign influence, it borrows unashamedly. That's why English has more than 500,000 words in its vocabulary, while French has little more than 100,000.

12 For me the rise and preeminence of English is an example to all cultures about how a language survives and thrives. When Julius Caesar invaded Britain 2,000 years ago, English did not exist. Fifteen hundred years later, Shakespeare had a potential audience of only five million English-speakers. Over the next 400 years, English would come to be spoken by more than one billion people. According to *The Story of English* (by Robert McCrum and Robert MacNeil), English is now "more widely scattered, more widely spoken than any other language has ever been."

13 Thanks to its versatility, shameless habit of appropriation and the violence and aggression of its people, English is now the *lingua franca* of the world. What is more remarkable is that despite its mongrel nature, the English world-view has persisted. Through all the mutations and adaptations it has still managed to service and protect a small island's place in the world.

14 The English people and the English language have survived by picking up influences and adapting words from dead languages, like Latin and Ancient Greek, and grafting elements from their world-views, religions and philosophies onto the English trunk.

15 English is both a lesson and an obstacle to the development of other languages and cultures. Which is why it strikes me that to lament the death of languages and to prescribe a solution that freezes language in time is to condemn a culture and a language to certain extinction.

16 If cultural diversity is so vital to our survival as a race, we must understand how languages work over time. After all, it only took English 400 years to achieve its current status. Who is to say that in another 500 years English will not go the same way as Greek, Latin or French? There is one more lesson that leaps out from my reading of the story of English. It is this: Languages and cultures don't die—they just get absorbed into something else.

Questions for Critical Thinking

1. In the first paragraph Ken Wiwa provides a number of statistics to underscore the prevalence of lost languages. In the second paragraph of Wade Davis's essay, "A Dead End for Humanity," he also cites statistics. Which set of numbers and statistics do you find more convincing? Why?

2. In both essays the writers use personal experiences. Why do you think they use their own experiences when discussing this topic? Is it effective? Why or why not?

3. Make two columns on a piece of paper. In one column, create a list of the arguments that Ken Wiwa makes in his article. In the other column, address these arguments using Wade Davis's examples. Which article do you think develops a better argument? Why?

4. In what paragraphs does the writer anticipate the position of the other side to his argument and then answer his critics? How effective is this technique? Why?

5. Ken Wiwa's conclusion is very effective. Study the last two paragraphs of his essay and discuss how he achieves his dramatic impact.

Writing in Response

1. Write an essay in which you agree or disagree that our world's languages must be protected.

2. Write an essay in which you discuss what you believe is the best way to promote cultural diversity.

Photo Credits

Literary Credits

INDEX